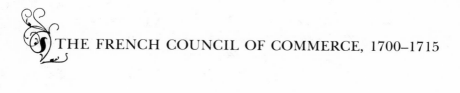THE FRENCH COUNCIL OF COMMERCE, 1700–1715

THE FRENCH COUNCIL OF COMMERCE, 1700–1715

A Study of Mercantilism after Colbert

Thomas J. Schaeper

OHIO STATE UNIVERSITY PRESS : COLUMBUS

The frontispiece is a detail from an engraving, "Le Conseil de Commerce," Bibliothèque Nationale, Cabinet d'Estampes, Collection Hennin, No. 6492. It is reproduced here by permission.

Portions of Chapters 1, 3, and 8 appeared earlier in the *European Studies Review*, the *Delta Epsilon Sigma Bulletin*, and the *Revue française d'histoire d'outre-mer*. They are reprinted here with permission.

Copyright © 1983 by the Ohio State University Press
All Rights Reserved.

Library of Congress Cataloging in Publication Data

Schaeper, Thomas J.
  The French Council of Commerce, 1700–1715

  Bibliography: p.
  Includes index.
  1. France. Conseil de commerce—History.
2. France—Commerce—History. 3. France—Commercial
policy—History. I. Title.
HF3555.S32 1983   354.440082'06   82-14523
ISBN 0-8142-0341-8

for my Mother and Father

CONTENTS

ABBREVIATIONS

AN	Archives Nationales
BN	Bibliothèque Nationale
Mar.	Archives de la Marine
Col.	Archives des Colonies
AD	Archives Départementales
AAE	Archives du Ministère des Affaires Etrangères
ACCM	Archives de la Chambre du Commerce de Marseille

ACKNOWLEDGMENTS

My work on this book would not have been possible without the advice and encouragement that I received from a wide circle of colleagues and friends. As my dissertation adviser and now as a friend, John C. Rule has been a generous and unfailing source of information, insights, and encouragement. Other persons who have read all or part of this study and who have shared their opinions with me include John Rothney, Frederick Snider, Charles Williams, Ragnhild Hatton, Pierre H. Boulle, and Paul W. Bamford. Through the years I have also benefited from the help that I have received from my good friends Ben Trotter and Gary McCollim.

The staffs of the various Parisian and departmental archives and libraries in which I have performed research have also been of great service to me. The travel necessary for the successful completion of this project was facilitated by grants from the Graduate School of the Ohio State University, the French government, the Interuniversity Centre for European Studies, and St. Bonaventure University.

I am grateful also to the editors of the *European Studies Review*, the *Delta Epsilon Sigma Bulletin*, and the *Revue française d'histoire d'outre-mer* for permission to reprint portions of chapters 1, 3, and 8 that appeared originally in these periodicals.

The final stages of the preparation of this book were made much more pleasant than one might have expected by the assistance that I received from my students and typists. In particular I must thank Cheryl Carr, Joanne Hastings, Flora Cooney, Lawrence J. Briggs, and Sean Kenny. I would be remiss if I did not also acknowledge the work of Robert S. Demorest, my patient and meticulous editor at the Ohio State University Press. Any infelicities that remain in the prose style and organization of the book are clearly the result of my own deficiencies.

Finally, I must express my warmest gratitude to my wife, Kathleen. Without ever showing signs of protest or boredom, she has listened for several years to my ideas about the Council of Commerce. Her patience and editorial assistance certainly have exceeded the bounds of matrimonial obligation.

INTRODUCTION

The Council of Commerce established in 1700 played an important role in the economic history of France until its dissolution in 1791. It was unique in the Old Regime because it consisted of government officials as well as merchant representatives from the more important French commercial cities. Although many historians have acknowledged the importance of this council, few have given it the attention it deserves.[1]

The study of the Council of Commerce provides one with a fresh vantage point for the study of that group of economic policies commonly referred to as mercantilism. Most works on this subject concentrate exclusively on such topics as the trading companies, the growth and regulation of French manufactures, tariffs, and so on. The present work, however, will deal primarily with the actual decision-making process within the upper levels of the government. By studying the Council of Commerce, one can better understand the bureaucratic machinery that enforced royal laws and ministerial orders, and one can see more clearly the relationship between the crown and the business community. The council's activities demonstrate that there was a far higher degree of cooperation and agreement between merchants and the crown than has heretofore been realized.

This book will treat the period dating from the council's creation up to the death of Louis XIV. These fifteen years form a discrete period in the history of France, comprising the Sun King's final years as well as the War of the Spanish Succession. They also form a distinct phase in the history of the Council of Commerce. The problems with which it dealt and the organization of the council made these years different from subsequent ones. After the king's death, this council was reorganized along with all the other royal councils. Although it survived in various forms and remained important until the end of the Old Regime, it never regained all the influence that it had had under Louis XIV.

Despite the many discussions that have arisen over the meaning and usefulness of the term *mercantilism*, I have intentionally placed that word in the title of this book. Some scholars argue that one should not use the word, since it did not even exist at the time for which it is meant to apply. But if historians were to limit themselves to the words existing during the epochs about which they write, their vocabulary would be sadly diminished. Furthermore, such an argument seems to deny one of the essential functions of the historian: namely, the tracing of ideas and patterns that might not have been evident to contemporaries. Others who dislike the word *mercantilism* assert that by creating an "ism" historians are establishing an artificial coherence that does not conform to the facts.[2]

I agree that mercantilism in France and elsewhere was largely empirical rather than theoretical. The great Swedish historian Eli F. Heckscher thus, for example, went too far in trying to make a unified system out of it.[3] But the vast majority of scholars dealing with early modern European history still employ the term, and I believe that this is justifiable. Although mercantilist statesmen and writers often contradicted themselves or each other, nevertheless they generally did follow a fairly uniform set of tendencies. These included the building up of colonial empires, the protection and encouragement of manufactures, the search for a favorable balance of trade, the creation of privileged trading companies, and the fostering of a nation's navy and merchant marine. Underlying these policies were a set of existing conditions and presuppositions: the growth and bureaucratization of the modern nation state, a basically hard-money economy, and a static view of the world's economy (which inevitably led to the conclusion that what helped one state must hurt another).

Among historians who agree that there was such a thing as mercantilism, the major debate has concerned the question of its goals. Over the past century, scholars such as Gustav Schmoller, William Cunningham, Eli F. Heckscher, Lionel Rothkrug, and D. C. Coleman have tended to argue that the basic aim of the mercantile system was state-building. Related to this is the argument of Herbert Heaton and Gabriel Ardant that mercantilism was at heart merely a fiscal instrument—that is, a means by which the state could increase its own wealth and power at the expense of the general economy.[4] In opposition to that point of view, other scholars have asserted that the goal of mercantilism was both power and plenty.[5] In other words, mercantilist statesmen and writers realized that the welfare of the state and the prosperity of the people went hand in hand because, as Martin Wolfe has said, the state could benefit only if the number of taxable transactions rose.[6]

As will become clear in the following pages, I believe that the latter interpretation is the one that most closely conforms to the story of the French Council of Commerce early in the eighteenth century. This is not to say that there was never any contention between the public and private sectors—far from it. But it does mean that there was no fundamental, theoretical contradiction between their needs and views.

For those readers who are still troubled by my use of the word *mercantilism*, let me say that for the purposes of this book mercantilism can be identified as Colbertism—that is, royal economic and financial policies from the 1660s through the 1680s, along with the various official and unofficial writings that supported them.[7] The Council of Commerce has almost always been described by historians as being part of a growing movement of opposition against Colbert's ideas. The following pages will assess this interpretation.

1. There exist several brief descriptions of the organization and work of the council. A good, short summary is in Louis de Rouvroy, duc de Saint-Simon, *Mémoires*, ed. A. de Boislisle, 7:415–33. Bernard Wybo's *Le Conseil de commerce et le commerce intérieur de la France* treats the entire eighteenth century, but is slender (113 pages) and was not based on any archival research. More substantive is Léon Biollay's *Etudes économiques sur le XVIII siècle: le pacte de famine; l'administration du commerce*. Also useful is Germain Martin's *La grande industrie sous le règne de Louis XIV*, pp. 262–73. There have been two historians who intended to produce major works on the Council of Commerce, but each, unfortunately, died before he could complete his project. One was Pierre Bonnassieux, a late nineteenth-century archivist at the Archives Nationales. Bonnassieux and Eugène Lelong did, however, edit the extremely valuable *Conseil de commerce et Bureau du commerce, 1700–1791: inventaire analytique des procès-verbaux*. The introduction and appendixes of this work provide a short history of the council and brief biographies of its members. I have had the good fortune to consult Bonnassieux's personal notes and papers, which are still conserved at the Archives Nationales. The second man who commenced a major study of this council was Warren Scoville. The only published fruits of his research are a section in his book *The Persecution of Huguenots and French Economic Development, 1680–1720*, chapter 11, and his article "The French Economy in 1700–1701: An Appraisal by the Deputies of Trade."

2. Scholars who would prefer to avoid using the term *mercantilism* or who have argued against attributing too much meaning to it have included Herbert Heaton, A. V. Judges, Raymond de Roover, E. A. J. Johnson, T. W. Hutchison, John F. Bosher and D. C. Coleman. Ralph Davis has managed to write the economic history

of early modern Europe without using the word (*The Rise of the Atlantic Economies*). The views of these historians and those who will be mentioned below are discussed in several books that treat this subject. See Walter E. Minchinton (ed.), *Mercantilism: System or Expediency?*; D. C. Coleman (ed.), *Revisions in Mercantilism*; Pierre Deyon, *Le Mercantilisme*; Fritz Blaich, *Die Epoche des Merkantilismus*; Jan Hajek, *Comparative Research into Mercantilistic Theories in Europe of the 16th and 17th Centuries*; Immanuel Wallerstein, *The Modern World System II: Mercantilism and the Consolidation of the European World-Economy, 1600–1750*.

3. Eli F. Heckscher, *Mercantilism*.

4. See note 2 above and Lionel Rothkrug, *Opposition to Louis XIV: The Political and Social Origins of the French Enlightenment*.

5. These include Jacob Viner, Jacob van Klaveren, Ingomar Bog, Charles H. Wilson, William Grampp, and Martin Wolfe. See note 2 above.

6. Martin Wolfe, "French Views on Wealth and Taxes from the Middle Ages to the Old Regime," in Coleman, *Revisions*, p. 204.

7. This working definition is borrowed from Wolfe, ibid., p. 196.

PART ONE

THE COUNCIL AND ITS PLACE
IN THE GOVERNMENT

1

THE CREATION OF THE COUNCIL

Historians have devoted more attention to the creation of the Council of Commerce in 1700 than to its subsequent ninety-one years of activity. This is not without some justification. The formation of the council fits into a general debate concerning the second half of the reign of Louis XIV. The more traditional view holds that the latter part of the reign (variously dated as beginning anywhere from 1679 to 1688) represented a decline—replete with economic and military disasters, an aging king, a mediocre, if not incompetent, corps of royal ministers, and the virtual bankruptcy of the state.[1] In recent years, however, several historians have viewed the second half of the reign more positively.[2] They have noted that Louis XIV's foreign policy, like the king himself, became more subdued and that several royal ministers and bureaucrats of this period were quite competent, imaginative, and eager to grapple with the difficulties besetting the government.

The creation of the Council of Commerce has been cited as evidence for the former point of view. Numerous historians have related the founding of this council to growing unrest over nettlesome regulations imposed on the economy by an increasingly reactionary government.[3] The strongest recent advocate of this position has been Lionel Rothkrug. In his influential book *Opposition to Louis XIV*, Rothkrug asserts that the French royal government after the deaths of the great Colbert in 1683 and war minister Louvois in 1691 faced "a crisis of confidence, existing in the highest circles of government and paralyzing the exercise of political authority."[4] Royal power was "rapidly declining,"[5] owing in part, to "the spectacle of ministerial uncertainty."[6] The successors of Colbert and Louvois sought futilely to remedy the economic depression of 1693–94 and meet the costs of the War of the League of Augsburg. In contrast to the sorry state of the government, Rothkrug portrays the French merchant community as growing in wealth and assertiveness in the 1690s. Merchants, who were "intoxicated with recently acquired wealth and exasperated at mercantilist restrictions,"[7] formed an "onslaught"[8] against the government, using "liberty of trade" as their "battle cry."[9] As a result, the government was "plunged into confusion,"[10] and overcome by "fatal indecisions."[11] After the conclusion of the War of the League of Augsburg in 1697, discontented nobles and merchants compelled the government, with "almost unseemly haste,"[12] to repeal the *capitation* and to grant trading concessions to the Dutch.[13] Royal ministers, who lacked Colbert's "supreme self-assurance," were for the first time asking businessmen for advice on commercial matters.[14] Merchants took advantage of this opportunity and "clamored for institutional reforms designed to give them an official voice in directing the economic affairs of the realm."[15] The government, "unable either to appease or to control the business community," established the Council of Commerce, "from which merchants publicly unleashed a torrent of pent-up criticism."[16]

This widely accepted interpretation of the events needs reconsideration. Three basic points should be acknowledged: first, that the idea of a Council of Commerce and of royal consultations with the merchant community was far from new in 1700; second, that there is little or no solid evidence of merchant demands for a Council of Commerce; third, that the government itself took the initiative in forming it.

PRECEDENTS FOR THE COUNCIL

To demonstrate the first point, one needs only to look at the several precedents for such a council. During the seventeenth century, there were at least six councils or commissions of commerce, established for varying lengths of time.[17] Henri IV, Marie de Medici, Cardinal Richelieu, Cardinal Mazarin, and Superintendant of Finances Fouquet all had assembled bodies of goverment officials to advise them on commercial matters. The most significant seventeenth-century effort to establish a permanent body to supervise trade, however, occurred under Colbert. In 1664 Colbert created a Council of Commerce that, unlike the earlier endeavors, had authority to issue *arrêts* on business and commercial affairs. Attached to this new council as advisers were three businessmen,[18] chosen by the king from nominations presented to him by the merchants and manufacturers of the eighteen major commercial and industrial cities of France.

For varying reasons, some not yet clarified by historians, none of these commissions or councils of commerce lasted more than a few years; but their very existence proves that since early in the seventeenth century the crown had sought a way to administer trade and industry more knowledgeably and efficiently.

The *assemblées représentatives du commerce* constituted another precedent for the council established in 1700. Colbert created these local assemblies in his famous manufacturing ordinance of August 1669. They were to meet periodically in all the major cities in France and were to be composed of municipal officials and representatives of local merchants and manufacturers. The members were expected to examine industrial and commercial problems and to recommend new regulations if they were considered necessary. Although Colbert repeatedly urged the larger cities to establish these assemblies, few were formed until the eighteenth century; but they offer further testimony of the crown's efforts to involve the business sector in goverment decisions.[19]

Quite frequently prior to 1700, the crown also turned to individual mechants for advice.[20] When Louis XI in 1470 met with merchants in the city of Tours to confer with them on ways to encourage trade, he established a precedent for royal or ministerial consultations with business groups.[21] Another of the many examples that one could cite involves Cardinal Richelieu's consultation on economic matters with Théophraste Renaudot's Bureau d'Adresse in the 1630s and early 1640s.[22] The papers of Colbert and his successors provide literally countless instances of the government asking merchants for their opinions on such issues as tariffs, textile regulations, and the general economic picture.[23] If the royal ministers of the 1690s relied on merchants for advice, they were therefore only continuing a tradition that had been followed by Colbert himself. One of Colbert's chief assistants was in fact a merchant, Jacques Savary. In addition to writing *Le parfait négociant*, a handbook for businessmen, Savary was the principal author of Colbert's commercial code, sometimes called the Code Savary.[24]

Royal concern for the business community was also evidenced late in the seventeenth century by the government's growing interest in obtaining accurate estimates of the condition of the economy as a whole. Colbert and his successors bombarded the provincial intendants, tax farmers, and inspectors of manufactures with demands for surveys and statistics on French manufactures, agriculture, trade, population, and the personnel in merchant and craft guilds.[25] Occasionally the government sent bureaucrats from Paris to report on the situation in the provinces, the most famous example of this being the inquest of 1687.[26] This royal concern for the gathering of information climaxed in the last two years of the century with the celebrated series of memoirs by the provincial intendants written for the instruction of the duke of Burgundy.[27] The reasons for all this activity were threefold: the realization that in order to govern efficiently the government needed accurate information about all aspects of the people and their activities, a genuine humanitarian concern for the welfare of Frenchmen,[28] and the belief that the good of the state depends upon the prosperity of the nation.[29]

This is not, of course, to deny that fiscal and military exigencies often led the government to disregard the economic needs of the country; but on the whole, French royal ministers acknowledged that helping trade and manufactures would increase the number of taxable transactions, thereby helping the goverment itself.

THE THESIS OF MERCHANT OPPOSITION

If one accepts then the notion that a council of commerce was not inherently an invasion of the prerogatives of an absolute monarch and that the crown had on many occasions in the past consulted the business community, the question still remains, Who was responsible for the creation of the new Council of Commerce in 1700? The argument that merchants or other supposedly anti-mercantilist forces somehow pressured the government into forming it proves, upon close examination, to be less than convincing. No exponent of this argument up to the present moment has presented any examples of a merchant or a group of merchants asking for a council of commerce or for any other sort of official forum in which their grievances could be voiced. The records of the secretary of state for the navy and of the controller general for the 1690s provide only one document that might support this argument.[30] On 16 February 1700, the officers of the *juridiction consulaire* of La Rochelle wrote to the new controller general, Michel Chamillart, to complain that Chamillart's predecessors had not listened to them.[31] They requested that several towns be permitted to send deputies to Paris so that commercial interests could be heard. Even this letter, however, does not totally conform to the thesis of a merchant opposition, for the officers clearly note that Chamillart had first let it be known that he wanted to hear from the merchant community.[32]

The archival records do present many examples from the 1690s of merchant complaints about various manufacturing regulations, tariff policies, and the farmers general (*fermiers généraux*). In this respect the 1690s were no different from preceding or succeeding decades: it is the nature of the correspondence of any government that most incoming letters deal with the problems and grievances of individual parties. It would be virtually impossible to analyze quantitatively the complaints, given the haphazard and incomplete nature of the archives of the Old Regime, but there seems to be no quantitative evidence of a deluge of unprecedented criticism by businessmen in the 1690s. The correspondence of that time does not show that merchants somehow felt themselves to be the masters of the situation. It is true that several merchants and bankers amassed great fortunes during the War of the League of Augsburg, but such profiteering occurred in all the wars of the Old Regime. Furthermore, there are no signs of ministerial panic or indecision resulting from the complaints received. If there was any period of the personal reign of Louis XIV when the crown was gravely threatened by a rising tide of opposition, it was the early part—not the later. The most serious popular revolts occurred in the 1660s and early 1670s. The number of political tracts raising complaints may also have been higher during this period than in subsequent years.[33]

There is no evidence that the goverment was aware of any sort of rising wave of discontent. Lionel Rothkrug, nevertheless, asserts that the crown felt the need to commission books supporting traditional mercantilist principles against mounting opposition. He cites as evidence the case of Gatien Courtilz de Sandras, a hack writer who supposedly was paid by the government to defend royal policies.[34] Rothkrug attributes two books to Courtilz de Sandras: *Testament politique de messire Jean Baptiste Colbert*, published in 1693,[35] and *Testament politique du marquis de Louvois*, published in 1695.[36] There is no evidence, however, that anyone in the government hired someone to write them. Furthermore, though the two works ostensibly defend royal policies, a casual perusal of them reveals that actually they are clever satires of the ministries of Colbert and Louvois, intended to criticize the government; and it is unlikely that Courtilz de Sandras was responsible for them: the authorship of both works is contested.[37] Also, Courtilz de Sandras's irreverent prose led the crown to imprison him in the Bastille from 1693 to 1699, at the very time when it is said to have engaged his services.[38]

One possible reason why there is only scant evidence of merchants demanding more influence in decisions made by the government of Louis XIV is that they were already well represented at Paris and Versailles. Provincial estates, large cities, and many important business and craft guilds already had permanent agents, or *syndics*, at the court to lobby for their interests.[39] And if these agents were not sufficient to do the job, special deputies were sent to deal with particular issues.[40] These private lobbyists used their skills of persuasion and the ever-present *pot-de-vin* in working to convince the royal ministers and their *commis* ("clerks") of the justice of their claims. The local interest groups for whom these various agents worked seem to have been quite content to continue this traditional manner of representing their grievances to the government.[41]

Those historians who have espoused the thesis of merchant unrest in the 1690s have generally had in mind the great shipowners and overseas traders. The government depended on these men during the War of the League of Augsburg to bring much-needed food supplies and naval stores to France. Also, during this war, the government gradually abandoned its big-fleet strategy and turned to a *guerre de course*.[42] Thus the crown came to rely more and more on the help of individual privateers for attacks on enemy shipping. Recently Geoffrey Symcox and Lionel Rothkrug have asserted that late in the 1690s these traders and privateers became increasingly dissatisfied with government regulations that prevented them from pursuing their business as they desired. This supposedly caused them to lead the merchant opposition that resulted in the assembling of the Council of Commerce.[43]

It is difficult to accept this interpretation: the very fact that these men were becoming wealthy as a result of their wartime enterprises is inconsistent with the picture of a beleaguered, discontented merchant community. Symcox himself demonstrates that in the years 1694–95 French privateers were highly successful in having their grievances settled by the government.[44] Furthermore, the investment of royal officials in privateering ventures seems to discount the fissure painted between privateers and the government.[45]

Even though there is little or no proof of merchants clamoring for a council of commerce, there were, nevertheless, at least three individuals who in the 1690s called for the creation of such a council. In 1692 an obscure noble by the name of Charles Paul Hurault de l'Hospital, seigneur de Belesbat,[46] presented to the king a series of memoirs in which he advocated a host of economic and administrative reforms, including the creation of a council of commerce.[47] Some historians include Belesbat among the leaders of the antimercantilist movement because of his espousal of certain free-trade ideas.[48] They fail to demonstrate, however, that any of the others in this "movement" ever read or knew Belesbat,[49] and they neglect to point out that Belesbat was among the staunchest supporters of royal absolutism. Furthermore, Belesbat specifically excluded merchant deputies from membership in his council of commerce. Jean Pottier de la Hestroye, a former admiralty officer at Dunkirk, wrote a series of memoirs in the late 1690s in which he discussed various means of improving French trade.[50] He suggested that a council of commerce be established, but, like Belesbat, he urged that merchants be excluded from it. Moreover, de la Hestroye did not submit his memoirs to the government until late in the year 1700, by which time the council was already in existence.[51] Marshal Vauban, France's great military engineer, likewise in his *Description géographique de l'élection de Vézelay* and in his *Dixme royale*, mentions a chamber of commerce as one of several possible remedies for the economic depression in France.[52] But Vauban does not elaborate his ideas about the form and responsibilities of such a chamber, and one could hardly include Vauban among the leadership of antimercantilist opposition to Louis XIV. It is thus highly unlikely that the ideas of these three men had any great bearing on the establishment of the Council of Commerce.

ROYAL INITIATIVE

The most convincing explanation for the creation of the council in 1700 is that the government itself took the initiative in forming it. There were three basic reasons for the government's decision: the return of peace, bureaucratic necessity, and the recent division of control over commercial affairs. With the signing of the Treaty of Ryswick in 1697, France was once again at peace, and the government used this opportunity to turn its attention back to the needs of the economy. That the entire nation expected a return to economic prosperity is reflected in an engraving preserved in the Collection Hennin in the *cabinet d'estampes* of the Bibliothèque Nationale in Paris.[53] The engraving, dating from 1698, is entitled "Les heureux fruits de la paix, par le rétablissemment du commerce universel." Pictured in it are ships being unloaded, stacks of barrels and packages ready for shipment, and several groups of French merchants carrying on their business affairs. The *arrêt* of 29 June 1700 that created the council affirms that the king of France had always been aware of the importance of trade for the good of the state.[54] It goes on to note that the return of peace would enable the king to testify once again to his esteem for businessmen and to give trade the protection it deserves. The *arrêt* makes no mention of merchant complaints as a motive for forming the council. Lest one suspect that the government intentionally omitted acknowledging such pressure, it should be pointed out that most, if not all, royal laws that were issued in response to protests or grievances by one group of Frenchmen or another freely admitted it.[55] It was, after all, good publicity for the government to show that it was responsive to the just complaints of the people.

The second factor leading to the creation of the Council of Commerce was bureaucratic necessity. One of the trademarks of the development of a sophisticated, "modern" bureaucracy, as outlined by Max Weber and others, is an increasing division of responsibilities, the assigning of narrower and more specific tasks to individuals and to councils.[56] This process was occurring in other areas of Louis XIV's government,[57] and the need for it was felt in commerce also. The *arrêt* of 29 June 1700 states clearly that the best way for the government to help commerce is to establish a special council to deal with it.

Since the dissolution of Colbert's Council of Commerce in the 1670s, there had been no group of officials charged specifically with such matters, and long before 1700 government was aware of this lack. In this regard one should note a memoir composed in 1690 by a secretary in the naval ministry.[58] The memoir, intended for the new secretary of state for the navy, Louis de Pontchartrain, describes the various bureaus within the ministry. It informs Pontchartrain that the supervision of all French overseas trade is in the hands of a single man. This man was Jean-Baptiste de Lagny, and he held the title of director general of commerce.[59] The memoir describes de Lagny's vast responsibilities within the naval ministry and notes that it is impossible for any one man to have all the experience and special knowledge needed to supervise French external commerce. The memoir then notes that discussions have been going on for some time concerning the possible establishment of a chamber of commerce in Paris, to be composed of retired businessmen who could share their experience with the secretary of state and the director general of commerce.[60] It is not known why immediate action was not taken on this proposal; perhaps the War of the League of Augsburg prevented any ideas of administrative reform from being put into effect.[61]

The need for a council of commerce was compensated for in the 1690s by a unique set of circumstances. Traditionally, French internal commerce and manufactures had been in the hand of the controller general of finances, and external commerce was the province of the secretary of state for the navy. This distinction was blurred, however, from 1690 to 1699, when both of these offices were held by the same person, Louis de Pontchartrain. To administer commerce, Pontchartrain relied on two men. As mentioned above, de Lagny dealt with the French colonies, the merchant marine, and foreign trade. For internal trade and manufactures, Pontchartrain relied on his cousin, Henri Daguesseau, a *conseiller d'état* and a member of the Council of Finances.[62] Daguesseau supervised internal trade and industries, corresponding with businessmen, tax farmers, provincial intendants, and manufacturers.[63] De Lagny and Daguesseau were men of exceptional talent, and between them they offset, at least temporarily, the need for a better institutional arrangement.[64]

Late in 1699, however, the situation changed. In September of that year, the chancellor of France, Louis Boucherat, died, and Louis de Pontchartrain was appointed to succeed him. This meant that control over commerce would be divided once again—between the new controller general, Michel Chamillart, and the new secretary of state for the navy, Jérôme de Pontchartrain, son of Louis. This was the third factor leading to the Council of Commerce in 1700.

Louis de Pontchartrain sought to prevent a recurrence of the problems that had plagued the administration of commerce from 1683 to 1691. Colbert had held simultaneously the offices of controller general, secretary of state for the navy, and superintendent of buildings—the latter office having charge over French manufacturers. On Colbert's death these three offices were divided between Le Peletier (controller general, 1683–89), Colbert's son Seignelay (secretary of state for the navy, 1683–90) and Louvois (superintendent of buildings, 1683–91). Late in the 1680s, these three men quarreled over the jurisdictions of their respective ministries. Administrative unity returned in the 1690s, when Louis de Pontchartrain assumed control over both internal and external commerce as well as over manufactures.[65] Early in 1699, even before the death of Boucherat, Pontchartrain sought to find a solution that would prevent the disputes of the 1680s from repeating themselves. In May of that year, he presented a memoir to the king in which he meticulously outlined the respective powers of the controller general and the secretary of state for the navy over commercial affairs.[66] Pontchartrain suggested the creation of a council of commerce as a means of preventing future conflicts between these two officials. He believed that such a council would give a central, united direction to trade. It would also constitute a standing body from which both the controller general and the naval secretary could get expert advice. This memoir is also noteworthy because in it Pontchartrain recalled that the king himself had originally requested him to reflect on the problem and to submit his suggestions.[67]

Although the primary impetus for the new Council of Commerce thus came from Louis de Pontchartrain, some historians have insisted that Controller General Chamillart inspired it.[68] This contention rests on the fact that the *arrêt* of 29 June 1700 states that the king established the council upon the report of Chamillart; it does not mention either of the Pontchartrains. The explanation for this is simple: the council that most properly should have issued this *arrêt* was the Council of Finances.[69] None of the other councils dealt with commercial matters as a general rule, except in cases involving foreign relations or legal disputes. The *arrêt* was thus issued as an *arrêt en finance*, and as such had to be signed by the controller general. The form of the *arrêt* is thus as should have been expected.

Far from creating the Council of Commerce, Chamillart actually disliked the institution. In 1707 he addressed a memoir to the king in which he contended that all commerce should be under the authority of the controller general. He argued that the sharing of power with a council and with the secretary of state for the navy was an encroachment on his own powers.[70] Chamillart's feeling toward the council did not, as will be demonstrated, prevent him from working with it, but it is highly unlikely that he would have contributed to its formation.

Even though the initial push for the Council of Commerce came from Louis de Pontchartrain, one should not ignore the assistance that he received from men working under him, including his son Jérôme, who succeeded him as secretary of state for the navy and who carried through to completion the plans begun by his father. The papers of the controller general and the secretary of state for the navy contain more than a dozen memoirs and letters written by royal officials or *commis* in 1698–1700 that discuss the possible duties and membership of a council of commerce.[71] Most of these documents are undated and unsigned. They are clearly *aide-mémoires* and rough drafts of position papers that were to be presented to Louis de Pontchartrain or to his son. All of them speak of a need for such a council, and most of them stress the importance of getting advice from the business community by having merchant deputies sit on the council. Some of these documents note that such a council could help settle disputes between businessmen and tax farmers. But there is no mention in the documents of pressure from merchants or from anyone else.[72]

Louis de Pontchartrain's principal collaborator on this project was Henri Daguesseau.[73] In May of 1699, he asked Daguesseau for his opinions concerning such a council. Pontchartrain himself favored a council similar to the one established by Colbert, but Daguesseau object to this.[74] As a member of the Pontchartrain clan, Daguesseau naturally favored the interests of the new secretary of state for the navy, Jérôme de Pontchartrain. Daguesseau told the elder Pontchartrain that a council such as Colbert's might eventually become the tool of the controller general. Daguesseau suggested that the new council be more of an advisory body, and he also urged that business interests be accorded more representation than they had had in Colbert's council. That these proposals were largely accepted is shown by the final shape that the council took.

To conclude, the Council of Commerce that was created in 1700 followed in a long tradition of royal consultation with the French merchant community. It was not the product of any movement of opposition to the crown. Historians should recognize the council for what it was: an enlightened reform by the government of Louis XIV.

1. Pierre Goubert, *Louis XIV and Twenty Million Frenchmen*; Ira Wade, *The Intellectual Origins of the French Enlightenment*, pp. 633 ff.; Lionel Rothkrug, *Opposition to Louis XIV: The Political and Social Origins of the French Enlightenment*. For an older generation of historians, see Philippe Sagnac and A. de Saint-Leger, "Louis XIV (1661–1715)," pp. 647 ff.

2. See Mark Thomson, "Louis XIV and William III, 1689–1697"; "Louis XIV and the Origins of the War of the Spanish Succession"; "Louis XIV and the Grand Alliance, 1705–1710." All three essays have been reprinted in Ragnhild Hatton and J. S. Bromley (eds.), *William III and Louis XIV: Essays by and for Mark Thomson*. In this same collection of essays, John C. Rule favorably evaluates the work of Louis XIV's last secretary of state for foreign affairs in his "King and Minister: Louis XIV and Colbert de Torcy," pp. 213–36. For general discussions of this historiographical debate, see Hatton, "Louis XIV: Recent Gains in Historical Knowledge"; Hatton, "Louis XIV et l'Europe: Eléments d'une révision historiographique"; Rule, "Royal Ministers and Government Reform during the Last Decades of Louis XIV's Reign"; Patrice Berger, "Pontchartrain and the Grain Trade during the Famine of 1693."

3. Pierre Goubert, *L'ancien régime*, 1:198; Pierre Léon, "La Crise de l'économie française à la fin du règne de Louis XIV, 1685–1715," p. 132; Charles Woolsey Cole, *French Mercantilism, 1683–1700*, pp. 230 ff.; Geoffrey Symcox, *The Crisis of French Sea Power 1688–1697: From the Guerre d'Escadre to the Guerre de Course*, pp. 186–87, 231, 233; Nannerl O. Keohane, *Philosophy and the State in France: The Renaissance to the Enlightenment*, pp. 312–57; Robin Briggs, *Early Modern France, 1560–1715*, pp. 73, 163, 206.

4. Rothkrug, *Opposition*, p. 464.

5. Ibid., p. 420.

6. Ibid., p. 434.

7. Ibid., p. 416.

8. Ibid., p. 420.

9. Ibid., p. 433.

10. Ibid., p. 420.

11. Ibid., p. 373.

12. Ibid., p. 449. Actually, the repeal of the *capitation* in 1698 was nothing unusual. The Old Regime's government often raised extraordinary taxes during wartime and then repealed them upon the return of peace.

13. Ibid., p. 434. In the Treaty of Ryswick and the Franco-Dutch tariff of 1699, France reduced its customs duties on many Dutch goods and exempted Dutch vessels from paying the tax of 50 *sous* per ton levied on all foreign ships entering French ports. Far from pressuring the government to make these concessions to Holland, French merchants opposed these measures. On numerous occasions after 1700, the deputies in the Council of Commerce criticized the fact that the Dutch, their chief competitors, enjoyed these special advantages.

14. Ibid., p. 413, 418.

15. Ibid., p. 392.

16. Ibid., p. 373.

17. See Bonnassieux and Lelong, *Conseil de commerce*, pp. vi–ix; Saint-Simon, *Mémoires*, 7:415–21; Charles Woolsey Cole, *Colbert and a Century of French Mercantilism*, 1:357–60.

18. The Old Regime's word for *businessman* or *merchant* was most commonly *marchand*. If one wanted to designate in particular a large wholesaler or an overseas trader, one could choose between *marchand en gros*, *négociant*, and *commerçant*. A manufacturer was a *fabricant*.

19. Pierre Bonnassieux, *Les Assemblées représentatives du commerce sous l'ancien régime*. Bonnassieux claims that these assemblies did not begin to meet until the eighteenth century. For evidence that some met prior to 1700, see Georg Depping (ed.), *Correspondance administrative sous le règne de Louis XIV*, 3:867–68; AN, G⁷ 8, Louis de Pontchartrain to Bignon (intendant of Paris), 14 May 1697. On the popular assemblies that the crown tried to establish in Canada in the latter part of the seventeenth century, see Cole, *French Mercantilism*, p. 73; Allana G. Reid, "Representative Assemblies in New France."

20. Concerning the cooperation between the government and the business community that was implicit in the very nature of mercantilism, see Introduction, n. 5, above. Jacob Viner in particular asserts that the influence of French merchants on royal policies has been underestimated by historians (Coleman, *Revisions*, pp. 68–69, 86–87).

21. Bonnassieux and Lelong, *Conseil de commerce*, p. vi.

22. Howard M. Solomon, *Public Welfare, Science, and Propaganda in Seventeenth Century France: The Innovations of Théophraste Renaudot*, pp. 89, 98–99.

23. Generally the controller general wrote to provincial intendants and other officials and asked them to consult with mechants. Many of these letters are reprinted in A. de Boislisle (ed.), *Correspondance des contrôleurs-généraux*; Pierre Clément (ed.), *Lettres, instructions, et mémoires de Colbert*.

24. Cole speaks of Savary and of the other merchant-advisers of Colbert in his *Colbert and a Century of French Mercantilism*, 1:325–27.

25. The government's interest in statistics is described by Hervé Hasquin, "Sur les préoccupations statistiques en France au XVIIᵉ siècle." Government surveys of manufactures are discussed by Louis Fontvielle, "Les premières enquêtes industrielles de la France, 1692–1703." Also see Pierre Goubert, *Beauvais et le Beauvaisis de 1600 à 1730: Contribution à l'histoire sociale de la France du XVIIᵉ siècle*, 1:249–65; Jacques Dupâquier, *La Population rurale du bassin parisien à l'époque de Louis XIV*, pp. 42–64; André Corvisier, *La France de Louis XIV, 1643–1715: ordre intérieur et place en Europe*, pp. 217–30.

26. See A. de Boislisle (ed.), *Mémoires des intendants sur l'état des généralités dressés pour l'instruction du duc de Bourgogne*. Volume 1, *Mémoire de la généralité de Paris*, pp. 781–86.

27. Louis Trenard discusses these memoirs and current research on them in *Les Mémoires des intendants pour l'instruction du duc de Bourgogne (1698): introduction générale*.

28. Marcel Giraud assesses the humanitarian ideals and the administrative reforms of Secretary of State for the Navy Jérôme de Pontchartrain in several articles: "Crise de conscience et d'autorité à la fin du règne de Louis XIV"; "La France et la Louisiane au début du XVIIIᵉ siècle"; and "Tendances humanitaires à la fin du règne de Louis XIV." The royal provincial intendants repeatedly made the crown aware of the poverty and injustices suffered by the *menu peuple*. See, for example, Boislisle, *Mémoires des intendants*, pp. 483–84, 524–25. The humanitarian concerns of Michel Bégon, intendant in the *généralité* of La Rochelle from 1694 to 1710, are described in Yvonne Bezard, *Fonctionnaires maritimes et coloniaux sous Louis XIV: Les Bégon*, chap. 7. Also see Patrice Berger, "Rural Charity in Late Seventeenth Century France: The Pontchartrain Case."

29. Two historians have stated that the Council of Commerce was related to the increasing concern for surveys and statistics. They claim, without documenting it, that the council was created in order to sift through and evaluate all the data coming in to the goverment. See Claude-Joseph Gignoux, *Le Commerce, du XVᵉ siècle au milieu du XIXᵉ*, pp. 244–45; David S. Landes, "Statistics as a Source for the History of Economic Development in Western Europe: The Protostatistical Era," p. 62.

30. I cannot claim to have checked every available source of information from the 1690s. This would entail exhaustive research in all the Paris archives as well as in every departmental archive. The materials that I have checked in the Archives de la Marine include a sampling of the B² and B³ series (outgoing and incoming correspondence), as well as a complete reading of B⁷ 495, 496, 497, 498, 499, 500 (diverse papers on commerce). In the G⁷ series at the Archives Nationales (controller general's papers), I have consulted most of the correspondence of the late 1690s from towns and provinces that eventually sent a deputy to the Council of Commerce. This includes the following cartons: G⁷ 115, 181–83, 259–60, 270–71, 304–6, 358, 431, 464–65, 496–97.

31. AN, G⁷ 339, *juge* and *consuls* of the *juridiction consulaire* of La Rochelle to controller general, 16 February 1700, and comte de Gacé to Chamillant, 20 February 1700.

32. Further research may produce other examples of merchants requesting some institutional arrangement with the government, but it is the burden of the proponents of the thesis of merchant opposition to produce this evidence. Even if a few other scattered letters supporting this view should some day be adduced, they would still be far from proving that the government was forced onto the defensive by a rising tide of opposition. As will be demonstrated below, the government seems to have been unaware of merchant "demands" for a council of commerce at the time it was making its own plans for such a council.

33. Martin Wolfe, "French Views on Wealth and Taxes," p. 471; Yves-Marie Bercé, *Croquants et nu-pieds: les soulèvements paysans en France du XVIᵉ au XIXᵉ siècles,* pp. 52–58; Klaus Malettke, *Opposition und Konspiration unter Ludwig XIV: Studien zu Kritik und Widerstand gegen System und Politik des französischen Königs während der ersten Hälfte seinen persönlichen Regierung;* Corvisier, *La France de Louis XIV,* pp. 78–81, 251.

34. Rothkrug, *Opposition,* p. 386.

35. *Testament politique de messire Jean Baptiste Colbert* (The Hague, 1693).

36. *Testament politique du marquis de Louvois* (Cologne, 1695).

37. This point is discussed by B. N. Woodbridge, *Gatien de Courtilz, sieur de Verger: étude sur un précurseur du roman réaliste en France,* pp. 206–7.

38. Woodbridge notes that Courtilz de Sandras may also have been sent to the Bastille a second time, remaining there from 1702 to 1709 (ibid., pp. 9, 12).

39. See L. J. Gras, "Les Chambres de commerce," pp. 500–51. For a description of the agent of Marseilles in Paris, see Joseph Fournier, *La Chambre de commerce de Marseille et ses représentants permanents à Paris, 1599–1875,* chaps. 1 and 2.

40. For example, in 1697 silk-manufacturing interests in Paris, Lyons, Tours, Amiens, and Rheims sent special deputies to the court to petition the government against permitting the sale in France of cloths from the East Indies that came to France in ships captured from the enemy. See Mar., B⁷ 498, fols. 212–14, "Mémoire sur les placets présentés par les marchans et ouvriers en soye des villes de Paris, Lion, Tours, Amiens et Reims."

41. Towns with deputies in the Council of Commerce continued to send special agents to Paris even after 1700. For example, see Jean-Auguste Brutails, "Etudes sur la Chambre du commerce de Guienne."

42. This episode in French naval history is best described in Geoffrey Symcox, *The Crisis of French Sea Power.*

43. Ibid., pp. 186–87, 203–5; Rothkrug, *Opposition,* pp. 392–419.

44. Symcox, *The Crisis of French Sea Power,* pp. 169–77. See also Claude-Frédéric Lévy, *Capitalistes et pouvoir au siècle des lumières: les fondateurs des origines à 1715,* pp. 49 ff. and passim.

45. On investment in privateering by royal officials, see Symcox, *The Crisis of French Sea Power*, pp. 173–74, 238–44; J. S. Bromley, "Projets et contrats d'armement en course marseillais, 1705–1712," p. 101; Bromley, "The French Privateering War, 1702–1713," pp. 208–9.

46. Saint-Simon mentions Belesbat only once in his memoirs, upon the occasion of his death in 1706. Saint-Simon's caricature of Belesbat is among his most sardonic: "He had the body of an elephant and the mind of an ox, and yet he continually thought of himself as a courtier, following the king in all his trips to the battle fronts. But all of this gained Belesbat very little. His family had been of the robe, yet Belesbat was of neither robe nor sword. He often caused himself to be laughed at, and occasionally he uttered some amusing crudities" (*Mémoires*, 13:305). Unless otherwise noted, all translations are by the author.

47. On Belesbat see Albert Schatz and Robert Caillemer, "Le Mercantilisme libéral à la fin du XVIIe siècle: les idées économiques et politiques de M. de Belesbat."

48. Rothkrug, *Opposition*, especially pp. 328–51, 372; Wade, *Intellectual Origins*, pp. 636–37; Werner Gembruch, "Reformforderungen in Frankreich um die Wende vom 17. zum 18. Jahrhundert: Ein Beitrag zur Geschichte des Opposition gegen System und Politik Ludwigs XIV," p. 269.

49. Rothkrug conjectures that Belesbat's ideas were "possibly" read at the weekly meetings of the *salon* of his cousin, the abbé de Choisy (*Opposition*, p. 330 n. 70). He cites the journal of the club (Bibliothèque de l'Arsenal, MS. 3186) as evidence that this group of intellectuals met to discuss contemporary political events. But a reading of the document shows that this weekly *salon* occupied itself with such "current" issues as ancient coinage, French grammar, dwarfism, and medieval history. Furthermore, the author of the journal often criticizes the other members for not taking the work of the assembly very seriously. On 5 August 1692, the club spent two hours discussing the recent French victory at Steinkirk, but this lapse into current events was clearly unusual. The journal's author admitted that "it is justifiable to sacrifice two hours to politics whenever there is a big battle or whenever we take a city," but he lamented this interruption in the club's scientific and historical discussions. (fol. 212v).

50. There exist several copies of these memoirs, each slightly different from the others. The author amended them on numerous occasions and resubmitted them to royal officials. See Bibliothèque de l'Arsenal, MSS. 4069, 4561; Bibliothèque Municipale de Poitiers, MS. 548; AAE, Mémoires et Documents, France, Supplément, 1999; BN, MSS. fr., 14294; Mar., B⁴ 14.

51. Rothkrug (*Opposition*, p. 435) says that Pottier de la Hestroye wrote his memoirs in June 1700 and implies that they had an impact on the establishment of the Council of Commerce. I found no evidence in the document Rothkrug cites to place it in June 1700. Furthermore, in another copy of these memoirs the author clearly states that he submitted them to Jérôme de Pontchartrain only after the Council of Commerce was already in existence (Bibliothèque de l'Arsenal, MS. 4561, p. E of Avertissement).

52. Vauban, "Description géographique de l'élection de Vézelay," in Boislisle, *Mémoires des intendants*, p. 743; Vauban, *Projet d'une Dixme Royale*, pp. 68–70. The former was written in 1696 and the latter, though not published until 1707, underwent its first draft in 1698. The chamber of commerce that Vauban speaks of should not be confused with the chambers of commerce that in the eighteenth century were established in several cities in France. Even afer its establishment in 1700, the Council of Commerce was often, erroneously, referred to as the Chamber of Commerce in Paris.

53. BN, Collection Hennin, MS. 6430. At least one historian has previously asserted that the Council of Commerce was part of a general plan to revive trade (John Bosher, *The Single Duty Project: A Study of the Movement for a French Customs Union in the Eighteenth Century*, p. 28).

54. This *arrêt* is reprinted in Boislisle, *Correspondence des contrôleurs-généraux*, 2: 476–77.

55. To cite just one illustration: the edict of February 1700 that established a consular jurisdiction and a chamber of commerce in Dunkirk. The edict cites the numerous requests from the people to Dunkirk that something be done to help their city as the primary motive for forming the new institutions. A copy of this edict can be found in AN, AD XI, 9.

56. Several of Weber's essays are reprinted in *The Theory of Social and Economic Organization*, trans. A. M. Henderson and Talcott Parsons, ed. Talcott Parsons; also see Michael T. Dalby and Michael S. Werthman, *Bureaucracy in Historical Perspective*; and Henry Jacoby, *The Bureaucratization of the World*.

57. On the foreign affairs ministry, see John C. Rule, "Colbert de Torcy, an Emergent Bureaucracy, and the Formulation of French Foreign Policy, 1698 to 1715," in Ragnhild Hatton (ed.), *Louis XIV and Europe*, pp. 261–88. For the naval ministry, see Albert Duchêne, *La Politique coloniale de la France: le ministère des colonies depuis Colbert*, pp. 28–35; John C. Rule, "Jérôme Phélypeaux, Comte de Pontchartrain, and the Establishment of Louisiana, 1696–1715."

58. Mar., B⁸ 18, "Mémoire sur le nouveau Département de Monseigneur," dated 9 November 1690. A note on the jacket of the memoir suggests that its author was probably Pierre Clairambault, the *premier commis* charged with maintaining the naval archives.

59. De Lagny was also a *fermier général*, and one of his duties was that of reconciling the interests of trade with those of the royal revenues. For more on him, see Rothkrug, *Opposition*, pp. 216–20, 377–78, 447, 448; Jacob M. Price, *France and the Chesapeake: A History of the French Tobacco Monopoly, 1674–1791, and of Its Relationship to the British and American Tobacco Trades*, 1:25, 55, 64, 98; Saint-Simon, *Mémoires*, 7:421. Symcox (*The Crisis of French Sea Power*, p. 200) states erroneously that de Lagny was named first head of the Council of Commerce; de Lagny was never a member of the council. He had been appointed director general of commerce by Seignelay in 1686. In addition to being a farmer general, he had formerly been a director of the Compagnie du Nord and of the Compagnie du commerce de la Méditerranée.

60. At about this same time (1690), former Controller General Le Peletier suggested a council of commerce in which merchants would be represented, but apparently Secretary of State for the Navy Seignelay opposed the idea. The anonymous memoir that describes this was written in 1698 or 1699 and purports to give a brief history of councils of commerce in the seventeenth century. This memoir, however, frequently errs, and therefore its account of the attempt to create a council of commerce in 1690 is unreliable. See Mar., B⁷ 499 "Sur un Conseil de Commerce," fols. 390–92.

61. The memoir in Mar., B⁸ 18 did stress that, in order to flourish, commerce always requires peace.

62. Henri Daguesseau (1635–1715) was the father of Henri-François Daguesseau (1668–1751), who served as chancellor of France from 1717 to 1750. The son wrote a full-length biography of his father in his *Oeuvres* (Paris, 1819), vol. 15. Many historians have confused the father and son. The source of this confusion lies in the fact that the two men held prominent positions concurrently for more than a quarter of a century. Daguesseau *père* was a *conseiller d'état* from 1694 to his death,

and president of the Council of Commerce beginning in 1700. He also belonged to several other councils and commissions. Daguesseau *fils* was *avocat général* (1691–1700), then *procureur général* (1700–1717) in the Parlement of Paris. Nineteenth-century activists frequently attributed the father's letters to the son, even though the signatures of the two men are easily distinguishable. The sad results of this mis-labeling are evident yet today in several volumes of the B⁷ series of the naval archives. Historians who have confused father and son include, among others, Philippe Sagnac, "La Politique commerciale," pp. 266–67; Charles Frostin, "Les Pontchartrain et la pénétration commerciale française en Amérique espagnole (1690–1715)," p. 312.

63. Daguesseau began his supervision of trade and industry within France in September 1691. See marquis de Dangeau, *Journal*, 3:378. Daguesseau held no official title, although contemporaries referred to him variously, as *directeur du commerce* or *surintendant du commerce*. Thus an untitled memoir dated 14 January 1699 in AN, F¹² 673, addressed Daguesseau by the latter title. Many of Daguesseau's letters and memos from the 1690s can be found in AN, G⁷ 1685.

64. See especially Mar., B⁷ 496, 497, 498, 499. De Lagny and Daguesseau worked well together, and they seem to have been the principal directors of French com-mercial policy in the signing of the Treaty of Ryswick in 1697 and in the 1699 commercial treaty with the Dutch.

65. After the death of Louvois in 1691, jurisdiction over manufactures was trans-ferred to the controller general. The new superintendent of buildings, the marquis de Villacerf, retained control over only the Gobelins and the Savonnerie. Further details on the ministerial conflicts of the 1680s can be found in Richard Bingham, "Louis XIV and the War for Peace: The Genesis of a Peace Offensive, 1686–1690," pp. 683–86. Concerning ministerial conflicts over the administration of commerce in particular, see "Mémoire de M. de Seignelay au sujet des contestations entre lui et le controlleur général sur l'administration des affaires du commerce," dated 21 September 1689, in Mar., B⁷ 495, fols. 550–52v.

66. Boislisle, *Correspondance des contrôleurs généraux*, 2:465–69. A *règlement* was issued on 13 September 1699 that divided control over commerce along the lines laid down by Pontchartrain. A copy of this *règlement* can be found in Mar., A² 21, pp. 161–65. On this see also BN, Joly de Fleury, MS. 1721, fols. 155–85. A second convention was signed between the controller general and the secretary of state on either 12 September or 12 December 1701; there is conflicting evidence concerning the date. See AN, G⁷ 1702, fols. 187–87v; Didier Neuville, *Etat sommaire des Archives de la marine antérieures à la révolution*, p. 249 n. 1; Biollay, *Etudes économiques*, pp. 296–97; Mar., A² 21, pp. 260–63.

67. Ella Lonn and D. Hauterive have conjectured that the French government formed the Council of Commerce in emulation of the English Board of Trade, which had been established in 1696; Ella Lonn, "The French Council of Commerce in Relation to American Trade," p. 193 n. 3; Mar., B⁷ 515, D. Hauterive to marquis de Clermont-Tonnerre, 8 January 1823, and the attached "Mémoire sur l'ancien conseil de commerce établi en France par Colbert sur le Board of Trade d'Angle-terre." The latter is especially unreliable, since Colbert actually died before the Board of Trade was created. I have found no evidence linking the two bodies.

68. For example, L.-J. Gras, "Les Chambres de commerce," p. 551; Paul Masson, *Histoire du commerce français dans le Levant au XVIIᵉ siècle*, p. 308; Jacques Saint-Germain, *Samuel Bernard le banquier des rois*, p. 93; Gaston Rambert, in Gaston Rambert (ed.), *Histoire du commerce de Marseille*, 4:242.

69. Michel Antoine has demonstrated, however, that most of the work of the conseil des finances was performed in the various bureaus of the controller general and the intendants of finances (*Le Conseil du roi sous le règne de Louis XV*, pp. 383–407.

70. Boislisle, *Correspondance des contrôleurs généraux*, 2:475.

71. These memoirs are in AN, F¹² 725, 908–9, 1903; G⁷ 1686 (piece 156); Mar., B⁷ 499 (fols. 380–402); BN, Joly de Fleury, MS. 1721, fols. 155–57, 183–85.

72. Nor do these papers discuss the need for revising Colbert's commercial ordinance of 1673. Without citing any evidence, Jacqueline-Lucienne Lafon contends that this issue was one of those that contributed most to the creating of the council (*Les Députés du commerce et l'ordonnance de mars 1673*, pp. v, 3).

73. Henri-François Daguesseau went so far as to credit his father with the honor of having established the Council of Commerce (*Oeuvres*, 15:335) This assertion has been repeated by Biollay (*Etudes économiques*, p. 295) and Cole (*French Mercantilism, 1683–1700*, p. 7).

74. Boislisle, *Correspondance des contrôleurs généraux*, 2:464–65, Daguesseau to Pontchartrain, 20 May 1699.

2

THE ORGANIZATION AND
FUNCTIONING OF THE COUNCIL

Before approaching the major problems on which the Council of Commerce worked during its first fifteen years, one must understand how the council operated. This chapter will therefore describe the organization and the workings of the council and its relations with the controller general and the secretary of state for the navy. It will also assess in general the role that the council played in French economic policies during this period.

THE ORGANIZATION OF THE COUNCIL

Although the *arrêt* establishing the council was issued on 29 June 1700, the council did not first assemble until 24 November 1700. Few of the commentators of the day mentioned it. In July 1700 the marquis de Dangeau briefly noted the creation of a "chambre pour le commerce,"[1] but the semiofficial *Almanach royal* did not start to list it among the royal councils until the year 1703.[2] This rather unspectacular beginning was reflective of the subsequent history of the council, for it always wielded more behind-the-scenes power and influence than the public generally recognized.

The council met at the home of its president, Henri Daguesseau, on the rue Pavée, in the Marais quarter of Paris. As prescribed by the founding *arrêt*, the council was composed of six *commissaires*, who were officers of the crown, as well as thirteen deputies from the major cities of France.[3] Daguesseau, as the senior *conseiller d'état*, presided over the meetings. The other *commissaires*, in order of seniority, were Controller General Michel Chamillart, Secretary of State for the Navy Jérôme de Pontchartrain, *conseiller d'état* Michel Jean Amelot de Gournay, and two *maîtres des requêtes*, François-Joseph d'Ernothon and Nicolas-Prosper Bauyn d'Angervilliers.[4] The deputies of commerce were to be "persons of recognized probity, ability, and experience in trade."[5] With the exception of the two Parisian deputies, who were chosen by the king, all the deputies were to be elected at town meetings composed of local municipal officers, consular officials, and prominent business leaders. The deputies who assembled on 24 November 1700 included Samuel Bernard and Antoine Peletyer (Paris), Nicolas Mesnager (Rouen), Léon de Rol (Bayonne), Jean-Baptiste Fénellon (Bordeaux), Noé Piécourt (Dunkirk), François-Eustache Taviel (Lille), (?) Mourgues (Languedoc), Jean Anisson (Lyons), Joseph Fabre (Marseilles), Joachim Descasaux du Hallay (Nantes), Antoine Héron (La Rochelle), and Alain de La Motte-Gaillard (Saint-Malo).[6]

The Council of Commerce also included two farmers general, who were summoned to meetings whenever an affair concerned their interests. The two tax farmers who served on the council during the reign of Louis XIV were Charles de Poyrel de Grandval and Jean-Rémy Hénault.[7] The last member of the council was the secretary, Jean de Valossière.[8] The secretary's duties, which were gradually expanded, included keeping the official minutes of the meetings.[9]

The Council of Commerce differed markedly from the other royal councils. Its chief task, as noted in the founding *arrêt*, was that of advising the controller general of finances and the secretary of state for the navy on all matters concerning French manufactures and commerce (both external and internal). Unlike other councils, therefore, the Council of Commerce had no administrative functions of its own; nor could it issue *arrêts* or any other sort of law or directive. The Council of Commerce was also of lesser authority because it lacked the royal presence. In all the other royal councils, either the king presided or he was at least counted as present by the empty armchair reserved for him at the head of the table; there was, however, no hint of royal presence at the Council of Commerce. This council is therefore noticeably different from Colbert's Council of Commerce, which was headed by the king and which did have the power to issue *arrêts* and other orders that were binding on provincial officials.[10] The fact that the Council of Commerce kept official minutes of its meetings further distinguished it from other royal councils. Part of the mystery of divine-right kingship consisted in the secrecy of all that occurred in the *conseil du roi*, the council to which all other councils were judged to belong.[11] This accounts for the absence of any *procès-verbaux* for the meetings of the *conseil d'en haut*, the Council of Finances, and the other royal councils.[12] The Council of Commerce was also peculiar because of the nonparticipation of royal ministers in its work. Although the controller general and the secretary of state for the navy were always counted as members of the Council of Commerce, they rarely attended its meetings. During the first fifteen years of the council's existence, these two officials attended only three times: the opening session of 24 November 1700 and the meetings of 23 June and 15 September 1701.[13] This was due not to the relative unimportance of the council but rather to an agreement made between Chamillart and Jérôme de Pontchartrain not to attend.[14] The purpose of this arrangement was to prevent one man or the other from gaining undue influence over the proceedings of the council. The two men further agreed that they would send to the council all matters that concerned commerce in general. This would keep each of them informed of the actions of the other.

All these considerations lead one to infer that the Council of Commerce was really more like a bureau or a permanent commission rather than a true royal council. Beginning in 1715, in fact, the *Almanach royal* classified it as the *Bureau pour le Conseil de Commerce* and listed it among the "Bureaux de Messieurs les commissaires du Conseil pour les commissions ordinaires et extraordinaires de Finances."[15]

The organization of the Council of Commerce underwent several modifications during the period under study. In 1701 two offices of directors of finances were created to serve the controller general. These two officials had the right of entry into all royal councils, including the Council of Commerce. The first two directors were Hilaire Rouillé du Coudray and Joseph-Jean Baptiste Fleuriau d'Armenonville.[16] In October 1703 the former was replaced by Nicolas Desmaretz, who attended the council regularly until he became controller general in February 1708.[17] Beginning in January 1705, the lieutenant general of police of Paris, the marquis d'Argenson, began to sit on the council.[18] He was given entrance to the council because of his control of trade and manufactures in the French capital. Early in 1708 the two offices of directors of finances were abolished, and the two persons who held these positions were replaced in the council by six newly created intendants of commerce.[19] The commissions of these six men were attached to six new positions of *maître des requêtes*, which offices were sold for 200,000 livres each.[20] The intendants of commerce were each given a department, consisting of several French provinces as well as certain parts of French foreign trade.[21] Whenever a matter was brought to the Council of Commerce, it went to the intendant in whose department it lay, and this individual was charged with studying the matter and reporting on it. In June 1708 another new *commissaire* was added to the council: Louis Béchameil de Nointel, brother-in-law of Nicolas Desmaretz. The *arrêt* appointing him said that the other *commissaires* were so busy on various affairs that they needed help in the Council of Commerce.[22] For this same reason, yet another *commissaire*, Jean-Baptiste Desmaretz de Vaubourg, younger brother of the controller general, joined the council in June 1715.[23]

During this period there were also two other members of the Council of Commerce, although one can seriously doubt that they ever actively participated in its work. In June 1700 the famous Rouen trader Thomas Le Gendre was given the title of inspector general of commerce. Along with this office went an annual pension of 12,000 livres and the freedom to attend the Council of Commerce whenever he wished.[24] The post that Le Gendre was given, however, seems to have been more honorific than substantial, and there is no evidence that Le Gendre ever attended the Council of Commerce.[25] The second rather shadowy member of the Council of Commerce was Philippe Millieu, who held one of the two offices of *directeur général des vivres, étapes, fourrages et lits des hôpitaux des armées et garnisons du roi*, which were created by edict in November 1703. By virtue of this office, he assumed a seat on the Council of Commerce on 16 January 1704,[26] but there is no further mention of him in any of the records or correspondence of the council.[27]

The paragraphs above describe the contours of the Council of Commerce up to the death of Louis XIV. The council was divided basically into two groups: the *commissaires* (including the six intendants of commerce), who sat in armchairs on one side of the table, and the deputies, farmers general, and secretary, who sat in armless chairs on the other side. The *commissaires* were the only ones who had the right to vote on matters being discussed at the meetings. It would be inaccurate, however, to conclude, as one historian has done,[28] that the deputies and farmers general were mere "auxiliaries" and not full members. As will become clear below, the *commissaires* depended upon the other members to do much of the work, and rarely did they fail to consider carefully the opinions of all the members of the council.

HOW THE COUNCIL FUNCTIONED

Generally the council met on Friday afternoon in the home of Henri Daguesseau.[29] If Daguesseau was ill or otherwise unable to attend, it met in the home of the second-ranking *conseiller d'état*. In the late summer and fall of each year, the *commissaires* followed the king to Fontainebleau, and the council was usually recessed for several weeks. This gave the deputies a chance to return to their homes and to conduct their own personal affairs.

At the meetings the deputies were allowed to speak only when called upon, although this happened frequently. At the opening of the council on 24 November 1700, it was decided that the deputies would need to meet on their own each week, apart from the council itself. This would permit them to have a full discussion of the matters introduced in the council. Chamillart proposed to ask the king for a pension for the secretary of the council, who would use it to rent a house where the deputies could meet and where all the records of the council could be stored.[30] Shortly thereafter the secretary was accorded an annual pension of 10,700 livres, and the deputies began to assemble at his home on Monday and Friday mornings.[31] If an urgent matter was being discussed, the deputies convened on other days as well. The secretary drew up a written *avis* of the deputies' opinions on each issue submitted to them and presented these *avis* at the next meeting of the council.

The affairs about which the controller general and the secretary of state sought the advice of the Council of Commerce had numerous origins. As a general rule, the ministers forwarded to the council the letters and petitions that they received from provincial intendants, inspectors of manufactures, traders, and manufacturers if the matters needed study and pertained to commerce. If the *commissaires* or deputies themselves wished to introduce a question to the council, they first had to have it approved by one minister or the other.[32]

The person who usually received the materials remitted by the controller general or the secretary of state for the navy was the secretary of the council, Jean de Valossière. Preserved in series G[7] and F[12] of the Archives Nationales are hundreds of letters and requests addressed to the controller general on which are added at the top "à M. Valossière." The secretary recorded every document he received in a register, and at the next meeting of the council he distributed these papers to the *commissaires* who would be charged with studying them. The controller general or the secretary of state could also choose, however, to present a matter directly to a *commissaire*, either in person or by letter. The *commissaires*, as *conseillers d'état* or *maîtres des requêtes*, generally served in several royal councils or commissions, and thus had frequent contacts with the two ministers.

With regard to the assignment of matters to the various *commissaires*, one must distinguish the period 1700–1707 from the period beginning with the creation of the intendants of commerce in May 1708. During the council's first seven years, there was no clear division of responsibilities among the *commissaires*. This left the door open for Amelot, capable and ambitious, to assume a leading role in the council's affairs. The records of the council clearly demonstrate that Amelot conducted a majority of the affairs treated in the council and that he was the chief link between the council and both Chamillart and Jérôme de Pontchartrain. In March 1705, however, Amelot was appointed ambassador to Spain, where he served until 1709.[33] During his long absence, his work in the council was taken over by the other *commissaires*—chiefly Henri Daguesseau, who remained surprisingly active in spite of his advanced age and frequent illnesses. The creation of the six intendants of commerce in 1708, however, regularized the procedures of the council and clearly distinguished the departments of the six new *commissaires*. Henceforth all of the investigations and reports were handled by these six men. The other *commissaires* still attended the meetings and participated in the debates and the voting, but they now had more time to devote to their other governmental responsibilities. The intendants of commerce, meanwhile, became "in effect the bureau chiefs of commercial affairs."[34] They had their own *commis* and as they accumulated correspondence and other papers, their own archives came to rival those kept by the secretary of the Council of Commerce as a documentary record of French economic developments.[35]

Once a matter had been introduced at a meeting and assigned to a *commissaire*, one of several things might happen to it. If the matter was simple and required no study, it was quickly voted on and reported back to the minister who had sent it. If the matter was complex or if additional information was required, it was dispatched to a provincial intendant, to an admiralty official, or to some other royal agent for study.[36] If the question concerned the king's revenues or the tax farmers, it might be sent to the farmers general, or the two farmers general assigned to the Council of

Commerce could be summoned to appear at the council.[37] After the royal officials or the farmers general had replied to the council's queries, the entire matter was then sent to the deputies. Most frequently, however, the affairs introduced at a meeting were referred immediately to the deputies, who discussed them at their next assembly in the home of the secretary. The *avis* of the deputies on each issue was then presented to the council by the secretary at the next meeting. If the deputies were divided on an issue, the views of each side were noted in the *avis*. Often, especially on controversial issues, the deputies drew up individual memoirs stating their particular views. These memoirs were then also presented to the *commissaires*. The secretary gave an oral report of the deputies' opinions, and occasionally the deputies themselves were called on to explain further their views.

Once the *commissaires* had heard the views of the deputies, they could decide to send the matter (along with the deputies' *avis*) to a provincial intendant or to some other royal official for his opinion. The council might also send the matter back to the deputies' assembly for more study. But most often the council decided to proceed with the debate and to vote on the matter. In extremely complicated and important issues, such as the question of French tariff policies, the whole process of seeking advice from experts, getting the opinion of the deputies, and discussing the matter in the council could be repeated numerous times over several months. But in the great majority of cases, the Council of Commerce required only two to three weeks to reply to the controller general or the secretary of state.

It is impossible to analyze quantitatively the voting patterns of the *commissaires* or the deputies on the affairs decided in the council. The *procès-verbaux* do not report which members were present at each meeting, much less how they voted. One can gather from memoirs of the deputies how they felt about certain issues, but there are only scraps of external evidence concerning how the *commissaires* voted. A plurality of voices carried an issue, and it was then generally presented to the royal ministers as the unanimous decision of the council. In some cases the *commissaires* did not vote, but merely forwarded to the ministers the opinions of the deputies.

The *avis* produced in the deputies' assemblies thus served as the indispensable foundation for virtually all work done by the Council of Commerce. The lawyers and bureaucrats who made up the voting half of the council depended heavily on the wide experience

TABLE 1
The Procedure Followed by the Council

The following diagram describes, in a general way, the course that was followed by most of the questions submitted to the council. The intendants of commerce, whose offices were created in 1708, are included here. Prior to that date one of the other *commissaires* acted as *rapporteur*. As noted in the text, a question could follow any of several paths through the council. Sometimes steps 2, 3, or 7 were eliminated. Step 7 often preceded step 6. Steps 6, 7, and 8 were occasionally repeated.

1. Request or complaint submitted by private individual, provincial intendant, or other royal official.

2. Decision by royal minister to seek advice of council.

3. Reception of the matter by secretary of the council.

4. Presentation of the matter to the intendant of commerce into whose department it fell. He directs the subsequent handling of the question.

5. Brief discussion of the matter in the council as a whole.

6. Deliberation of the question in the deputies' assembly at the home of the secretary. The secretary drafts a written summary of the deputies' views.

7. Solicitation of additional information or evidence from interested parties or royal officials.

8. Final discussion in the council as a whole. Vote by the *commissaires*. The two farmers general attached to the council may be asked to attend and partake in the discussion if the subject pertains to the king's revenues.

9. Final report to the royal ministers. This was done in person (by an intendant of commerce or other *commissaire)* and in writing (by the secretary).

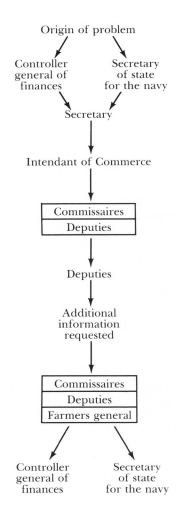

that the deputies had in trade and manufactures, the problems faced by the merchant marine, and the disputes that often erupted between merchants and tax farmers.

Out of the thousands of affairs discussed in the Council of Commerce during this fifteen-year period, I have uncovered only ten instances in which the *commissaires* rejected an *avis* that had the unanimous support of the deputies.[38] Most of these instances involved only minor points or procedural matters. It would be impossible to see in them an unsuccessful campaign by the deputies to defend the rights of free trade and unhampered private enterprise against encroachments of the royal government. In at least two of the cases, the *commissaires*, in fact, were the ones who defended the cause of free trade against the proposals of the deputies. One such case involved the plague that was ravaging much of Europe in the winter of 1711–12. The deputies pushed for stronger, more severe safeguards, including the cutting off of all trade with Baltic cities for three months. The *commissaires* felt that such an action would unduly harm French commerce, and they decided that the less drastic safety measures already enacted in French ports on orders from Jérôme de Ponchartrain were sufficient.[39] In another case the *commissaires* decided in July 1708 to permit French merchants to import *fils de dentelle* (lace thread) from Holland because it was needed for French manufactures. The deputies of commerce, on the other hand, had hoped that prohibiting its import would contribute to the destruction of Dutch trade.[40]

The differences between the deputies and the *commissaires* were thus extremely few in number, and none involved broad, fundamental disagreements over royal economic policies. The general harmony between the deputies and the representatives of the government in the Council of Commerce thus further discounts the notion that this council was a forum for protest against the crown. In later chapters when it is noted that the Council of Commerce took a stand on a particular issue, this should be understood to include both the *commissaires* and the deputies, unless otherwise noted.

Even though the deputies formed an integral, indispensable part of the council, the *commissaires* occasionally assembled apart from them. The minutes of the council record twenty-three occasions in the period under study when the *commissaires* met alone or when the deputies were asked to retire from a meeting so that the *commissaires* could discuss something in private. It should be pointed out, however, that the minutes are careful not to refer to these sessions as the Council of Commerce. On these occasions simply a "committee" was meeting.

Why did the *commissaires* feel the need to meet apart from, or to exclude, the deputies from some discussions? On two occasions the explanation is simple: the *commissaires* assembled to discuss some unfinished business while at Fontainebleau during the autumn recess in the council's schedule.[41] The things that they discussed there were fairly routine, and the deputies had already expressed their views on them. Thirteen of the other twenty-one special meetings involved highly charged, controversial issues on which the deputies were sharply divided. These issues included disputes between Marseilles and the Atlantic ports concerning Marseilles's privilege as a free port and its advantages in the Levant trade, a debate between Dunkirk and La Rochelle concerning Dunkirk's request to be able to trade directly with the French West Indies, and the rivalry between sugar refiners in La Rochelle and Bordeaux.[42] In each of these cases, the council weighed the opinions of both sides, and then the *commissaires* decided to have the deputies leave the room so that they could debate the matter in a calm, dispassionate manner. On the eight other occasions when the *commissaires* met alone, it is not clear why they felt the need to discuss matters apart from the deputies. In two cases the *procès-verbaux* report only that the *commissaires* assembled to examine an "extraordinary document" sent by the king.[43] In the six remaining instances, the matters discussed do not appear to have been unusual or any more crucial than the host of other subjects for which the deputies were permitted to remain present. For example, the deputies retired from the meeting of 18 June 1704 so that the *commissaires* could privately consider a proposal drawn up by several deputies for a new *arrêt* relating to French privateers.[44] The *commissaires* agreed with the definitions drawn up by the deputies on the questions of what constituted neutral commerce and of what ships could be legally seized as prizes by French *corsaires*. The *commissaires* decided to forward the proposal to Jérôme de Pontchartrain, and it was eventually issued as an *arrêt* on 23 July 1704. On this occasion, as well as on several others, the *procès-verbaux* do not explain why the deputies were not permitted to witness the *commissaires*' debate. What is clear, however, is that the twenty-three occasions on which the deputies were not present were rare breaches in the ordinary operating procedure of the Council of Commerce.

Once a decision was made on an issue, the council reported it ("rendre compte" was the phrase continually used) to the two royal ministers. Regardless of which one sent the matter to the council, both the controller general and the secretary of state for the navy received reports on all matters decided by it. This "rendering account" to the government took place in two ways. First, the secretary to the council, Valossière, was charged with keeping both ministers informed of the activities of the council. He sent a weekly summary of the council's meeting to each of the two ministers. In addition, he often wrote letters to them on particular issues. Almost invariably he included with his letters and his reports a copy of the *avis* of the deputies.[45] The reports and letters sent by the secretary to the controller general became even more numerous and more detailed starting in 1708. This was another of the changes brought to the Council of Commerce by Desmaretz, who wanted to keep closer control over its workings.[46] Desmaretz was also primarily responsible for the *règlement* of 9 October 1708,[47] which made more explicit the procedures to be followed by the council in examining and reporting the matters sent to it.

After 1709 Valossière's reports to the two ministers became less detailed, and fewer of them can be found in the archives. One reason for this was, perhaps, that there was a second manner in which the ministers kept abreast of the activities of the council. From the council's inception in 1700, the *commissaires* were also important links between it and the two royal ministers. Daguesseau and Amelot in particular worked closely with Chamillart and Pontchartrain, and they reported to them on the activities of the council. This practice was formalized with the creation of the six intendants of commerce in 1708: these new members were charged with informing the two ministers on all the affairs that concerned their individual departments. The archives of the controller general and of the secretary of state for the navy contain hundreds of letters both to and from the intendants of commerce, but it is impossible to gauge the full depth of the contacts between the *commissaires* and the ministers because the *commissaires* usually made their reports in person. Letters from the intendants of commerce to the royal ministers (or to their *premiers commis*) frequently allude to their weekly discussions about matters examined in the council.[48] That the two ministers met in person virtually each week with these representatives of the council further reflects the value that the crown attached to the work that the council was performing.

THE COUNCIL'S IMPORTANCE

The Subjects Discussed

The wide spectrum of subjects treated in the council is certainly one measure of its importance.[49] In the realm of commercial institutions, the council dealt with provincial chambers of commerce, consular tribunals (*juridictions consulaires*), guilds and merchant associations, trading companies, banks, bourses, and royal monetary manipulations. With regard to internal commerce, the council studied matters relating to such topics as fairs, internal customs duties and tolls, roads and navigable rivers, public transportation, the postal system, and confrontations between merchants and *commis* of the farmers general. In the area of foreign trade, the council examined questions on fisheries, tariffs, the rights of enemy and neutral shipping, free ports, French consulates, French colonies, imports, exports, and the grain trade. On the subject of French manufactures, the council considered the general state of the French economy, the inspectors of manufactures, textile regulations, privileges and monopolies for manufactures, and dangers from foreign competition. In addition, the council considered such diverse problems as the frequent fires aboard ships in the port of Saint-Malo,[50] the replenishing of French forests,[51] and the possible dangers to health caused by the use of oxblood in the sugar-refining process in La Rochelle.[52]

This work will not endeavor to treat of all the thousands of affairs introduced in the council from 1700 to 1715; rather, it will concentrate on those subjects to which the council devoted the greater part of its time.[53]

Its Personnel

One can also appreciate the council's importance by looking at its personnel. From the council's inception in 1700 until the year 1744, the man who held the post of director of commerce in the controller general's ministry was always a member of the Council of Commerce.[54] From 1691 to 1699 this position had been filled by Henri Daguesseau. In 1699 Daguesseau stepped down from it in order to permit his nephew, Michel Amelot, to assume it.[55] Amelot held this post until his death in 1724, with Daguesseau substituting for him during his ambassadorship to Spain. Thus during the period under study here, the man who was charged by the controller general with supervising all internal trade and industry was also, conveniently, a leading member of the Council of Commerce. Daguesseau and Amelot were responsible for corresponding with provincial officials and the farmers general, as well as for the drafting of *arrêts* and edicts on all matters of trade and industry. They were thus in a unique position to see that the advice of the Council of Commerce was carried through to execution. In the letters, orders, and *arrêts* concerning trade and industry that Daguesseau and Amelot sent out each week, one can find concrete evidence of the direct impact of the Council of Commerce on government decisions. A summary of each piece of correspondence was preserved in the controller general's office; at the bottom of virtually every item, a notation was made stating that the subject had been decided "on the advice of the Council of Commerce."[56] If such a notation is absent, a glance at the *procès-verbaux* of the council usually confirms that the matter had indeed been discussed there.

The director of commerce was not the only influential government official to sit in the council. As mentioned earlier, the two directors of finances sat on the council from 1701 until the dissolution of their offices in 1708. These two men were charged by Chamillart with directing the finances of the realm, and their attendance at the council gave added luster to that body. Nicolas Desmaretz held one of these offices from 1703 until his appointment as controller general, and we have every indication that he took seriously his work on the council. The archives reveal numerous letters addressed to him from Valossière and others concerning his work in the meetings of the council.[57] After Desmaretz assumed the controller generalship and thus stopped attending the council in person, he maintained his personal contacts with it by appointing two of his relatives to it: his brother-in-law Béchameil de Nointel in June 1708 and his younger brother Desmaretz de Vaubourg in June 1715. Jérôme de Pontchartrain already had familial ties with the council in the persons of Daguesseau and Amelot, who were both related by marriage to the Pontchartrain clan.[58]

Each of the *commissaires* in the council was either a *maître des requêtes* or a *conseiller d'état*, which offices afforded access to several of the royal councils and their bureaus. Of the seventeen individuals who at one time or another served as a *commissaire* in the council during this period, four had served earlier as royal provincial intendants, and four became intendants upon leaving the council.[59] One intendant of commerce (Machault) went on to succeed d'Argenson as lieutenant general of police in Paris. Two *commissaires* were later appointed *garde des sceaux* (d'Argenson, Fleuriau d'Armenonville). One *commissaire* eventually became controller general of finances (Desmaretz); a second became secretary of state for war (Bauyn d'Angervilliers). The Council of Commerce was thus not staffed with nonentities.[60] Rather, its membership included some of the ablest and most influential servants of the crown.

The Services Rendered by the Council

Throughout the period under study here, the controller general and the secretary of state for the navy demanded and received from the council a steady stream of advice on economic matters. Each minister required that the council keep him fully informed on all its activities. Pontchartrain in particular continually bombarded secretary Valossière with requests for more details on decisions made by the council.[61] One of the first things that Desmaretz did as controller general in 1708 was to ask that Valossière draw up and present to him a copy of the minutes of all the meetings of the council held since its establishment.[62] Desmaretz also, it will be recalled, in 1708 created the six intendants of commerce in an effort to expedite the conduct of affairs in the council.[63]

To what extent did Chamillart, Desmaretz, and Jérôme de Pontchartrain follow the advice that they so keenly sought from the Council of Commerce? The records are clear: the council played a decisive, and often central, role in the vast majority of decisions made concerning trade and industry during this period. Most of the *arrêts*, edicts, and ordinances concerning French manufactures, French overseas trade, and other areas of the economy were in fact drafted in the council itself.

The ministers also relied on the council as a storehouse of information. The archives of the secretary of the council and the files kept by the intendants of commerce were the most extensive record of past decisions and laws that the royal ministers had at their disposal. One can gather some idea of the size of these archives by looking at the lists of letters and documents sent to the secretary each week. The Archives Nationales possess, for the period of Desmaretz's ministry, a nearly complete set of the lists of remissions to Valossière.[64]

On the basis of these documents, it is calculated that the average number of distinct items being sent to Valossière from the controller general each week was nearly fifteen.[65] Judging from Pontchartrain's correspondence and the *procès-verbaux* of the council, it appears safe to assume that the secretary of state for the navy sent approximately an equal number of items each week to the council. This means that altogether Valossière received about thirty items every week from the royal ministers; these papers were either stored in the secretary's own files or distributed to the various *commissaires* at the next meeting. Included in these papers were such standard items as the monthly reports that the controller general received from the inspectors of manufactures. The controller general had these forwarded immediately to the Council of Commerce, where the intendants of commerce retained them and used them as a basis to judge matters that came before the council. In addition to papers sent by the royal ministers, the secretary of the council received one hundred copies of every *arrêt* issued on commercial matters.[66] He kept some for his own files, gave some to his colleagues in the council, and dispatched the remainder to individuals, cities, or provinces affected by the legislation.

The result of all this stockpiling of data was that the Council of Commerce became the government's library of information on all commercial affairs. When Desmaretz, in 1714, wanted a description of the functions and the mode of payment of the inspectors of manufactures, he discovered that his own ministry was unable to provide this information, and he therefore had to turn to the Council of Commerce for help.[67] Jérôme de Pontchartrain repeatedly asked Valossière to keep him informed, not only of decisions reached in the council itself, but of all papers, letters, and other documents that he received.[68] Pontchartrain also ordered Valossière to send him periodically a register of all *arrêts*, ordinances, and edicts that were issued on the advice of the council.[69]

The secretary of the council eventually compiled an alphabetized listing of all the various subjects introduced in the council.[70] This catalog permitted the council to review quickly all past laws and decisions concerning any particular topic. The controller general was thus, for example, able to depend on the Council of Commerce to keep track of the dozens of *arrêts* and ministerial decisions made concerning the many merchandises that different enemy and neutral nations were permitted to introduce into France during the War of the Spanish Succession.

In addition to using the Council of Commerce as an adviser, as a drafter of laws, and as an archive, the controller general and the secretary of state for the navy frequently empowered it to act as a court. Some of the original proposals for a council of commerce had, in fact, suggested that its major function be that of an arbitrator, judging disputes among merchants or between merchants and tax farmers.[71] A contemporary engraving, still preserved in the Bibliothèque Nationale, celebrated the opening of the council and pictured it as a place where merchants could enter and seek redress of their grievances.[72] Although this is not how the council normally operated, nevertheless it happened on dozens of occasions during the period being considered here. Usually it occurred in particularly complex or touchy legal suits involving merchants, trading companies, or the farmers general. In each such case, an *arrêt* of evocation was issued that lifted the case from the ordinary jurisdiction (e.g., an admiralty court) and brought it to the Council of Commerce. This might be done for several reasons: to eliminate the red tape and delays of the ordinary courts; to save private individuals the financial burden of pursuing a case in the normal channels because the case involved "the general good," or because the Council of Commerce was believed to be less partial. On these occasions the council met as usual, with the deputies attending and presenting their written *avis*, and with the *commissaires* alone judging. The individuals involved in a dispute appeared in person to argue their cases. The decision of the council was, as a general rule, not open to appeal.[73]

Limits on Its Powers

Although the importance of the Council of Commerce to the administration of Louis XIV cannot be disputed, one must acknowledge that there were definite limits on its powers. As noted earlier, the council could discuss only such matters as were submitted to it by the controller general or the secretary of state for the navy. On several occasions Jérôme de Pontchartrain reminded Daguesseau or Valossière of this rule and gently reprimanded the council for having discussed an issue or an incident that had not been sent to it by one of the two ministers.[74] Although it appears that an overwhelming majority of all matters concerning trade and manufactures were referred to the council for deliberation, there was nothing that obligated a minister to forward something to it.

This fact is clearly revealed in the correspondence of the Chamber of Commerce of Bordeaux with its deputy in Paris. The chamber frequently sent grievances and requests to the two royal ministers whenever it felt that Bordeaux's trade was suffering from an injustice. The city's deputy, Fénellon, continually had to remind the chamber, however, that he could not defend the city's interests in the Council of Commerce until the items in question were forwarded to it by one minister or the other. And, as Fénellon noted, there was never any guarantee that a minister would do so.[75]

In some areas this discretionary prerogative of the ministers became very evident over the years. A look at the chart in the appendix reveals several topics about which the voice of the Council of Commerce was seldom heard. The administration of the privileged trading companies, for example, was generally kept under the close supervision of the royal ministers, and the council usually dealt with these corporations only in questions concerning exports or imports. The economic life of the French colonies was another question seldom introduced into the council. Colonial commerce lay entirely under the authority of the secretary of state for the navy, and Jérôme de Pontchartrain jealously guarded his private control of it as much as possible. Thus questions concerning the colonies were never introduced in the council more than a handful of times a year. A memoir written by the Council of Commerce in September 1717 bitterly accused Pontchartrain of having decided too many commercial matters on his own.[76] As the memoir pointed out, this was contrary to the spirit of the Council of Commerce, which had been intended to act as a centralizing force, giving united direction to all French trade. It was also against the *règlement* of 1701 signed between the controller general and the secretary of state for the navy, in which the two ministers vowed to keep each other fully informed of all important commercial affairs that lay within their respective jurisdictions. Pontchartrain's reluctance to communicate colonial affairs to the Council of Commerce was in marked contrast to his eagerness to share with it all other matters that fell into his department.

The Council of Commerce was further limited by the fact that the ministers were in no way obliged to follow the advice that they so avidly sought from it. Some historians have suggested, to varying degrees, that the council had very little influence on government policies.[77] Other historians have asserted, however, that the government seldom departed from the will of the council.[78] The truth lies somewhere in between these two positions, though certainly much closer to the latter than to the former. The ministers as a general rule did accept the views of the council, but they were sometimes compelled by fiscal, military, or other exigencies to disagree with it. In some of these instances, a minister flatly rejected the will of the council, but in others the council was able to prevail and have its own view accepted. Sometimes a compromise solution was worked out.

During the fifteen years under consideration here, there occurred approximately three dozen examples of ministerial disagreement with the Council of Commerce.[79] Most of these involved small incidents in which a minister wished to make an exception to a rule or a law that the council wished to enforce. Other cases were broader. In the fall of 1710, Desmaretz and Pontchartrain, in an attempt to bring the Dutch to their knees, cut off all trade with Holland despite the objection of the Council of Commerce that France desperately needed Dutch trade.[80] In 1709 Pontchartrain granted passports to Dutch vessels to carry food supplies to the starving French Caribbean islanders; he thereby overrode the council's opposition to the entry of foreign traders into French colonies.[81]

In other cases, however, the Council of Commerce prevailed. As mentioned previously, the council's protests helped force the crown in 1704 to abolish the newly created offices of inspectors and controller-visitors of manufactures. In another instance Jérôme de Pontchartrain, for altruistic reasons, proposed in 1711 that shipowners be obliged to provide financial assistance to the families of sailors on merchant vessels that were away on cruises of a year or longer. The deputies to the Council of Commerce, most of whom were wealthy, conservative armateurs, objected that this would unduly burden traders such as themselves.[82] Despite Pontchartrain's insistence on the issue, he was unable to overcome the opposition of the council, and no action was taken on the matter.

R. B. Grassby has lucidly described a good example of the kind of give-and-take that often occurred between the crown and the Council of Commerce in the process of working out the details of a controversial decision.[83] One of the proposals that the deputies of commerce campaigned hard for in the first two years of the council's existence was a higher social status for the profession of merchant. They envisaged a *noblesse commerçante*. The edict of August 1669 had already exempted from derogation any nobles engaging in overseas trade, but the deputies now wished that nobles should be able to partake in any type of wholesale trade (*commerce en gros*) without loss of status. In addition, they complained of the disdainful ways in which merchants were treated by the *commis* of the farmers general. In April 1701 the deputies drafted a general memoir in which they listed twenty-one specific demands.[84] They argued, among other things, that there should be a legal distinction between great overseas and wholesale traders on the one hand and small shopkeepers and peddlers on the other; henceforth the word *négociant* should be reserved solely for the former, and *marchand* for the latter. Certain municipal offices should be reserved for important merchants, who should also be granted exemptions from such obligations as the *ban* and the *arrière ban* (if they owned noble land) and from billeting, watch, and guard. The deputies asked that they themselves be granted the title of *conseiller du roi*. Finally, they requested that hereditary nobility be granted automatically to any man whose family had been engaged in wholesale trade for four successive generations. The lack of such marks of recognition, asserted the deputies, was leading thousands of merchants each year to buy offices, lands, and *rentes* and to abandon their business careers.

Grassby traces the developments and modifications in the deputies' program as the *commissaires* in the council, the crown, and even some cities and provincial merchants voiced objections to various aspects of it. The *commissaires* basically supported the clauses protecting nobles from derogation but opposed many of the suggestions for privileges and exemptions for merchants.

The edict that the crown finally issued on 30 December 1701 was remarkable for its good will but also for its blandness.[85] Previous edicts honoring trade and protecting nobles from derogation were confirmed and broadened. Wholesale trade within France was now opened to nobles. The edict gave firm, though vague, promises that the king would grant nobility and other favors to merchants as the opportunities presented themselves. But the *noblesse de robe* was still excluded from all trade, and the edict said nothing of the deputies' suggestion that nobles' sons be apprenticed to merchants to learn the profession. No official distinction was made between *négociant* and *marchand*. There was to be no automatic granting of nobility to fourth-generation wholesale-trading families. In short, the document was a compromise. Even though the deputies failed to obtain many of their specific demands, the government did begin increasingly to protect merchants from harassment by tax collectors and to grant nobility to merchants—including several of the deputies themselves.

Contributions by Individual Members

There was yet one other way in which the council helped the crown. The personnel of the council, more knowledgeable in matters of trade and industry than any other group of men in France, often served the controller general and the secretary of state in a private capacity. Several of the *commissaires* and deputies worked as personal advisers, special agents, or diplomatic envoys for Chamillart, Desmaretz, and Pontchartrain. Since they performed this work apart from the council itself, it is only tangential to the present study. But it was the Council of Commerce that provided these men with much of their expertise and brought them to the attention of the ministers, and for this reason note should be made here of these activities.

Why did the controller general and the secretary of state for the navy frequently turn to individuals rather than to the council as a whole? There are several answers. Some issues were so delicate or secret that the crown did not wish an open debate on them in a council. At times a minister required an answer in a hurry and could not wait for a council to examine an affair.[86] At other times a minister needed to dispatch a special representative to study a commercial problem outside of Paris. Thus the controller general frequently had individual members of the council examine such subjects as manufactures[87] or trade with the enemy.[88] Many times the royal ministers honored individual deputies by inviting them to Marly or Fontainebleau, where they worked with the ministers on special projects.[89] On several occasions Jérôme de Pontchartrain issued *arrêts* appointing deputies of commerce to judge disputes between individual merchants.[90] Several deputies—Anisson and Héron in particular—were called to meet privately with the farmers general concerning revisions of the general tariffs.[91] Finally, the ministers also turned to the *commissaires* and deputies to serve on diplomatic missions in other countries.[92]

Of all the deputies, Anisson of Lyons and Mesnager of Rouen were the two who were closest to the royal ministers.[93] They owed their privileged status to their native abilities, their personal contacts at court, and their longevity in the council. Mesnager was an old acquaintance of Chamillart; the two had met early in the 1690s when Chamillart served as intendant in Rouen. Anisson was on intimate terms with Desmaretz's *premier commis* Clautrier.[94] The latter was the *premier commis* who worked most closely with the controller general and determined who was to gain an audience with him.[95] Both Mesnager and Anisson were at liberty to share with the ministers their opinions on virtually all important economic and financial matters.[96]

From all the above, it should be clear that, in one way or another, the Council of Commerce rendered an invaluable service to the government of Louis XIV. It operated as a regular part of the decision-making process in the upper echelons of the bureaucracy. The royal ministers could, and did, draw upon it as a source of counsel, of information, and of experienced men who could serve as economic troubleshooters.

1. Dangeau, *Journal*, 7:341.

2. *Almanach royal*, 1703, p. 36.

3. The *arrêt* of 29 June 1700 called for only twelve deputies, but the Estates of Languedoc, upon hearing of the creation of the council, requested the right to send a deputy to it. The government consented and issued an *arrêt* to this effect on 7 September 1700.

4. All of the *commissaires* who served in the council during the period 1700–1715 are listed in the Appendix.

5. *Arrêt* of 29 June 1700.

6. A list of the deputies of trade for the years 1700–1715 can be found in the Appendix.

7. Both men represented the United General Farms in the Council of Commerce until 1716.

8. The *arrêt* of 29 June 1700 named as secretary Charles-Léonard Cruau de la Boulaye, a *correcteur ordinaire* in the *Chambre des Comptes* of Paris. But he died in early October of that year, before the opening of the Council of Commerce. An *arrêt* of 4 October 1700 appointed Valossière, who served in this post until December 1720. Valossière formerly had been a *commis* of Colbert in the department of the navy, a *procureur du roi* of profits from the sale of prize ships in Provence and Languedoc, and a controller general of the navy. See Bonnassieux and Lelong, *Conseil de Commerce*, p. lxii.

9. The *procès-verbaux* of the Council of Commerce for the years 1700–1791 are located in AN, F[12] 51–108. They are complete for the reign of Louis XIV, but there are some volumes missing from the second half of the century. The Archives du Ministère des Affaires Étrangères possess several volumes of *procès-verbaux* for the years 1700–1719. These do not provide an exact copy of the original *procès-verbaux* but rather a summary of each of the affairs as described in the F[12] series in the AN. See AAE, Mémoires et documents, France, 1984–89, 2000–2003. Another copy of the *procès-verbaux*, for the years 1700–1716, can be found in the Bibliothèque de la

Chambre des députés, B^c 147–52; these registers, like the ones in the foreign affairs archives, do not preserve the exact wording of the original. A similar copy for the years 1700–1716 is in the Bibliothèque de l'Assemblée nationale, MSS. 1040–45. The last reference was brought to my attention by Gary McCollim.

10. Those historians who claim that the council formed in 1700 was a revival of Colbert's council are therefore wrong. For instance, Emile Levasseur, *Histoire des classes ouvrières en France avant 1789*, 2:342; Sagnac, "La Politique commerciale," p. 268; Henri Sée, *Histoire économique de la France*, 1:265; R. B. Grassby, "Social Status and Commercial Enterprise under Louis XIV," p. 26; Pierre Léon, in Fernand Braudel and Ernest Labrousse (eds.), *Histoire économique et sociale de la France*, vol. 2: *1600–1789*, p. 222; Corvisier, *La France de Louis XIV*, p. 237.

11. See Michel Antoine, *Le Conseil du roi sous le règne de Louis XV*, p. 31.

12. This practice was ended in 1722 when the meetings of the Council of Finances began to be recorded by a *premier commis* of the controller general. Only one of the registers in which these minutes were kept has been preserved—that of 1736. Consult Michel Antoine, *Le Conseil royal des finances au XVIIIe siècle*.

13. On the latter two meetings, see below, p. 90.

14. Biollay (*Etudes économiques*, pp. 296–97) quotes in its entirety a convention to this effect signed by Chamillart and Jérôme de Pontchartrain on 12 September 1701. He gives as his source AN, G^7 1697, but I have found no such document in this carton; the citation is probably an error, for this particular carton concerns commerce in the years 1712–13.

15. *Almanach royal*, 1715, p. 63. In 1722 the *Conseil de Commerce* was officially changed to the *Bureau du Commerce*. See the Appendix.

16. They took their seats in the council on 8 July 1701 (AN, F^{12} 51, fol. 51).

17. His first attendance at the Council of Commerce was recorded on 23 November 1703 (ibid., fol. 222).

18. Meeting of 14 January 1705 (ibid., fol. 299).

19. The original intendants of commerce were Denis-Jean Amelot de Chaillou, Louis-François Lefèvre de Caumartin de Boissy, Louis-Charles de Machault, Jean Rouillé de Fontaine, Charles Boucher d'Orsay, and César-Charles Lescalopier.

20. "Edit du Roy, portant création de six commissions d'Intendans du Commerce," Versailles, May 1708. A copy can be found in AN, AD XI, 9.

21. These departments are described in AN, F^{12} 55, unnumbered folios at front of volume.

22. A printed copy of the *arrêt* of 5 June 1708 is located in Mar., A^2 22. De Nointel assumed his place in the council on 22 June 1708; AN, F^{12} 54, fol. 215.

23. Meeting of 28 June 1715, AN, F^{12} 58, fols. 363v–64.

24. These facts are recorded by Brother Joseph Léonard, an Augustinian monk, in his *Recueil de quelques faits historiques*, AN, MM 825, fol. 36. Jean Meuvret errs in saying that Le Gendre actually did attend the Council of Commerce whenever he liked ("The Condition of France, 1688–1715," in J. S. Bromley (ed.), *The Rise of Great Britain and Russia, 1688–1715/25*, p. 337). Le Gendre was appointed inspector general to succeed de Lagny (on him see Chapter 1, n. 59). De Lagny did not die until December 1700, but apparently he fell into disgrace about 1698 and gradually had most of his duties stripped from him. Although Le Gendre received the title of inspector general, most of the duties of that office went to others. These included the following persons in the naval ministry: Des Haguais, who took charge of issuing passports and corresponding with French merchants; de la Touche, already director of the Bureau du Ponant, who assumed control of French colonies and French trading companies; Charles de Sallaberry and Michel Bégon de Mont-

fermeil, each a *premier commis* of Jérôme de Pontchartrain. See circular letter of Pontchartrain, 23 January 1701, in Mar., B² 153, fols. 136–36v; Neuville, *Etat sommaire*, pp. 250–51; Price, *France and the Chesapeake*, 1:97–98.

25. On at least one occasion, the controller general forwarded to the Council of Commerce a letter from Le Gendre—a further indication that Le Gendre did not actually attend the council. In May 1701 Le Gendre proposed the establishment of formal commercial relations with Muscovy (meeting of 13 May 1701, AN, F¹² 51, fols. 34v–39). In December 1701 Chamillart proposed that Le Gendre be appointed to one of the newly created positions of *inspecteurs marchands* in Rouen (AN, F¹² 115, fols. 201–1v, Chamillart to *juge* and *consuls* of Rouen, 15 December 1701, and Chamillart to Le Gendre, same date). Even if Le Gendre did not accept the job, it is clear from these letters that his chief residence was in Rouen, not Paris.

26. AN, F¹² 51, fol. 233v.

27. Secretary of State for the Navy Jérôme de Pontchartrain seems himself to have been equally unsure of Millieu's position in the council. In a letter of 23 January 1704 to Valossière, Pontchartrain said that he had just received notice of the November edict and of Millieu's entry into the Council of Commerce; he asked Valossière what purpose Millieu could serve there (Mar., B² 174, fols. 228–28v). Valossière's reply has not been preserved.

28. John Bosher, *The Single Duty Project*, p. 28.

29. This was not, however, a strict rule. The council frequently changed its meeting to other days of the week, due to illnesses, the pressure of important business, or other reasons.

30. AN, F¹² 51, fol. 4v.

31. Bonnassieux and Lelong, *Conseil de commerce*, p. lxii. Valossière was paid regularly from the *trésor royal* until 1712. In 1715 he complained that he had not been paid for the past three years. See AN, G⁷ 1704, piece 152.

32. The term *minister* is used here in a very general sense. Technically speaking, only those who were called to sit in the *conseil d'en haut* were *ministres*. Jérôme de Pontchartrain did not sit in this council, but, nevertheless, contemporaries often referred to him as a minister.

33. On Amelot in Spain, see Chapter 8.

34. Bonnassieux and Lelong, *Conseil de commerce*, p. xviii.

35. Much of the F¹² series at the Archives Nationales is composed of the remains of the *dépôts* of the intendants of commerce. Some information on the organization of these papers at the time of the French Revolution is provided by the "Mémoire concernant les bureaux de l'ancienne administration du commerce, et les différens papiers qui y sont déposés" (F¹² 725). I thank Pierre H. Boulle for bringing this memoir to my attention.

36. The Council of Commerce did not correspond with these officials in its own name. Rather, a *commissaire* would draft a letter and have either the controller general or the secretary of state for the navy sign it. It would then be returned to the *commissaire* to send out.

37. On the farmers general and the tax farms in general, see Chapter 7.

38. There were many cases in which the deputies were divided. On these occasions, of course, the *commissaires* had to reject the views of one group and side with the views of the other.

39. Meeting of 17 January 1712, AN, F¹² 58, fols. 3v–4.

40. Meeting of 20 July 1708, AN, F¹² 54, fol. 235v. Also see AN, G⁷ 1691, piece 276.

41. Meetings of 26 October 1701 (AN, F^{12} 51, fol. 73v.) and 25 August 1712 (F^{12} 58, fol. 74).

42. These disputes will be discussed in Chapter 4, below.

43. Meetings of 3 December 1706 (AN, F^{12} 51, fol. 466v.), and 22 July 1707 (F^{12} 54, fol. 85).

44. AN, F^{12} 51, fols. 267v–268v.

45. Valossière's correspondence with the controller general is preserved in the papers on commerce located in AN, G^7 1686–1704. The naval archives, although as a general rule much better preserved than the financial archives, do not contain these weekly reports or the voluminous correspondence between Pontchartrain and Valossière; but the letters between the two men that we do possess frequently allude to Valossière's weekly reports to Pontchartrain. See, for example, Mar., B^2 230, p. 459, Pontchartrain to Amelot, 8 June 1712, which refers to Valossière's reports; and B^2 187, fol. 115v, Pontchartrain to Valossière, 13 January 1706.

46. The increased tempo of contacts between the controller general and the Council of Commerce in the period 1708–9 is reflected in AN, G^7 1692–94. It is impossible to measure such a phenomenon in the naval archives because of the circumstances explained in note 45. The fact that even before 1708 Jérôme de Pontchartrain's letters referred to the detailed weekly reports and to his considerable correspondence with Valossière suggests that he did not need to request more extensive accounts on the council's doings.

47. A copy can be found in the unnumbered pages at the front of AN, F^{12} 55.

48. For example, AN, G^7 1702, piece 27, de Machault to Clautrier, 21 February 1714; G^7 1695, piece 85, d'Orsay to Desmaretz, 2 May 1710; G^7 1696, piece 166, Landivisiau to Desmaretz, 5 July 1711.

49. Anyone doing research on French trade and manufactures in the eighteenth century will likely find that the Council (later, Bureau) of Commerce at one time or another dealt with his topic. The alphabetical index presented by Bonnassieux and Lelong should be consulted for an extensive (but not complete) list of topics introduced in the council.

50. Meeting of 10 March 1702, AN, F^{12} 51, fol. 104.

51. Meeting of 10 June 1701, AN, F^{12} 51, fol. 43, and on several other occasions in 1701 and 1702.

52. AN, F^{12} 55, fols, 2v–3; AN, G^7 1694, fols. 65, 82.

53. The chart in the Appendix gives a more graphic impression of the variety of the topics discussed in the council.

54. As noted above (Chapter 1, n. 63) there was, officially, no title accompanying this position. Contemporaries referred to the person exercising it variously as the *directeur du commerce*, the *directeur général du commerce*, or the *surintendant du commerce*. The position generally went to someone close to the controller general, usually a *conseiller d'état* or an intendant of finances. The directors of commerce in the eighteenth century are briefly discussed in Bonnassieux and Lelong, *Conseil de commerce*, p. xvii. The director of commerce under the controller general should not be confused with the director general of commerce in the naval ministry (see above, p. 10).

55. See Dangeau, *Journal*, 7:155. An inscription added to the frontispiece of a memoir submitted to the controller general early in the eighteenth century says that Chamillart forwarded it to "M. Amelot, conseiller d'état, surintendant du commerce" (Bibliothèque Mazarine, MS. 2762). The only study of Amelot is Roger Gaucheron, "Etude sur Michel Amelot et l'administration du commerce (1699–1724)," an unpublished thesis at the Ecole des Chartes (1913). Unfortunately, no

copies of this work can be located. It is summarized, however, in *Ecole des Chartes. Positions des thèses* (Paris, 1913), pp. 41–49.

56. The director of commerce met once a week with the controller general and had the latter sign all the correspondence that had been drafted that week. The director then dispatched the letters and *arrêts* to the various provincial officials concerned. Each week's correspondence was summarized in an "Etat des Expéditions concernant le commerce et les manufactures." Many of these have been preserved in AN, F¹² 662–70; G⁷ 1691, pieces 100, 282–95; G⁷ 1692, pieces 242–55.

57. AN, G⁷ 1687, Valossière to Desmaretz, 15 June 1705, and 12 May 1707; G⁷ 552, Mayet to Desmaretz, 13 March 1705.

58. Consult the genealogical tables in BN, *pièces originales*, 14; *dossiers bleus*, 16; *nouveau d'Hozier*, 264.

59. These 17 do not include Chamillart and Jérôme de Pontchartrain, who were official members of the council but never really participated in its work. Desmaretz is included because he did serve on the council for five years as a director of finances.

60. One might also consider the offspring of the *commissaires*. For example, the sons of Daguesseau, Amelot de Chaillou, and de Machault became, respectively, chancellor, secretary of state for foreign affairs, and controller general of finances. One son of d'Argenson later served as secretary of state for foreign affairs, and another held the position of secretray of state for war.

61. For illustrations, see Mar., B² 154, fol. 441v, Pontchartrain to Valossière, 18 May 1701; B² 176, fols. 480v–81, Pontchartrain to Valossière, 20 August 1704.

62. AN, G⁷ 1695, piece 176, Valossière to Desmaretz, 13 August 1710.

63. Biollay (among others) has suggested that Desmaretz created the six intendants of commerce in a move to decrease the power of Amelot in the Council of Commerce (*Etudes économiques*, pp. 313–14). Amelot at the time, of course, was in Spain. But we know from contemporary accounts that he was well respected by Louis XIV and that several royal ministers and other high officials were jealous of him. His successes at the court of Philip V were well known at Paris and Versailles. The marquis de Sourches says that Amelot "avoit toujours été l'âme du conseil du roi Philippe V" (*Mémoires*, 11:336). In speaking of Amelot after his return to France in 1709, Marshall Villars states that "après avoir regné en effet en Espagne il fait trembler tous les ministres" (Saint-Simon, *Mémoires*, 6:494 n. 8). Biollay's conjecture is plausible. The presence of six intendants of commerce, who were henceforth charged with giving all reports in the council and who had their own bureaus, certainly prevented Amelot from dominating the council as he had prior to his departure for Spain. It is also true that Amelot was in a mild form of disgrace after his return to France, as a result of rumors that he had Jansenist sympathies. The king did not grant him a place on the Council of Finances as he had earlier promised him. But the reasons for the creation of the six intendants of commerce would seem to lie elsewhere. They were truly needed in the council to augment the number of *commissaires* there. With Amelot absent, Daguesseau frequently ill, and the other *commissaires* occupied with other government duties, the affairs of the council often went slowly. Also, one should not overlook a fiscal motive for creating the six positions. The six offices of *maître des requêtes* to which the six intendants were attached were sold for 200,000 livres apiece. I have found no evidence of personal rivalry between Desmaretz and Amelot. They frequently corresponded on commercial and other matters after Amelot's return from Spain.

64. This weekly record of items sent to the Council of Commerce was entitled "Propositions, lettres et mémoires renvoyez au Conseil de Commerce," after which was written the date. Two hundred sixty-eight of these, dating from 14 November

1708 to 13 September 1715, are located in AN, G⁷ 1693. These communications are also recorded in the "Registre des renvois faits à M. de Valossière, secrétaire général du commerce," located in G⁷ 736.

65. The 268 weekly summaries list 4,010 items that Desmaretz sent to the Council of Commerce; if all the weekly lists from Desmaretz's ministry were preserved, the total would probably be over 5,000. Dividing 4,010 by 268, one arrives at a weekly average of 14.96.

66. This is mentioned in AN, G⁷ 1696, piece 4, Mesnager to de la Garde, 2 January 1711.

67. AN, G⁷ 1703, piece 6, Valossière to de la Garde, 18 July 1714; piece 195, untitled note by de la Garde.

68. See for example, Mar., B² 226, p. 169, Pontchartrain to Valossière, 14 January 1711; also B² 176, fols. 545v–46, same to same, 27 August 1704.

69. Mar., B² 176, fols. 405–5v, Pontchartrain to Valossière, 13 August 1704; B² 217, p. 500, Pontchartrain to Valossière, 30 October 1709; B² 220, p. 427, Pontchartrain to Valossière, 29 January 1710; B² 241, p. 134, Pontchartrain to Valossière, 23 January 1715.

70. AN, F¹² 671ᴬ, 671ᴮ, 672ᴬ, 672ᴮ, "Déliberations du Conseil de Commerce, 1700–1740." These cartons contain thick packets, each devoted to a single letter. Each packet is divided into all the subjects beginning with that letter. The packet for "I," therefore, includes folders on the *Indes espagnoles*, the *Indes orientales*, the *inspecteurs des manufactures*, *Irlande*, etc. Below each topic are subtopics and the dates when they were discussed in the Council of Commerce. These records were begun early in the eighteenth century and then augmented each year as more things were discussed. It is not known why this catalog ends in 1740. See also F¹² 662–70, "Inventaire des propositions et mémoires examinez au Conseil de Commerce establ y suivant l'arrest du Conseil d'Etat du 29 juin 1700, depuis le 24 novembre 1700 jour de la première séance jusqu'à la fin de 1706," and in the same carton, the "Inventaire des Papiers de Mʳ de la Vigne." De la Vigne was Amelot's secretary, in the latter's capacity as director of commerce. De la Vigne worked hand in hand with the Council of Commerce on many commercial problems.

72. BN, Collection Hennin, no. 6492.

73. See Bonassieux and Lelong, *Conseil de commerce*, p. xxxi. Judging by the correspondence that has been preserved, it appears that Jérôme de Pontchartrain used the Council of Commerce as a court much more often than did Chamillart or Desmaretz. He sent the council hundreds of cases involving merchants and shipowners or the trading companies. Pontchartrain did all that he could to encourage the merchant marine and overseas commerce, and he felt that the Council of Commerce could judge these cases more quickly and inexpensively. Few of these cases appear in the actual minutes of the meetings of the council. Affairs such as these, which were of the same nature and therefore repetitive, were usually included in the "diverses autres choses" that the *procès-verbaux* say were discussed at many meetings. For an illustration of such a case, see Mar., B² 216, pp. 542–43, Pontchartrain to Daguesseau, 24 July 1709.

74. For example, Col., B 33, p. 294, Pontchartrain to Daguesseau, 17 October 1708; Mar., B² 217, p. 693, Pontchartrain to Daguesseau, 6 November 1709; B² 221, pp. 194–95, Pontchartrain to Anisson, 9 April 1710.

75. In AD, Gironde, C 4301, see Fénellon to Chamber of Commerce, piece 25, 15 June 1709; piece 30, 20 September 1709; piece 47, 7 August 1710.

76. AN, F¹² 14, pp. 156–57, "Mémoire du Conseil de Commerce tendant à faire voire qu'il seroit à propos qu'il y eut au moins un de Mʳˢ les conseillers de ce conseil

qui assistat au Conseil de Marine, afin que la connoissance réciproque de ce qui se passe, et se resout, dans l'un, et dans l'autre de ces deux conseils fuss un nouveau moyen de consiliation," dated September 1717.

77. Scoville, "The French Economy," pp. 249–52; François Dumas, *La Réglementation industrielle après Colbert*, pp. 50 ff.; Pierre Clément, *Histoire du système protecteur en France depuis le ministère de Colbert jusqu'à la révolution de 1848*, pp. 56–58; Lafon, *Les Députés du commerce*, pp. 2, 9.

78. Bonnassieux and Lelong, *Conseil de commerce*, p. xxx; Paul Masson, *Histoire du commerce français dans le Levant au XVIIIᵉ siècle*, p. 44; Laurence B. Packard, "Some Antecedents of the Conseil du Commerce of 1700," 1:280.

79. Lack of information on some cases and various ambiguities or other problems with the documents prevent me from giving an exact number. Also, if the Council of Commerce was itself divided on an issue, then the royal ministers had to disagree with at least some of its members when making a decision.

80. See Chapter 5.

81. See Chapter 8.

82. AN, F¹² 55, fols. 253–54v, meeting of 24 April 1711; ibid., fol. 278, meeting of 12 June 1711.

83. Grassby, "Social Status and Commercial Enterprise under Louis XIV," pp. 19–38.

84. AN, F¹² 51, fols. 30–32, "Mémoire sur les veües que le Roy a d'exciter ses sujets au Commerce et à la Navigation," meeting of 22 April 1701.

85. A copy can be found in Isambert et al. (eds.), *Recueil général des anciennes lois françaises*, 20:400–402.

86. On several occasions Pontchartrain complained of the slowness of the Council of Commerce. See Mar., B² 241, p. 672, Pontchartrain to Daguesseau, 29 May 1715; B² 242, pp. 27–28, Pontchartrain to de Landivisiau, 3 July 1715.

87. See AN, G⁷ 1695, piece 70, Mesnager to Desmaretz, 7 April 1710.

88. Out of many examples, see AN, G⁷ 1696, piece 101, Mesnager to Desmaretz, 21 April 1711; ibid., piece 203, Anisson to Desmaretz, 15 August 1711; G⁷ 577, Anisson to Desmaretz, 18 June 1705.

89. Mar., B² 208, p. 542, Pontchartrain to Daguesseau, 1 August 1708; B² 239, p. 151, Pontchartrain to Amelot, 20 October 1714; AN, G⁷ 1696, piece 157, Anisson to Clautrier, 2 July 1711.

90. See Col., B 24, fols, 445–46, *arrêt* of 16 August 1702 naming Mesnager to help judge a dispute involving the costs of outfitting a ship owned by the Chevalier Damon; see also ibid., fol. 470v., Pontchartrain to Héron and Mesnager, 10 September 1702, which concerns a similar case.

91. See AN, G⁷ 1695, piece 129, notes for a letter to be sent from Desmaretz to the *échevins* of La Rochelle concerning the important work that their deputy is doing in Paris (July 1710); see also AN, F¹² 51, fol. 42v; AN, G⁷ 1694, piece 91, Anisson to Desmaretz, 30 March 1709; Bosher, *The Single Duty Project*, p. 36.

92. See Chapter 8.

93. One must also acknowledge the close relations that Samuel Bernard had with the royal ministers. Bernard, however, owed most of his influence to his position as banker and financier.

94. AN, G⁷ 1696, piece 157, Anisson to Clautrier, 2 July 1711, and passim.

95. The workings of the controller general's office remain the least known of any of the ministries of the royal government. The three most important *premiers commis* used by Chamillart and Desmaretz were Clautrier, Le Cousturier, and de la Garde.

Clautrier worked as a sort of personal aide to the controller general. Although de la Garde handled a majority of the dealings with the Council of Commerce, there was not a precise division of responsibility between the bureaus of the three men—at least as regards the Council of Commerce. Each handled questions of trade, manufactures, and finance. For an account of the organization and the archives of the finance ministry, see Boislisle, *Correspondance des contrôleurs généraux*, 1:iii–xlvii; and Gary McCollim, "The Formation of Fiscal Policy in the Reign of Louis XIV: The Example of Nicolas Desmaretz, Controller General of Finances (1708–1715)," pp. 178–97.

96. See AN, G⁷ 1696, piece 270, Anisson to Desmaretz, 9 November 1711. The letter begins: "I use the liberty that you gave me to share with you everything that I learn concerning matters of trade; if I abuse your kindness, then tell me to stop. But I assure you that I have nothing in view but the general good, which I know you desire. At the same time I want to help you in a portion of your department, which contains an infinite number of details, whose good results are not always evident."

3

THE DEPUTIES OF TRADE AND THEIR GENERAL MEMOIRS

The factor that gave the Council of Commerce its uniqueness was the presence on it of merchants representing various local and regional interests in France. This chapter will examine the background of the deputies, and analyze the series of general memoirs that they presented to the council shortly after its establishment.

THE DEPUTIES OF TRADE

Before the Council of Commerce was formed, the government feared that no prominent, knowledgeable merchants would give up their business interests in order to move to Paris to work in such a body,[1] but the fear proved to be groundless. The deputies of trade were, invariably, among the wealthiest and most important members of their communities. Rich businessmen eagerly sought election to the position: not only was it a great honor to be chosen to represent one's city in the capital, but it could put one in a position to cultivate friendships with government ministers and their *commis*. Nor did serving as a deputy in any way force an individual to neglect his private concerns. Françoise Giteau has aptly described the office of deputy as "the highest level of the *cursus honorum* that a businessman could attain."[2]

The *arrêt* of 29 June 1700 declared that the deputies should be replaced each year in a new election held by local assemblies or chambers of commerce, but this practice never came about. Generally, the government was very satisfied with the caliber of the men elected and asked the local bodies to retain them in office indefinitely. Thus when a deputy left the council, it was usually through his voluntary retirement. Only three of the original deputies served until 1715 or beyond: Anisson, of Lyons (to 1721), Fénellon, of Bordeaux (to 1718), and Bernard, of Paris (to 1720).

During the period 1700–1715, thirty-three different men served as deputies.

Virtually nothing is known of the personal background of eight of them, but there is enough information available on the twenty-five others to give a composite picture of this group.[3] The overwhelming majority were prominent merchants, usually with extensive interests in overseas trade. Two deputies also were involved directly in manufacturing: Joseph Fabre owned a silk factory in Marseilles, and Simon Gilly, of Languedoc, operated a sugar refinery in Sète. The only deputies who appear not to have been personally involved in trade or manufacturing were Anisson (Lyons), François Philip (selected deputy of Marseilles in 1714), and the *syndics généraux* who represented Languedoc from 1703 to 1709. Anisson's family was important in the publishing industry in Lyons, and in 1691 he himself was appointed director of the *Imprimerie royale* in Paris. Although Anisson was succeeded in that post by his brother-in-law Rigaud in 1702, he remained active in publishing throughout the rest of his life.[4] Despite the fact that he was not a merchant himself, he was knowledgeable in trade and in affairs of state. Even before the creation of the Council of Commerce, the crown employed him to work with the farmers general on tariff questions and on disputes arising between merchants and tax farmers.[5] Philip likewise had no personal experience in trade; but he had served as an archivist in the Chamber of Commerce in Marseilles, and this had provided him with much expertise in business affairs. There were six *syndics généraux* who served, each for one year, as deputies from Languedoc during the period 1703–9. The *syndic général* was a man elected annually by the Estates of Languedoc to represent that province's interests in Paris. Very little is known of these men, and thus their experience in trade cannot at present be ascertained.

Of the twenty-five men about whom we do have information, over half held some sort of appointive or elective office in their respective cities prior to entering the Council of Commerce. Fénellon, for example, had been a *jurat* in Bordeaux, Mathieu Fabre an *échevin* in Marseilles, and La Motte-Gaillard the *maire* of Saint-Malo. Mesnager had served as a *quartenier*[6] in Rouen and Chauvin as an *échevin* in Paris. Nine of the deputies had served as either *juge* or *consul* in a local *juridiction consulaire*.

Joseph Fabre, at 66, was the oldest of the deputies in 1700, and already he had enjoyed a long and illustrious career. He had been

Marseilles's official representative in Paris in 1660, when his city sought forgiveness for the role it had played in the Frondes. From that time through the 1680s, he had worked as an agent of Colbert and Seignelay in Marseilles. In the mid-1680s, he had become the director of French consulates in the Mediterranean. As part of his duties in that post, he had traveled to the Levant and opened up French commerce with several areas—most notably Salonika. In the 1670s and 1680s, he also had invested in the Levant Company and the Mediterranean Company. At one point he had held the office of *trésorier de la marine* in Marseilles.[7]

Several of the deputies had distinguished themselves in yet other ways. Peletyer, of Paris, had served capably as one of the three French negotiators of the 1699 tariff with the Dutch Republic.[8] When the council first met in 1700, two of the deputies (Bernard and Peletyer) were directors of the East India Company, and Bernard was the principal director of the royal tobacco monopoly (the *parti du tabac*). In 1701 Mesnager, of Rouen, became a director of the Asiento Company. Seven of the deputies had acquired nobility prior to joining the council through *lettres patentes* from the king or by purchase of the office of *secrétaire du roi*, and at least two of them were granted letters of nobility directly as a result of their service on the council (Fénellon and Piou). Three others were rewarded for their work in the council with the coveted title of *chevalier* and membership in the exclusive *ordre de Saint-Michel* (Bernard, Moreau, Mesnager). After leaving their posts as deputies, two men later became farmers general (Piou and Godeheu), and four (Piou, Descasaux du Hallay, Mouchard, Godeheu) became directors of the East India Company. Three also later became directors of John Law's Company of the Occident (Piou, Moreau, Mouchard). All of this presents a curious paradox if one argues that the deputies were ardent foes of tax farmers and exclusive companies.

As noted above, serving on the Council of Commerce in no way prevented the deputies from keeping up with their personal business activities. The special knowledge to which they were privy in the council and their close contacts with ministerial officials were, in fact, a definite aid in helping them enhance their private affairs. Descasaux du Hallay, of Nantes, was probably the only one during this period who resigned because of his need to devote more time to his business pursuits. But even in his case, the Council of Commerce proved helpful: during his two years in Paris, he lived in the

Hôtel d'Orléans on the rue d'Orléans (near the present-day Palais Royal, the quarter where most royal ministers and other top of-ficials resided).[9] In Paris he befriended Chamillart, Desmaretz, and Jérôme de Pontchartrain, and after his return to Nantes, he was able frequently to request favors from them. These included spe-cial permissions for trade with the *mer du Sud* (the Pacific coast along Peru and Chile) and with Holland. He also asked the minis-ters to intervene on his behalf in disputes he was having with other merchants or with the *commis* of various tax farmers.[10] But Descasaux du Hallay's closest contact in Paris was his friend and associate Samuel Bernard, who used his position on the Council of Commerce and at court to obtain privileges and exemptions for his partner in Nantes.[11]

Descasaux du Hallay was not alone in his commercial enter-prises. Fénellon, Héron, Piécourt, and Piou (deputy of Nantes, 1705–19) also were important *armateurs*. Their correspondence in the marine and financial archives reveals again and again that their trading ventures did not suffer as a result of their having to reside in Paris. They were all involved in the lucrative, but officially pro-scribed, trade with the *mer du Sud* and with the Spanish West Indies.[12] In the Mediterranean, Joseph Fabre kept up his vast trading operations and continued to serve as a *fournisseur de la marine*.[13] In 1709 the government loaned him royal ships so that he could bring badly needed grains from Italy and the Levant to France.[14] Nicolas Mesnager used his diplomatic forays into Holland as opportunities for some profitable horse-trading.[15] Finally, the commercial and banking activities of Samuel Bernard during his two decades as a deputy are too well documented to require description here.[16] The royal ministers did all that they could to ensure that the deputies' work in the Council of Com-merce interfered as little as possible with their personal affairs. If a deputy needed to return home on urgent business, they generally granted him a short leave of absence.[17]

The personal relationships that several deputies had with the royal ministers have already been mentioned. Some of them fre-quently were called to Fontainebleau or to Marly to advise the ministers, and on at least a few occasions some of the deputies were invited to the country estates of Chamillart and Desmaretz.[18] Joseph Fabre, of Marseilles, was close enough to Jérôme de Pontchartrain to visit him virtually every time that the secretary of state was in Paris.[19] Each of the deputies at one time or another felt close enough to the ministers to request favors for himself or for a friend. Anisson in particular was guilty of this; he repeatedly asked the controller general to have all *arrêts en finance* printed at the Imprimerie royale rather than at other publishing houses.[20]

Judging from the above, one can infer that the men who served as deputies in Paris were well qualified to evaluate commercial problems and to transmit the opinions of their localities to the central government. Soon after the council began to meet, they were given a splendid opportunity to do this.

THE GENERAL MEMOIRS OF THE DEPUTIES

Perhaps the best way to approach the study of the deputies and the issues that they discussed in the Council of Commerce from 1700 to 1715 is to begin with a look at the series of general memoirs written by the deputies in the winter of 1700–1701. When the council assembled on 24 November 1700, the first official action taken by President Daguesseau was to ask that each deputy submit "a memoir on the general state of trade."[21] Over the next several months, the deputies composed their memoirs and presented them individually to the council. This was one of the rare occasions[22] when the deputies were asked to consider the economy as a whole and were not restricted to commenting on a unique problem referred to them by the *commissaires*. The memoirs therefore offer a valuable appraisal of the French economy at the turn of the century, and they also reveal a great deal about merchants' expectations concerning the Council of Commerce.

These memoirs have, in fact, attained such notoriety that a discussion of them is indispensable. Historians have devoted an inordinate amount of attention to them, often neglecting the council's subsequent ninety-one years of activity.[23] The reasons for this attention are easy to explain. The memoirs were written by experienced businessmen, and they do offer a valuable analysis of the French economy at a critical moment.[24] Furthermore, the memoirs are attractive because they were part of a new and unique type of royal council, one in which the governed themselves had an important voice. But the principal cause for all the interest in the memoirs is that historians have tended to see in them evidence of merchant opposition to the mercantilist policies of the crown. Authorities as diverse as Philippe Sagnac, Jean Meuvret, and Pierre Goubert have portrayed the deputies as harbingers of the physiocrats and of laissez-faire economics.[25] Lionel Rothkrug asserts that the deputies "argued vehemently and eloquently against the established doctrines of political economy."[26] Claude-Frédéric Lévy declares that they presented "a manifesto of Physiocratic liberalism."[27] These historians have fondly quoted the anguished cries of the deputies, for "liberté du commerce," for "liberté générale," and for "entière liberté." Such phrases, which the deputies did indeed use in their general memoirs, have been taken as *post hoc* evidence of the collective merchant unrest that supposedly compelled the government to establish the Council of Commerce.

Although it is true that the deputies did catalog a long list of merchant grievances, the standard interpretation of these memoirs is in need of sharp revision. The deputies spoke of liberty of trade and of more freedom from government restrictions, but their *liberté* was much closer to *Colbertisme* than to the twentieth-century conception of laissez-faire.

Before looking at the ideas contained in the memoirs, one should first consider how they were composed. Charles Woolsey Cole says that the deputies "could scarcely wait" to write their memoirs and that "it was as if a dam had burst,."[28] If this was true, then Cole had in mind a very slow dam. The first memoir was submitted by Mesnager on 3 December 1700, but over the next several months, Daguesseau repeatedly had to solicit the other deputies to finish their memoirs and submit them.[29] The final ones were not presented to the council until 8 April 1701.[30] There were twelve such memoirs in all; Samuel Bernard did not write one. They varied in length from six folio pages (Mesnager) to sixty-nine (Descasaux du Hallay). A few of the deputies supplemented their principal memoirs with additional ones on specific topics.

We know little about how the memoirs were composed. The deputies of Lille and Dunkirk probably collaborated on theirs; the two memoirs are remarkably similar in style and phraseology. Most of the deputies had received written instructions from their local electors to guide them. The Chamber of Commerce of Marseilles, for example, presented their new deputy (Joseph Fabre) with a list of instructions 445 pages long![31] The departmental archives for Nantes contain several rough drafts, extracts, and copies of the memoir that Descasaux du Hallay submitted to the council in April 1701.[32] It is clear that the municipal officials and important merchants in Nantes participated in instructing their deputy and perhaps in composing his memoir.

There are several manuscript copies of the memoirs located in Parisian depositories, which leads one to suppose that they attained a high degree of attention early in the eighteenth century. The only reliable and complete collection is in the Bibliothèque Nationale, MSS. fr., 8038.[33] Incomplete manuscript copies of them can likewise be found at the Bibliothèque Nationale, as well as at the Bibliothèque de l'Arsenal and the Archives Nationales.[34]

The memoirs, though varying in length, organization, and style, were nevertheless fairly similar. There was, one must admit, much evidence in them of opposition to restrictive royal policies. All but one of the deputies (Mesnager) made repeated calls for greater liberty for the merchant. Descasaux du Hallay eloquently declared that "liberty is the soul and body of commerce"[35] and that "all of France aspires for this liberty,"[36] "a liberty without limits."[37] La Motte-Gaillard, of Saint-Malo, vowed that his city's economy would revive only through "a complete freedom of trade."[38] Taviel, of Lille, affirmed that two prerequisites for a flourishing economy were "peace and freedom."[39] Several deputies pointed admiringly to the example set by Holland, where much greater liberty existed. They lamented that perhaps trade could prosper only in republics, for monarchies were far too prone to war.[40]

According to the deputies, what were the chief obstacles to the freedom so necesssary for commerce? The deputies were virtually unanimous in their criticism of privileged trading companies.[41] The monopolies enjoyed by these companies profited a small clique of private directors who, the deputies asserted, cared little for "the general good." Descasaux du Hallay admitted that at one time these companies had perhaps been needed to open up new areas of trade, but he argued that this was no longer true.[42] The China, East India, Senegal, Canada, and tobacco companies each had exclusive privileges in its respective area of trade; and this, according to the deputies, prevented free and open competition. Piécourt, of Dunkirk, complained that if the number of monopolies in France continued to grow, one would have to purchase from the government the right to enter into any kind of trade whatever.[43] The deputies accused the companies of purposefully keeping the volume of trade low in order to keep prices up and of not developing French colonies. They further charged that the Guinea and Senegal companies failed to honor their commitment to supply the French colonies with an adequate number of slaves. Piécourt alleged that these companies would rather send 1,500 slaves a year to the colonies, selling them for 400 to 450 livres apiece, than send 4,500 yearly and be able to get only 200 to 250 livres each.[44] The deputies decried the East India Company for its failure to supply France with enough spices; as a result Frenchmen had to purchase great quantities from the Dutch. The French company preferred to bring to France, in fraud, large quantities of Indian calicos (*toiles peintes*), which did considerable harm to the nation's textile industry. The deputies also castigated the tobacco company for preferring to buy tobacco from the Dutch rather than cultivate it in Saint-Domingue. They argued that if all these trades were opened to everyone, then French commerce and the French colonies would prosper, and that the coffers of the king would grow as a result of the increased number of imports and exports. At the very least, the deputies pleaded, these companies should be deprived of their exclusive monopolies, so that individuals could buy passports from them to partake in these areas of trade.[45]

Another obstacle to the freedom of trade, in the eyes of the deputies, was the high tariffs on imports and exports adopted by the French government in the decades preceding the creation of the Council of Commerce. The deputies, with the exception of Mesnager, argued that French tariffs were exorbitant and that they were cutting off trade with foreigners. In addition, high tariffs actually decreased rather than augmented the revenues of the king, for they encouraged frauds.[46] The deputies sang paeans to the beauty, richness, and productivity of France; but they all realized that autarky was impossible: France needed foreign trade. Fénellon, of Bordeaux, moralized that

> God has distributed his gifts in such a way as to make men love one another. He did not wish for the same things to be produced everywhere on earth because he wanted men to seek the help of each other by a mutual exchange of the goods they possess.[47]

Thus it was unrealistic for France to hope to produce all the manufactures and other goods it needed. Even if the country were self-sufficient, it would still require foreign trade. Many provinces, noted the deputies, depended on the sale to foreigners not only of their manufactures but also of their agricultural products. Virtually every year such things as wine, brandy, salt, and honey were produced in superfluity in France, and the economic prosperity of much of the country depended on their export to other nations.

High tariffs, however, were rebuffing foreigners and leading to reprisals against French exports. If other countries could not easily sell their products in France, then they would not willingly buy French merchandise.

Several of the deputies argued that French textiles were overprotected and that French viniculture, "our precious treasure,"[48] was much more in need of help. Already the English were adapting themselves to the taste of Portuguese and Spanish wines. Descasaux du Hallay contended that French textiles needed few laws to protect them. French styles were always the vogue in Europe, he said, and therefore the nation's textiles would always have a brisk market.[49]

Anisson, of Lyons, perhaps expressed the will of all the deputies when he said, "It is necessary to reject the maxim of Colbert which claimed that France could do without the rest of the world and which wanted to oblige foreigners to buy from us."[50] This was against nature and against divine providence, he claimed. The fruits of the earth were distributed in such a way as to force people to partake in "a reciprocal trade." It would not be reciprocal, he noted, if France wished to sell its manufactures to foreigners only in return for their gold and silver.

The deputies further deplored the multitudinous internal duties and tolls that had to be paid on goods traveling between cities and provinces within France. Descasaux du Hallay estimated that the river tolls collected on goods traveling on the Loire River from Nantes to Orleans amounted to 15 pecent of their total value, not to mention the costly delays encountered at each collection point.[51] Two deputies ventured to recommend a complete reformation of the internal tariff structure.[52] They suggested that all regional tariffs be superseded by a uniform tariff wall on the frontiers of France. This would remove the internal impediments to the free flow of goods and help unite France.

Another object of the deputies' scorn was the favors and privileges that certain cities possessed to the exclusion of others. All the deputies from the Atlantic ports, for example, attacked Marseilles's virtual monopoly of trade with the Levant.[53] Marseilles was one of only three cities that could trade directly with that area; but the other two, Rouen and Dunkirk, had to pay a 20 percent duty on all Levantine goods, whereas Marseilles was a free port. This meant that all other French cities were virtually compelled to purchase their Levantine goods through the merchants of Marseilles, and they were thus forced to pay whatever prices Marseilles was asking for them.

Most of the deputies were equally severe in their opposition to Lyons's unique position in the silk trade. All raw silk coming from Italy and the Mediterranean had to enter France through Marseilles or Pont-de-Beauvoisin and from there pass through Lyons. Silk was thus subject to a host of local customs duties and extra transportation costs before it reached manufacturing towns such as Tours and Nîmes. Several deputies charged that this arrangement had already caused the number of silk looms in Tours to drop from 12,000 to fewer than 1,200.[54] To remedy this they asked that all French cities be permitted to import silks directly from their sources of origin.

The deputies also had a number of other grievances or requests. La Motte-Gaillard, of Saint-Malo, urged, for instance, that the number of free ports be increased to include other cities besides just Dunkirk and Marseilles.[55] Naturally he hoped that one of these additional free ports would be his own city. Together with the deputy of Dunkirk, La Motte-Gaillard likewise objected to the fact that direct trade with the French West Indies was open only to Rouen, Dieppe, Nantes, Bordeaux, La Rochelle, and Marseilles.[56] This, according to the two deputies, was an unfair restriction of the trade that should be open to all French ports. In a like spirit, several deputies criticized the granting of various manufacturing monopolies to private individuals or to friends of the court; these were viewed as pernicious constraints on the enterprising spirit of all Frenchmen.[57] Another practice deplored by the deputies was the continual monetary instability caused by an increase or decrease in the value of metallic currency with respect to the livre (the money of account.)[58] The government's tinkering with the money supply made foreign merchants reluctant to trade with Frenchmen. Other complaints by the deputies concerned the growing shortages of wood and coal in France,[59] the delays and excessive fees incurred in commercial legal suits,[60] the exorbitant prices being charged by the tax farmers operating the postal system,[61] and the growing wealth of the clergy.[62] Also, the deputies bemoaned the sad effects of the revocation of the Edict of Nantes.[63] Although they did not openly criticize it, they did note that it had caused many Huguenots to flee to England and Holland, taking their skills with them. The deputies hoped that the government might induce many of these refugees to return to France.

One last point on which the deputies agreed, and on which they expounded at great length, was the need to honor commerce and to grant marks of distinction to merchants. The outcome of these demands has already been mentioned above. The deputies declared that unless the low status of trade was rectified, the sons of merchants would continue in increasing numbers to leave the profession, and France would thus lose all of its experienced traders. One of the chief obstacles to treating them with the respect they deserved was the behavior of the *commis* of the tax farmers. These clerks were "burning with insatiable desire for personal profit" and had "ready-made pretexts for irritating merchants." They caused innumerable delays at the check points where merchandise was unloaded and appraised, and often an honest merchant had to bribe them in order to get his goods through. But what was hardest to tolerate was the disdain and the hauteur with which the *commis* treated merchants.[65]

These then were the opinions of the deputies that many historians have viewed as a frontal assault on that vast body of economic policies brought to maturity by Colbert that we now call mercantilism. If one examines the memoirs more closely, however, one can see that there is little in them with which Colbert would have disagreed. Several historians have already noted the traditional or mercantilist nature of parts of the memoirs and have attributed this to the transitional nature of the memoirs or to the deputies' hesitancy in voicing new ideas.[66] The fact is, however, that the deputies were more Colbertian than historians have heretofore been willing to admit.

In calling for greater freedom of trade, the deputies were no different from Colbert himself. The historians who quote Descasaux du Hallay's proud cry that "freedom is the soul and body of trade" could also cite Colbert's letter to the intendant d'Herbigny in 1671, in which Colbert opposed restraints on "this freedom which is the soul of trade."[67] Colbert's correspondence is filled with such references to freedom of trade.[68] One might protest that Colbert's definition of liberty differed from that of the deputies. After all, Colbert certainly did regulate, inspect, and limit trade as he considered it necessary. In actuality, however, Colbert's conceptions were not far removed from the "complete freedom" desired by the deputies. This "freedom" of which they spoke was, in practice, far from complete.

On the question of French tariff policies, for example, the deputies were in reality very close to Colbert's position. Anisson, of Lyons, argued that the country must abandon the "maxim" of Colbert that France was self-sufficient and could survive without importing things from other countries. Actually, Colbert never said anything of the sort. To the contrary, he realized that France needed to export its superfluous goods and that it could not do without foreign imports. In addition, since France had no gold or silver mines, foreign trade was the only means by which she could build up stocks of these precious metals. Colbert's general tariffs of 1664 and 1667 were certainly protective of French industries, but Colbert did not wish to drive away foreign trade. His tariffs encouraged the import of foodstuffs and raw materials and the export of French manufactures.[69] The deputies of commerce in 1700–1701 were in complete agreement with this aim, and several of them actually praised Colbert's tariff policies. They merely asked that the duties added to the tariffs since 1683 be lowered.[70]

Despite the claims of a few of the deputies that the wine industry was more important to France than were its textiles, all the deputies agreed that French manufactures required some protection against foreign competition. Fabre, of Marseilles, proclaimed that "manufactures are the soul of trade," and that as such they deserved important consideration.[71] Even Descasaux du Hallay admitted that it was necessary to protect "our useful establishments."[72] Taviel, of Lille, suggested that duties of 12 to 15 percent on foreign manufactures should suffice to protect those in France; any French manufacturer who demanded more than this was "a man who wants to enrich himself at public expense."[73] Several deputies urged that the bans on the importation and use of Indian calicos be continued; otherwise, they asserted, French manufactures would surely be ruined.[74] They also argued that the export of raw materials needed for French manufactures should be prohibited and that French workers should be discouraged from settling abroad.[75] The deputies castigated those small merchants (*détailleurs, boutiquiers*) who heedlessly imported huge quantities of foreign merchandise and made no attempt to export French products in return.[76] Several deputies lamented the imperfections that were developing in French textiles and urged that the regulations established by Colbert and his successors be enforced and even increased in number and in severity.[77] Mourges, of Languedoc, for example, proposed the creation of eight new inspectors and assistant inspectors in every province to police the silk and woolens industries; he also wanted new laws to guarantee the quality of these products. In addition, he asked the government to force Frenchmen to plant mulberry trees so that silkworms could be raised in France. Finally, he urged that the crown protect the wool supply by restricting the slaughter of lambs for food and by prohibiting the growing of crops in sheep pastures.[78] Anisson recommended that fines be levied on all persons wearing certain foreign cloths. He likewise suggested that the new king of Spain, Louis XIV's grandson Philip V, compel Spaniards to dress *à la française* and to stop purchasing English woolens.[79]

On the question of money, the deputies were every bit as bullionist as Colbert had been. Gold and silver were, according to Anisson, "without contradiction the sole nerve of states."[80] In contrast to Descasaux du Hallay's claim that liberty was the soul of trade, Rol, of Bayonne, exclaimed that "money is the soul and fuel of trade."[81] One of the deputies' chief objections to the East India Company and to Marseilles's trade with the Levant was that they were sending much specie out of France. The deputies did not wish to prohibit completely the export of precious metals, but they did seek some means of compelling merchants to sell more to foreigners than they purchased from them. Several of the deputies expounded on ways to establish a balance of commerce that would protect France's stores of bullion.[82] Descasaux du Hallay, usually cited as the most liberal of the deputies, proposed that every merchant who imported things from the Dutch be forced to export to Holland an amount of goods equal or greater in value.[83] Most of the deputies recommended new sumptuary laws to supplement those of Colbert; these would greatly restrict the amount of gold and silver that could be used in clothing, jewelry, and tableware and prevent the use of foreign luxury fabrics.[84]

There was, at least on the surface, a difference between Colbert and the deputies on the question of granting special privileges or exemptions to individuals or to cities. As noted earlier, the deputies all opposed such favoritism—in theory at any rate. If one considers each memoir more closely, however, one can see that in reality each deputy was pleading for the special interests of his own region. Joseph Fabre agreed that special favors granted to one city always hurt others, but almost within the same breath he defended Marseilles's monopoly of the Levant trade.[85] La Motte-Gaillard pleaded for the opening of the West Indies trade to all French cities, but when he requested that Saint-Malo's status as a free port be reestblished, it was clear that he did not want the privilege to be shared by every city.[86] The deputies of La Rochelle, Bordeaux, Rouen, and Nantes railed against the privileges of Marseilles and Lyons, but never once did they suggest that their own cities surrender their monopoly of trade with the West Indies and thus open it to Bayonne, Dunkirk, and other ports. In short, the deputies were rather hypermetropic, seeing clearly the abuses and privileges of other cities but overlooking or even defending the favors and monopolies of their own localities. The excuse was always that it was in the interest of the common good: each deputy's city or region was so well-endowed or conveniently located for a particular trade that it merited special consideration.

Concerning internal duties and tolls, Colbert would have been in complete accord with the sentiments of the deputies. Colbert had worked diligently throughout his ministry to diminish the number of customs barriers and privately owned tolls within France. His 1664 tariff had been designed originally for the frontiers of France, but the resistance to it by several outlying provinces had led to the failure of the plan. The result was that France was divided fiscally into three basic regions: the *cinq grosses fermes*, the *provinces réputées étrangères*, and the *provinces de l'étranger effectif*.[87] Similar resistance by local and private interests had prevented Colbert from abolishing all internal tolls. Colbert would thus have been sympathetic to the deputies' complaints about the host of taxes encountered on French rivers, canals, and roads. In fact, Colbert was even more liberal in this respect than some of the deputies. Descasaux du Hallay, for example, bemoaned the excessive number of tolls on the Loire River, yet Nantes became the most vehement opponent in the Council of Commerce of the proposal to establish a uniform tariff wall around the borders of France.[88] The city did not want to relinquish the fiscal privileges it enjoyed as part of a *province réputée étrangère*.

The deputies' criticisms of the *commis* of the tax farmers were not so much an attack on the system itself as on the abuses of the personnel who ran it. Descasaux du Hallay made clear that he was not criticizing the tax farmers; he said they were probably unaware of the misconduct of their employees.[89] But the crown did not need the Council of Commerce in order to find out about the abuses present in the tax-collection machinery. Throughout the seventeenth century, the government had received complaints similar to those of the deputies; often these came from the royal provincial intendants.[90] During the period under consideration here, Secretary of State for the Navy Jérôme de Pontchartrain was himself one of the most vocal critics of the *commis* of the farmers general. He frequently informed the controller general of the vexations and delays that these *commis* were causing the shipments of goods destined for the navy.[91] Whenever possible the controller general took steps to correct the abuses—whether by the launching of investigations[92] or by the firing of miscreant *commis*.[93] To find fault with the tax-gathering machinery in France thus did not necessarily mean that one was an antimercantilist or a leader of opposition to the government.

Historians have generally agreed that one of the most serious flaws in Colbert's economic policies was that they contributed, logically and inevitably, to war. This flaw was likewise shared by the deputies of commerce. Colbert's static view of the world's resources is well-documented. He believed that one nation could prosper only at the expense of others, and he argued that Holland was doing just that, to the detriment of France. In his famous 1669 memoir, he estimated the total number of ships in the world to be twenty thousand; of these, he noted enviously, the Dutch owned fifteen to sixteen thousand, whereas France, with a population ten times larger than Holland's, possessed only five to six hundred.[94] Although recent research has shown that Colbert may not have actively supported the Dutch War at its commencement,[95] soon thereafter he did become one of its strongest proponents. Even before the war broke out, Colbert had acknowledged that at some point France would have to take drastic steps to overcome the predominance of the Dutch merchant marine. It is, of course, ironic that the Dutch War actually helped undercut all of Colbert's financial and commercial achievements.

The deputies of commerce were every bit as hostile to the Dutch as Colbert had been, and they agreed with him that trade was only war in a different guise. Although they admired the commercial know-how of the Dutch, they loathed their "pernicious designs"[96] for reducing France to dependency on Holland. The Dutch had demanded and received in the Treaty of Ryswick concessions that, according to the deputies, enabled them to dominate French trade. That treaty, for example, had exempted Dutch vessels from the duty of 50 sous per ton that had been collected since 1659 on all foreign ships entering French ports. The deputies urged that this duty be totally abolished so that the ships of other nations might successfully compete with the Dutch.[97] They also recommended that the crown induce French shippers to engage in direct trade with the Baltic, thereby eliminating the Dutch middlemen. Piécourt (Dunkirk) affirmed that the only way to humiliate the Dutch and to destroy their commerce would be to prohibit them from bringing to France anything but their own goods and manufactures.[98] This would certainly destroy the Dutch carrying trade, and it would not hurt France, since, as Piécourt assured the council, the Dutch would still need to buy French products for their commerce. At the very least, he continued, France should put Dutch trade back on the same footing it had had prior to the concessions granted at Ryswick. In brief, the deputies fully adhered to Colbert's chauvin-istic resentment of Holland.

There was perhaps only one area of genuine difference between the deputies and Colbert: the deputies' opposition to exclusive trading companies and to monopolistic privileges of any kind. Yet even here the disagreement is not so great as it might at first seem. Neither Colbert nor any of his successors was unalterably com-mitted to the principle of exclusive privilege. Colbert had with-drawn such monopolistic favors whenever he considered them to be unnecessary or detrimental to the common good—thus the re-moval of the exclusive rights of the West Indies Company in 1671.[99] In fact, the government often seems to have resorted to such monopolies only as a last resort, when it became clear that individual initiative alone was not sufficient to develop a trade or an industry. In this regard Charles Frostin has shown that Jérôme de Pontchartrain preferred private enterprise for developing the French colonies but was forced by lack of this to turn to trading companies.[100] The deputies of commerce did not wish to abolish these companies or to end all privileges for manufactures; they merely wanted to remove their exclusiveness. In their general memoirs, for example, they admitted that the Senegal Company deserved certain exemptions and favors because of its vast ex-penses in maintaining forts on the African coast and in transport-ing slaves to the colonies. The deputies asked only that private individuals be able to enter into such areas of trade if they desired to do so.

If there was so little basic disagreement then between Colbertian policies and the ideas of the deputies, one might then ask why the deputies presented so many grievances in these memoirs. This can be explained in several ways. First, no general policy ever suits all parties; and regardless of how prosperous a country is, some special interest groups or localities will always have complaints or believe that another city or area has an unfair advantage. Second, France had recently emerged from a long and relatively unsuccessful war and from several years of poor harvests. Although the economy as a whole was not suffering as badly as many scholars have asserted, nevertheless the return of peace led many people to call for more governmental attention to trade and industry. Third, the very nature of the memoirs lent itself to the airing of grievances. As noted earlier, the deputies did not so much seek to offer a dispassionate analysis of the economy as a whole as to present a series of *cahiers de doléances* on behalf of their regional interests.

A fourth possible explanation lies in the fact that the deputies were complaining not about Colbertism but about the practices of Colbert's successors—Le Peletier, Seignelay, Louvois, and Louis de Pontchartrain. French historians have labeled the economic policies of the late seventeenth century as *Colbertisme à outrance* or *protectionisme à outrance*—that is, taken to its extreme.[101] Charles Woolsey Cole has devoted an entire book to this period, detailing the rigidification, the overregulation, the lack of imagination, and the higher tariff duties that crept into the administration of trade and industry during these years.[102] This interpretation of the work of Colbert's successors is in some ways just, although it is not totally convincing. The commercial and financial policies of Le Peletier and Louis de Pontchartrain (the controllers general of these years) are sorely in need of thorough research; and until it is completed, no definite judgment can be made.

Often the royal ministers themselves were not to be blamed for the higher tariffs. The increased import duties on foreign woolens of 1687, for instance, resulted from pressure by manufacturers who demanded more protection against foreign competition.[103] Most of the higher tariffs and import restrictions on enemy and neutral commerce during the 1690s had the full support of French *armateurs*, whose privateering vessels preyed upon the trade of other nations. Ironically, and somewhat inconsistently, many of these same *armateurs*, several of whom became deputies of commerce in 1700, reversed their position upon the return of peace and called for greater freedom of trade. Concerning manufactures, the increasing severity of laws regulating French textiles during this period were not thrust on an unwilling merchant community by an overbearing government, but rather were usually

requested by the merchants themselves in order to stop the growing abuses that were damaging the reputation abroad of French
cloths. [104]

Nevertheless, the deputies of commerce in 1700 did criticize
what they considered to be the excessive tariffs and the lack of
flexibility of Colbert's successors. Time and again the deputies acknowledged that protection was necessary—but in moderation.
There was thus no difference between the *liberté* of Colbert and
that of the deputies. No one wished to eliminate all controls. What
the deputies wanted, rather, was a system of reasonable government regulations and moderate, though protective, tariffs. Even
Descasaux du Hallay, who called for a "freedom without limits,"
admitted in other places that this was not practicable. Just after he
saluted liberty as the soul of trade, he conceded: "One must admit,
however, that it is sometimes necessary to place restrictions on this
general freedom. . . ." [105]

Three of the deputies (Mesnager, Rol, and Fabre) actually went
out of their way to praise Colbert, speaking of him as "enlightened"
and imbued with "penetration" and "insights," [106] As a whole the
deputies shared the same *Weltanschauung* as Colbert, and one must
scrupulously avoid making them appear too liberal. If one seeks to
find in the late seventeenth century early signs of classical economic thought, one must turn to England. In the 1680s and 1690s,
English writers such as Dudley North, Nicholas Barbon, Dalby
Thomas, and others were abandoning such mercantilist standbys as
bullionism, the balance of trade, the static view of a nation's economy, and protective tariffs. [107] In comparison with these men, the
French deputies were still thoroughly traditional. This fact will
become clearer as one examines more closely the work of the
Council of Commerce in the years following 1700.

1. Biollay, *Etudes économiques*, pp. 411–13; Bibliothèque de l'Arsenal, MS. 4561,
avertissement, fols. F–G.

2. Giteau, in Robert Boutruche (ed.), *Histoire de Bordeaux, de 1453 à 1715* (Paris,
1966), p. 464.

3. All the deputies are listed in the Appendix. I have gathered information on
them from a variety of archival sources and printed works. See especially Bonnassieux and Lelong, *Conseil de commerce*, pp. lxiv–lxxii.

4. See Mar., B² 170, fols. 338v–39, Pontchartrain to Anisson, 4 November 1703;
B² 182, fol. 534, same to same, 12 September 1705.

5. AN, G⁷ 532, Anisson to Chamillart, 20 November 1699, with accompanying
memoir.

6. The *quarteniers* were minor police officials in several of the larger cities in France. Formerly they had commanded the *milice bourgeoise*, but by the late seventeenth century, their power had greatly diminished. They retained certain police powers in cases of fires, epidemics, and other exceptional circumstances.

7. Fournier, *La Chambre de commerce de Marseille*, pp. 39–44; Rambert, *Histoire du commerce de Marseille*, 4:219, 284–86; AN, G⁷ 645, Fabre to Le Peletier, 29 October 1685 and 15 December 1685; Cole, *French Mercantilism, 1683–1700*, p. 23.

8. The other two were Jean-Baptiste de Lagny, director general of commerce in the naval ministry, and Jean-Rémy Hénault, a farmer general ("Tarif arresté entre la France et la Hollande, 8 Decembre 1699"; several copies are in AN, G⁷ 1685).

9. Pierre Bonnassieux reports a letter dated September 1702 addressed as follows: "Monsieur Descasaux, député de la Chambre de commerce de Nantes, rue d'Orléans, à l'hostel d'Orléans, à Paris" (AN, AB XIX, 368 [Bonnassieux Papers]).

10. See, for example, AN, G⁷ 1695, piece 22, Descasaux du Hallay to Desmaretz, 25 January 1710; G⁷ 598, same to same, 11 July 1715; Mar., B² 187, fols. 428v–29, Pontchartrain to Descasaux du Hallay, 17 February 1706; B² 231, p. 157, same to same, 27 July 1712. For additional information on his commercial activities, see Lévy, *Capitalistes et pouvoir*, pp. 403, 406–7; Charles de La Morandière, *Histoire de la pêche française de la morue dans l'Amérique septentrionale (des origines à 1789)*, 1:448, 461, 463–64.

11. Saint-Germain, *Samuel Bernard*, p. 52; AN, G⁷ 1694, piece 30, (Berkley?) to Desmaretz, 26 January 1709.

12. Letters to and from them are scattered throughout the financial and naval archives. Some illustrations: Mar., B² 222, pp. 980–81, Pontchartrain to Piécourt, 24 September 1710; B² 223, p. 433, Pontchartrain to Héron, 12 November 1710; B² 197, p. 86. Pontchartrain to Piou, 6 April 1707; B² 217, p. 998, Pontchartrain to Fénellon, 11 December 1709; B³ 140, f. 34, "Liste des particuliers à qui le Roy a accordé des permissions pour envoyer aux decouvertes." Also see Lévy, *Capitalistes et pouvoir*, pp. 403–15. Scoville therefore errs in saying that the deputies were merely merchants and not shippers or shipowners ("The French Economy," p. 240). On trade with the *mer du Sud*, see Chapter 8, below.

13. Mar., B⁷ 502, fol. 24, Fabre to Pontchartrain, 2 January 1702; ibid., fols. 110–11, "Mémoire pour avoir la permission d'une barque," 1702, by Fabre; ibid., fols. 112–13, Fabre to Pontchartrain, 3 December 1702.

14. Mar., B² 219, fols. 296v–97v, 359v–60v, Pontchartrain to Fabre, 2 October and 25 October 1709.

15. Herbert Lüthy, *La Banque protestante en France de la révocation de l'édit de Nantes à la révolution*, 1:175.

16. Ibid., passim; Saint-Germain, *Samuel Bernard*, passim; Lévy, *Capitalistes et pouvoir*, especially pp. 49 ff.

17. See Mar., B² 217, p. 998, Pontchartrain to Fénellon, 11 December 1709; B² 208, p. 1124, Pontchartrain to Piou, 5 September 1708; AN, F¹² 115, fol. 163v, Chamillart to Basville, 11 October 1701; F¹² 121, fol. 58v, Chamillart to de la Bordonnoye, 7 September 1705.

18. For example, ACCM, B 157, Joseph Fabre to Chamber of Commerce, 7 August and 11 August 1703; AN, G⁷ 1696, piece 167, Anisson to [Clautrier], 11 July 1711; Col., B 30, pp. 127–28, Pontchartrain to Mesnager, 10 June 1709.

19. See Mar., B⁷ 502, p. 47, Fabre to Pontchartrain, 7 April 1702; B⁷ 504, f. 409, same to same, 11 January 1706.

20. AN, G⁷ 1695, piece 225, Anisson to [Clautrier], 6 November 1710; G⁷ 1696, piece 167, same to same, 17 July 1711.

21. AN, F¹² 51, fol. 4.

22. At a later date Daguesseau asked the deputies to submit general memoirs on the problems that they felt most urgently required the council's attention. Meeting of 30 May 1704, ibid., fol. 258v.

23. At least five scholars have reprinted parts of the memoirs. Laurence B. Packard includes a transcription of all of them in "Some Antecedents of the Conseil du Commerce of 1700," volume 2. The dissertation itself is of minimal worth. Packard explains in his preface that he was forced to abandon his research in France soon after arriving there because of the eruption of World War I. A. de Boislisle has printed four of the memoirs in his *Correspondance des contrôleurs généraux*, 1:477–504. Extracts of most of the memoirs can be found in the following: Pierre Clément, *Histoire du système protecteur*, pp. 285–95; C. Dareste de la Chavanne, *Histoire de l'administration en France et des progrès du pouvoir royal, depuis le règne de Philippe-Auguste jusqu'à la mort de Louis XIV*, 2:392–421; Martin, *La grande industrie sous le règne de Louis XIV*, pp. 374–91.

24. Warren Scoville correctly points out the limitations of the memoirs in "The French Economy in 1700–1701," pp. 232, 249–50. Most of the deputies concentrated on issues that affected their own local interests rather than trying to evaluate the economy as a whole. Paul Masson, however, clearly exaggerates in claiming that the deputies' memoirs contained "peu d'idées fécondes" (*Histoire du commerce . . . XVIIe siècle*, p. 310).

25. Sagnac, "La Politique commerciale de la France," pp. 265–69, and in Ernest Lavisse (ed.), *Histoire de France depuis des origines jusqu'à la révolution*, vol. 8, pt. 1, pp. 215–17; Jean Meuvret, "Les Temps difficiles," p. 79; Pierre Goubert, *L'Ancien Régime, 1: la société*, p., 198; Goubert, *Louis XIV and Twenty Million Frenchmen*, p. 280. See also, among others, Auguste Dubois, *Précis de l'histoire des doctrines économiques dans leurs rapports avec les institutions*, vol. 1: *L'Epoque antérieure aux Physiocrates*, pp. 273–74; Emile Levasseur, *Histoire du commerce de la France*, 1:420–21; Henri Sée, *Histore économique*, 1:274; Marcel Giraud, *Histoire de la Louisiane française*, 1:234; Merle L. Perkins, *The Moral and Political Philosophy of the Abbé de Saint-Pierre*, pp. 74–80; Laura Bernardini, "Le Conseil du commerce," pp. 37–38; Pierre Deyon, *Le Mercantilisme*, p. 62; Abel Poitrineau, *Le premier XVIIIe siècle: 1680 à 1750* (Paris, 1971), p. 61; Hubert Méthivier, *Le Siècle de Louis XIV*, p. 121. Warren Scoville ("The French Economy") and Charles Woolsey Cole (*French Mercantilism, 1683–1700*, chap. 5) present the best accounts of the deputies' memoirs. Both men treat the ideas in them evenhandedly, though they do argue that the memoirs reflect an incipient attack on royal mercantilist policies.

26. Rothkrug, *Opposition*, p. 416.

27. Lévy, *Capitalistes et pouvoir*, p. 297.

28. Cole, *French Mercantilism, 1683–1700*, p. 231.

29. Meeting of 10 December 1700, AN, F^12 51, fol. 8; 28 January 1701, fol. 18v; 10 February 1701, fol. 21.

30. On that date memoirs were presented by Descasaux du Hallay (Nantes), Peletyer (Paris), and Piécourt (Dunkirk) (ibid., fol. 27).

31. ACCM, B 152; partially reprinted in Fournier, *La Chambre de commerce de Marseille*, pp. 249–63.

32. AD, Loire-Atlantique, C 694, pieces 5–14; C 700, piece 77.

33. The copies of the memoirs located in the Bibliothèque Nationale are described in Julien Cain, "Les Mémoires des députés au conseil de commerce de 1700." Cain demonstrates that the only reliable copy is MS. 8038. This register includes a memoir written by the deputies in 1708 concerning the importation of Dutch merchandise, and the register's frontispiece bears the inscription "Mémoire présenté à M. le duc d'Orléans, régent, par les Députés du Commerce." Thus the

memoirs were probably bound together into this volume sometime between 1708 and 1715.

34. BN, MSS. fr., 18597; MSS. Fr., nouv. acq., 885. See also the copy of Ezechiel Spanheim's *Relation de la cour de France* (MSS. fr., nouv. acq., 6838, pp. 499–579), which contains notes on several of the memoirs. These notes are not included in any of the published editions of the *Relation*. Spanheim, who was in Paris at the time, apparently received copies of the memoirs as a result of his acquaintance with some of the deputies. A copy of these notes can be found in the Seligman Collection at Columbia University. Several of the memoirs can also be found in Bib. de l'Arsenal, MS. 4496. Scattered copies or extracts of individual memoirs are located at various places in the BN and AN. For example, AN, G⁷ 1686 (Descasaux du Hallay and La Motte-Gaillard); BN, MSS. fr., 14294, fols. 16–27 (Anisson). At Harvard University (Kress Collection, no. 4346) and at the Library of Congress (Rare Book Collection, HF 3555 F 81), one can find a volume entitled *Memorials Presented by the Deputies of the Council of Trade in France, to the Royal Council in 1701. Being the Year after the Establishment of the said Council of Trade by King Lewis XIV* (London, 1736). The title of this work is a misnomer. It does not contain the general memoirs of 1700–1701, but rather an assortment of other memoirs, many of which were written after 1701. Most of the memoirs in this work can also be found in BN, MSS. fr., nouv. acq., 6828. Copies of the general memoirs of various deputies can also be found in several departmental archives.

35. BN, MSS. fr., 8038, fol. 224v.

36. Ibid., fol. 271.

37. Ibid., fol. 288v.

38. Ibid., fol. 293.

39. Ibid., fol. 105v.

40. Ibid., fols. 105v, 124, 225, 425v.

41. The two Parisian deputies, Antoine Peletyer and Samuel Bernard, were actually directors of the East India Company. Bernard, as noted above, wrote no general memoir. Peletyer's memoir studiously neglected to criticize the large trading companies. Peletyer did, somewhat contradictorily, however, object to exclusive privileges in other fields. For example, he attacked the tobacco company and a proposed monopoly of all public transportation in France; "complete freedom for passenger coaches," he proclaimed (ibid., fol. 90). Mesnager was undoubtedly the most conservative of the deputies. He had the fewest number of criticisms of exclusive trading companies (whose utility he noted) and privileged manufactures. In several places he unabashedly praised the work of Colbert. It is thus difficult to understand how Hubert Méthivier (*Le Siècle de Louis XIV*, p. 121) can say that Mesnager was one of the most vocal opponents of "un Colbertisme périmé." Also see Lévy, *Capitalistes et pouvoir*, p. 396. Charles Frostin claims that Mesnager and Daguesseau were the leaders in a campaign against all monopolies (Frostin, "Les Pontchartrain et la pénétration commerciale," p. 311 n. 2). I have not seen the letter of Mesnager from which Frostin quotes, but Mesnager's memoir of 1700 and his subsequent activities in the Council of Commerce demonstrate that he did not object to monopolies (in trade or in industry) if he felt they were necessary. He supported, for example, the privileges of the East India and Senegal companies (BN, MSS. fr., 8038, fol. 158v).

42. BN, MSS. fr., 8038, fol. 268v; see also 166v.

43. Ibid., fol. 148.

44. Ibid., fol. 131v.

45. Ibid., fols. 129–33v, 159, 166, 269–87, 302–9v, 316–18, 420v–22, 437v–41, 464–65.

46. Ibid., fols. 106v, 119v–20.

47. Ibid., fol. 405.

48. Ibid., fol. 245v.

49. Ibid., fol. 255v.

50. Ibid., fol. 245v.

51. Ibid., fol. 237v.

52. Ibid., fols., 120v–21, 181–84.

53. Ibid., fols., 111–11v, 134, 158–58v, 195–96, 263–64, 319–20, 415v–16, 444.

54. Ibid., fols. 134v, 197, 264–65v, 444–45, 449, 476.

55. Ibid., fols., 292–94, 299; see also fols. 251, 450.

56. Ibid., fols. 134v, 312–13v.

57. Ibid., fols. 58, 159v, 170, 287–87v.

58. Ibid., fols. 106, 113v–14v, 145–48, 255, 507v.

59. Ibid., fols. 286v–87v.

60. Ibid., fols. 322v–23, 172–72v, 235–35v.

61. Ibid., fols. 91–93v.

62. Ibid., fol. 105.

63. Ibid., fols. 14v–15, 62–63, 156v, 164v, 170v, 434, 467, 476, 506.

64. Ibid., fol. 234v.

65. Ibid., fols. 89v, 93v–95, 106–7, 122–24, 148, 153, 160v, 165–66, 172–72v, 215v–16, 234–36v, 326–27, 329–30, 348–55, 388–89, 391–93, 397–99, 442, 451–52, 455, 503, 513, 517.

66. Cole, *French Mercantilism, 1683–1700*, pp. 238, 239–40; Scoville, "The French Economy in 1700–1701," pp. 235, 244, 248; Sagnac, "La Politique commerciale de la France," pp. 265, 271; Schatz and Caillemer, "Le Mercantilisme libéral," pp. 565–66.

67. Pierre Clément (ed.). *Lettres, instructions, et mémoires de Colbert*, vol. 2, pt. 2, p. 632, Colbert to d'Herbigny, 1 September 1671.

68. This fact has not been lost on some historians: see Rambert, *Histoire du commerce de Marseille*, 4:210–12; Heckscher, *Mercantilism*, 2:280; Pierre Clément, *Histoire de Colbert et de son administration*, 1:366; Emile Levasseur, *Histoire du commerce de la France*, 1:296–97, 362. Martin, *La grande industrie sous le règne de Louis XIV*, p. 16; Pierre Léon, in Braudel and Labrousse, *Histoire économique et sociale*, 2:224. See also Clément, *Lettres, instructions, et mémoires de Colbert*, vol. 2, pt. 2, p. 68, Colbert to d'Herbigny, 15 September 1673; p. 473, Colbert to Colbert de Terron, 24 June 1669. Louis XIV speaks of liberty of commerce in Depping, *Correspondance administrative*, 3:xxix, Louis XIV to *corps de la ville* of Paris, 27 August 1664. Seignelay also speaks of it in ibid., p. 626, Seignelay to de Morant, 8 August 1684.

69. See Clément, *Histoire du système protecteur*, pp. 42–43, 235–37. The best general account of Colbert's tariffs is S. Elzinga, "Le Tarif de Colbert de 1664 et celui de 1667 et leur signification."

70. BN, MSS. fr., 8038, fols. 96–97v, 135, 239, 409–10, 428v; see also Clément, *Histoire du système protecteur*, pp. 54, 237.

71. BN, MSS. fr., 8038, fol. 504.

72. Ibid., fols. 249v, 250v.

73. Ibid., fol. 113.

74. Ibid., fols. 133–33v, 158v, 165, 272.

75. Ibid., fols. 136–36v, 171, 173.

76. Ibid., fols. 107, 244, 252v, 254v.

77. Ibid., fols. 98v–99, 137, 173.

78. Ibid., fols. 456v, 459, 460–63.

79. Ibid., fols. 174v, 175v.

80. Ibid., fol. 163.

81. Ibid., fol. 441. The same was said by the magistrates and principal merchants of Dunkirk in 1699: see Mar., B⁷ 499, fols. 231–35, "Mémoire à Monseigneur de Pontchartrain de la part des principaux négotians de la ville de Dunkerque."

82. BN, MSS. fr. 8038, fols. 66, 98, 139, 155, 156v, 160, 165, 169, 176, 243–43v, 254–55, 268, 283, 285, 287–89, 364v, 406–7, 480.

83. Ibid., fols. 261–62v.

84. Ibid., fols. 103–3v, 133, 165, 174, 175, 272, 315, 423, 435–36, 460, 464, 493–94.

85. Ibid., fols. 497–99v, 517v–18v.

86. Ibid., fols. 293v–94.

87. See Cole, *Colbert and a Century of French Mercantilism,* 1:416–36; Bosher, *The Single Duty Project,* pp. 2–9.

88. See Chapter 7.

89. BN, MSS. fr., 8038, fol. 236.

90. For example, AN, G⁷ 271, Barentin to Chamillart, 5 April 1700.

91. See Mar., B³ 111, fol. 99, Chamillart to Pontchartrain, 22 August 1700; B² 150, fol. 270v, Pontchartrain to Chamillart, 5 May 1700; ibid., fol. 411v–12, Pontchartrain to Daguesseau, 16 June 1700.

92. One purpose of the famous 1678 inquest, in which several *conseillers d'état* were sent on missions to various provinces, was to investigate abuses in the tax-gathering machinery: see Boislisle, *Mémoires des intendants,* p. 781; also see circular letter of the controller general to the intendants, 12 May 1684 (ibid., p. 483).

93. AN, G⁷ 339, Bégon to Chamillart, 8 June 1700.

94. "Dissertation sur la question: Quelle des deux alliances de France ou de Hollande peut estre plus avantageuse à l'Angleterre," Clément, *Lettres, instructions, et mémoires de Colbert,* 6:264.

95. Paul Sonnino, "Jean-Baptiste Colbert and the Origins of the Dutch War," paper presented at the annual meeting of the Society for French Historical Studies, Washington, D.C., 22 March 1980. Sonnino's forthcoming book on this subject should shed further light on this question.

96. BN, MSS., fr., 8038, fol. 260v.

97. Ibid., fols. 244v, 259–63, 142v–43v, 318v–19.

98. Ibid., fol. 144v.

99. See Martin, *La grande industrie sous le règne de Louis XIV,* p. 95; Levasseur, *Histoire du commerce,* 1:297–98; Cole, *Colbert and a Century of French Mercantilism,* 2:12–18, 539; Depping, *Correspondance administrative,* 3: 869, Colbert to Archbishop of Lyons, 20 May 1672.

100. Frostin, "Les Pontchartrain et la pénétration commerciale," pp. 311 ff.; Jérôme de Pontchartrain's liberal ideas are also described in P. Sagnac, "La Politique commerciale de la France," pp. 271 ff.

101. Sagnac, ibid., p. 265; Sagnac, in Lavisse, *Histoire de France,* vol. 8, pt. 1, pp. 202, 208, 209–10, 234; Masson, *Histoire . . . XVIIᵉ siècle,* p. 240; Martin; *La grande industrie sous le règne de Louis XIV,* pp. 232–37; Clément, *Histoire du système protecteur,* pp. 46–48, 56–59; Depping, *Correspondance administrative,* 3:lvi; Dubois, *Précis,* p.

213; Scoville, *Persecution*, pp. 391–93; J. S. Bromley, "Le Commerce de la France de l'ouest et la guerre maritime, 1702–1712," p. 50; Jules Chinault, *La Chambre de commerce de Toulouse du XVIIIe siècle, 1703–1791*, p. 5.

102. Cole, *French Mercantilism, 1683–1700.* This is likewise the theme of François Dumas, *La réglementation industrielle après Colbert.* The latter is especially biased against Colbert's successors, and it is based on flimsy research.

103. Clément, *Histoire du système protecteur*, p. 46.

104. Ibid., p. 47.

105. BN, MSS. fr., 8038, fol. 226.

106. Ibid., fols. 156v, 426v, 499.

107. W. J. Ashley, "The Tory Origin of Free Trade Policy," pp. 268–303; Joyce Appleby, "Ideology and Theory: The Tension between Political and Economic Liberalism in Seventeenth-Century England"; Joyce Appleby, *Economic Thought and Ideology in Seventeenth Century England.* For a different view see Emory Crockett Bogle, "A Stand for Tradition: The Rejection of the Anglo-French Commercial Treaty of Utrecht," pp. 38–39.

4

THE CHAMBERS OF COMMERCE
AND LOCAL PRIVILEGES

Even though the government called upon them to work for *le bien public*, one must remember that the deputies of trade were elected by local bodies and that they were expected to uphold the particular interests of their constituents. Who were these constituents? The *arrêt* of 29 June 1700 stipulated that the nomination of the deputies was to be done "without intrigue" by assemblies consisting of the city magistrates and the prominent merchants in each of the cities to be represented. Such an assembly elected the first deputies in all but three of the selected cities. The two Parisian deputies (Bernard and Peletyer) were chosen personally by the king.[1] In Dunkirk and Marseilles, the local chambers of commerce did the electing; these were the only two cities with such bodies in 1700.

Soon after the Council of Commerce was created, several of the deputies called for the establishment of chambers in other cities.[2] According to the deputies, these chambers would do on a local level what the council was doing nationally: that is, listen to the complaints of merchants and advise the government on whatever was needed to promote commerce. Also, the chambers could correspond with the council in Paris, and they could elect the deputies who went there. After discussing the possible creation of chambers of commerce in numerous meetings throughout the early months of 1701, the council finally decided to ask that they be formed.[3] Its decision was ratified by an *arrêt* issued on 30 August 1701.[4] This *arrêt* called for the establishment of a chamber of commerce in each of the following cities: Lille, Rouen, Bordeaux, La Rochelle, Nantes, Saint-Malo, Bayonne, and one city in Languedoc (to be chosen by the provincial estates). The form of each chamber was left up to the cities themselves.

For one reason or another, however, there were delays in establishing these chambers. Those created by the time of Louis XIV's death were, in order of formation: Lyons, 20 July 1702; Rouen, 19 June 1703; Toulouse, 29 December 1703; Montpellier, 15 January 1704; Bordeaux, 26 May 1705; and Lille, 31 July 1714.

Up until the time that a city formed a chamber of commerce, it elected its deputies in the manner laid down in the *arrêt* of 29 June 1700. Every time that a new election had to be held, the city magistrates and the *juge* and *consuls* of the *juridiction consulaire* called together a group of former *juges* and *consuls* as well as a number of prominent local businessmen. Together they nominated a list of candidates for the position of deputy, and then they voted. The man with a plurality of votes won.

The person elected was in a real sense the representative of his locality, but it was a very elite group that actually elected him. The records of a handful of the special town meetings in which deputies were elected have been preserved. We have, for example, the transcript of the meeting in Rouen of 4 August 1700 that elected Nicolas Mesnager.[5] The *premier échevin* of the city presided, and the assembly consisted of representatives of the wholesale merchants' guilds. With "a uniform voice," Mesnager was elected. At the end of the manuscript are the signatures of all the "marchands négociants" who participated: 44 men in all. Similarly, one could cite the election held in Nantes on 5 October 1702 to choose a successor to Descasaux du Hallay.[6] The man elected was a former consul in the *juridiction consulaire*, Germain Laurencin. There were a total of 79 electors, all either former members of the *juridiction consulaire* or prominent businessmen.[7]

Because some cities lacked chambers of commerce, and because the chambers of commerce varied in organization, there was no uniform pattern followed for the election and control of deputies to the Council of Commerce. Virtually the only thing that every locality had in common was royal supervision. From the very beginning, the controller general and the secretary of state for the navy rigorously supervised the operations of the chambers of commerce and the elections of the deputies of trade. The royal provincial intendants were authorized to preside over the local bodies whenever they wished, and it was up to them to ensure that qualified persons were chosen to attend the council in Paris. The crown did not impose its own choices on the localities,[8] but it did reserve the right to reject a candidate if it found him unsuitable.[9] Each prospective deputy had to get the personal approval of the controller general and, if he were from a port city, from the secretary of state for the navy.[10]

CITIES WITHOUT CHAMBERS OF COMMERCE

Four of the cities named in the *arrêt* of 30 August 1701 did not form chambers of commerce during the years under consideration here. La Rochelle did not establish one until 1719, and Bayonne not until 1726. Nantes and Saint-Malo did not have any at all in the eighteenth century. Paris was not named in the 1701 *arrêt*, and so it likewise did not have a chamber. Bayonne did not form one simply because it could not afford one. Its trade was damaged by Louis XIV's final two wars, and perhaps even more by competition from the city's larger rivals—Saint-Malo, Bordeaux, Nantes, and La Rochelle. For most of this period, in fact, Bayonne did not have a deputy of trade. When its first deputy, Léon de Rol, left the council in September 1702, Bayonne obtained permission temporarily to withdraw its deputation from the council. From 1703 to 1711, therefore, the city had no representative. In 1711 Bayonne was allowed to elect a Parisian merchant, Gérard Heusch de Janvry. This saved the city the expense of sending a man from Bayonne and supporting him in the capital.[11]

Several factors prevented Saint-Malo and Nantes from forming chambers, even though both cities initially showed interest in having one. In 1702 the Council of Commerce sent out a circular letter to all cities with deputies of trade; the letter concerned the possible shape that the new chambers would take. Both Saint-Malo and Nantes responded favorably to the letter, adding their own ideas for their respective chambers.[12] Financial considerations, however, proved to be a major stumbling block. Every city that formed a chamber of commerce feared that it would cost too much, especially in wartime. Plans in Saint-Malo and Nantes were also stymied by the question of how these chambers would be organized. The intendant of Brittany and the deputies of the Council of Commerce objected that the proposed forms of the chambers in the two cities were unworkable.[13] Saint-Malo and Nantes also seem to have feared that if they complied with the *arrêt* of 30 August 1701 and established chambers of commerce, somehow the cities would lose some of their provincial autonomy and be subjected to "a vexing and despotic surveillance" by royal agents.[14] In Saint-Malo the powerful Magon family, which directed much of that city's trade, feared that a chamber would vie with it for control of the city's commercial affairs.[15] In both cities, therefore, the *juridictions consulaires* assumed the duties of a chamber of commerce and supervised the cities' deputies in Paris. A document preserved in the departmental archives in Nantes describes the commanding role which that city's *juridiction consulaire* exercised in the election of deputies throughout the first half of the eighteenth century.[16] Not only did the *juridiction consulaire* (conjointly with the *maire* and *échevins*) convoke the special electoral assemblies but it drew up the lists of nominees from which deputies were chosen. These lists consisted almost exclusively of former *juges* and *consuls* of the *juridiction consulaire*.

Like Saint-Malo and Nantes, La Rochelle initially showed an early interest in forming a chamber of commerce. On 23 September 1701 the *juge* and *consuls* met with the principal merchants of the city to draw up a plan for such a body. This assembly sent a proposal to the local intendant, who forwarded it to Chamillart. The latter in turn referred it to the Council of Commerce. The deputies of trade thereupon rejected it. They noted that it failed to describe, among other things, how the members would be chosen, how the chamber would be funded, and when it would meet.[17]

The whole question therefore was sent back to La Rochelle, where for the next eight years a series of local squabbles prevented the merchants there from coming up with a suitable plan. The business community, ever status-conscious, engaged in seemingly endless debates concerning membership and rank in the proposed chamber. Would the *juridiction consulaire* automatically sit in it? Would former *juges* and *consuls* outrank ordinary merchants? Would merchants who had nobility outrank former consular officials? Could *marchands en détail* (retail merchants) be elected to the chamber? Who would sit closest to the head of the table when the body met? Wrangling over such questions prevented any decisions from being made until 21 October 1710, when an *arrêt* was issued creating a chamber of commerce.[18]

This chamber, however, never came into being: the war helped divert attention to other matters, and the only building where the chamber could have met (the hall of the *juridiction consulaire*) had burned down in 1705.[19] La Rochelle did not finally get its Chamber of Commerce until 15 July 1719, when a second *arrêt* was issued.[20] Up until that time the *juges* and *consuls* largely controlled the deputy in the Council of Commerce, as they did in Bayonne, Saint-Malo, and Nantes.

Paris likewise had no chamber of commerce. Since it was the home of the Council of Commerce, it was believed that the capital had no need of a separate such body. As noted above, the king appointed the first two Parisian deputies. Samuel Bernard sat in the council until he retired in 1720. After his departure he was not replaced, and thereafter Paris had only one deputy. Antoine Peletyer retired in January 1702, and his successors were henceforth chosen by the *gardes* of the *six corps des marchands* of Paris.[21] This body controlled the deputy, paid him, and corresponded with the Council of Commerce.

THE CHAMBERS OF COMMERCE

Now that we have considered how deputies were elected in towns or provinces that did not have chambers of commerce, we can briefly look at the places that did have such bodies.[22] By reason of its age and its extensive powers, the Chamber of Commerce of Marseilles stood apart from all the others. This chamber was created in 1650.[23] Although theoretically it was distinct from the *conseil de ville*, in practice it was not. The city's five principal magistrates sat in the chamber, and they selected its other members—four deputies and eight councillors. In addition to its members, the chamber employed a secretary, an archivist, and dozens of treasurers and tax collectors.

The chamber was charged with a host of administrative duties. Its major responsibility was that of supervising and regulating Marseilles's trade with the Levant. It administered the city's port, and it controlled the French consulates that were scattered throughout the Mediterranean. Among other things, the chamber also was charged with protecting French shipping from the Barbary pirates and with paying the salary of the French ambassador in Constantinople (16,000 livres annually). The chamber's expenditures averaged more than 150,000 livres per year. To meet these expenses, it collected a variety of taxes on goods and ships entering and leaving Marseilles and various eastern Mediterranean ports.[24]

Dunkirk was the other city that had a Chamber of Commerce prior to the establishment of the Council of Commerce. This chamber was instituted by an edict issued in February 1700.[25] Its creation was part of the same governmental drive to revive the economy at the end of the War of the League of Augsburg that contributed to the creation of the council later in that year. The principal event that led to the formation of the chamber in Dunkirk was the signing of a new Franco-Dutch tariff in December 1699 that gave Dutch shippers extensive trading privileges in France. It also reaffirmed the severe restrictions placed on the kinds of Dutch goods that could pass through French Flanders into the rest of France. These provisions dashed Dunkirk's hopes for becoming a middleman between the United Provinces and France. Soon after the publication of this agreement, Dunkirk merchants barraged the government with complaints and demanded favors of some sort to help the city recover from the war.[26] The result was the edict of February 1700, which created both a *juridiction consulaire* and a chamber of commerce. The edict was rather vague concerning the organization of the chamber. It was to consist of six persons: a president, four deputies (two current and two former *échevins*), and one *pensionnaire*, whose function was to prepare reports on the various matters brought to the chamber. It was to meet twice weekly. Its ordinary sources of revenue were a series of small duties placed on various goods (especially fish) passing through Dunkirk's port; these sufficed to pay the salary of the deputy in Paris, plus three to four thousand livres a year for the expenses of the chamber. Everything else was left to the discretion of the provincial intendant, who selected the members, supervised the raising of funds, and directed its work.

During the War of the Spanish Succession, the chamber's revenues were augmented so that it could arm frigates to protect the coast from enemy *corsaires*.[27] Otherwise, the chamber appears to have led a rather somnolent existence—certainly it did not meet twice a week as had been prescribed by the founding edict. In 1715, when Dunkirk's commerce was ruined by the destruction of its port, the chamber requested permission to withdraw its deputation from the Council of Commerce.[28] Permission was granted, and Dunkirk was not again represented in the council until 1781.

There were six chambers of commerce formed between 1701 and 1715.[29] Even for those cities that were eager to have one, various obstacles hindered immediate compliance with the *arrêt* of 30 August 1701. Many of the same problems that delayed or prevented the creation of chambers in Bayonne, La Rochelle, Nantes, and Saint-Malo also arose in other cities. Disputes about funding, organization, and rank occurred in virtually every city. The War of the Spanish Succession also served to deflect attention and money to other matters. In Languedoc difficulties appeared when the provincial estates tried to decide which city should have the chamber of commerce prescribed by the *arrêt* of 1701. Nîmes, Carcassonne, Toulouse, and Montpellier all vied for it. In the end the estates received permission to establish two chambers, in the latter two cities.[30]

Albeit some of the delays in forming chambers of commerce were unavoidable, a perusal of the materials available gives one the distinct impression that most cities were not overly anxious to comply with the *arrêt* of 1701. They often chose to procrastinate rather than to appropriate the several thousand livres that a chamber would cost each year. This brings one back to the questions posed in the first chapter. Were commercial centers actively campaigning at the turn of the century for greater representation before the central government? Or did the crown take the initiative with regard to the chambers of commerce just as it did with the Council of Commerce? Although several of the deputies called for local chambers in their general memoirs of 1700–1701, government officials had already begun laying plans for them in the 1690s.[31] After the *arrêt* of 30 August 1701 was issued the central government was the force that constantly pushed the cities to pursue their plans for such bodies. The Council of Commerce and the royal provincial intendants supervised every step in their creation.[32] If it had not been for this royal prodding and continued support, it is likely that few chambers of commerce would have been created in the eighteenth century and that most of those established would soon have slipped into desuetude.

Little needs to be said here about the actual organization of the chambers established in Rouen, Lyons, Bordeaux, Lille, Toulouse, and Montpellier. They consisted of from five (Lille) to nine (Rouen) members, who called themselves either deputies, syndics, or directors of commerce. Generally they assembled once a week in the *hôtel de ville* or in the *maison consulaire*. Lyons's chamber was the only one that, like those in Dunkirk and Marseilles, included members of the magistracy; its chamber was presided over by the *prévôt des marchands* and one *échevin*. In Rouen, Bordeaux, Toulouse, and Montpellier, the chambers were presided over by the three members of the local *juridiction consulaire*. Lille's chamber was the only one that was completely separate from both the city magistrates and the *juridiction consulaire*; it was headed by a merchant of the town. Each chamber included four or five merchants, who could debate and vote on all issues discussed in the meetings. In addition, each group employed a secretary, who kept the archives and handled correspondence. The provincial intendants were free to attend (and preside over) the chambers whenever they wished, though this did not occur often.

The members of the chambers were usually chosen through a system of co-optation. The electors consisted of present and former member of each chamber; in some cases former consular officials and a handful of important merchants also could participate. The members served for two years, with the possibility of being reelected for an additional two years. They served without pay, although in Lille, Toulouse, Montpellier, and Rouen, members received two silver *jetons* (tokens) worth from six to ten *deniers* for each meeting they attended and a gold medal equivalent to five *louis d'or* when they left office.

The chambers were funded in a variety of ways. The one in Lyons received 13,000 livres annually from the city treasury— 8,000 for its deputy to the Council of Commerce and 5,000 for the chamber's expenses. The bodies in Toulouse and Montpellier had to subsist on a meager yearly stipend of 600 livres each, which they received from the Estates of Languedoc. The chamber in Bordeaux was given funds by the city and by the *receveur général* of the *généralité*: 6,000 livres for its deputy and 4,086 for the chamber itself. Rouen's institution collected its own duties on foreign goods entering the city; these produced a yearly income of about 12,000 livres, 8,000 of which was for the deputy in Paris.

The chambers served four main functions. First, they received memoirs from local businessmen and debated commercial afairs; they then sent these matters to the provincial intendant, the controller general, or the secretary of state for the navy. Second, they elected and supervised the work of their deputies in Paris.[33] Third, the chambers approved all *parères* before they could be introduced into their respective cities.[34] Fourth, the chambers of commerce provided the royal ministers and the Council of Commerce with a standing body of local economic experts from whom they could quickly obtain advice or information.

The valuable service provided in this final respect was exemplified in the debate that erupted throughout France in 1713 concerning the importation of foreign-made silks by the East India Company. Controller General Desmaretz asked all the provincial intendants to find out how local businessmen felt about the question. Those intendants who could turn to chambers of commerce for advice were able to respond swiftly,[35] but the intendant of Dauphiné had to apologize to the controller general for his tardy reply.[36] Dauphiné had no chamber of commerce, he said, and it therefore took him much longer to survey the opinions of that area's traders and manufacturers.

RELATIONS BETWEEN THE DEPUTIES AND THEIR CONSTITUENTS

The primary way in which the chambers of commerce (and in cities without chambers, the *juridictions consulaires*) made themselves heard by the central government was through their deputies in Paris. This posed a vexing problem for the deputies. On the one hand, they had an obligation to represent the interests of their localities; but on the other hand, they were constantly urged by the royal ministers and the *commissaires* in the Council of Commerce to work for *le bien public*. The crown wished to divest gradually the deputies of selfish local interests that contradicted the general welfare. This was why the government usually asked the cities represented in the council to reelect their deputies indefinitely: in this way the deputies would not be subject to recall by their constituents if they did not defend local causes fervently enough. To a limited extent the government succeeded in its aim. Deputies such as Mesnager, Piécourt, Fénellon, and Anisson were sufficiently imbued with an allegience to the general good that they could be entrusted with sensitive diplomatic missions; but even these men worked hard to defend vital regional interests.

Each of the deputies maintained a lengthy correspondence with his local chamber of commerce or *juridiction consulaire*. These bodies insisted that they be kept well informed of all the activities of the Council of Commerce. The deputies took great pains to assure their constituents that they were working assiduously to uphold the rights and privileges of their respective provinces, but the chambers of commerce and consular officials never hesitated to bombard their deputies with lengthy instructions or with complaints about real or imagined threats to local prerogatives.[37]

The blatant partisanship of the cities represented in Paris cannot be doubted. What Ernest Pariset has said concerning the Chamber of Commerce of Lyons can be applied to all of its counterparts: "In all of its deliberations one sees that the chamber of commerce had only one goal: the interests of Lyons."[38] Occasionally the deputies in Paris gathered enough courage to reprove their constituents for their selfish desires. In May 1708 Fénelon responded to a passionate, one-sided memoir sent to him by the chamber in Bordeaux by reminding it that "one can go a little too far."[39] Generally, however, the deputies were loathe to offend their electors, and their desire to please local interests sometimes led to lamentable excesses. André de Joubert, the *syndic général* of Languedoc who sat in the Council of Commerce in 1704 and again in 1707, so irritated the king with his intemperate demands on behalf of his province that Louis XIV sent Intendant Basville a *lettre de cachet* for Joubert's arrest, but the intendant never used it.[40]

No deputies of trade worked harder for the concerns of their localities than did the Fabre brothers (Joseph and Mathieu), who represented Marseilles in succession fron 1700 to 1714. Although each man spouted slogans concerning the general good, they both toiled endlessly to protect Marseilles's privileges, and all their work was done in close conjunction with the chamber in Marseilles. Joseph Fabre served in the council less than three years, but during that time he wrote 257 letters to his chamber of commerce—an average of about two a week.[41] This is even more impressive in view of the great length of many of the letters. Fabre's campaign in defense of Marseilles's privileges began on the day that he arrived in Paris in January 1701. As soon as he reached the capital, he outfitted his valet in Marseilles's colors and decorated his carriage with his city's coat of arms. Complaining of how hard he labored, he once wrote to Chamillart: "Remember that I have much work and will continue to have it and that I will have only Sundays free; and on that day I have to write more than St. Augustine."[42] Mathieu Fabre was no less an upholder of Marseilles's interests. Not to be outdone in classical allusions by his brother, he boasted to his chamber: "My strategy is to imitate Horace, that great Roman, who, in withdrawing, was able to fight his enemies one after the other."[43]

But despite the services rendered by all the deputies in Paris, their cities were rarely content with their accomplishments. The mutual jealousies of the cities led them each to believe that the others were benefiting more from the Council of Commerce than they themselves were. This helps explain why most of the cities represented in the council were at one time or another reluctant to pay the salaries of their deputies.[44] Time and again one deputy or another was forced to inform the controller general that he had not been reimbursed for his services. On each occasion the minister either wrote to a provincial intendant to see that the matter was taken care of or issued an *arrêt* ordering that the deputy be paid.

In some cases the disenchantment of the local merchants is understandable. Rouen, for example, complained of the fact that it had to pay Nicolas Mesnager's salary of 8,000 livres a year even though the deputy spent almost as much time on diplomatic missions in Spain, Holland, and England as he did in Paris.[45] To make matters worse, while Mesnager was absent from the council the job of safeguarding Rouen's interests was assigned, at different times, to the deputies of Lyons, La Rochelle, and Saint-Malo—cities whose interests sometimes directly opposed those of Rouen.

La Rochelle's unhappiness with its deputy (Héron) was, however, less excusable. In 1703 and again in 1708 and in 1710, the merchants of that city wrote to the controller general and to the secretary of state for the navy requesting permission to replace Héron with someone else or to withdraw their deputation from the council altogether.[46] They claimed that the 6,000 livres paid him each year was an undue burden on the municipal treasury; but they also bemoaned the fact that Héron seemed to be more concerned about the good of France in general than the good of La Rochelle in particular. They accused him of negligence and cited several commercial conflicts in which La Rochelle's rights were suffering due to advantages won by other cities. In view of these factors, the city wished to remove "an unfruitful deputation." On each occasion, however, the royal ministers demanded that Héron be continued as deputy; he was working on several important projects, they said, especially the reform of French tariffs.[47]

Even the Fabres encountered difficulties in being paid by their chamber of commerce. This was caused not so much by dissatisfaction with the work they performed in Paris as by the tangled affairs of the municipality and the chamber of commerce. Both Joseph and Mathieu Fabre were embroiled in the cabals and political factions that divided Marseilles at that time.[48] Neither man remained untainted by the seamy corruption infesting the city, and each one had acquired a long list of enemies. They managed to win election as deputies to the Council of Commerce largely because they were known to have powerful friends at court. But immediately upon becoming deputy, each man encountered opposition in the chamber in Marseilles; and as early as December 1700, that body delayed in paying Joseph Fabre's salary.[49] According to the Fabres, their enemies in the city council and in the chamber continually spread malicious lies about them.[50] Neither man ever succeeded in being fully remunerated for his services in the capital. When Joseph Fabre left office late in 1703, he presented the chamber with a bill for 4,897 livres still due him for his salary and expenses.[51]

Mathieu Fabre in particular had bad luck with the Chamber of Commerce. Not only did he fail to collect all the money that he claimed was owed him, but after 1710 his role as Marseilles's representative in Paris lost any real importance.[52] In 1710 the Chamber of Commerce sent to Paris its assistant archivist, François Philip. He took with him many of the chamber's account books, which he was charged with presenting to the royal commission then examining the affairs of Marseilles in general.[53] Philip remained in Paris for several years, representing Marseilles before the commission. During this time the Chamber of Commerce began to rely on him rather than on Mathieu Fabre to manage its affairs. Philip gradually came to the attention of Controller General Desmaretz, who was favorably impressed by his abilities. In August 1714 Desmaretz asked the chamber to replace Fabre with Philip.[54] The chamber soon after complied, but the minister's request sparked an abrupt reversal in the chamber's attitude toward Philip. Up to this time it had had a cordial rapport with him, but the chamber bitterly detested the fact that Philip had been virtually imposed upon them by the crown. This was felt to be a grave encroachment on the chamber's right to select independently its own candidates, and a blow to Marseilles's privileges in general. Philip's term as deputy thus was even less pleasant than those of the Fabres had been.

DEFENSE OF LOCAL PRIVILEGES

Given the highly self-centered attitudes of all the cities represented in the Council of Commerce, it is no surprise to learn that interregional rivalries occupied a good deal of the council's time during this period. The very first topic ever introduced in the council gives an indication of this tendency. In December 1700 the Chamber of Commerce of Dunkirk asked that an exclusive whaling company be established in that city.[55] Such a company would have seriously harmed such cities as Saint-Malo and Bayonne, whose fishing fleets derived great profits from their whaling expeditions. It was perhaps for this reason that nothing ever came of the proposal.

The general memoirs written by the deputies in 1700–1701

abounded with attacks on the privileges of other cities and with
requests for the granting of privileges to one's own city or province.
These same sorts of conflicts continued during the subsequent
fifteen years. Although it would be misleading to portray the
Council of Commerce as merely a forum for intercity and interregional debates, these rivalries reflected the ways in which provincial businessmen often viewed the council and its usefulness to
them.

The deputies defended local interests in several ways. They
wrote memoirs and debated their colleagues in the council. They
also pleaded for their cities' interests during their many private
work sessions with the royal ministers or the *commissaires*. In a letter
to the Bordeaux Chamber of Commerce in September 1710,
Fénellon revealed one of the parliamentary tactics that could be
used to further one's argument.[56] He noted that he was clearly
outnumbered by the *commissaires* and the other deputies on the
question of permitting the export of linseed (*graine de lin*) from the
country. Bordeaux, which had an oversupply of it, wanted permission to sell it to other nations. Most of the members of the council,
however, wanted to prevent it from leaving France, where it was
needed for the preparation of textiles. In order to postpone a vote
on the issue—which Bordeaux would surely lose—Fénellon was
able to get the question sent to Guienne's intendant, de Courson,
who could be expected to defend Bordeaux's interests. Through
this maneuver Fénellon managed to win time and to fortify his
position with testimony from a royal official. Such ploys were often
used by the deputies.[57]

Yet another means of furthering one's local interests was the
pot-de-vin, which could range from an apparently innocent gift to
outright bribery. All the deputies seem to have used it at one time
or another. The recipients of these gratifications, *présents*, and
pensions were fellow deputies, *commissaires*, *commis* in the royal
ministries, and ministers themselves.[58] Some of these gifts were
relatively simple. Fénellon often asked his Chamber of Commerce
to send him Gascony hams and Bordeaux wines, which were as
prized in the Paris of that period as they are today. Fénellon
laconically explained: "I can have them distributed; it will not do
any harm."[59] In December 1707 Mathieu Fabre complained to the
chamber in Marseilles that, because he had not received all the
money due him for his expenses in Paris, he would not be able to
dispense 300 to 400 livres worth of gifts to the *commissaires* of the

Council of Commerce as was expected on the occasion of a new year.[60] He pointed out that the other deputies would be presenting gifts to them, so in order to save face he would have to feign illness and stay at home.

These practices seem to have been customary, if not exactly laudable, but there were more serious cases that approached pure bribery. Moreau, of Saint-Malo, for example, was suspected of offering money to naval officials in return for the granting of passports to Malouin merchants who wished to send ships to the *mer du Sud*—which trade was off-limits for Frenchmen.[61] The *six corps des marchands* of Paris on at least one occasion presented a gift of twenty *louis d'or* to de la Vigne, *commis* of Amelot, in return for "the cares he will have for preserving the interests of these corporations."[62]

None of the other cities, however, came close to matching the "generosity" of Marseilles. It is impossible to document fully the gifts and bribes that the chamber and the city council distributed in Paris during these years. Much of this money was included in the hundreds of thousands of livres that royal investigators reported were unaccountably missing from the treasuries of the two bodies.[63] One of the reasons why Joseph and Mathieu Fabre were always in debt was the presents and pensions that they doled out to "secret agents" in Paris. In his report of 1703 to the Chamber of Commerce, Joseph Fabre recorded that during his three years as deputy he had distributed 23,500 livres to private agents and "important personages."[64] Although this sum was considerable in itself, other testimony shows that it only skims the surface of the largesse that Marseilles showered on royal officials during this period. The money and the gifts of fine cloths and Mediterranean fruits probably amounted to well over 100,000 livres during the period under consideration here. The Marseilles deputies were aided in the distribution of these gratifications by the city's chief agent in the government, François Blondel, a *premier commis* of the secretary of state for foreign affairs, the marquis de Torcy. Blondel and the deputies of trade gave regular pensions or periodic gifts to persons in every ministry and at every level—from doormen to royal ministers. There can be no doubt about the fact that these gratifications were essential for the preservation and enhancement of Marseilles's privileges.[65]

The Council of Commerce also was not untouched by the financial influence of Marseilles. When Joseph Fabre tallied up his expenses at the end of his three years in Paris, he included among them

> gifts to diverse persons, including the Seigneurs of the Royal Council of Commerce, as well as Messieurs the Farmers General who had been so against us, as well as all the deputies, in order to lessen a little the haughtiness with which they handled things contrary to Marseilles.[66]

In 1703 the Chamber of Commerce ordered Fabre to give up to 100 *louis d'or* to Rouillé du Coudray, the *commissaire* who most vehemently criticized the city's privileges.[67] The secretary of the council, Valossière, frequently received free supplies of cloth and food from Marseilles.[68]

Royal ministers likewise appear to have been swayed by the city's generosity. Although the foreign minister, Torcy, appears to have been the only one to accept a regular pension, all of them received sizable gifts on a periodic basis. In 1715, for example, the Chamber of Commerce sent Jérôme de Pontchartrain a shipment of thirteen crates of various foods weighing a total of 1,880 pounds.[69]

Not even Louis XIV himself was free from the influence of Marseilles's lobbyists. Somehow the city managed to win the sympathies of the king's Jesuit confessors, Père La Chaise and Père Fleuriau. Gaston Rambert avers that through "spiritual means" these two priests apparently succeeded in impressing both the king and his grandson, the duke of Burgundy, with the justice of many of the city's claims.[70]

THE PRIVILEGES OF MARSEILLES

In view of the above, it is not surprising to learn that Marseilles's deputies had great success in defending that city's privileges against attacks by other cities. Marseilles was helped by the fact that Joseph Fabre had managed to win the two major figures in the Council of Commerce (Daguesseau and Amelot) over to his side.[71] But the city's chief support came from Jérôme de Pontchartrain, who came to be regarded as its protector. Whether his friendly attitude toward Marseilles resulted from his patriotic desire to see France dominate Europe's trade with the Levant or from the gifts that he received from the city, or both, is open to conjecture. The Marseilles Chamber of Commerce or its deputy frequently asked the minister to intercede with *commissaires* of the Council of Commerce on its behalf. Both Joseph and Mathieu Fabre had easy access to Pontchartrain, and they saw him often.[72] When Joseph arrived in Paris in January 1701, Pontchartrain obtained for him an audience with the king—an honor bestowed on no other deputy.[73] And when he retired from the council in 1703, Pontchartrain presented him with a portrait of the king.[74]

With such help as this, the Fabre brothers were able to protect and to bolster Marseilles's two principal commercial privileges: its status as a free port and its virtual monopoly of the Levant trade. The city had obtained these two advantages through the edict of March 1669.[75] This edict withdrew all royal tax farmers from the city and placed them around its borders. Merchandise entering Marseilles for local consumption or for transshipment elsewhere henceforth was not subject to royal taxes of any kind; customs duties were collected only on goods transported inland to other areas of France. The edict also gave Marseilles what amounted to a monopoly on trade with the Levant. Every other French port, whether on the Atlantic or the Mediterranean, in the future had to pay a 20 percent duty on all Levant goods that it did not get from Marseilles.[76] These measures were designed to compel the rest of France to purchase Levant goods at Marseilles rather than at their places of origin.

Colbert's reasons for granting Marseilles these privileges are easy to understand: he hoped that by favoring this city he could drive the English and the Dutch out of the Levant trade. He wanted Marseilles to become a great entrepôt, where French, Italian, English, and even Dutch ships would come to exchange goods. Finally, Marseilles's trade with the Levant would provide a sure outlet for the woolens manufactures that Colbert was establishing in Languedoc, Provence, and Dauphiné.

During the final decades of the seventeenth century, Marseilles's status as a free port suffered various infringements. Financial needs forced the crown to levy taxes on all goods entering and leaving the port,[77] and various tax farmers set up bureaus within the city to supervise the collection of these duties. Special entrepôts were established for tobacco as well as for Brazilian sugars and coffee.[78] In 1691 the crown prohibited the entry into Marseilles of any *toiles peintes* (printed calicos) and similar light printed fabrics from the East; these items posed a threat to France's own textiles.

Late in the century, Marseilles also suffered from the frauds perpetrated by merchants in the various Atlantic ports. Rather than purchase Levant goods in Marseilles, these traders often preferred to smuggle them into France from England or Holland. Not only did this practice foster the commerce of France's competitors, but it reduced the demand for Marseilles's supply of Levant goods.

Despite all these infringements on its privileges, however, Marseilles's position in the Levant trade remained preponderant. As mentioned earlier, the deputies of trade from the Atlantic ports and from Languedoc unleashed a bitter assault on the city's privileges in their general memoirs of 1700–1701. This attack continued throughout 1701 and 1702. They charged that Marseilles's merchants often paid for Levant goods with gold and silver rather than with French manufactures. They further accused the Marseilles traders of overcharging for the Levant goods that they sold to businessmen from other parts of France.

Finally, the deputies contended that such a monopoly was destructive of the general good. They argued that if all Frenchmen were permitted to trade directly with the Levant, they could do so more cheaply than they did through middlemen at Marseilles. French businessmen could thereby transport their manufactures, agricultural products, and fish directly to the eastern Mediterranean and assure all French provinces of a market for their goods.

The deputy of Marseilles, although greatly outnumbered in the council, answered these arguments with an impressive volley of evidence and invective. He deluged the ministers and the members of the council with countless memoirs and letters.[79] He was aided, of course, by the financial inducements that he liberally proffered to all takers.

Joseph Fabre contended that his city did not export an excessive amount of precious metals from France, but that it did export huge quantities of French manufactures. To back up this claim, Fabre and Intendant Lebret supplied the controller general with records of Marseilles's exports and imports.[80] On several occasions Fabre lauded Colbert, whose wisdom had perceived that Marseilles's strategic location made it a natural center for the Levant trade.[81] As for the other deputies' demands that their cities be allowed to trade with the Near East, Fabre asserted that if this were done these cities would merely purchase Levant goods from England and Holland. It was to prevent such an occurrence that Colbert had established Marseilles's privileges in the first place.

With telling effect Fabre also pointed out that if all French cities were freed from paying the 20 percent duty then the Dutch would likewise be freed from it. According to article nine of the Treaty of Ryswick, Dutch traders were to be treated exactly the same as Frenchmen in French ports, and thus they had to pay only those duties that Frenchmen themselves paid. Although this provision was not in effect during the War of the Spanish Succession, it seemed likely that the Dutch would regain their old trading concessions in any future peace treaty. To accede to the other deputies' demands would therefore, according to Fabre, be to put "the wolf in with the sheep."[82] Dutch shippers could navigate much more economically than could Frenchmen, and they would be able to sell Levant goods in French ports at prices far lower than those offered by French merchants.

Finally, the Marseilles deputy argued that the Levant trade was not large enough to warrant opening it up to all French cities. Already there was an oversupply of Levant goods sitting in Marseilles waiting to be sold; if all French cities entered the trade, this glut would increase.[83]

Joseph Fabre and the Chamber of Commerce of Marseilles demanded not only the preservation of the 20 percent surtax but the removal of all impingements on the free-port status of the city. Only by granting both of these requests, they claimed, could France come to dominate trade with the *Grand Seigneur* and the rest of the eastern Mediterranean.

The crown considered the debate over Marseilles's privileges to be so important that on two occasions in 1701—23 June and 15 September—Controller General Chamillart and Secretary of State Pontchartrain attended the Council of Commerce in person to discuss the issue.[84] Amelot, who was known to be favorable to Marseilles, was charged with conducting the affair. Because of a prolonged illness that struck Amelot in 1702, a decision was delayed for several months.[85]

The entire question was settled by an *arrêt* issued on 10 July 1703,[86] which basically reaffirmed the edict of 1669. Goods entering Marseilles's port were freed from all taxes until they crossed the border into other French territories. The special entrepôt on tobacco, coffee, and sugar was removed.[87] The city's monopoly in the Levant was underscored: no other French Mediterranean port could enter this trade. All the Atlantic cities could once again trade directly with the Levant, but only upon payment of the 20 percent surtax—which meant that few Atlantic merchants would ever participate in this trade. This 20 percent duty also had to be paid for all Levant goods imported from England, Holland, and other non-Levant nations. To ensure that this duty was paid, Marseilles won the right to employ a *contrôleur* in each of the Atlantic ports to supervise its collection by tax farmers. Finally, Marseilles and Pont-de-Beauvoisin remained the only two cities where silk could enter France. The *arrêt* therefore was an overwhelming triumph for Marseilles.[88] Indeed, Joseph Fabre had helped draft it.[89]

Although the *arrêt* of July 1703 marked a tremendous victory for Marseilles, the city's privileges were somewhat compromised in succeeding years. This was partly because Marseilles's new deputy, Mathieu Fabre, was a less capable, though no less fervent, upholder of his city's cause. His hot temper and his strident defense of Marseilles's local interests alienated even those in the Council of Commerce who were sympathetic to his city's views. But it also was evident that Marseilles's claims sometimes clearly contradicted the general good.

Thus in 1704 the Council of Commerce and the royal ministers decided against Marseilles on the question of whether or not Levant goods entering France in enemy prize ships had to pay a 20 percent duty. Marseilles, wishing to protect its special position as a supplier of Levant goods, argued that the surtax had to be paid. But deputies from other cities pointed out that the survival of the French *guerre de course* depended on the sale of prize goods within France; Levant goods from prize ships therefore should not be subject to this added imposition. The latter argument prevailed, and French privateering got a much-needed stimulus at a crucial moment.[90]

Marseilles also suffered another setback in 1704, this time at the hands of its sometime ally, Lyons. When Colbert established a Levant trading company in 1670 to stimulate French trade with the Near East, one of the privileges that he gave it was a *transit* from Marseilles to Geneva, by way of the Rhône River and Lyons.[91] After the Levant Company expired a few years later, another company, under a Sieur Magy and associates, purchased the *transit* and retained it until 1704. By means of this *transit*, Marseilles found a rich market for its Levant goods in Switzerland and Germany.

In 1704, however, Anisson, of Lyons, complained that this right of free passage cheated his city of the customs duties that it normally collected on all goods passing through its territory.[92] Lyons merchants, he expostulated, were already suffering from the decline of their fairs, and the Marseilles *transit* gave that city's traders an even greater advantage over them. Before 1670 many of Lyons's merchants had participated in the sale of Levant goods, purchasing them in Marseilles and transporting them to Germany and to various French provinces. Since the establishment of the free passage, they had been unable to compete with Marseilles merchants in this trade. Furthermore, Anisson claimed, this *transit* caused the king to lose much money. Once Levant goods reached Geneva, he said, many of them were shipped fraudulently back into France, where they were sold. Anisson asserted that if Lyons merchants could enter this trade once again, they would transport the merchandise directly to the French provinces, paying many royal customs duties along the way.

Mathieu Fabre argued vehemently that Marseilles needed the free passage in order to assure itself of the rich Genevan and German market for Levantine goods. Ultimately, however, his pleas were only partially successful. The *arrêt* issued on 15 October 1704 abolished the Rhône *transit*,[93] but Marseilles' shipments up the river to Geneva continued to be exempted from about half of the full amount of the tolls and duties ordinarily collected on the river and at Lyons.

In addition to these mild defeats, in 1712 Marseilles lost a quarrel with the East India Company. In 1710 this company, along with some private individuals, had begun to bring coffee to France from Moka (Mocha, on the Red Sea, in present-day Yemen). This coffee was transported to Nantes and other ports by way of the ocean. The Chamber of Commerce of Marseilles was quick to decry this as a threat to the coffee that it imported from Egypt. Mathieu Fabre declared in the Council of Commerce that Moka was a part of the Levant and that therefore its coffee was subject to 20 percent duty. The other deputies retorted that Moka was not in the Levant but belonged properly to the trading concessions of the East India Company. The Council of Commerce at length decided in favor of the Atlantic ports, but it assured Marseilles that its interests would not be hurt.[94] The Moka coffee would always be more expensive than that of Egypt, said the council, because of the high costs of shipping it around the continent of Africa. The council likewise stated that the Egyptian coffee was far superior in taste and would always be preferred by the vast majority of the public over the coffee brought by the East India Company.

Marseilles had better luck in defending its interests in other areas during this period. It effectively rebuffed the repeated attempts of

Sète and Toulon to enter the Levant trade.[95] Working with the deputy of Lyons, the Marseilles deputy similarly quashed proposals of the deputies from Bayonne, Saint-Malo, and Le Havre that their cities be granted free-port status. Marseilles and Lyons feared that any increase in the entrepôt trade of these cities would hurt their own commerce and industries.[96]

In 1714 Marseilles was able to avenge its 1712 defeat by the East India Company; this time the question concerned the importation by that company of silk thread from the Orient. Once again Mathieu Fabre allied with Jean Anisson in waging his fight. The entire episode was sparked in October 1713 when the *Grand-Dauphin*, a ship belonging to the company, arrived in Saint-Malo from China with a cargo including more than 30,000 pounds of silk.[97] Fabre and Anisson pointed to the various laws dating all the way back to 1669 that stipulated that silk could enter France only through Marseilles and Pont-de-Beauvoisin, from there to be transported through Lyons. According to Fabre and Anisson, these laws were well founded. The two deputies contended that by restricting the importation of silk to two cities it was easier for duties to be collected on them and for frauds to be controlled, but their principal argument concerned the protection of Lyons's famed silk manufactures. Thanks largely to Colbert's encouragements, these manufactures had attained a high degree of perfection and great popularity, both within and without the country. In the eyes of the deputies of Lyons and Marseilles, they therefore merited special favors. These manufactures could not withstand competition from other areas that received raw silk from the Atlantic ports. Each quintal (100 kilograms) of raw silk going from Marseilles to Lyons was charged more than 93 livres in various internal duties, whereas silk entering Atlantic ports was charged on the average only 16 livres per quintal before reaching the manufactures of Tours and other areas. The Lyons silk industry thus would not be able to compete and would soon be ruined.

The East India Company obtained the support of most of the deputies and *commissaires* in the Council of Commerce. They felt that the company had the right to bring raw silk to France, and they also hoped that this would help silk manufacturers in areas such as Champagne and Tours hold their own against those in Lyons and Languedoc.[98]

Controller General Desmaretz, however, sympathized with Lyons and Marseilles, and he vetoed the council's decision.[99] In part this was because Desmaretz was angered by the East India Company's attempt in 1713 to export French workers to China, where they could teach the Chinese to manufacture finished silks in the French manner. The company had hoped to sell these finished silks in France, but exporting a nation's workers and encouraging foreign industries were sacrilegious to mercantilist policies. When news of the company's plans reached Paris, the crown set up a huge manhunt, finally capturing the workers in Saint-Malo before they could embark.[100] At least one of the company's directors was imprisoned as a result of the affair. This episode, along with Anisson's arguments on behalf of Lyons's silk industry, led Desmaretz to decide against the company. An *arrêt* issued on 13 March 1714 reaffirmed the monopoly of Marseilles, Pont-de-Beauvoisin, and Lyons on the importation of silk into France.[101]

OTHER LOCAL PRIVILEGES

Although the conflicts that posed the Atlantic deputies against those of Marseilles and Lyons were the most prominent during this period in the Council of Commerce, there were others that were no less harsh. At regular intervals, for example, the cities of Dunkirk, Saint-Malo, and Bayonne requested the right to trade directly with the French West Indies. This subject had come up in the general memoirs of 1700–1701, and it remained a sticky issue throughout the eighteenth century. The only cities that could trade directly with the islands were Rouen, Dieppe, La Rochelle, Bordeaux, Nantes, and Marseilles. Merchants from other ports who wished to trade with the islands first had to ship their goods to one of these six cities. All returning ships likewise first had to put in at these ports, where their cargoes were examined and marked. The net result of this situation was that a few cities were able to monopolize the rich colonial trade. The crown had adopted this system in order to prevent fraud. Rouen, Dieppe, and La Rochelle were located within the *cinq grosses fermes*, and thus the farmers general could be sure to collect the necessary duties on goods entering France at these points. Bordeaux, Nantes, and Marseilles were not in the *cinq grosses fermes*, but they were ringed by a tight network of farmers' bureaus, which made smuggling difficult.

Although the deputies of Nantes, Bordeaux, and La Rochelle staunchly defended "liberty of trade" whenever their own cities stood to gain by it, they were quick to point up the necessity of preserving their monopoly of trade with the Antilles. If all cities could deal directly with the islands, they warned, then the revenues of the king would surely suffer; the farmers general would not be able to guard the entire coastline of France to prevent the fraudulent entry of goods into the country. This argument prevailed, and those cities excluded from the West Indies trade had to content themselves with other areas of commerce—at least for the period under review here. [102]

Although the six cities that shared the Caribbean trade united in keeping other cities out of it, these cities themselves split over another issue. The most profitable aspect of the West Indies trade was the sale of sugar, which was brought to France and refined in these six cities as well as in a few others. [103] Every sugar refinery received certain favors, such as a remission of most export duties for refined sugar sold to other countries. But by the final decade of the seventeenth century, Bordeaux's refineries had clearly surpassed all others in France, and that city was able to obtain special privileges for its sugars.

This naturally led other cities to be jealous. In December 1704 the deputies of La Rochelle and Nantes began to complain about the *arrêt* of 11 August 1699. This *arrêt* permitted Bordeaux's sugar refiners to transport their product to Valence, Lyons, Franche-Comté, and Alsace without paying the greater part of the internal tolls that normally would have been levied on them. La Rochelle and Nantes demanded that this privilege be extended to their sugars also. Despite the protests of Bordeaux's deputy, the Council of Commerce sided with the other deputies, and their request was granted in 1705. [104]

In 1706 Mathieu Fabre insisted that Marseilles's sugar refinery also was suffering as a result of the extensive favors granted to the refineries in Bordeaux. An *arrêt* of 30 June 1671 had granted Bordeaux's refined sugar a virtually duty-free *transit* all the way to Marseilles, from which it could be transported to Italy and other points in the Mediterranean. Fabre contended that this was unfair competition for the relatively new and inexperienced refinery situated in Marseilles. Fénellon (Bordeaux) countered this by pointing out that Marseilles was already blessed with a tremendous geographical advantage. Early in 1707 the sugar refiners of Sète and Nîmes joined Marseilles in arguing that at the very least the refineries in these cities should share some of the tax exemptions enjoyed by those in Dieppe, Rouen, La Rochelle, and Bordeaux. [105]

Passions rose so high over the issue that on 7 January 1707 Fénellon and Mathieu Fabre very nearly came to blows over it. The pugnacious Fabre later described the incident in a letter to the Chamber of Commerce of Marseilles. [106] He reported that Fénellon, a man "vain and violent," had submitted to the council a memoir that spoke of "the ignorance of all the merchants of Marseilles." Filled with "just resentment," Fabre rose to speak and deplored the selfish motives of the Bordeaux deputy. Turning to Fénellon, Fabre exclaimed: "The very least of our merchants is a more able man than you." He then declared that the only thing that Fénellon knew anything about was barrel staves, which were so essential for Bordeaux's wine industry. Fénellon thereupon cried out that his honor had been sullied, and the two men rushed upon each other. The other members of the council quickly separated them, and Daguesseau forced the two men to shake hands. Upset by this breach in the decorum of the council, Daguesseau adjourned the meeting. Fabre reported triumphantly to the chamber in Marseilles, however, that he succeeded in getting Fénellon's offensive phrase scratched from the memoir. One can be sure that when Fénellon related this incident to his chamber of commerce it was he, not Fabre, who was the hero. In the long run, Bordeaux preserved her privileges but the Mediterranean refineries attained additional favors and also were able to prosper in the eighteenth century.

There were numerous other conflicts between the cities represented in the council, but none of them was as violent or as recurrent as those mentioned above. As a general rule, deputies from agricultural or commercial areas (e.g., Bordeaux, La Rochelle, Saint-Malo) were less concerned about protecting French textiles than were deputies from areas with strong manufacturing interests (Rouen, Lyons, Languedoc). Deputies from areas not in the *cinq grosses fermes* (Nantes, Marseilles) opposed the efforts of other deputies (Anisson, Mesnager, Fénellon) to bring about an internal customs union. [107]

Such disputes were not, of course, limited to the cities represented in the council. Other cities and regions voiced their opinions through memoirs that merchants, magistrates, and intendants sent to the council or to the royal ministers. Thus, for example, throughout the early years of the century Bordeaux carried on a debate with the provinces of Alsace, Normandy, and Champagne over the question of brandy production. [108] Bordeaux insisted on upholding the various existing laws requiring that brandy be produced solely from wine. If these laws were not enforced, said Bordeaux's deputy, the reputation of French brandies would suffer both within France and abroad. Merchants from the other provinces maintained that equally good brandies could be extracted from such things as honey, apple cider, or grape skins (*marc de raisin*). The Council of Commerce upheld the bans against brandy made from apple cider and honey, but in 1712 and 1713 it granted permission for its manufacture from grape skins at Rheims, Besançon, and Metz. The council stipulated, however, that the brandy produced in these three areas had to be consumed entirely in the provinces of Champagne and Franche-Comté and the territory of Metz.[109]

Despite the recurrent lack of agreement among the deputies of trade, it would be wrong to portray the council as merely a soapbox for the airing of local grievances and the defense of regional privileges. The issues on which the deputies quarreled were in a clear minority. Also, the deputies sometimes disagreed simply because they judged matters differently and not because they were defending opposing local interests. For the most part, they were able to conciliate private concerns with the general good, and on many occasions they sounded like Colbert as they rebuked those merchants who were always out for their own selfish profit, regardless of *le bien public*.[110] Even the local chambers of commerce and *juridictions consulaires* were often on friendly terms with each other, exchanging information and addressing one another as "Messieurs nos chers confrères."[111]

In this respect one might cite the way in which the deputies regarded Samuel Bernard, one of the two deputies from Paris. Bernard was a director of the tobacco and East India companies, as well as a director or partner in several other exclusive or privileged trading ventures. His commercial and financial interests made him a natural foe of many of the views of the other deputies, yet all available evidence shows that he was one of the hardest working and most respected among them.

In November 1708 Bernard wished to retire from the council, claiming that it took too much time away from his other interests. As soon as the other deputies who were in Paris at that moment heard of this, they wrote to Controller General Desmaretz and asked him to persuade Bernard to remain on the council. Nothing could be worse for their plans to reestablish commerce, they said, than Bernard's departure. They lauded him as a man of "probity, . . . exactitude, . . . disinterestedness, . . . firmness . . . and courage."[112] His experience, his talents, his reputation, and his international contacts made him indispensable, they affirmed. Whether Desmaretz actually interceded is not known, but Bernard did, however, remain on the council another twelve years.

From all the above, one might conclude several things. To ensure the election of the deputies of trade and to guarantee that important commercial centers would have an influence on royal economic policies, the crown pushed for the establishment of local chambers of commerce. The war, local squabbles over rank, and other factors frequently prevented the quick formation of such bodies. Even so, by 1715 a total of eight existed in France; later in the century, several more would be created. Although the crown exercised constant surveillance over the chambers as well as over the _juridictions consulaires_, these local institutions were nevertheless surprisingly active and independent. They maintained close connections with their deputies in Paris. To a greater extent than the government had wished, the cities represented in the Council of Commerce used that body to carry on regional rivalries rather than to pursue national goals, but to a large degree the crown did achieve its aim. It had broadened the decision-making machinery, both on the local and the national levels. It had found a way to coordinate, and sometimes to conciliate, the desires of businessmen from all over the country. And finally it had created a two-way channel by which it could obtain the information it required to administer the economy and by which merchants could voice their needs and grievances.

1. AN, F^{12} 114, fol. 93, Chamillart to Bernard and Peletyer, 21 September 1700.
2. BN, MSS. fr., 8038, fols. 124, 172–73, 228.
3. AN, F^{12} 51, fols. 74, 78v, 84v, 115v, and passim.
4. A copy can be found in AN, AD XI, 9.
5. Charles Beaurepaire, "Election d'un député au conseil du commerce."
6. AD, Loire-Atlantique, C 695, piece 71, "Liste de Messieurs. . . ."
7. A word should perhaps be said about the _juridictions consulaires_. Most large cities had such a tribunal. It usually consisted of one _juge_ (or _prieur_) and two to four _consuls_. All the members were merchants elected by their fellow businessmen, and they served without pay for one year. The _juridiction consulaire_ judged civil cases concerning commercial matters, and the decisions it made in suits involving less than 500 livres could not be appealed to higher courts. On many occasions during

this period, the Council of Commerce strengthened the powers of these commercial courts. In particular see AN, F^{12} 51, fols. 249–50, 261–61v, 267, 269v–70, 275v, 280, 286v; F^{12} 58, fols. 358v–61, 377v–78, 380–80v, 387–91v.

8. Sometimes the municipal assembly or chamber of commerce selected three candidates and let the government choose the new deputy from among them. This was often the case in Bordeaux and Rouen. See, for example, V. Lebraque-Bordenave, "Histoire des députés de Bordeaux au conseil du commerce, au comité national, et à l'agence commerciale à Paris, 1700–1793," p. 293; AN, G^7 1697, piece 68, Anisson to Desmaretz, (day and month missing) 1712.

9. This occurred once during this period, when Desmaretz in 1715 nullifed the election of a man named Vaultier selected by the Chamber of Commerce of Lille. The chamber had chosen Vaultier because of his connections at court, but Desmaretz rejected him because he was not a native or a resident of Lille. See the numerous letters concerning this episode in AN, F^{12} 692 and F^{12} 908–9.

10. See AN, G^7 496, Mesnager to Chamillart, 5 August 1700; G^7 339, Le Comte to Chamillart, 28 November 1700; Mar., B^2 177, Pontchartrain to Piou, 19 November 1704; Boislisle, *Correspondance des contrôleurs généraux*, 2:124, Laurencin to Chamillart, 7 October 1702.

11. Bonnassieux and Lelong, *Conseil de commerce*, p. lxiv; AN, F^{12} 908–9, "Proposition pour l'establissement des chambres de commerce dans les principales villes du Royaume."

12. AN, F^{12} 908–9, "Proposition pour l'establissement . . ."; AD, Loire-Atlantique, C 700, piece 3, "M. les juges consuls et tous les négotians de Nantes . . . ," 23 February 1702.

13. See the dossiers on Saint-Malo and Nantes in AN, F^{12} 880–907, 908–9.

14. Quoted in Léon Vignols, "Jean-Paul Vigneau, secrétaire de la représentation commerciale de Nantes (1730–1746)," p. 46; also see Maurice Quénet, "Un Exemple de consultation dans l'administration monarchique au XVIIIe siècle: les nantais et leurs députés au Conseil de Commerce."

15. Vignols, "Jean-Paul Vigneau," p. 47.

16. AD, Loire-Atlantique, C 695, piece 54; "Observations sur la manière de procéder à l'élection d'un député du commerce tirées des procès-verbaux des quatre élections portés sur les livres du commerce."

17. See the letters and memoirs on La Rochelle in AN, F^{12} 880–907.

18. Reprinted in Emile G. Garnault, *Le Commerce rochelais au XVIIIe siècle*, 1:15–20.

19. Ibid., p.21.

20. Reprinted in ibid., pp. 27–33.

21. The *six corps* was the governing body of the six principal merchant guilds in Paris. These included the wood merchants, spice merchants, haberdashers (*merciers*), hosiery dealers (*bonnetiers*), fur and pelt traders, and goldsmiths. These six guilds were largely distinguished from the others by the places they received in civic ceremonies. The records of the meetings of the *six corps* for this period are in AN, KK 1340, 1341.

22. On the chambers of commerce in general, see L.-J. Gras, "Les Chambres de commerce," pp. 550–89, 680–740; Léon Poinsard, "Les Chambres de commerce: étude sur leur rôle financier et sur les récents projects de réforme soumis au parlement français." The existing state of the records of the various chambers is briefly described in Félix Reynaud and G. Vinay, "Les Archives des chambres de commerce de France." The only chambers whose archives remain virtually intact are those of Bordeaux and Marseilles. The records for the others have suffered, in varying

degrees, from wars, natural disasters, and neglect. Thanks to the work of Pierre H. Boulle, the greater part of the records of most of the chambers has been copied on microfilm, and this collection is deposited in Montréal. See my article "The Interuniversity Centre for European Studies/Le Centre interuniversitaire d'études européennes."

23. The best introduction to this chamber is Joseph Fournier, *Inventaire des archives de la chambre de commerce de Marseille*. Four deputies of trade were appointed beginning in 1599, but the Chamber of Commerce proper was created only in 1650.

24. See ibid. and Masson, *Histoire du commerce . . . XVIIe siecle*, pp. 338–43, and appendix, pp. viii–x; Rambert, *Histoire du commerce de Marseille*, 4:304; J. Marchand, *Un Intendant sous Louis XIV; etude sur l'administration de Lebret en Provence, 1687–1704*, pp. 326–28; BN, MSS. fr., 16736, fols., 273–78, "Mémoire donné par le Sr. Philip sur l'establissement de la chambre du commerce, les droits qui s'y persoivent et les changemens dans la perception des dits droits."

25. A copy is in AN, AD XI, 9.

26. These complaints are noted in the edict itself. See also the memoir in Mar., B⁷ 499, fols. 531–32. The provincial intendant in Dunkirk (Barentin) was principally responsible for drafting the parts of the edict that concerned the Chamber of Commerce (see AN, F¹² 1646–50, Barentin to Chamillart, 2 January 1700).

27. See Mar., B⁷ 503, fols. 18–21, "Articles et conditions que la chambre de commerce de Dunkerque suplie très humblement Sa Majesté de luy accorder pour la construction et armement de deux fregattes . . . ," 13 June 1704; B⁷ 505, fols. 31–32, untitled memoir from Chamber of Commerce of Dunkirk to Pontchartrain.

28. Piécourt, Dunkirk's deputy since 1700, died in 1715; thus Dunkirk actually had no deputy at the time of its request (see Bonnassieux and Lelong, *Conseil de commerce*, p. lxi).

29. In Lyons, Rouen, Toulouse, Montpellier, Bordeaux, and Lille. Only those of Montpellier and Lille have escaped extended study. On Toulouse see Jules Chinault, *La Chambre de commerce de Toulouse*, and Henri Rozy, *La Chambre de commerce de Toulouse au XVIIIe siècle: esquisse historique*. On Rouen: Henri Wallon, *La Chambre de commerce de la province de Normandie*. Three works deal with Bordeaux's chamber: V. Labraque-Bordenave, "Histoire des députés de Bordeaux au conseil de commerce"; Michel Lheritier "Histoire des rapports de la chambre de commerce de Bordeaux avec les intendants, le parlement, et les jurats, de 1705 à 1791"; Jean–Auguste Brutails, "Etude sur la chambre du commerce de Guienne." Concerning Lyons, see Ernest Pariset "La Chambre de commerce de Lyon au dix-huitième siècle: étude faite sur les registres de ses délibérations."

30. See the dossiers relating to each city in AN, F¹² 880–907, 908–9.

31. Several of the memoirs that discussed the formation of a council of commerce also mentioned chambers of commerce; See above, Chapter 1, n. 71. Boislisle, *Correspondance des contrôleurs généraux*, 2:464; Chinault, *La Chambre de commerce de Toulouse*, p. 8.

32. AN, F¹² 880–907, 908–9.

33. Two exceptions to this were the chambers of Toulouse and Montpellier. The deputy from Languedoc was chosen and paid by the Estates of Languedoc.

34. A *parère* was a local usage or law concerning relations between merchants (e.g., practices surrounding the question of liability, investment in commercial ventures, payment of debts, etc.).

35. Many of these responses are in AN, G⁷ 1701.

36. Ibid., fol. 119, d'Angervilliers to Desmaretz, 6 December 1713.

37. For example, each time that a new deputy was elected in Nantes, the electoral assembly presented him with a hefty stack of papers consisting of all the important memoirs and instructions that Nantes officials had sent to his predecessors (see AD, Loire-Atlantique, C 700, pièce 76, "Mémoire des juges consuls et des négotians de Nantes pour Monsieur Piou à l'occasion de sa députation au conseil de commerce à Paris en l'année 1705, avec des instructions relatives au bien général du commerce").

38. Pariset, "La Chambre de commerce de Lyon," p. 145.

39. AD, Gironde, C 4300, Fénellon to Chamber of Commerce of Bordeaux, 25 May 1708.

40. Chinault, *La Chambre de commerce de Toulouse*, p. 59.

41. ACCM, B 153–57.

42. Quoted in Fournier, *La Chambre de commerce de Marseille*, p. 49.

43. Ibid., p. 64.

44. These ranged from 6,000 to 8,000 livres annually. Out of this money, each deputy had to pay for a secretary, an apartment, and postage for his correspondence with his city's officials.

45. Wallon, *La Chambre de commerce de la province de Normandie*, pp. 36–37.

46. Mar., B⁷ 502, fols. 292–93, the *corps de ville* and principal merchants of La Rochelle to Pontchartrain, 12 August 1703; ibid., fols. 294–99, same to same, 29 October 1703; AN, G⁷ 341, Bégon to Desmaretz, 28 July 1708; G⁷ 1695, pièce 128, *maire* and *échevins* of La Rochelle to Desmaretz, 12 July 1710; G⁷ 341, Beauharnais to Desmaretz, 21 October 1710.

47. AN, G⁷ 1695, pièce 129, draft for a letter from Desmaretz to *maire* and *échevins* of La Rochelle. In 1712 La Rochelle again balked at paying Héron (Mar., B² 230, p. 87, Pontchartrain to Daguesseau, 13 January 1712).

48. Most of the information dealing with this episode has been collected in BN, MSS. fr., 18979. See my forthcoming article "Government and Business in Early Eighteenth-Century France: The Case of Marseilles."

49. AN, G⁷ 464, Lebret to Chamillart, 9 December 1700.

50. Fournier, *La Chambre de commerce de Marseille*, p. 52; Mar., B⁷ 502, fols. 36–37, Joseph Fabre to Pontchartrain, 11 February 1702; AN, G⁷ 1691, pièce 37, *négociants* of Marseilles to Desmaretz, 8 March 1708; BN, MSS. fr., 18979, fols. 92, 104v.

51. Fournier, *La Chambre de commerce de Marseille*, pp. 264–65; also see various items in ACCM, A 17–19; B 153–65.

52. Mar., B⁷ 502, fols. 339–42, untitled memoir on behalf of Mathieu Fabre addressed to Pontchartrain; B⁷ 507, fol. 94, Fabre to Pontchartrain, 10 August 1709, and fol. 52, de Machault to Pontchartrain, 23 August 1709; B⁷ 508, fols. 330–31, Fabre to Pontchartrain, 30 January 1712; ibid., fols. 348–49, memoir from Fabre to Pontchartrain; ibid., fols. 350–51, Fabre to Pontchartrain, 10 October 1712; B⁷ 509, fol. 261, Fabre to Pontchartrain, 25 September 1714. Also, AN, G⁷ 1703, pièce 31, Harley to Desmaretz, 11 September 1714; ibid., pièce 32, *projet d'arrest*. Mathieu Fabre's letters to the Chamber of Commerce of Marseilles are in ACCM, B 158–64.

53. Fournier, *La Chambre de commerce de Marseille*, pp. 71–82; ACCM, B 165–67.

54. Desmaretz to Chamber of Commerce of Marseilles, 30 August 1714, reprinted in Fournier, *La Chambre de commerce de Marseille*, p. 270; ACCM, B 165, Philip to Chamber of Commerce, 14 September 1714.

55. AN, F¹² 51, fol. 5.

56. AD, Gironde, C 4301, piece 51, Fénellon to Chamber of Commerce, 5 September 1710.

57. All royal provincial intendants actively defended what they perceived to be the legitimate rights of their *généralités* and provinces; see, for example, Marchand, *Un Intendant sous Louis XIV*, p. 328.

58. Quénet, "Un Exemple," p. 459; Jean-Auguste Brutails, *Inventaire du fonds de la chambre du commerce de Guienne*, p. xxviii. On the general subject of gratifications and pensions in both diplomacy and domestic politics, see J. Levron, "Louis XIV's Courtiers," in Ragnhild Hatton (ed.), *Louis XIV and Absolutism*, pp. 142–46; Janine Fayard, "Attempts to Build a 'Third Party' in North Germany, 1690–1694," in Ragnhild Hatton (ed.), *Louis XIV and Europe*, pp. 213–40; Hatton, "Gratifications and Foreign Policy: Anglo-French Rivalry in Sweden during the Nine Years War," in Hatton and Bromley (eds.), *William III and Louis XIV*, pp. 68–94.

59. Quoted in Labraque-Bordenave, "Histoire des députés de Bordeaux," p. 279. Also see Brutails, "Etude sur la Chambre de commerce de Guienne," pp. 302–3.

60. Fournier, *La Chambre de commerce de Marseille*, p. 68.

61. Mar., B² 234, p. 277, Pontchartrain to Moreau, 10 May 1713.

62. AN, KK 1340, p. 510.

63. BN, MSS. fr., 18979, passim.

64. ACCM, A 17, "Compte de la récepte et dépense faite par Mr. Joseph Fabre, député du commerce de Marseille à Paris," Marseille, 29 March 1704.

65. For an extended treatment of this topic, see my "Government and Business in Early Eighteenth-Century France."

66. ACCM, A 17, "Compte de la récepte."

67. Masson, *Histoire du commerce ... XVIIe siècle*, pp. 317–18.

68. See various pieces in ACCM, A 49, B 153–59.

69. ACCM, B 7, fol. 201v, Chamber of Commerce, meeting of 22 August 1715.

70. Rambert, *Histoire du commerce de Marseille*, 4:220–21.

71. Ibid., p. 220.

72. Mar., B⁷ 502, fols. 30–31, Joseph Fabre to Pontchartrain, 22 January 1702; ibid., fols. 78–79, same to same, 21 May 1702; B⁷ 503, fol. 186, Mathieu Fabre to Pontchartrain, 18 April 1705; B⁷ 504, fol. 409, same to same, 11 January 1706; B⁷ 509, fols. 230–33v, *maire, échevins*, and deputies of trade of Marseilles to Pontchartrain, 15 September 1714; ACCM, B 153–65.

73. ACCM, B 153, Joseph Fabre to Chamber of Commerce, 1 March and 15 March 1701.

74. Rambert, *Histoire du commerce de Marseille*, 4:288.

75. Reprinted in Isambert, *Recueil général*, 18:205; it is discussed in Rambert, *Histoire du commerce de Marseille*, 4:204 ff.

76. By 1700 the number of Atlantic ports that could trade with the Levant had been reduced to two: Rouen and Dunkirk. These two cities continued to pay the 20 percent duty on articles coming directly from the Levant. By 1700 in the Mediterranean, only Marseilles could engage in this trade. Any Levant goods that entered France—even at Marseilles—after touching down in a foreign port were likewise subject to a 20 percent duty. This was done to encourage Frenchmen to trade directly with the Levant, rather than purchasing Levant goods from Italian, Dutch, and English merchants.

77. Rambert, *Histoire du commerce de Marseille*, 4:215–16; Cole, *French Mercantilism, 1683–1700*, pp. 28–29.

78. The word *entrepôt* usually designates a commercial center where goods are received for distribution or transshipment, but the word was sometimes used—as it

is here—to refer to the storage of goods in a warehouse guarded by customs officials. Although the fee for such storage was minimal, Marseilles's citizens considered it to be a violation of the free-port status of the city. These three types of merchandise were placed in entrepôt in order to prevent their fraudulent entry into other parts of France.

79. In addition to the *procès-verbaux* for the years 1701–3 (in AN, F¹² 51), see Mar., B⁷ 502, fols. 49–52, "Raisons du Sr. Fabre député au Conseil de commerce sur la franchise de Marseille," April 1702; BN, MSS. fr., 16909, fols. 12–84, various memoirs; AN, F¹² 1908, dossier on Marseilles.

80. AN, F¹² 51, fol. 72; G⁷ 1686, piece 199, Fabre to Chamillart, 14 February 1703.

81. For example, BN, MSS. fr. 16909, fols. 61–62, "Motifs qui ont obligé le Roy en 1669 sous la direction de Mr. Colbert de préférer. . . . "

82. Quoted in Masson, *Histoire du commerce . . . XVIIᵉ siècle*, p. 314.

83. That Marseilles was suffering from an oversupply of Levant goods was also noted by other authorities: see AN, G⁷ 1685, Pontchartrain to Chamillart, 18 November 1699; G⁷ 533, same to same, 13 January 1700; Mar., B⁷ 499, de Lagny to Pontchartrain, 10 November 1699; Boislisle, *Correspondance des contrôleurs généraux*, 2:77, Lebret to Chamillart, 20 June 1701.

84. AN, F¹² 51, fols. 44v. 70v.

85. Mar., B⁷ 502, fols. 96, 98, 104, 106, Joseph Fabre to Pontchartrain, 6 August 1702, 13 August 1702, 2 October 1702, and 11 October 1702.

86. A copy can be found in AN, F¹² 1910.

87. It was repealed for three years only. The revocation was renewed every three years until 1717, when the entrepôt was abolished permanently.

88. The *arrêt* did not remove all restrictions on Marseilles's freedom. Prohibitions against the entry of foreign-made woolens, Indian calicos, dried cod, and tanned hides remained in effect. Tax farmers continued to maintain two bureaus in the city: one to prevent the entry of dried cod and tanned hides, another to prevent the importation of any tobacco not belonging to the royal tobacco monopoly.

89. Mar., B⁷ 502, fols. 76–77, 329–30, Fabre to Pontchartrain, 21 May 1702, 2 June 1703.

90. AN, F¹² 1910, Pontchartrain to Amelot, 25 June 1704; ibid., "Sur la question proposée, si les marchandises du Levant provenant des prises . . . ," by the deputies of trade, 14 July 1704; ibid., "Copie de l'ordre de Mgr. Chamillart aux fermiers généraux," 22 January 1705; F¹² 51, fol. 277.

91. *Transit* referred to the right of free passage, exempting merchandise from all internal tolls and customs duties.

92. Actually Lyons had voiced objections to the free passage as early as the 1680s, but to no avail (Mar., B⁷ 495, fols. 533–37, "Mémoire concernant le transit . . . "). On this entire affair see Mar., B² 176, fols. 545v–46, Pontchartrain to Valossière, 27 August 1704; also see various materials in AN, F¹² 1908, 1910; and F¹² 645, "Mémoire de la chambre du commerce de Marseille, sur les marchandises du Levant qui vont de cette ville aux pays étrangers par terre."

93. A copy is in AN, AD XI, 53.

94. AN, F¹² 55, 212v–16v, meeting of 26 September 1710; AN, G⁷ 1701, fol. 22, de Machault to Desmaretz, 31 May 1713; ibid., fol. 207, Daguesseau and Amelot to Desmaretz, 23 May 1713; Masson, *Histoire du commerce . . . XVIIᵉ siècle*, p. 321.

95. AN, F¹² 55, fols. 237–39v; F¹² 58, fols. 396–96v; Masson, *Histoire du commerce . . . XVIIᵉ siècle*, p. 320.

96. AN, F¹² 58, fol. 181v; AN, G⁷ 1693, piece 157, notice concerning a *placet* by merchants of Saint-Malo; ibid., piece 166, notice of a letter from magistrates of Le

Havre; AN, F¹² 1646–50, *maire, échevins*, and *syndics* of Havre de Grace to Desmaretz, 5 May 1713, with accompanying memoir; ibid., "Résponse des habitans de St. Malo à la demande de préférence pour l'entrepost que font les habitans du Havre." The greater part of the general memoir written in 1701 by Saint-Malo's deputy was devoted to the proposed reestablishment of that city's *franchise* (BN, MSS. fr., 8038, fols. 291–314). The Chamber of Commerce of Toulouse also feared that increasing the number of free ports would endanger French manufactures by facilitating the entry of foreign-made products into the country (Chinault, *La Chambre de commerce de Toulouse*, p. 93).

97. Much information on this affair is in AN, G⁷ 1701, pieces 106–37, and fols. 1–200. Also see Masson, *Histoire du commerce . . . XVIIᵉ siècle*, pp. 321–22.

98. AN, G⁷ 1701, fol. 71v, Caumartin de Boissy to Desmaretz, 10 September 1713.

99. Desmaretz's insistence led the council to reverse its position and decide in favor of Lyons, Marseilles, and Languedoc (AN, F¹² 58, fols. 241v–46v, 9 March 1714).

100. AN, G⁷ 1701, fols. 51 ff.

101. A copy is in ibid., fol. 200.

102. AN, F¹² 51, fols. 69, 87v, 104v, 256, 261v–62, 363; F¹² 55, fol. 323; AN, G⁷ 1704, piece 88, extract of a memoir by Chamber of Commerce of Bordeaux; G⁷ 1686, piece 60, "Mémoire des motifs qui prouvent la nécessité de permettre aux négocians de St Malo d'envoyer leur vaisseaux faire le commerce des isles françoises de l'Amérique, et Guinée, et faire leur retour avec leur chargement dans leur ville" (ibid., pieces 181–83); Col., F² B 1, fols. 32–35, "Mémoire de la Chambre de commerce de Dunkerque;" AN, F¹² 644, pieces 308–12.

103. At the end of the seventeenth century, the only other sugar refineries were in Sète, Nîmes, Orléans, Lille, and Dunkirk (see Paul-M. Bondois, "Les Centres sucriers français au XVIIIᵉ siècle").

104. AN, F¹² 51, fols. 228, 279–79v, 322, 378. In the interests of simplified tax-collection procedures, even the farmers general favored granting Bordeaux's privileges to other cities; see their "Mémoire sur la contestation qui est entre les raffineurs de la Rochelle, et ceux de Bordeaux," 1705 (BN, MSS. fr., 14294, fols. 126–28v).

105. AN, F¹² 1903, "Les députez au conseil de commerce sur le différend d'entre le raffineur de Marseille et les négocians de Bordeaux," 19 January 1707; also see various pieces in F¹² 1908.

106. The *procès-verbaux* report the debate that took place on that date but do not allude to the fight between the two deputies (AN, F¹² 54, fols. 1–2). See Fabre to Chamber of Commerce, 25 January 1707, ACCM, B 161.

107. See Chapter 7.

108. AN, F¹² 51, fols. 14, 181v, 194, 224v, 227, 228, 262v, 278–78v; F¹² 55, fols. 203–4, 217v, 293, 344–45v; F¹² 58, fols. 98–100v, 200v–201v, 287–89v, 395.

109. AN, G⁷ 1697, piece 158, Wilquin to Desmaretz, 11 December 1712; G⁷ 1703, piece 44 *bis*, Wilquin to [?], 13 October 1714; ibid., piece 101, extract of a memoir by de la Garde; AN, F¹² 58, fols, 200v–201v, 287–89v.

110. AN, G⁷ 1691, piece 210, *avis* of deputies on the request of Sieur Loyseau, 18 May 1708; G⁷ 1692, piece 259, fols. 318v–19, 332v; F¹² 51, fol. 45v; F¹² 54, fol. 238v; G⁷ 1695, piece 308, Anisson to Desmaretz, 14 December 1710.

111. For example, AD, Loire-Atlantique, C 611, *juge* and *consuls* of Bordeaux to *juge* and *consuls* of Nantes, 30 May 1710.

112. AN, G⁷ 1692, piece 79, Anisson, Héron, Mesnager, Fénellon, and Piécourt to Desmaretz, 11 November 1708.

PART TWO

THE WORK OF THE COUNCIL

5

ENEMY AND NEUTRAL TRADE

The question of trade with enemy and neutral powers was the topic
that occupied more time than any other in the Council of Commerce during the War of the Spanish Succession.[1] This subject has
already received excellent treatment from Sir George Clark and J.
S. Bromley,[2] but both of these historians have left largely unex-
plored an important dimension of this question: namely, the development of French trading policies during this period. Clark has
concentrated mostly on English and Dutch policies, and Bromley
has generally focused upon the impact that privateering had during each war. This chapter therefore will deal with French policies
and the role of the Council of Commerce in their formulation.[3]

PREPARATIONS FOR A WAR ON TRADE

If the War of the League of Augsburg can be described as a war
against French trade,[4] then the War of the Spanish Succession can
be termed—from the French viewpoint—a war on allied trade. The
Council of Commerce viewed this war as an opportunity to strike at
the European and worldwide commerce of France's chief competitors, England and Holland. In keeping with this aim, the council
worked to establish proper guidelines for French economic relations with other nations. It also did all that it could to encourage the
French *guerre de course*.

Trade wars were not new to Europe,[5] but two factors helped
magnify their severity during this period. First of all, the final two
wars of Louis XIV's reign witnessed the apogee of the *guerre de
course*, which by definition was a war on enemy commerce. This was
the "glorious" age of Jean Bart, Guay-Trouin, and a host of other
freebooting buccaneers stationed in ports all over Europe. Second,
the quest of European powers for colonies and for a larger share of
international trade led almost inevitably to attacks on enemy commerce.

Trading with the adversary during wartime had been a long-standing custom among European merchants. During the War of the League of Augsburg and the War of the Spanish Succession, however, the belligerent powers endeavored to cut off or severely limit this traffic. Each side also sought to limit the commerce of neutrals with the other camp.

The policies that became clear during the succession war were adumbrated during its predecessor in the 1690s. In 1689 England and the Dutch Republic signed a series of four agreements, one of which called for a complete embargo on trade with France. It was to apply to neutrals as well as allies.[6] This had been insisted on by Louis XIV's inveterate opponent William III.

Neither the Dutch nor the Spanish nor the Scandinavian neutrals were happy with this interdiction. Merchants from all nations (including England) continued to deal with France throughout the war, often surreptitiously. Allied privateers tried to coerce Denmark and Sweden into obeying the convention, despite the vehement protests of these neutral powers, and hundreds of Scandinavian vessels were brought to English and Dutch ports. The neutrals very nearly came to blows with the Atlantic powers over the issue.[7] Gradually England and Holland gave in, and by 1693 they admitted the right of neutrals to trade with France in anything but contraband.[8]

In addition to these measures, the allies, of course, also attacked French trade directly. Clark has estimated that between 900 and 1,000 French ships were captured by the enemy during the war. This was not enough to cripple French trade, but it was sufficient to inflict serious damage.[9] As much as was possible, the allies tried to boycott French merchandise throughout the war.[10]

The French policy at the beginning of this war was much less severe than that of its adversaries. Louis XIV did not at first wish to cut off all trade with the enemy, nor did he wish to press neutrals to do so. Only as the sea powers began to impinge on neutral commerce did France itself decide to cut off trade with the enemy and to attack illicit trade by neutrals. When France switched eventually from a *guerre d'escadre* to a *guerre de course*, French privateers proceeded to inflict heavy losses on allied shipping. It is possible that by the end of the war in 1697 French corsairs may have done more damage to allied commerce than was done to French trade by enemy ships.[11]

In the Treaty of Ryswick (1697) and the subsequent tariff of 1699, France and the United Provinces agreed to a *modus vivendi*.

The Dutch were guaranteed that their traders would receive all the same privileges in French ports that Frenchmen themselves received, and the heavily protective tariff of 1667 was lowered for Dutch goods. France, in return, was able to reestablish contact with the Dutch carriers, on which it depended heavily for the export of many of its manufactures and agricultural products. The two nations likewise agreed, in the event of future wars, to the principle of "free ship, free goods." This ensured the rights of neutral ships to trade with belligerents of either side.

There was no such commercial agreement between France and England in 1697, and the two nations returned to the mutually hostile trade restrictions that had soured relations between them since the 1660s. Each side declared that its cross-channel competitor had been the first to adopt a hostile trade posture.[12]

The situation was such that by 1700 a series of outright prohibitions or exorbitant customs duties prevented English woolens and other manufactures from entering France. England, on the other hand, had outlawed the export of raw wool from any of the British Isles, not wishing to contribute to her competitor's manufactures. Furthermore, most French textiles were prohibited in England. What especially irked the French were the seemingly outrageous duties placed on their wine in England: by the year 1693 for a *gallon impérial* (about 4.5 liters) of Bordeaux one had to pay more than 19 shillings in duties, roughly twice as much as for wine from other countries. In addition, French goods could enter England only on English or neutral ships, and French merchants had to conduct all their business through English brokers[13]

The need to correct this situation was clearly recognized in France. In 1699–1700 Louis XIV's ambassador to England, the comte de Tallard, worked feverishly, but unsuccessfully, to negotiate a trade agreement with William III.[14] Several of the deputies of commerce expressed the hope in their general memoirs that a treaty of commerce might be signed with England.

But nothing of that sort came about. Soon after the Council of Commerce was created, the long-anticipated death of King Carlos II of Spain occurred. Although war was not officially declared until May 1702, the eighteen months that elapsed between the monarch's death and the commencement of hostilities were filled with diplomatic and military maneuvering that foreshadowed the upcoming struggle. That left little time or desire to think about trade agreements.

There can be no doubt about the fact that the Council of Commerce was the principal organ charged with determining French trade policies during this war. On a few occasions, as will be noted, the royal ministers departed from the council's advice. The crown neverthelsss relied chiefly on this body to examine French policies and to determine a proper course of action.

When the war erupted, trade with every European nation was put on a different footing. The process of deciding which trades were permissible and which were not was complex. The council had to decide whether certain goods were needed in France (for manufactures or shipbuilding) and whether other goods could be permitted to leave France. It also had to decide what forms passports would take and to whom they would be granted. [15] The thousands of requests that poured into the government from foreign and native merchants to bring goods to France were generally forwarded to the council for consideration. [16]

The *commissaires* and deputies drew up lists (*états*) enumerating all the goods that each nation was permitted to send to France. The controller general then ratified these *états*, either by letter or by *arrêt*. No merchandise could be imported from abroad unless it was included on these lists.

In addition to these lists, merchandise coming from enemy states likewise required a special permit or passport before entering France. Each passport for goods entering by sea had to be signed by three people: the admiral of France (the comte de Toulouse), the secretary of state for the navy, and the controller general. [17] The Council of Commerce also determined the policies that were followed for overland trade. In such cases the controller general merely wrote to the farmers general and informed them that a particular merchant had permission to import certain items into France through a specified customs bureau on the frontiers of the country. [18]

TRADE WITH ENGLAND, SCOTLAND, AND IRELAND

The Council of Commerce assumed an antagonistic position toward English trade even before the war began. On 6 September 1701 the crown issued an *arrêt* that was openly hostile to English commerce. [19] It absolutely forbade the importation from England of all textile products of any kind, as well as alcoholic beverages, tin, lead, drugs, spices, and hardware products. In addition, import duties were sharply raised on thirteen other articles that England often sent to France (alum, glass bottles, salted meat, coal, dried cod, and others). The *arrêt* struck at the English carrying trade by declaring that henceforth English merchants could bring to France only goods that were of English production or manufacture. Finally, all English merchants now had to go through French brokers. All these provisions applied equally to Scotland and Ireland also.

Sir George Clark explains the provenance of this *arrêt* as follows:

> . . . Louis XIV prohibited the importation of British manufactured articles, not, it seems, with the intention of hastening the war, but in order to keep the English traders out of war by giving them a foretaste of what they might expect. His action had the contrary effect. It made English opinion more hostile.[20]

Clark is certainly correct about the British reaction to the French *arrêt*, but along with others he has overlooked the role of the Council of Commerce in formulating it. Late in June 1701 Louis XIV requested that the council examine the question of French-English commerce.[21] He wanted to know how France should respond to the exorbitant duties and the prohibitions that England had imposed on French products. The matter was discussed briefly in the council and then referred to the deputies for further study.

In the meeting of 8 July 1701, the deputies gave their response.[22] Of the eleven deputies present, all desired a treaty of commerce with England, but only four urged constraint on the part of France.[23] These four argued that many English measures had been adopted only in reprisal against earlier French actions, and they suggested that France unilaterally reduce its tariffs on English goods, in the hope that England might do the same. In this more conciliatory atmosphere, they argued, a treaty of commerce would more likely be possible. The seven other deputies, however, pushed for even harsher regulations against English goods. They stubbornly insisted that only by assuming a hard line would France be able to force England into signing a treaty of commerce, and they recommended a prohibition against all English manufactures.

The council accepted the majority view of the deputies, and the *arrêt* proclaiming this policy was, after a brief delay, issued on 6 September. One knows from hindsight, of course, that the policy advocated by most of the deputies did not succeed. Rather than forcing England into submission, it only alienated British opinion. The new law remained the basis for French commercial relations with England until the Eden Treaty of 1786 liberalized trade between the two nations. From 1701 until that date, such trade as there was between the two countries was mostly carried out illegally.

After war was officially proclaimed in May 1702, England prohibited all trade with France. Anyone from England, Scotland, or Ireland who was caught trading with France was subject to the death penalty. England also endeavored to make its chief ally, the Dutch Republic, agree to cut off all trade with the enemy. Under strong urging from English ministers, the Dutch reluctantly agreed to such a ban. It went into effect on 1 June 1703 and lasted one year. Dutch merchants disliked it from the very beginning. Their carrying trade depended heavily on the voluminous quantity of goods that Dutch vessels normally transported to and from France, and their government therefore refused to renew the ban when it expired in 1704. Thereafter England was thus alone in its severance of trade with France.[24]

These measures had their counterparts in France. On 11 April 1702 the crown issued an *arrêt* that prohibited the entry into France of any manufactures from England, Scotland, and Ireland.[25] In response to the Anglo-Dutch agreement of June 1703, France prohibited all trade with enemy powers through an *arrêt* of 28 August 1703.[26] This marked a high point in the French attempt to wage an all-out war against its adversaries.

Although the deputies of trade and *commissaires* had strongly supported the first of these two *arrêts*, only reluctantly did they approve of the second.[27] They realized that France was not self-sufficient and depended on foreign trade. The Anglo-Dutch convention of June 1703, however, finally spurred them to adopt a similarly harsh strategy. The new *arrêt* ended trade not only with England and its dependencies but with Holland and Germany as well.

Soon after the *arrêt* was issued, its impracticality became clear: French privateers demanded the right to sell in France certain goods found on English prize ships.[28] In order to promote the French *guerre de course*, the Council of Commerce therefore decided to permit the entry into France of lead, tin, cod, and other nonmanufactured products found in English prize vessels. Any English manufactures, however, still had to be reshipped out of France.

In other ways it also became clear that France could not do away completely with trade with the enemy. For example, France had come to rely on Scotland and Ireland for various foodstuffs. The salted meat imported from Ireland was sent to feed colonists in the West Indies, and thousands of the *menu peuple* in France depended on the relatively inexpensive butter imported from both Scotland and Ireland. These reasons made trade with these two English dependencies a necessity. Also, there was the obvious political advantage of further weakening Scottish and Irish allegiance to England by encouraging them to break English law through trading with France. Lastly, both areas would provide an outlet for French products; French wines might even be able to enter England through these two channels.

Because of these considerations, the Council of Commerce decided that passports should be granted for trading with both Ireland and Scotland. In 1702 there had already begun a brisk trade with Ireland, despite the recent English prohibition of trade with France. The council had decided at that time to limit Irish imports to salted meat and butter.[29] Notwithstanding the *arrêt* of 28 August 1703, the council let it be known that it was willing to reopen trade with both of the English dependencies, and soon it was flooded with requests for passports from Frenchmen and from expatriate Irish and Scottish merchants residing in such ports as Rouen, Nantes, and Saint-Malo.

The *commissaires* and deputies were especially sympathetic to Ireland. There were thousands of Irish refugees in French ports. These people were all Catholics, and, what is more, they supported the claims of the Pretender, James III, then residing in France.[30]

At first the council was very selective about the Scottish and Irish articles that could enter France. It did not wish to permit merchants from these two areas to send to France any products that it suspected came originally from England. Thus, for example, throughout the war it refused to permit the importation of lead from Ireland, for Ireland produced no lead.[31] Beginning in 1705, however, the council did permit the entry of 360 tons of lead a year from Scotland. It judged that this was about how much exportable lead Scotland produced in a year; anything in excess of this probably would have come from England.[32]

Because of the pinch of war, the list of Scottish and Irish goods permitted in France was gradually expanded, but the council always insisted that the merchant or merchants who bought these goods be obligated to take out of France an amount of French goods of equal or greater value. This was part of the council's program of "equivalent," about which more will be said later. By 1710 Ireland could export to France ten varieties of goods, including butter, tallow, salted meat, wool, animal skins, leather, and cheese.[33] Scotland by that time could bring lead, hobnails, wool, coal, and salted salmon.[34] Although trade with these two countries was not up to prewar levels, nevertheless several hundred passports were granted to their vessels throughout the war.[35]

Long before 1710 the Council of Commerce also found it necessary to relent somewhat on its outright prohibition of trade with England. There were hundreds of English merchants and shippers willing to run the risks of trading illicitly with France, and France undeniably needed several English products. In the early years of the war, the Council of Commerce refused to grant passports to Englishmen themselves; wool and the few drugs used in preparing textiles whose importation was permitted had to enter in Irish and Scottish ships. But late in 1706 the council decided to permit direct contacts with Englishmen. In November of that year, Jérôme de Pontchartrain forwarded to the council a letter from the inspector general of the navy at Bordeaux.[36] The man who held this office, Lombard, had received a letter from a London merchant requesting a passport to bring some merchandise to France; in return the merchant proposed to take a cargo of wine back to England. The council debated the issue and decided that such passports should indeed be granted.[37]

The council's decision, however, ran into the stiff opposition of the secretary of state for the navy, who opposed it on grounds of principle. He felt that the granting of passports to subjects of Queen Anne would be "an open recognition" of the legitimate rule of "the Princess of Denmark," as the French government called her.[38]

Chamillart, on the other hand, supported the contention of the Council of Commerce that such passports to Englishmen could only be beneficial to France. The issue was bruited about for several more months. Finally, in the spring of 1707, Pontchartrain relented, and limited numbers of such passports began to be issued.[39]

From this time through 1710, English vessels were thus permitted to bring to France wool and limited quantities of dyeing materials. English ships were especially encouraged to come to France empty, which they did in large numbers. In this way France did not need to worry about the entry of prohibited goods, but it could send wines and other goods to England. English and Channel Islands vessels that returned French prisoners of war to their native country were also encouraged to take out French products.[40] Eventually, lead and some spices were also permitted to enter from England. Of course, since England still prohibited commerce with France, these traders received harsh punishments from their own government if they were caught.

In 1709 French Flanders requested permission to add coal to the list of goods permitted to enter from England. The Council of Commerce opposed the proposal. The deputies wished to maintain as hard a line as possible against England, and they argued that Flanders could obtain enough coal from elsewhere in France. Desmaretz, however, overrode the council's proposal. The harsh winter of 1709 had caused a depletion of wood supplies used in Flemish *brasseries*, and in order to keep workers occupied the controller general decided to permit the importation of coal.[41]

The French position on English trade was drastically liberalized in December 1710. Because this development was directly tied to French policies toward the Dutch, however, it is better to delay its discussion.

TRADE WITH HOLLAND

If the Council of Commerce wished to limit trade with England during the war, in the hope that somehow this would damage the English economy, it wished, literally, to destroy Dutch commerce and navigation. Its desire to humble *les hollandois* was so strong that it influenced French trade policies in general.

As noted earlier, the deputies' general memoirs of 1700–1701 reflected their jealousy of Dutch merchants. The French feared that the skillful, economical traders from the provinces of Holland and Zeeland would soon be the "sole masters" of all European seaborne commerce.[42] Time and again during the War of the Spanish Succession, the deputies railed against the Dutch in a fashion that would have warmed Colbert's heart. Echoing Louis XIV's own sentiments, they frequently denounced the Dutch as *ces républicains*,[43] a term that did not lose its derogatory connotation in France until much later in the eighteenth century.

Although French enmity toward Dutch commerce remained constant during the war, the actual policy toward trade with

Holland shifted several times from 1702 to 1713. Throughout 1702 and 1703 the Council of Commerce discussed possible stances to be taken with regard to the Dutch. Much of this discussion stemmed from a dispute that had been stirring since 1700 between the deputy of Nantes and the other deputies from Atlantic ports.[44] Although Descasaux du Hallay had railed against the "pernicious designs" of the Dutch in his general memoir, he soon after softened his tone.[45] Nantes desperately needed Dutch vessels to carry its wine and other agricultural products to the North, and therefore it did not wish to alienate the little republic too much. The deputy feared that French shippers would never be able to oust the Dutch from French trade; they were much too economical and highly skilled as seamen, needing far smaller crews to man their ships than did Frenchmen. He complained that Dutch shippers "live on their ships with their wives and their children."[46] Nearly every one of them was thereby born a natural sailor.

Descasaux du Hallay did agree, however, that ships from Denmark, Sweden and Hamburg should be exempted from the 50-sous-per-ton duty.[47] This exemption would encourage vessels from these nations to seek French goods in France rather than in the great entrepôt of Amsterdam.

The other Atlantic deputies—led by Piécourt (Dunkirk) and Mesnager (Rouen)—argued for a harsher stand against the United Provinces.[48] Dutch ships already controlled five-sixths of France's trade, they expostulated, and unless something was done soon, they would have all of it. The deputies contended not only that the exemption from the 50-sous duty should be extended to all nations and cities of the North, but that the Dutch should be prohibited from bringing to France anything that was not of their own cultivation or manufacture. This, they believed, would drive a nail right into the heart of the Dutch carrying trade.

During the first year and a half of the war, the number of Dutch ships entering French ports certainly decreased from prewar levels; but decisions as to what merchandise they could bring were made on a purely *ad hoc* basis. In order to protect the French fishing industry and French manufactures, the Dutch were prohibited from bringing such goods into the country.[49] Otherwise, passports were granted to the Dutch on a fairly regular basis.

There were, however, other forces pushing the Council of Commerce to adopt a harsher policy toward Holland. Many private individuals bombarded Chamillart and Jérôme de Pontchartrain with memoirs on ways to destroy the Dutch economy, and the royal ministers quickly forwarded these proposals to the council. The two chief exponents of this total-war strategy were Jean Pottier de la Hestroye[50] and Denis Faulconnier.[51] Both men were from Dunkirk, and both deplored the stranglehold that the Dutch had acquired over French commerce. Pottier de la Hestroye limited his proposals to ways in which Dutch imports into France and the Dutch carrying trade could be curtailed without discouraging Holland from taking out French wines and manufactures.

Faulconnier, however, was a fanatic patriot whose memoirs virtually dripped with venomous schemes for destroying the merchant republic. Chamillart and Pontchartrain each showed interest in Faulconnier's ideas, and they encouraged the council to study them carefully. Faulconnier recommended, among other things, that all passports to the Dutch be revoked, that Spain be encouraged likewise to end all commerce with the republic, and that a host of favors be extended to neutral vessels to encourage them to come directly to France.[52]

In May 1702 the deputies of commerce voiced objections to these plans.[53] They considered them impracticable and even dangerous. There was no guarantee that Spain would go along with them, and it seemed unlikely that neutral vessels would be able, on such short notice, to muster enough ships to take out France's vast stores of wines, brandies, and other goods traditionally exported to northern Europe.

Chamillart and Pontchartrain, however, were clearly sympathetic to Faulconnier's views, and at least two provincial intendants also agreed that drastic measures were imperative.[54] The Anglo-Dutch convention of 1 June 1703 provided the final push that was needed to convince the council to adopt a strong position against enemy trade, and it responded by drafting the *arrêt* of 28 August 1703, already mentioned above. By its terms France vowed to end all commerce with enemy powers. Together with the Anglo-Dutch convention, the *arrêt* marked a significant escalation of the concept of warfare. Virtually every major war thereafter would include attempts to destroy not merely the armies of an enemy prince but entire national economies as well.

Although concessions would later have to be granted to the Dutch, the *arrêt* nevertheless gave France a brief opportunity to end Holland's domination of the European carrying trade. The Council of Commerce sought to do this by promoting direct contacts between nonbelligerent nations and France. We must now therefore turn to the overtures that France made to neutral commerce.

ENCOURAGEMENT TO NEUTRALS

In their general memoirs, the deputies already had expressed the hope that direct commerce might be fostered between France and northern Europe. In these memoirs and in their discussions during the next couple of years, the deputies especially pushed for removal of the 50-sous-per-ton duty on merchandise entering in foreign ships.[55] The Dutch were already exempted from this tax, and this gave their ships an unfair advantage over the ships of other nations. Most of the deputies likewise recommended that merchandise from the North be permitted to enter France only if it had not been *entreposée* anywhere else. In other words, the deputies wanted these countries to bring their goods directly to France, not to Amsterdam, whence they would be reshipped to France.[56] In April 1702 Héron, of La Rochelle, even suggested that a special trading company be created for commerce with the Baltic lands, but nothing came of the proposal.[57]

No decision was made concerning Swedish and Danish commerce until the summer of 1703—at the moment when the general prohibition of trade with the enemy was being deliberated. This prohibition was finally approved only because the council believed that neutral vessels could supply France with her needs and would be able to take out her excess wines, brandies, salt, and other merchandise. Through the *arrêt* of 14 June 1703, the council established a list of goods that Danish or Swedish ships could bring to France. This list included wood for building ships, barrel staves, tar, hemp, and copper. What is more, ships bringing these goods were exempted from paying the duty of 50 sous per ton. The list was expanded by the *arrêts* of 19 June 1703, 1 September 1703, and 4 March 1704.[58] For those goods that France most desperately needed, the exemption from the 50-sous tax continued to be granted, although the other ordinary import duties had to be paid. Goods that were less urgently needed remained subject to the 50-sous tax. These included such things as wool, amber, starch, cereals, azure, white lead (*céruse*), *cornes à lanterne*, animal skins, feathers, salmon, and small hand tools. In the years after 1704, a few other items were added to the list permitted from these two countries.

The Council of Commerce was always careful to restrict this list to merchandise that it was sure were products of the North. Otherwise it would have been easy for the Dutch to send things into France on Swedish and Danish ships.[59] Upon arrival in France, all neutral vessels had to present certificates from their nations' port officials; these certificates listed the ships' cargoes and stipulated that the ships would not stop in Holland on their way to or from France.

The Danish and Swedish ships that brought goods to France were always required to take out an amount of French products of equal or greater value. They could get this equivalent value of goods either in their port of entry or another French port.

The favors bestowed on Danish and Swedish ships were not extended to those from Poland. This was due primarily to letters of reprisal that had been granted by Louis XIV to the abbé de Polignac in 1701 against all ships of Danzig. The origins of this affair went back to the mid 1690s, when Polignac had served as French ambassador to Poland. After the death of John Sobieski in 1696, the two chief candidates for the throne of Poland were Augustus, duke of Saxony, and Louis XIV's cousin, the prince of Conti. Although Polignac succeeded in getting a majority of the Polish diet to choose the prince of Conti as king, the duke of Saxony invaded Poland and by force of arms and personal contacts with several Polish nobles succeeded in reversing the election. The Polish people swiftly gave their allegiance to the new king (Augustus II). In June 1697 great numbers of people in Danzig went on a rampage against all Frenchmen in the city, arresting them and looting their homes. Although Polignac escaped without personal harm, a mob destroyed or stole all his possessions. He estimated his losses at 162,000 livres. At first the abbé received no solace from Louis XIV; for a period after 1698, in fact, he was in disgrace. While campaigning for the prince of Conti, he had made promises to the Poles that went far beyond his official instructions, and this had greatly irritated the king. By 1701, however, Polignac had returned to court, and Louis XIV granted him the letters of reprisal.[60]

Of course, these letters directly contradicted the efforts of the Council of Commerce to stimulate contacts with northern neutrals. The council, along with French merchants, often complained of this obstruction to trade.[61] The few Danzig ships that did enter France during the war were usually able to do so only with the special permission of Polignac.[62] These exceptions were few in number, though Danzig ships were given tacit permission to bring grains to France in 1709–10.[63]

In 1708 the crown began to seek funds with which it itself could reimburse Polignac for his losses.[64] Apparently a solution was eventually arrived at, for Polignac gave up his letters of reprisal (probably in 1710). In 1711 Danzig ships were welcomed in France on terms nearly as favorable as those extended to the ships of Denmark and Sweden.[65]

The Council of Commerce also wished to promote trade with neutral Italian states—principally Venice and Genoa. France depended on the silk thread and alum that it imported from Italy, and during the crisis of 1709–1710, it encouraged Italian ships to bring grains from the Levant to France. But French trade with the Italian neutrals never reached the scale attained by trade with Denmark and Sweden.

The Council of Commerce, with good reason, suspected the Italians of violating their neutrality whenever it suited their pocketbooks. Italian merchants frequently carried on illegal trade with the enemy. They were suspected of supplying those Spanish forces under the Archduke Charles with munitions and of helping to provision and repair English and Dutch privateers.[66] Italian traders were known to disguise their ships as French in order to benefit from the special privileges granted to Frenchmen in the lands of the Turkish sultan.[67]

As a result of these activities, French privateers were constantly stopping Italian vessels to check on their cargoes and to discover their destination. The Italian cities responded by repeatedly complaining to the French court of the unjust seizures of their vessels by French corsairs.[68] In 1711 Genoa requested French passports for its vessels so that they would not be bothered by privateers, but the Council of Commerce rejected this demand.[69] It said that neutrals did not require passports, no matter with whom their commerce was; and as long as they were engaging in legitimate neutral trade, they had nothing to fear from privateers.

Louis XIV, nevertheless, bowed to Genoese demands, and the passports were issued.[70] It was not long, however, before this decision was regretted: as the Council of Commerce had feared, the Genoese proceeded to use their passports to protect their ships from French privateers while they engaged in illicit trade with the enemy. The council reminded the government that it had predicted this would happen, and no more such passports were issued.[71]

In addition to promoting trade with neutral states, the Council of Commerce helped determine exactly which countries and territories were to be considered neutral. There was, of course, no difficulty in acknowledging the neutrality of such states as Venice, Denmark, and Sweden, but there was a host of small islands and territories whose status was rather dubious.

In 1705 the island of Ameland—off the coast of the Dutch province of Friesland—petitioned to be considered neutral.[72] The deputies of trade argued that Ameland was indisputably a Dutch territory and that the request was merely a ruse used by Holland in the hope of obtaining greater security for its own trade.[73] The request was therefore rejected.

On the other hand, however, the council in 1705 decided that ships from the tiny Adriatic republic of Ragusa (present-day Dubrovnik, in Yugoslavia) should be recognized as neutral.[74] Jérôme de Pontchartrain had opposed this, arguing that Ragusa was under the sway of the emperor. But the council's views prevailed, and Ragusa's small merchant fleet received the same rights as those of Venice, Genoa, and other neutrals.

In 1705 the Hanseatic towns of Hamburg, Lübeck, and Bremen also requested the privilege of neutral status. These towns were admittedly a part of the empire, but they claimed to have no real allegiance to it and to be virtually independent states. At first the Council of Commerce argued that they should be granted the same rights as Denmark and Sweden,[75] but only a few weeks later, on 26 August 1705, the council reversed itself and decided that the cities really were enemy territory.[76] It argued that if they were given extensive rights to trade with France, this would only provide the Dutch with ample opportunity to mask their own ships under the Hanseatic flags. Furthermore, the extensive granting of passports to ships from Hamburg, Lübeck, and Bremen would only serve to reduce the number of potential prizes for French privateers.[77] Throughout the first half of 1706, the question continued to be brought before the council. In July of that year, the deputies of trade decided to permit the Hanseatic vessels to obtain passports to come to France empty; this was done in order to guarantee that French goods (especially Bordeaux wines and the plentiful grains of that year's harvests) would find foreign markets.[78] Because of the pleading of Pontchartrain and various French shippers, in November 1706 the council relented even further. It decided that henceforth ships from the three cities in question could bring about a dozen different types of articles to France—mostly timber and naval stores. But these ships would have to pay the duty of 50 sous per ton and would be required to purchase at least an equivalent value of French merchandise.[79] As a result of the council's decision, trade with the Hanseatic cities almost immediately began to grow, and hundreds of their ships visited French ports throughout the remainder of the war.[80]

To protect the legitimate rights of neutral ships against French privateers during the war, the Council of Commerce helped formulate the *arrêt* of 23 July 1704.[81] This *arrêt* delineated and defined in careful detail the nature of neutral commerce. It stated that Louis XIV wished to defend neutral rights, whereas England and Holland continued to violate them. A neutral vessel was defined as one that was either built by a neutral or purchased from a belligerent power prior to the declaration of war.[82] The ship's owner and the captain, as well as the owners of the cargo, likewise had to be natives of a neutral country, or to have been naturalized prior to the war. Sailors of enemy nationality could serve on neutral ships, but they could never comprise more than one-third of the total crew.

Neutral ships were free to leave their own country, loaded with that country's products, and sail to any other nation—be it enemy, neutral, or ally; and they were likewise free to transport cargo from enemy states directly back to their own country. They could sail between neutral and allied ports, provided that they did not transport merchandise grown or manufactured in enemy lands. If a neutral vessel was caught transporting enemy goods anywhere except back to its own country, the ship and its entire cargo were a *bonne prise*. No neutral vessel leaving a French port with a *congé* (permission to depart) from an admiralty official could be stopped by French privateers unless there was strong evidence that it was breaking the rules outlined above.

Finally, to guarantee all these rights, the *arrêt* stipulated that if a neutral vessel was seized unjustly by a French privateer, the vessel would not only be released, but the privateer would be forced to pay for any damages.

This *arrêt* was a landmark in the history of neutral rights. It did not, of course, end all conflicts between neutrals and French corsairs. Italian vessels, as well as Danish and Swedish ships, were sometimes unjustly seized by the intrepid buccaneers from Dunkirk, Saint-Malo, Marseilles, and other ports. But the records of the French Prize Council reveal that it was commendably scrupulous in its judgment of captured ships. In more than three hundred cases, it forced privateers to release their prizes, and on many occasions it further ordered the privateers to recompense the owners for the interruption of their commerce.[83]

It is impossible to gauge quantitatively the degree to which neutrals took advantage of these various inducements to come directly to France, thereby skipping the traditional Dutch middlemen. Since neutral ships required no passports to enter French ports, the records of their comings and goings have not been as well preserved in the local admiralty archives. Certainly their vessels made several thousand trips to France during the war.

What one can say for sure is that the high point for commerce with the northern neutrals came during the years 1705–9. The *arrêts* issued in 1703 and 1704 to encourage neutral trade had only minor impact until late 1705. Up to that time English and Dutch privateers preyed upon their vessels, violating their neutrality, just as they had in the previous war.[84] Once in port, the English and Dutch gave the neutrals a fair price for their goods and then permitted the ships to leave. Late in 1705, however, they gave in to Danish and Swedish complaints, and from then on neutral vessels were relatively free to enter French ports. They proceeded to do so in increasing numbers until 1710, when the Northern War again interrupted trade in the Baltic.

CONCESSIONS TO THE DUTCH

Long before 1710, however, it had become clear that Denmark, Sweden, and other neutrals could not compensate for the loss of trade with Holland. The Council of Commerce had hoped to destroy Dutch trade by means of the neutrals, but the *arrêt* of 28 August 1703 prohibiting trade with the enemy soon proved to be impracticable. Guienne, Saintonge, Brittany, and other provinces that traditionally depended on Dutch vessels to carry out their surplus goods could not afford to wait several years to build up a new clientele.[85] Furthermore, French manufactures desperately needed the raw materials and semifinished goods traditionally imported from Holland.

In 1704 pressure began to mount for a modification of the 1703 *arrêt*. The Council of Commerce reviewed dozens of requests by merchants and manufacturers to import various products from Holland. Controller general Chamillart was sympathetic to these

pleas, and the council was charged with reevaluating French policy
with regard to the republic.[86] The result was the *arrêt* of 11 October 1704,[87] which permitted the importation from Holland of
cheese, *rabes* (?), borax, box-wood (*bois de buis*), and tar. Soon merchants from both countries were requesting hundreds of passports,
and they wanted to expand the list of goods permitted from
Holland.

In brief, the war on Dutch trade envisioned by the Council of
Commerce was soon reduced to a shambles. Once the government
had reopened the sluices to Dutch trade, there was no way to prevent a flood. From 1705 through 1710, the topic of trade with
Holland far outweighed any other question discussed in the council. During 1708 alone this subject came up in the council 121
times.[88] As they had done earlier, the deputies continued to ful-
minate against *ces républicains*, but again and again they had to
recognize that France could not do without them.

The attempt to restrict the types of merchandise that were allowed to enter from Holland became a farce. *Arrêts* were issued on
24 March 1705 and 16 May 1705 expanding the list of permitted
goods to include azure, glue, dyeing materials (*bois de teinture,
garance*), barrel staves, and wild boar skins.[89] These permissions
only whetted the appetites of French traders and manufacturers
even further, and one by one the Council of Commerce was forced,
grudgingly, to add others to the list. Its decisions were always ratified by the controller general, either in an *arrêt* or in an *état*. He, in
turn, sent copies of the lists of permitted goods to the farmers
general, who were charged with checking all imports and exports
in the ports and on the borders of the country.

By 1708 the list of goods officially permitted from Holland numbered more than three dozen, and by 1710 more than 50.[90] But
this list was only a face-saving device. In 1705 the Council of Commerce had begun to build a second list, consisting of "nonpermitted" merchandise, which nonetheless was permitted to enter.[91] In
order to import these goods, a merchant had to obtain a *passeport de
grâce*, and he had to pay an extra five percent *ad valorem* duty on
them.[92] These "nonpermitted" goods numbered more than fifty,
and they included steel, alum, quicksilver, ferrous sulphate
(*couperose*), hemp, elephant teeth, tallow, and small hand tools. As
was true for imports from all other countries, the ships bringing
goods from Holland were compelled to take out French products
of equal or greater value.

The net result of all these special and not-so-special permissions for importations from Holland was that thousands of Dutch vessels came to France during the war years. J. S. Bromley has tabulated the figures for Bayonne (and surrounding ports), Bordeaux, La Rochelle, Nantes, and Saint-Malo, and has shown that for the years 1702–12 more than 4,000 Dutch ships came to these ports.[93] Bordeaux especially welcomed Dutch ships, which came to take out wine and brandy. In each of the years 1706–7, more than 500 such vessels entered its port. Dutch ships also frequented France's northern ports, but we do not as yet have statistics to document the volume of this traffic. Although historians may argue about the general state of the Dutch economy early in the eighteenth century, Dutch trade with France generally prospered, thanks to the myriad French passports.[94]

The trade war against Holland was weakened in other ways as well. Throughout the war the tax farmers of the *gabelles*, as well as the directors of Asiento company and the tobacco company, occasionally used Dutch vessels to transport their goods from one French port to another. This was done because French ships would easily have fallen prey to the English and Dutch privateers that plied the French coast. The Council of Commerce did not like the idea of using Dutch bottoms—because of the boost it gave to Dutch navigation—but it generally relented and approved the passports.[95]

For similar reasons the council decided in 1710 to permit a few Dutch ships to go to Canada and buy beaver skins from the French Beaver Company,[96] which was heavily in debt and needed an outlet for its product. Threats from enemy corsairs made the journey too dangerous for French ships.

The council, however, opposed the granting of passports to Dutch vessels to go to the French West Indies.[97] Jérôme de Pontchartrain was always concerned about the problem of supplying the colonists there with the food they needed; but enemy privateers made the crossing from France to the islands hazardous, and the poor harvests of 1709 made the export of provisions out of the question in that year and in the following one. Throughout the war numerous Dutch merchants requested the right to carry food to the French colonies. The Council of Commerce, however, seems to have preferred that the colonists starve rather than that foreign ships be permitted to trade with the French islands; but Pontchartrain overrode this objection and granted several such passports to Dutch vessels.[98]

The council also failed to prevent Dutch ships from sailing

to Marseilles. That city's deputy, Mathieu Fabre, argued that Marseilles's traders needed to acquire from Holland various raw materials for the manufactures of Provence as well as spices, cloths, and small manufactured goods that would then be traded in the Levant. The other deputies opposed this. If Dutch vessels received passports to go to Marseilles, they could stop to trade with Portugal, the rebel Spanish provinces, and other parts of the Mediterranean, and their passports would serve to protect them from French privateers. Marseilles's influence at court prevailed, however, and a handful of Dutch ships were permitted to go there from 1706 to 1708.[99]

Even after it had become obvious that France could not survive without Dutch trade, the Council of Commerce vainly sought to hurt the Dutch in other ways. After the fall of much of the Spanish Netherlands to the enemy in the summer of 1706, France declared the captured areas to be enemy territory and therefore subject to the same trade restrictions as was Holland.[100] The council had hoped thereby to stamp out the illicit Franco-Dutch trade passing through Flanders. Even in peacetime that area always had been notorious as a nest for smugglers.

In addition, the council eased trade restrictions with other enemy nations in the hope that their competition would cut into the Dutch share of the market. Beginning in 1706, the council decided to stimulate a limited amount of commerce with Germany and Portugal (which perforce had switched to the allied side in 1703). Coming overland from Germany, such metal goods as awls, scythes, files, sword blades, and certain types of thread (such as *fil de Cologne, fil d'or*) were henceforth permitted to enter France.[101] Portuguese merchants were allowed to send certain fruits and oils, as well as goat skins, sumac, dyes, and a few other types of raw materials used in French manufactures.[102]

As noted above, in 1706 the council also permitted trade with Ireland and Scotland, and early in 1707 it encouraged the granting of passports to Englishmen. Although the council wished to hurt England's trade just as much as Holland's, it would much rather have granted passports freely to English ships. Unfortunately, however, the English government officially forbade trade with France, whereas the merchant republic to the north encouraged it. The council's preference for England is easy to explain: the English, unlike *ces républicains*, did not appear to be trying to capture all the world's commerce for themselves. In addition, the English were not afraid to pay a high price for the goods they bought in France "because they are less thrifty and perform trade more nobly than the Dutch."[103]

Ironically, the Council of Commerce was accused in 1708 of being too soft on Holland. An anonymous memoir submitted to the council on 22 August 1708 charged not only that it had done nothing to stimulate French trade but that it had in no way hurt the commerce of the Dutch.[104] The memoir was referred to the deputies, who on 14 September presented a memoir rebutting the charges.[105] The deputies were clearly angered by what they considered groundless, irresponsible accusations. They pointed to the work the council had performed in reforming French tariffs and in facilitating the free flow of goods within the country, and they also mentioned the difficulties of stimulating trade during wartime. But they were particularly incensed by the charge that the council had done "no damage to Dutch trade." They noted the steps that the council had taken to promote trade with neutrals as well as with other enemy nations. All of this had been designed to hurt Dutch trade. The deputies noted further that they had supported the 1703 cut-off of trade with Holland. It was not the council but rather French merchants who campaigned to reopen the commerce with the republic. The deputies charged that most French merchants were lazy: they preferred to purchase goods from "these bold republicans" rather than seek out the goods themselves in their places of origin. The deputies pointed out that at least the council had stood firm against permitting the entry of spices and fish from Holland—the two trades that occupied more than one-third of Dutch citizens. By cutting these articles off from the French market, the deputies were confident that at least some significant damage was being inflicted on that nation's economy.

Despite this ringing defense of the council's actions, one gets the impression from reading the deputies' reply that they in part agreed with the anonymous memoir's allegation that the trade war against Holland was a complete failure. It was perhaps this realization that spurred the council, and the government as a whole, in 1709 to reconsider another cut-off of trade with Holland. The deputies of commerce had since 1705 consistently urged that trade with the Dutch be restrained to as narrow a limit as possible. It had been the *commissaires* who generally took a less doctrinaire position; they were concerned lest French manufacturers and wine producers lack the raw materials or the markets that they needed.[106]

Late in 1709, however, the council as a whole seemed to agree that something was necessary to bring the Dutch to their knees.

Perhaps the *commissaires* and deputies were infused by the hearty resolve that filled many of their countrymen that year. Several things occurred in 1709 to give Frenchmen pride and to instill in them a sense of daring. First of all, most of them had had to endure poor harvests and a fierce winter and yet had survived.[107] Second, the crown had firmly rejected the humiliating peace terms proposed by the Dutch in the peace preliminaries at The Hague in June 1709. Third, French armies had given excellent accounts of themselves in the battles of the Rhine (August) and Malplaquet (September). Finally, the Dutch showed "alarming signs of weakness" late in 1709:[108] several provinces clamored for acceptance of French peace proposals.

Whatever the reason, the council began, in August 1709, to consider proposals to cut off all trade with Holland. The first such proposal was submitted by a man named Sossiondo, a French official stationed in Amsterdam and charged with supervising the exchange of prisoners of war between France and Holland.[109] Sossiondo wrote to Pontchartrain in June 1709, recommending that either France cut off all trade with Holland or that the Dutch be compelled to permit French ships to enter their ports (throughout the war Holland had insisted that all Franco-Dutch commerce take place in Dutch vessels). The deputies of commerce, to whom the letter had been submitted, replied on 9 August that the two alternatives were equally impossible.[110] Concerning the first suggestion, they noted how French merchants and manufacturers in 1704 had overturned the earlier attempt to do without Dutch trade; and the deputies ruefully acknowledged that indeed the country did depend on Dutch navigation. As to the second proposal, the deputies pointed out that even if the Dutch agreed to it, English privateers would seize French merchant ships before they could ever reach Holland.

But the matter was not permitted to rest. In October 1709 Duguay, intendant of the navy at Dunkirk, likewise proposed that all commerce with the Dutch be ruptured.[111] The Council of Commerce this time decided that the matter needed a complete review, and letters were sent to all provincial intendants in areas that traded heavily with Holland.[112] The council wished to know, with as much assurance as possible, whether the French economy could survive without the carrying trade of its northern neighbor.

During the first eight months of 1710, the council continued to study this question but was unable to come to a decision. It was concerned lest French manufactures starve for lack of raw materials and agricultural regions suffocate under the weight of their unsold wine, brandy, honey, salt, and other products. The council also feared that any hostile French action against Dutch trade would lead Amsterdam bankers to cut off their money market to French bills of exchange. The *commissaires* and the deputies also examined the question of whether France could further liberalize trade regulations with other enemy powers and with neutrals, thereby compensating for the loss of Dutch trade.

Throughout the months of debate on the issue, the council reversed itself on several occasions. Sometimes a majority favored the cut-off, sometimes not. If the council had been completely free to decide, it probably would not have elected to reestablish the prohibition on trade with Holland. With the resumption of the Northern War in 1709, the number of Swedish and Danish ships coming to France had slowed to a dribble, and France seemed to need Dutch navigation more than ever. On 30 May 1710 the council once again rejected the notion of revoking all passports to the Dutch,[113] but both the controller general and the secretary of state for the navy insisted that the council continue to reconsider this question. Jérôme de Pontchartrain wished to give a boost to the French *guerre de course* by allowing privateers to feast on the thousands of Dutch merchant vessels plying European coastal waters.[114] On 21 June 1710 Desmaretz informed Daguesseau that the Council of Finances had agreed that a total suppression of passports to the Dutch "could produce an effect all the more advantageous in that by troubling its commerce it would make that Republic feel the inconveniences of war."[115]

On 11 July 1710 the Council of Commerce therefore drew up a lengthy memoir on this issue to be submitted to the king.[116] It listed several reasons why commerce with the Dutch should be discontinued. No other nation in the universe, said the memoir, would be hurt so much as Holland by loss of its commerce, which was for it "an absolute necessity." The revocation of passports to their ships would mean that the Dutch would have to resort to costly convoys to protect their trade from French privateers. Also, France did not need to worry so much at that time about how to send out its agricultural surpluses; after the poor harvests of 1709, there was little left of anything to be exported. The council followed these arguments by repeating the traditional argument for continuing trade with Holland, but it agreed that these factors now had to give way to the political and military imperative of bringing the Dutch into total submission.

By the late summer of 1710, virtually all the *commissaires* and deputies had made up their minds to support once again a total ban on commerce with the republic.[117] The crucial step was finally taken on 19 November 1710: the ordinance issued on that date stopped the issuance of all passports to the Dutch and severed all ties between that nation and France.[118] It should be remarked that this ordinance was drafted by Daguesseau and several deputies of trade.[119]

NEW FAVORS GRANTED TO OTHER NATIONS

To compensate for the loss of Dutch ships, the council hoped to stimulate commerce with the rest of Europe, including both neutral and enemy powers. From December 1710 to April 1711, it drafted a series of *arrêts* aimed at achieving that result. The chart in the Appendix clearly reveals how the question of trade with neutral and non-Dutch enemy powers came to occupy more and more of the council's time in 1711.

France relied chiefly on the neutral states to make up for the loss of Dutch trade. To this effect the council helped draft the *arrêt* of 30 December 1710, which was intended to encourage northern neutrals to send their ships to France.[120] The list of goods that Denmark and Sweden could bring into France was enlarged to include nearly one hundred types of items.[121] Also, Danish and Swedish ships were exempted from paying the 50-sous duty on any of these goods; formerly this tax had been removed only for certain products. What is more, all Danish and Swedish vessels were henceforth freed from the often troublesome obligation of taking out of France an equivalent value of French merchandise.

The Italian neutral states were likewise invited to increase their trade with France. At the behest of Venice and Genoa, an *arrêt* was issued on 28 April 1711 declaring that the benefits of the *arrêt* of 30 December 1710 applied to all neutral ships, not just those of the North.[122] Italians were therefore exempted from the 50-sous tax and from taking out the irksome equivalent of goods entering France. Further, the list of goods that Italians could bring to France was extended to comprise eighteen other sorts of products, all of which were produced in Italy. As always, Italian and other neutral ships were prohibited from stopping in enemy ports on their way either to or from France.

In addition to encouraging neutral traffic, the council endeavored to stimulate business with France's enemies as well—all in the hope of ruining Dutch trade. On 30 December 1710 it drew up a new *état* of things permitted from England.[123] As noted above, the council since 1707 had encouraged English ships to come to France; they were permitted to bring wool, coal, lead, and a few other items. The new *état*, however, included more than ninety types of goods, including many that had been prohibited in the *arrêt* of 6 September 1701. In addition, the exorbitant import duties of the 1701 *arrêt* were set aside for the remainder of the war, and the English had to pay only the duties paid by most other nations. The English, however, still were obliged to pay the 50-sous-per-ton duty and to take out an equivalent value of French goods. Furthermore, English manufactures continued to be banned in France.

Despite the fact that their government still prohibited them from trading with France, English shippers increasingly braved the channel crossing in order to trade with the enemy. Franco-British trade grew even more after the Parliament in London, on 15 March 1711, passed a bill permitting neutral vessels to bring French wines to England.[124] These wines still were subject to the high import duties set up in the 1690s, but many Englishmen were becoming so tired of inferior—or at least unfamiliar—Portuguese, Spanish, and Italian wines that they were willing to pay the higher prices for the French product.

In June 1711 the Council of Commerce decided that this step by the British Parliament was sufficiently friendly toward France to merit an equally favorable response. Once again the council compared English traders favorably to the Dutch, noting that

> no nation in the world trades more nobly. That is a truth generally recognized in every place where the English go. They spend a lot of money, thereby causing prices of goods and merchandises to rise. They seek out the most expensive and the most perfect articles. This is just the opposite of the Dutch, who live very frugally, accustom themselves to thriftiness and pay less attention to good quality than to a low price.[125]

The council therefore decided that neutral ships would henceforth be allowed to bring to France from England all the items that

English ships themselves were permitted to bring; these ships would still, however, have to take out an equivalent value of French goods. This was a breach in the *arrêt* of 23 July 1704, which had said that neutral vessels could come to France only from a neutral or an allied port.

It soon proved to be a wise decision by the council, for there were many—perhaps hundreds—of Danish, Swedish, and Polish ships that were reluctant to return to their native lands, lest they be taken prize by one side or another in the Northern War. These ships were now able to partake in the growing Franco-English trade.

The council did not actually expand the lists of things that Scotland, Ireland, Portugal, and Germany could send to France, but it did reaffirm the privileges that it had already granted to traders from these nations. In December 1710 the council drew up *états* summarizing the types of merchandise from these nations for which passports would be granted.[126]

Perhaps the most significant step taken by the council in 1711 in an effort to bypass the Dutch was the move to widen trade with the Hanseatic cities of Hamburg, Bremen, and Lübeck. The outbreak of war in the North and the revocation of Dutch passports meant that Danish, Swedish, and Dutch ships would no longer be bringing to France the timber, naval stores, metals, and agricultural products that the country needed. France therefore hoped to get them from the Hanseatic ports. In December 1710 the council drew up an *état* that expanded from about a dozen to more than ninety the items that these cities could bring to France.[127] Although ships from these cities would still be required to obtain French passports, they were exempted from the 50-sous-per-ton duty and from the obligation of taking out an equivalent value of French goods. Strict regulations were established to ensure that ships or cargoes coming from these cities were not actually coming from Holland.

The council also opened up a limited trade with other Baltic areas that formerly could not send ships to France.[128] In part this was done because the Northern War prevented many Swedish and Danish vessels from coming to France. Areas that were formerly regarded as belligerent were now declared to be neutral. Thus the Danish duchy of Holstein-Gottorp, technically a part of the empire, now received all the privileges accorded to Denmark itself. Other areas to which the council granted neutral status in 1711 included Danzig,[129] Königsberg, and Rostock.[130] The latter two cities belonged, respectively, to the duke of Brandenburg and to the duke of Mecklenburg.

This liberalization of trade with various European nations, coupled with the prohibition of trade with Holland, was not, however, a complete success from the French standpoint. Immediately following the publication of the ordinance of 19 November 1710, there were grumblings about it. Bordeaux merchants were quick to complain that without the Dutch they would never be able to sell all of their stocks of wines and brandy.[131] The result was that in 1711 and 1712 a limited number of passports were granted to Dutch ships to bring a small variety of goods to France. J. S. Bromley records that in 1711 a total of 103 Dutch ships entered the ports of Bordeaux, Nantes, and Saint-Malo, whereas only one entered in 1712 (at Nantes.)[132] The 1711 figure is misleading, however, for many of these ships came to France by virtue of passports issued prior to the ordinance of 19 November 1710. The 1712 figure, though accurate for the three ports mentioned here, does not include the handful of Dutch vessels that entered other ports during that year.

Ironically enough, it was Jérôme de Pontchartrain, the man who had campaigned hardest to prohibit trade with Holland, who was the first to dilute the interdiction. Late in November 1710, and at several other points during the next two years, he granted special passports to Dutch vessels to bring various naval stores to Rochefort and other French arsenals.[133]

Pontchartrain's example was followed by others. In February 1711 the royal tobacco monopoly complained that it would go bankrupt unless it could refurbish its supplies of the commodity. In that same month, the company obtained passports for three Dutch ships to bring tobacco to France.[134] A few passports were likewise granted to bring small manufactured items, cloths, and metals from Holland for use in the African slave trade, but French port authorities took strong precautions to guarantee that none of these goods entered France.[135] In 1711 a few individuals received permission to import from Holland, by land, certain types of yarn needed for manufactures.[136]

These permissions for trade with Holland made the trade embargo less than absolute; but even though several dozen Dutch ships did come to France during this period, this was a sharp decline from the thousands of Dutch ships that had crowded French ports in previous years. There can be little doubt that the republic was hurt by the reversal of French policy. The frantic attempts of the Dutch in 1711 and 1712 to disguise their ships as Danish, Swedish, or Hanseatic testify to the impact that the ordinance of November 1710 had on their economy.[137]

The influence that the trade embargo had on bringing the Dutch to the conference table has yet to be fully documented: historians of the peace negotiations have generally overlooked this question. The Council of Commerce, at any rate, worked hard to uphold the ban on trade with the republic. In December 1711, at the moment when the French plenipotentiaries were preparing to leave for Utrecht, the council reaffirmed its confidence in the fact that this ban had been decisive in compelling Holland to seek an end to hostilities.[138]

The apparent success of the embargo on trade with the Dutch was probably one factor that led to the ban on trade with the empire in 1713–14. After the various treaties were signed at Utrecht in April 1713, the empire—having refused to participate in the peace congress—remained as France's sole enemy. Treaties between these two powers were signed in 1714 at Rastadt (March) and Baden (September). With the support of the Council of Commerce, France cut off all trade with the German states (except those considered to be neutral) from August 1713 to June 1714.[139]

ENFORCEMENT OF TRADE POLICIES

The bulk of this chapter has been devoted to an analysis of French commercial policy during the war and to the role of the Council of Commerce in shaping it, but the picture would be incomplete without looking briefly at the means by which these policies were enforced. There were two basic ways of doing this: one was bureaucratic or legal; the other was military, by means of French privateers.

Not only did the Council of Commerce decide what merchandise neutrals or enemies could bring to France, but it helped formulate all the other regulations concerning commerce during the war. The council, for example, helped establish the form of the passports needed for trade with the enemy. Merchants from hostile states had to go through a French partner or *commissionnaire* (broker), who formally requested the passport. To obtain one, the Frenchman had to sign a surety (*soumission*), obliging him to pay a large fine if the foreign ship somehow violated the terms of its passport. Generally these sureties amounted to 3,000 livres per 100 tons of vessel. Passports were usually valid for a period of five (sometimes six) months from date of issue. Thus a Dutch ship that had a passport dated 1 January usually had to arrive in France by 1 May. The same passport would protect the ship on its return journey, with no time limits set for that. Each passport also specified the cargo that the ship would bring as well as the name of the French port of destination.

If any of these and other conditions were violated, the surety had to be paid. More serious infractions could lead to confiscation of a ship by a French privateer. Such infractions might include the carrying of contraband or the use of a passport to carry on trade from one French port to another.

Throughout the war the council deliberated hundreds of cases involving real or supposed violations by enemy ships of their passports. Often an enemy ship would not go to the French port listed in its passport. Poor weather or unfavorable winds could, for example, force a ship to put in at La Rochelle rather than at Bordeaux. Another frequent violation involved ships bringing merchandises not listed in their passports and perhaps not even included on the list of goods permitted to enter from the ship's home country. In such cases the council had to decide whether an honest mistake had been made or if actual fraud had been intended.

The most frequent complaint against enemy (especially Dutch) ships was either that they arrived in France after the expiration date of their passports or that they failed to arrive in France at all. There could be several reasons for this: unavoidable delays in the outfitting of a ship in its port of departure, poor weather conditions, loss of the ship at sea. What most concerned Pontchartrain, however, was that hundreds of Dutch vessels were obviously using their French passports to protect them while they traded with Baltic countries and with England; only later would they come to France—if at all. This illicit trade was depriving the French *guerre de course* of many of its prey. Technically, the French merchants who had put up the sureties for these enemy ships were obliged to pay them to the *trésorier* of the navy, but the merchants complained that if they were obliged to do so they would be forced into bankruptcy.

By 1707 there were literally hundreds of cases pending in the admiralty courts concerning violations or inexecution of passports. In order to expedite the hearing of these disputes, an *arrêt* was issued on 6 August 1707 designating the *commissaires* of the Council of Commerce as the sole judges in all cases involving inexecution of passports.[140] From that date to the end of the war, the council devoted a hefty portion of its time to deciding these suits. They are not generally recorded in its *procès-verbaux*, but other evidence testifies to the hard work of the council in this regard. We know, for example, that at one point Intendant of Commerce Amelot de Chaillou had as many as eighty such cases for which he was charged with leading the examination.[141]

Generally the council tended to side with the French merchants. It often decided that they did not have to pay a surety if they were not part of the fraud devised by the Dutch traders who had obtained the passports (or if legitimate reasons for the late arrival of a ship could be proven). With the interests of French privateers at heart, Jérôme de Pontchartrain usually urged a harsher stand against all abuses of passports, but he abided by the council's decisions.[142]

Another aspect of wartime trade with which the council was intimately involved was the system of the equivalent. As has been mentioned before, every neutral or enemy ship entering France during the war was obliged to take out an amount of French goods equal to, or greater in value than, the goods it brought into the country. Although this practice had been enforced somewhat in the War of the League of Augsburg,[143] the Council of Commerce defended it with relentless insistence. In their general memoirs of 1700–1701, the deputies had already expressed their concern for establishing a balance of commerce, which would prevent gold and silver from escaping the country. The outbreak of hostilities gave them a perfect opportunity to put it into practice.

In the early years of the war, the system was rather flexible. If a foreign ship could not find enough French goods in the port where it entered, it could return at a later date to obtain them or it could go to another port to purchase them. Many times it was physically impossible to send out the equivalent on the same ship. French exports were often bulk items (agricultural products) that required more space than an equivalent value of incoming goods. Whereas one ship might bring a cargo of wool, cheese, and dyes to France, two ships (or one larger ship) might be needed to take out an equal value of French wine, salt, and grains. In such cases a second ship was permitted to carry out all or part of the equivalent.

As a guarantee that the equivalent went out, the ship's captain signed a surety agreement obliging him to take out the equivalent within a certain time limit (usually three months). This system was, however, open to many abuses. The ships that went from one port to another to obtain the equivalent frequently ended up transporting French goods from port to port. As has been noted above, this practice was illegal because of its detrimental impact on small French coastal shippers. When a ship delayed taking out the equivalent until a later date or when it went to another port to get it, this caused a large amount of paperwork. The confusion that often ensued made it impossible to check to see that the equivalent eventually did go out.

The council was aware of these abuses, and in October 1708 it acted to stop them.[144] A majority of deputies agreed that henceforth all foreign traders should be obliged to take out the equivalent in the same ship and from the same port. The deputies from Rouen, Dunkirk, and Paris, however, vehemently opposed this proposal.[145] These cities imported great quantities of raw materials for their manufactures, but they had relatively fewer things to export. Thus these cities always had great difficulty in fulfilling the equivalency requirements, and they generally sent foreign ships to other ports to obtain all or part of their cargoes of French goods. But the other deputies supported the measure—in particular the deputies from Nantes, La Rochelle, and Bordeaux. Having rich agricultural hinterlands, these ports never had any trouble in sending out the equivalent. They argued that the same-ship, same-port requirement was the only way to stem the abuses committed by both enemy and neutral ships. The latter argument held sway in the council, and the controller general ordered the farmers general to enforce the new measure.[146]

Economic and political necessities, however, compelled the council to modify the equivalency system later in the war. After the disastrous harvests of 1709, the council waived the equivalency requirement for all grains that foreign ships brought to France.[147] When the council acted, late in 1710, to revive its trade war against Holland, it decided to exempt neutral ships altogether from the obligation of taking out the equivalent. The *arrêts* of 30 December 1710 and 28 April 1711 included this exemption along with the other above-mentioned inducements to neutral nations.

It is interesting to note that throughout the war the council vigorously defended its restrictive bullionist position on the "equivalent" question, despite the complaints against it by foreign ship-

pers and the immense problems involved in enforcing it. Only the
disastrous harvests of 1709 and the French desire to wreck the
Dutch economy finally persuaded the government to sacrifice,
temporarily, its desire to establish a favorable balance of commerce.

The French *guerre de course* was the second means by which the
government enforced its trade policies. The *arrêts, états,* and other
regulations that, on the one hand, defined the limits of neutral and
enemy commerce had the obverse effect of outlining the rights of
the French privateers.

Thanks to the work of J. S. Bromley, we now know that the
French *guerre de course* had a far greater impact on allied commerce
than had heretofore been realized.[148] During the war the daring
corsairs from Dunkirk, Saint-Malo, and other ports captured
nearly seven thousand enemy and neutral vessels.[149] The depredations that these privateers inflicted on English shipping were so
great that London merchants nearly rioted in 1707, and virtually
forced the Parliament in that year to issue the Cruisers and Convoy
Act.[150] Among other things, this law declared that henceforth no
fewer than forty-three English ships of war were at all times to
cruise along the English coast in order to ward off French privateers.

The point to be made here is that virtually all the laws and
regulations issued by the crown to regulate or encourage the *guerre
de course* were first deliberated in the Council of Commerce. There
were two basic issues involved in the effort to aid privateers. The
first surrounded the question of what constituted a valid prize ship.
By the *arrêt* of 23 July 1704, the council defined the nature and the
rights of neutral ships. If any ships from neutral nations violated
the provisions of this *arrêt,* they forfeited their rights. French privateers therefore confiscated several hundred such vessels during
the war. All enemy ships were valid prizes, unless, of course, they
carried French or Spanish passports, but even these ships could be
seized if in some way they violated their passports.

A second question concerned the sale of prize goods in France. If
the French *armateurs* were to profit from their investments, they
needed a ready market for the merchandise brought to France in
captured ships. But the interests of privateers clashed with two
other cherished aims of the Council of Commerce: protection of
French manufactures from foreign competition and an end to
dependence on goods from enemy nations. The council's solution

to this conflict of goals was not easily achieved. Throughout the war it struggled to satisfy both sides.

Due to the insistent urging of Jérôme de Pontchartrain, the council drafted several *arrêts* that facilitated the sale of prize goods. The *arrêt* of 20 June 1702 established the basic policy of the crown in this regard.[151] All foreign textiles and other manufactures as well as tobacco that entered on prize ships could be sold, but generally on the condition that they be exported out of the country. If necessary, such goods received a complete tax exemption for their passage overland through France on their way to their foreign destination. With regard to goods for which entry and consumption in France were permitted, import duties were reduced. English goods entering on prize ships therefore did not have to pay the elevated duties called for in the *arrêt* of 6 September 1701. The *arrêt* of 20 June 1702 also established the principle that whatever items a foreign nation could export to France during the war could also enter France on prize ships. The list of goods that could enter on prize ships thus fluctuated as commercial policies with respect to enemy and neutral nations changed in the course of the war.

The *arrêts* of 24 March 1703, 25 November 1705, 9 July 1709, and 29 April 1710[152] reaffirmed or broadened the advantages given to privateers by the 1702 *arrêt*. The *arrêt* of 9 July 1709 was especially important in this regard: it declared that many foreign textiles that entered on prize ships could now for the first time be sold and used in France, paying reduced import duties. The only textiles whose sale was still prohibited in France were expensive luxury fabrics as well as silks and printed cottons from the Far East and the Levant.

This chapter has endeavored to illustrate the role of the Council of Commerce in directing French commercial policies during the War of the Spanish Succession, but it has not tried to assess the ultimate success of any of these policies. To do that would require years of research on the trade of every nation in Europe. Nor has it discussed the changes made in France's wartime policies during the commercial and peace negotiations of 1712–14; these will be touched upon briefly in a later chapter.

The council, and the government as a whole, viewed this war as an opportunity to damage the commerce of France's adversaries. The deputies, who in 1700 had spoken eloquently of the need for reciprocal, unlimited international trade, became the strongest advocates of a trade war against England and the Dutch Republic.

If Colbert had been alive, very probably he would have warmly applauded the policies advocated by the council.

1. See the chart in the Appendix.

2. Their many works on this topic are listed in the Bibliography.

3. French trading policies during the war are discussed very briefly and sometimes erroneously in Henri Sée, "Notes sur le commerce des ennemis en France pendant la guerre de la succession d'Espagne."

4. See Sir George N. Clark, *The Dutch Alliance and the War against French Trade, 1688–1697.*

5. For an introduction to this subject, see Gaston Zeller, "Le Commerce international en temps de guerre sous l'ancien régime," reprinted in Gaston Zeller, *Aspects de la politique française sous l'ancien régime,* pp. 185–96.

6. Clark, *Dutch Alliance,* pp. 22 ff.

7. Ibid., pp. 92 ff; Ragnhild Hatton, "Gratifications and Foreign Policy," p. 85.

8. Contraband was normally defined as military supplies or equipment of any sort, as well as timber and naval stores. Neutral ships were always prohibited from going port to port in a belligerent country. Thus, for example, a Swedish ship going from London to Bristol or from Nantes to Saint-Malo was subject to seizure by the privateers of one side or the other. Such port-to-port traffic, if permitted, would have enabled a country to transport its own goods from province to province without danger of enemy attack. In order to prevent France from importing needed food supplies, the Atlantic powers added grains to the list of contraband items in 1693–94 and 1709–10.

9. Clark, *Dutch Alliance,* p. 62.

10. Jonathan Webster, "The Merchants of Bordeaux in Trade to the French West Indies, 1664–1717," pp. 279 ff.

11. Clark estimates that the English and the Dutch together lost about the same number of ships to privateers as did France—between 900 and 1,000. He insists, however, that the commerce of the allied powers suffered much less from the *guerre de course* than did that of France. He calculates that the total value of French prizes captured by Dutch and English privateers was approximately £543,000 (£100,000 for the Dutch and £443,000 for the English). The English pound at that time was worth approximately 18 French livres. Multiplying 543,000 by 18, one arrives at 9,774,000 livres. Clark's figures, in ships and in money, are probably much too low (*Dutch Alliance,* pp. 61–62, 128). Symcox evaluates the role of French privateers much more favorably, though he is quick to point out the limitations of the *guerre de course.* He estimates that the total value of prize ships taken by French corsairs may have exceeded 100 million livres (*The Crisis of French Sea Power,* pp. 222–26). Likewise, David Ogg cites figures which show that French privateers did more damage to allied shipping than their English and Dutch counterparts did to that of France (*England in the Reigns of James II and William III,* pp. 296–99). On French trade policies during the war, see Webster, "The Merchants of Bordeaux," pp. 279–342; Rambert, *Histoire du commerce de Marseille,* 7:658; AN, F^{12} 125, fol. 49v, Daguesseau to Desmaretz, 30 August 1708.

12. On Franco-English commercial relations late in the seventeenth century, see Clément, *Histoire du système protecteur,* pp. 47–49; Cole, *French Mercantilism, 1683–1700,* pp. 12–14; Webster, "The Merchants of Bordeaux," pp. 283 ff.; Viviane

Barrie, "La Prohibition du commerce avec la France dans la politique anglaise à la fin du XVIIe siècle"; AN, F¹² 125, fol. 49v, Daguesseau to Desmaretz, 30 August 1708; Mar., B⁷ 500, fols. 43–67, various memoirs on this subject.

13. The figures on English trade kept by England's inspector general of commerce reveal how small the volume of Anglo-French trade actually was. From Michaelmas (29 September) of 1697 to Michaelmas 1698, England's exports to, and its imports from, France were worth £61,441 and £48,806 respectively. Corresponding figures for some other countries follow: Germany (£694,349 and £525,734); Holland (£1,507,177 and £649,348); Spain (£580,499 and £354,164); Spanish Flanders (£547,033 and £81,741); see Newberry Library, Case, Manuscript H 7045.372, "An Abstract of the Inspect.ʳ Gen.ˡˡˢ accounts of import.ˢ and export.ˢ from Mich.ˢ 1697 to Mich.ˢ 1698." Of course, there was much illicit Anglo-French trade, but it would be impossible to estimate its extent. Despite official proscriptions, many Englishmen smuggled raw wool from their country to France. Many Frenchmen, on the other hand, secretly conveyed wines, brandies, silks, and other goods into England. On this subject see Henri Sée, "Aperçu sur la contrebande en Bretagne au XVIIIe siècle," in Hayem, *Mémoires et documents*, 9:227 ff.

14. See, for example, AN, G⁷ 1686, Tallard to Chamillart, 28 April 1700.

15. Neutral ships did not require passports, but they had to follow the rules set down by the council (these will be described below). All enemy ships had to obtain passports before coming to France.

16. The correspondence concerning all these affairs can be found in AN, G⁷ 1686–1704 and Mar., series B² and B³, passim. Many of the original *placets* by French merchants for trade with the enemy or neutrals can be found in AN, F¹² 646, 799A, 1903, 1908, 1910, 1920–24, 1933A. Only a small minority of these requests receive special mention in the *procès-verbaux* of the Council of Commerce.

17. The process of issuing passports was rather complex. After the Council of Commerce had determined a policy concerning trade with another state, merchants' requests that fell within this policy did not need to go to the council for approval. Rather, the controller general usually sent them directly to the *premier commis* in his ministry who was charged with supervising their expedition. Under both Chamillart and Desmaretz, this man was de la Garde. He worked closely with the Council of Commerce, and he could quickly approve a passport if it was within the guidelines already set down by the council. He recorded every such passport in a register (which, unfortunately, has not been preserved). Once de la Garde recorded a passport, he sent it to the *premier commis* in the naval ministry who was charged with drawing up the final copy. Until 1710 this man was Des Haguais; on him see Chapter 2, n. 24. In 1710 Des Haguais retired and was succeeded by Fontanieu. Sometimes passport requests were sent directly to Des Haguais or Fontanieu, who also worked closely with the Council of Commerce. They had each passport signed by Jérôme de Pontchartrain and the comte de Toulouse. They then sent it back to de la Garde, who had the controller general initial it. Finally, the passports were returned to the naval secretary, who dispatched them to the person or persons who had requested them. For some illustrations of de la Garde's activities, see AN, G⁷ 1692, piece 123, Desmaretz to de la Garde, 13 May 1711; piece 124, de la Garde to Desmaretz, 23 May 1711; piece 258, Anisson to Desmaretz, 26 October 1711. On Des Haguais see Mar., B⁷ 506, "M. de Richebourg, contestation entre le secrétaire d'état de la marine, et le controlleur général des finances au sujet des passeports," dated 10 December 1710; B² 191, fol. 292, Pontchartrain to Fénellon, 15 September 1706; B² 199, p. 743, Pontchartrain to Des Haguais, 16 November 1707. Daguesseau's importance in the decisions as to what was permitted to enter by passport is reflected in his letters to Pontchartrain and the farmers general, which are preserved in AN, F¹², 121–22.

18. Communication with the farmers general was usually done through the director of commerce (Daguesseau or Amelot). Consult the "Etats des expéditions concernant le commerce et les manufactures" (see Chapter 2, n. 56) and AN, F[12] 122–25[A].

19. A copy is in AN, F[12] 694.

20. Clark, "War Trade and Trade War, 1701–1713," p. 268.

21. AN, F[12] 51, fols. 50–50v.

22. Ibid., fols. 52v–53.

23. The names of the deputies who were in each faction are not provided.

24. See Douglas Coombs, *The Conduct of the Dutch: British Opinion and the Dutch Alliance during the War of the Spanish Succession*, pp. 41–84; G. N. Clark, "War Trade and Trade War" pp. 271–73.

25. A copy is in AN, F[12] 1933[A]; also see BN, MSS. fr., 21776, fols. 159–60.

26. A copy can be found in AN, F[12] 1924.

27. See AN, F[12] 1921, "Avis de Mrs les députez du commerce sur la proposition su Sr Gordon banquier à Paris pour la continuation du commerce en Angleterre, Ecosse, Irlande et Hollande pendant la guerre," 23 August 1702; F[12] 51, fols. 168–69.

28. See the *arrêt* of 24 March 1703, articles 2–4, in Sylvain Lebeau (ed.), *Nouveau code des Prises*, 1:268–69.

29. See AN, F[12] 51, fols. 137–38; Mar., B[2] 162, fols. 318v–321, Pontchartrain to Chamillart, 2 August 1702; ibid., fols. 398–98v, Pontchartrain to Fénellon, 9 August 1702; B[3] 119, fol. 209, Chamillart to Pontchartrain, 3 August 1702.

30. Concerning the many Irish immigrants residing in French ports, see Ragnhild Hatton, *Louis XIV and His World*, p. 94; J. S. Bromley, "The Jacobite Privateers in the Nine Years War"; Claude Nordmann, "Louis XIV and the Jacobites," in Hatton, *Louis XIV and Europe*, p. 95.

31. AN, F[12] 54, fols. 178–79; F[12] 55, fol. 41v.

32. AN, F[12] 51, fols. 338, 349–49v 432–32v; F[12] 55, fol. 4; F[12] 121, fol. 73v, Chamillart to Pontchartrain, 26 September 1705.

33. AN, F[12] 51, fols. 462–64; F[12] 1903, "Etat des marchandises qui pourront être apportées en France d'Angleterre, Ecosse, Irelande, Hambourg et autres ennemis qui ont reçu les avocatoires de l'Empereur, de Portugal, et par terre en vertu des passeports qui seront accordés par la Roy;" AN, G[7] 1687, piece 167, *états* of goods permitted from various countries; G[7] 1692, fol. 259, *avis* of deputies; G[7] 1695, piece 287, "Estat des marchandises d'Irlande."

34. AN, F[12] 1903, "Etat des marchandises qui pourront être apportées en France"; G[7] 1687, piece 167; G[7] 1695, piece 288, "Estat des marchandises d'Ecosse."

35. J. S. Bromley has tabulated some figures concerning this traffic ("Le Commerce de la France de l'ouest," p. 64 n. 68). For the years 1707–10, Irish ships with passports entered three French ports in the following numbers: 174 (Bordeaux), 164 (La Rochelle), 164 (Nantes). From 1702 to 1712, 387 Irish and 109 Scottish ships entered Bordeaux with passports.

36. Meeting of 19 November 1706, AN, F[12] 51, fol. 464v.

37. Meeting of 26 November 1706, AN, F[12] 51, fols. 465v–66.

38. Mar., B[2] 196, pp. 864–65, Pontchartrain to Daguesseau, 19 February 1707.

39. BN, MSS. fr., 14294, fols. 80–82, "Sentiment des députez au conseil de commerce, sur les passeports demandez par des négocians anglois;" AN, F[12] 54, fols. 8v–11, 38v–39v, 279–79v; Huetz de Lemps, *Géographie du commerce*, pp. 116 ff., 174, 179, 188, 200, and passim.

40. AN, F¹² 1903, de la Bucaille to Pontchartrain, undated; ibid., avis of deputies, 23 July 1706.

41. AN, F¹² 1921, "Les Députez au conseil de commerce sur la demande que fait le Sʳ Jacobus Janssen de Dunkerque;" Mar., B³ 175, fols. 105–6, Desmaretz to Pontchartrain, 19 April 1709; B⁷ 507, fol. 40, Lescalopier to Pontchartrain, 20 April 1709.

42. AN, F¹² 51, fol. 39.

43. See, for example, BN, MSS. fr., 14294, fol. 82, "Sentiment des députez au conseil de commerce sur les passeports demandez par des négocians anglois," 28 March 1707. AN, F¹² 54, fols. 38v, 277; F¹² 55, fol. 232v; AN, G⁷ 1695, piece 274, Piécourt to Desmaretz, 2 November 1710; G⁷ 1695, piece 303, a summary of memoirs presented by Mesnager to Desmaretz, prepared by *premier commis* de la Garde.

44. This dispute is summarized in Henri Sée and Léon Vignols, "Quelques documents sur les relations commerciales entre la France et la Hollande au début du XVIIIᵉ siècle."

45. See AD, Loire-Atlantique, C 754, piece 1, "Mémoire du Sieur Descaseaux (*sic*) du Hallay député de Nantes pour justifier qu'il est important de laisser vaisseaux estrangers nous aporter leurs marchandises en France pour leur propre compte et par leurs propres navires, sans nous piquer de les aller chercher chez eux par nos vaisseaux"; piece 33, "Réflexions du Sieur des Caseaux député de Nantes au conseil de commerce sur la proposition faitte par Mrs. Mesnager et Piécourt."

46. Ibid., piece 1.

47. Beginning in 1659 a tax of 50 sous per *tonneau* was collected on all foreign ships entering French ports. In nautical terms a *tonneau*, or ton, is a measure of volume, not weight; it is equivalent to 2.83 m.³ or about 50 cubic feet. By terms of the Franco-Dutch tariff of 1699, Dutch ships were exempted from paying this duty. The *arrêt* of 6 September 1701 raised it from 50 sous to 3 livres 10 sous for English ships.

48. See Sée and Vignols, "Quelques documents."

49. AN, F¹² 51, fol. 151v, 15 December 1702; fols. 161, 162v, 9 February 1703; fol. 218v, 12 March 1704.

50. On Pottier de la Hestroye, see above p. 9. Throughout the war years, he presented to the crown several revised versions of his original set of memoirs. See also AN, G⁷ 1687, piece 33, Pottier de la Hestroye to Chamillart, 9 September 1704; also piece 34, "Mémoire de M. de la Hestroye touchant le commerce."

51. Faulconnier's memoirs include AN, F¹² 1903, "Proposition touchant la navigation des estrangers pour la paix;" F¹² 693, "Mémoire pour diminuer le commerce et la navigation en Hollande et les augmenter très considérablement en France," and "Explication du mémoire donné par le soussigné pour l'establissement de la navigation en France"; AN, G⁷ 1686, piece 140, "Mémoire sur la guerre présente"; G⁷ 696, Pour entreprendre l'exécution du projet présenté par le soussigné à Mgr. de Chamillart pour ruiner le commerce et la navigation des hollandois."

52. See AN, F¹² 693, Faulconnier to Chamillart, 2 April 1702; ibid., same to same, 13 April 1702 and 15 April 1702. Mar., B² 171, fols. 327v–28, Pontchartrain to Valossière, 3 May 1702 (Valossière's copy of this letter is in F¹² 693); B² 168, fol. 58–58v, Pontchartrain to Amelot, 4 April 1703, and fol. 62, same to same, 12 April 1703. See also AN, G⁷ 1686, piece 136, "Réponse à un mémoire touchant le commerce, qui m'a esté addressé par Monseigneur de Chamillart," 16 August 1702.

53. AN, F¹² 693, "Avis des députez du commerce sur la proposition du Sr. Faulconnier de diminuer le commerce et la navigation des hollandois, et de les

augmenter en France," 3 May 1702. Also see AN, F¹² 51, fol. 115v, 28 April 1702; fol. 121v, 26 May 1702; fol. 126v., 30 June 1702.

54. AN, F¹² 644, piece 284, *avis* of Barentin, dated 9 August 1703; F¹² 646, piece 193, memoir by de Bagnols, dated 21 July 1702.

55. See AN, G⁷ 1686, piece 91, "Mémoire sur la supression du droit de 50 sous per tonneau," a copy of which can also be found in AN, F¹² 644, piece 186. Also F¹² 51, fols. 25v, 28v, 37, 43–43v, 69v, 127v, 129v, 143, 179v, 217, 232–32v, 244v.

56. AN, F¹² 51, fols. 37, 43, 50.

57. Ibid., fols. 11v, 115.

58. All these *arrêts* were reaffirmed by the general *arrêt* of 18 August 1705, which summarized current policies concerning trade with Denmark, Sweden, and Holland. A copy of this *arrêt* can be found in AN, AD XI, 9.

59. English and Dutch merchants did, nevertheless, trade with France by means of the Scandinavian neutrals. They either disguised their own ships as Danish or Swedish or they secretly transported their goods to neutral ports, whence they were shipped to France. See Huetz de Lemps, *Géographie du commerce*, p. 90; J. S. Bromley, "The North Sea in Wartime (1688–1713)," pp. 278, 286.

60. *Recueil des instructions données aux ambassadeurs et ministres de France*, Vol. 4, *Pologne*, pp. 209–43; Pierre Paul, *Le Cardinal Melchior de Polignac (1661–1741)*, pp. 23–85; Lévy, *Capitalistes et pouvoir*, pp. 72–75; AN, G⁷ 544, dossier 17, "Mémoire pour Mr l'abbé de Polignac."

61. AN, F¹² 51, fols. 102, 177v; F¹² 54, fol. 20.

62. Mar., B² 168, fol. 820–20v, Pontchartrain to Fénellon, 27 June 1703; B² 169, fol. 54v, same to same, 4 July 1703.

63. See Mar., B³ 175, fol. 115, Desmaretz to Pontchartrain, 1 June 1709; and fols. 163–64, same to same, 6 September 1709; Shelby McCloy, *Government Assistance in Eighteenth-Century France*, p. 14.

64. AN, G⁷ 544, "Mémoire pour Mr l'abbé de Polignac."

65. See "Le Commerce des ennemis," p. 108.

66. See, for example, AAE, Correspondance politique, Venise, 160, fols. 50–54, Pontchartrain to Torcy, 3 April 1709; Bromley, "The French Privateering War," p. 225; Mar., B³ 132, fols. 8–9, Torcy to Pontchartrain, 5 February 1705; AN, F¹² 54, fols. 199–200.

67. Mar., B⁷ 507, fols. 55–57, Machault to Pontchartrain, 23 October 1709; ibid., fols. 66–68, same to same, 8 November 1709; B⁷ 508, fols. 146–53, same to same, 20 February 1712, with two accompanying memoirs.

68. AN, F¹² 51, fols. 301v–3, 309v, 318v, 356; F¹² 54, fol. 14; F¹² 55, fols. 275–76, 289v–90v, 299, 304–5v.

69. AN, F¹² 55, fols. 288v–90v (24 June 1711), 320v–21 (11 September 1711).

70. Ibid., fols. 331–32v, 10 October 1711.

71. AN, F¹² 58, fols. 19v–20v, 19 February 1712.

72. AN, F¹² 54, fol. 137, 2 March 1705.

73. Ibid., fols. 144 (9 March 1705), 211v (15 June 1705). This question was raised again in 1708: see Mar., B² 206, pp. 690–92, Pontchartrain to Daguesseau, 29 February 1708.

74. AN, F¹² 51, fol. 335, 10 June 1705.

75. AN, F¹² 51, fols. 325, 333v, 6 May and 10 June 1705.

76. Ibid., fol. 351v.

77. See Mar., B² 181, fols. 510v–11v, Pontchartrain to Daguesseau, 13 May 1705.

78. AN, F¹² 51, fols. 396, 425v–27.

79. Ibid., fols. 436, 460v–61v; F¹² 123, fols. 11, 75, Chamillart to Pontchartrain, 6 November 1706, 4 January 1707.

80. See, for example, the monthly records of ships entering and leaving Bordeaux in 1709 in AN, G⁷ 1694, pieces 682–86; Huetz de Lemps, *Géographie du commerce*, pp. 69–70 and passim.

81. See AN, F¹² 51, fols. 267–68v, 18 June 1704. The *arrêt* is reprinted in Lebeau, *Nouveau code des prises*, 1:283–89. It makes specific mention of the work of the deputies of commerce in helping to draw it up.

82. At the behest of Denmark, Louis XIV in January 1705 extended this to include all ships purchased from the enemy up to 23 November 1704, provided that these recently purchased vessels were used solely in trade with France (see Lebeau, *Nouveau code des prises*, 1:290–91, Louis XIV to comte de Toulouse, 28 January 1705).

83. J. S. Bromley reports that 312 ships were released by the *conseil des prises* during the war ("The French Privateering War," p. 213).

84. See Clark, "Neutral Commerce in the War of the Spanish Succession," pp. 72–76; Bromley, "Le Commerce de la France de l'ouest," pp. 53–54. Zeeland privateers continued to harass neutral shipping throughout the war, to the consternation of the other Dutch provinces and England. This is discussed in Bromley, "Les Corsaires zélandois." Also consult Bromley, "The North Sea."

85. For a graphic illustration of Bordeaux's dependence on the Dutch to carry out its wine, see the map in Boutruche et al., *Bordeaux de 1453 à 1715*, p. 462.

86. AN, F¹² 51, fols. 236, 237v, 241v, 248v.

87. A rough draft of the *arrêt* prepared in the Council of Commerce can be found in AN, F¹² 1903.

88. See the chart in the Appendix. As noted there, the council's *procès-verbaux* do not specifically mention every matter discussed at each meeting. The figure 121 probably is slightly below the true number.

89. The *arrêts* of 11 October 1704, 24 March 1705, and 16 May 1705 were all summarized and reaffirmed by the *arrêt* of 18 August 1705, a copy of which is in AN, AD XI, 9.

90. For merchandise added to it from 1705 to 1708, see AN, F¹² 54, fols. 265v–67v, 31 August 1708. For items added after 1708, see F¹² 1903, "Etat des marchandises qui pourront être apportées en France."

91. See AN, F¹² 799ᴬ, "Etat des marchandises pour lesquelles il a esté accordé des passeports pour les faire venir d'hollande, outre celles comprises dans les arrests en payant les droits extraordinaires de cinq pour cent de la valeur"; also F¹² 1903, "Etat et estimation des marchandises venant d'hollande pour lesquelles il sera accordé des passeports, en payant le droit extraordinaire de cinq pour cent de la valeur," dated 9 May 1707.

92. It should be noted that during the war Dutch merchants did not enjoy the privileges granted to them in the 1699 Franco-Dutch tariff agreement. Instead they had to pay the same duties that applied to goods from other nations, including the 1667 tariff schedule as well as the subsequent additions to it.

93. Bromley presents a yearly breakdown for each of these ports in "Le Commerce de la France de l'ouest," p. 66. By adding up these figures, one arrives at a total of 4,069; but since there are some gaps in the records, it is current that the actual number of Dutch ships entering these ports was slightly higher than this.

94. Evidence for this is presented in "Le Commerce de la France de l'ouest," and also in Bromley, "The French Privateering War," p. 231.

95. For example, Mar., B² 221, p. 537, Pontchartrain to Amelot, 3 April 1710; B² 223, p. 472, Pontchartrain to Desmaretz, 19 November 1710.

96. AN, F¹² 55, fols. 169–70, 176–77v (16 May and 20 June 1710); AN, Col., B 32, fols. 392–94v, Pontchartrain to Amelot, 25 May 1710; ibid., fols. 529–30, Pontchartrain to Aubert de Forillon, 28 September 1710; Mar., B² 221, pp. 871–74, Pontchartrain to Daguesseau, 21 May 1710; ibid., pp. 1130–31, same to same, 10 June 1710.

97. AN, F¹² 55, fols., 16v–18 (4 January 1709), 111–12 (8 November 1709); AN, G⁷ 1693, piece 49, letters and memoirs sent to the Council of Commerce, 7 January 1710; there is much correspondence concerning this question in AN, Col., B 29, 31, and Mar., B² 217; see also Mar., B⁷ 507, fols. 138–43, Chamber of Commerce of Bordeaux to Pontchartrain, 12 October 1709, with accompanying memoir.

98. In 1705 seven such passports were granted, but there do not seem to have been this many in succeeding years (see Mar., B⁷ 504, fol. 133, anonymous memoir). See also Mar., B⁷ 503, fols. 193–93v, Fabre to Pontchartrain, 9 November 1705, with accompanying memoir; Mar., B² 196, p. 676, Pontchartrain to Daguesseau, 2 February 1707; B² 211, pp. 612–13, same to same, 25 July 1708.

99. AN, F¹² 54, fols. 37, 42v, 46–46v, 49–50, 269–70, 291.

100. AN, F¹² 51, fols. 441–45, 1 September 1706.

101. AN, F¹² 124, fol. 164, Chamillart to farmers general, 24 April 1708; F¹² 54, fol. 267v, 31 August 1708.

102. AN, F¹² 124, fol. 12, Chamillart to Pontchartrain, 30 June 1708; F¹² 55, fols. 79v–80, 12 July 1709.

103. AN, F¹² 55, fols. 79v–80, 12 July 1709.

104. Ibid., fol. 261v.

105. Ibid., fols. 274v–78v.

106. See, for example, AN, F¹² 54, fol. 235v, 20 July 1708; the original copy of the deputies' *avis* is in AN, G⁷ 1691, piece 276. In this case a Rouen merchant wished to import some thread (*fil à dentelle, fil de Cologne*) from Holland. The deputies wanted to refuse the request, but they were overruled by the *commissaires*, who believed that these articles were necessary for French manufactures.

107. Furthermore, historians are now coming to recognize that the effects of the 1709 winter were not as dire as had formerly been believed: see my monograph *The Economy of France in the Second Half of the Reign of Louis XIV*, pp. 19–23.

108. John C. Rule, "France and the Preliminaries to the Gertruydenberg Conference, September 1709 to March 1710," p. 108. In addition to Rule, other scholars also have viewed the years 1709–10 as a turning point for France: John B. Wolf, *Louis XIV*, pp. 566–77; Joseph Klaits, *Printed Propaganda under Louis XIV: Absolute Monarchy and Public Opinion*, pp. 241–43.

109. AN, F¹² 55, fols. 90v–91v, 9 August 1709.

110. Ibid.; the original copy of the deputies' *avis* is in AN, G⁷ 1694, piece 459. Concerning another proposal for ending commerce with the Dutch submitted to the council at about the same time, see Mar., B⁷ 507, fols. 7–12, Caumartin de Boissy to Pontchartrain, 12 August 1709; also Mar., B² 216, pp. 404–5, Pontchartrain to Daguesseau, 17 July 1709.

111. See AN, G⁷ 1693, piece 41, letters and memoirs sent to the Council of Commerce on 23 October 1709.

112. Ibid.

113. AN, F¹² 55, fols. 174–75v.

114. Ibid.; AN, G⁷ 1695, piece 157, Pontchartrain to Desmaretz, 23 July 1710.

115. AN, F¹² 55, fols. 182v–83, 11 July 1710. Only a few days earlier, Desmaretz had opposed cutting off commerce with Holland: see Mar., B³ 189, fol. 165–65v, Desmaretz to Pontchartrain, 8 July 1710.

116. AN F¹² 55, fols. 182–88v.

117. Daguesseau was virtually alone in counseling moderation: see AN, G⁷ 1695, piece 223, Daguesseau to Desmaretz, 4 November 1710, and piece 273, same to same, 7 November 1710. Copies of both of these letters are in Mar., B⁷ 507, fols. 307–9, 320–21. On the support that the others in the council gave to the revocation, see AN, G⁷ 1695, piece 274, Piécourt to Desmaretz, 2 November 1710, recopied in Mar., B⁷ 507, fol. 291; G⁷ 1695, piece 268, Mesnager to Desmaretz, 3 November 1710; also see piece 224, same to same, 27 October 1710. Both of these are recopied in Mar., B⁷ 507, fols. 287–90. In addition consult B⁷ 507, fols. 311–19, "Mémoire sur la proposition de ne plus accorder des passeports du Roy aux vaisseaux hollandois," by Anisson, Fénellon, Fabre, Héron, Piécourt, and Mesnager, dated 4 November 1710; and fols. 297–306, memoir beginning "La proposition de ne plus accorder des passeports aux hollandois"; fols. 268–77, "Mémoire sur les passeports." A copy of the letter is also in BN, MSS. fr., 16737, fols. 110–14.

118. Reprinted in Lebeau, *Nouveau code des prises*, 1:354–55.

119. See Mar., B² 223, p. 431, Pontchartrain to Daguesseau, 12 November 1710.

120. A copy can be found in BN, MSS. fr., 21776, fols. 77–78. Also see AN, G⁷ 1695, piece 284, "Etat des marchandises qui pourront être apportées en France par les vaisseaux neutres."

121. An *arrêt* issued on 20 January 1711 added to the list ferrous sulfate (*couperose*), needed for dyeing textiles. This *arrêt* likewise reiterated that neutral ships were not permitted to stop in enemy ports while going to or from France. A copy can be found in Bibliothèque Historique de la Ville de Paris, NF 35-380, volume 75, no. 22, fols. 74–75. On the increase in neutral traffic with France, see Webster, "The Merchants of Bordeaux," p. 400; Huetz de Lemps, *Géographie du commerce*, p. 88.

122. Copies of the *arrêt* of 28 April 1711 can be found in Bibliothèque Historique de la Ville de Paris, NF, 35-380, volume 76, no. 21, fols. 65–66, an BN, MSS. fr., 21776, fols. 75–76. See also AN, F¹² 55, fols. 259v–60v, 29 April 1711.

123. AN, B² 189, fols. 112–13, "Etat des marchandises qui pourront estre apportées d'Angleterre en France par les navires anglois en vertu des passeports qui seront accordez par le Roy," signed by Desmaretz.

124. See AN, F¹² 55, fol. 282v, 26 June 1711.

125. See AN, F¹² 55, fol. 283; Neuville, *Etat sommaire*, p. 261. On the Dutch and their various cost-cutting techniques, see Paul Bamford, "French Shipping in Northern European Trade, 1660–1789."

126. These can be found in AN, G⁷ 1695, pieces 283, 285, 287, 288.

127. Ibid., piece 286; also see Mar., B³ 189, fols. 116–17.

128. For a list of northern cities and territories that were now to be considered neutral, see AN, F¹² 55, fols. 317–18, 22 August 1711.

129. Ibid. As noted earlier, it seems that the abbé de Polignac had by this time relinquished his letters of reprisal against Danzig ships; but I have as yet found no direct evidence to prove this.

130. See AN, F¹² 55, fols. 317v–18, 22 August 1711. I have not found any documents detailing the limitations on trade with these cities, but almost certainly their trade with France was much more restricted than was that of the Hanseatic cities.

131. Mar., B⁷ 507, fols. 330–31, Fénellon to Pontchartrain, 4 January 1711, with accompanying memoir; Huetz de Lemps, *Géographie du commerce*, pp. 86–88.

132. Bromley, "Le Commerce de la France de l'ouest," p. 66.

133. See, for example, Mar., B² 223, p. 471, Pontchartrain to Desmaretz, 19 November 1710, and p. 477, same to same, 22 November 1710; B³ 202, fol. 158, Desmaretz to Pontchartrain, 23 February 1711.

134. Mar., B³ 202, fol. 158, Desmaretz to Pontchartrain, 23 February 1711.

135. See, for example, AN, G⁷ 1695, pieces 313 and 314, concerning passports issued to a Sieur Jacquin to import various merchandises.

136. AN, F¹² 55, fol. 258v, 24 April 1711; F¹² 58, fol. 78, 12 October 1712.

137. The Council of Commerce frequently worked to tighten up controls to prevent the Dutch from carrying on clandestine or fraudulent trade with France: for example, AN, F¹² 55, fol. 337v (24 October 1711); F¹² 58, fol. 47 (13 May 1712).

138. AN, F¹² 55, fols. 351–52, 18 December 1711. The fact that the Dutch economy suffered during the war, especially in its final years, has been indicated in various ways. See Bromley, "The North Sea," pp. 272–73; Michel Morineau, "La Balance du commerce franco-néerlandais et le resserrement économique des Provinces-Unies au XVIIIᵉ siècle"; J. Aalbers, "Holland's Financial Problems (1713–1733) and the Wars against Louis XIV." A differing view is expressed in Goubert, *Louis XIV and Twenty Million Frenchmen,* p. 266.

139. AN, G⁷ 1693, piece 223, items referred to Council of Commerce, 28 June 1714.

140. A copy can be found in AN, AD XI, 9.

141. Mar., B² 234, pp. 120–21, Pontchartrain to Amelot de Chaillou, 18 January 1713.

142. The bulk of Pontchartrain's correspondence with the members of the council concerning this subject is scattered throughout Mar., B² 209, 222, 226, 227, 228, 230, 231, 234, 237, 241. The responses of the intendants of commerce and the other *commissaires* can be found in the B³ series. For a good illustration of the manner in which the council made its decisions, see B³ 189, fols. 240–43, Caumartin de Boissy to Pontchartrain, 6 July 1710. Also see AN, G⁷ 1692, piece 103, "Mémoire des députez au conseil de commerce servant de réponse à celui de M. le controlleur général de la marine."

143. See AN, F¹² 662–70, "Traité des marchandises de la flandre espagnole par terre."

144. AN, F¹² 54, fols. 301–1v, 24 October 1708; see also the untitled memoir by Daguesseau in AN, G⁷ 1694, piece 132.

145. AN, G⁷ 1692, piece 65, memoir by *syndics du commerce* of Normandy, dated 25 October 1708; and piece 212, "Mémoire sur la contestation qu'il y a entre le député de Rouen et les députez des autres villes au sujet de la sortie des équivalents," 26 September 1708.

146. AN, G⁷ 1692, piece 246, "Expéditions concernant le commerce et les manufactures du 10 octobre 1708"; AN, F¹² 125, fol. 89, Desmaretz to farmers general, 11 October 1708.

147. AN, F¹² 55, fols. 58–59, 107–8 (3 May and 23 October 1709).

148. Bromley, "The French Privateering War," especially pp. 227–31; "The North Sea," p. 292 and passim.

149. J. S. Bromley reports that the total number of prizes was actually 7,220, but from this number one should subtract 245 recaptures and 312 releases (because the captures were judged invalid). Thus the total number of bona fide prizes was 6,663. Of this number 2,118 ships were ransomed at sea, and the remaining 4,545 were brought to French (or allied) ports. ("The French Privateering War," p. 213.)

150. Partially reprinted in J. H. Owen, *War at Sea under Queen Anne, 1702–1708,* pp. 284–85.

151. Reprinted in Lebeau, *Nouveau code des prises,* 1:256–64.

152. See ibid., pp. 267–73, 340–43, and AN, AD XI, 53.

6

REGULATION OF MANUFACTURES

Next to the question of determining commercial policies concerning enemy and neutral trade, the topic that most often occupied the Council of Commerce during the years 1700–1715 was the regulation and encouragement of French manufactures. In particular the council concerned itself with textiles, which constituted by far the largest industrial sector in the French economy throughout the entire early modern period.

This chapter will demonstrate two basic points. First, it will show that the Council of Commerce was thoroughly Colbertian in its policies, using government intervention whenever it was felt to be necessary and employing all the modes of encouraging industry that had been used by Colbert and his immediate successors. Second, it will argue that these royal policies concerning manufactures were far more enlightened than most historians have taken them to be.

The concern here chiefly will be with the regulation and encouragement of manufactures, not with manufactures themselves or their growth or decline during this period. This regulation had two chief components: the royal statutes in which royal policies were embodied and the inspectors of manufactures charged with enforcing the statutes. The government (with the aid of the Council of Commerce) also used other means to encourage manufactures, and these are treated elsewhere in this book. It should be clear from the previous chapter, for example, that the crown took advantage of the war to exclude foreign manufactures while encouraging the importation of raw materials. A later chapter will discuss tariff policies, which were also essential to the government's promotion of native textile production.

There can be no doubt that the Council of Commerce had a major voice in formulating and promulgating royal policies concerning manufactures during this period. The council helped draft virtually every important *arrêt* or ordinance on the subject. Furthermore, the official who was charged by the controller general with administering French manufactures—the director of commerce—was a leading member of this council. As noted earlier, this position was held by Michel Amelot (1699–1705 and 1709–24) and Henri Daguesseau (1705–9).[1] Fortunately for the historian, several of the letter books of Amelot and Daguesseau have been preserved in the Archives Nationales.[2] From them one can get a firm grasp of how the machinery of bureaucratic controls operated. The director of commerce supervised the work of the provincial intendants on matters concerning manufactures, and he appointed and directed the work of the inspectors of manufactures.[3] Often the director mentioned the work of the Council of Commerce in his letters, and it is clear that many of the guidelines or decisions that he handed down were drawn up in the council.

As is true with any of the subjects discussed in the Council of Commerce, it is impossible to ascertain in precise numbers or percentages the full importance of the council on manufacturing issues. Not every matter that the council discussed is represented in its *procès-verbaux*, and frequently individual members worked on problems outside the council on the direct command of the controller general. It is clear that the council did not participate in the day-to-day administration of manufactures. This was the work of the provincial intendants, the inspectors of manufactures, and the director of commerce. But the council was, invariably, called upon to deliberate important matters involving the issuance of new regulations, the granting of privileges to new or to established manufactures, and the execution of royal laws. The presence of the director of commerce on the council helped ensure that the council's advice would be acted on.

MANUFACTURING REGULATIONS

Turning directly to the questions of royal regulation of manufactures, one can say that, as a general rule, historians have allowed their liberal biases to slant their views on the subject. They argue that strict control of manufactures, with few exceptions, limited the freedom and cramped the initiative that workers needed to develop their crafts. The prolific nineteenth-century historian Pierre Clément, who was favorable to Colbert in most ways, nevertheless decried what he called "this mania for regulating and tormenting industry."[4] Twentieth-century historians have largely agreed with this view. Alfred Cobban has asserted that "French industry had in fact been put into a strait-jacket by Colbert just at the time when a continual stream of new technical inventions was to call for the greatest flexibility and liberty."[5] Eli Heckscher devoted a large section of his influential *Mercantilism* to a comparison of industrial policies in England and France.[6] He concluded that a lesser degree of regulation in England was an important factor in helping manufactures there develop faster than they did in France in the eighteenth century.

Although historians grudgingly admit that several of Colbert's measures were necessary, Colbert's successors are uniformly depicted as unimaginative emulators who enlarged Colbert's heavy-handed bureaucracy and increased the number of irksome laws controlling every phase of the manufacturing process. A number of authorities have dutifully recorded Pierre Clément's assertion that during Colbert's administration some forty-four royal laws were issued to regulate manufactures, whereas from 1683 to 1739 the number jumped to 230.[7] Thus, as noted earlier, historians have come to describe the policies of Le Peletier, Seignelay, Louvois, and Louis de Pontchartrain as *Colbertisme à outrance, protectionisme à outrance,* or *Colbertisme exagéré.*[8]

If the standard interpretation of the Council of Commerce were correct, then one would expect it to have clamored loudly against this supposed strangulation of French industry. Such was not the case. In their general memoirs of 1700–1701, not one of the deputies of commerce complained about any overregulation of manufactures. Virtually all of them mentioned the need to protect and encourage industry, and some of them spoke admiringly of regulations initiated by Colbert.[9] Examination of the council's records for the next fifteen years confirms this impression. The council—with the full support of the deputies—worked to consolidate the system of regulation instituted by Colbert.

Prior to the 1660s textile regulations had largely been under the authority of local guilds. What Colbert did was to rationalize and bring uniformity to these controls. With some justification, he believed that a major reason why Dutch and English cloths were outselling French-produced ones on the world market was that a great many defects had crept into the latter, and he therefore set about to correct these abuses. Beginning in the late 1660s, his ministry issued a long series of statutes that covered, in minute detail, every stage of the manufacturing process for all types of cloths. For example, the great ordinance of 1669 for woolens, consisting of 59 articles, ordered that each variety of woolen cloth— whether it be high-quality *ratines* or low-quality serges—have the same length, width, number of threads, quality of wool, and type of dye, no matter where it was produced in France.[10]

Colbert's successors, it is true, did multiply the number of laws over textiles and make the regulations much more detailed. Accordingly, they have been accused of exaggerating the Colbertian system in what amounts to an *esprit de réglementation*. Charles Woolsey Cole speaks for many historians when he claims that after Colbert "there was a tendency to make the regulations more numerous, more meticulous, more detailed, and more rigid. There was less willingness to make exceptions or to grant or use discretion."[11] Thus, whereas Colbert's regulations for woolens being produced for the Levant had specified only two general types of cloth, the *arrêt* of 22 October 1697 further divided these basic types into *londrines premières larges, londrines secondes, londres larges, londres, mahous, seizans,* and *abouchokous,* with specific requirements for each kind.[12]

Although the regulatory system established in France in the second half of the seventeenth century may strike the modern reader as burdensome and inhibitive, some qualifications are necessary. Although textile regulations did tend to become longer after 1683, some of Colbert's own laws were among the lengthiest ever issued; one might cite, in particular, his compendious 1669 ordinance on dyeing, which included fully 317 articles.[13] To label the policies of Colbert's successors as *Colbertisme à outrance* is unfair. Although his successors did multiply the number of industrial statutes, they had good reason for doing so. Colbert's laws were for the most part intended to cover the entire nation. Furthermore, his laws spoke only of a few dozen basic types of textiles. But these laws were clearly impracticable. Many cities in France were accustomed, from time immemorial, to producing their own special variations of the standard types of cloths, and these products had, over the years, acquired a loyal clientèle, whether in France or abroad. To have forced all these cities and individuals to conform to the new national norms would have wrecked their businesses. In addition, Colbert's laws left no room for changing styles and new varieties of cloths, and late in the seventeenth century dozens of new cloths were devised. Amiens, for example, was producing more than sixty types of fabrics by the early eighteenth century.[14] To accomodate these new innovations and local variations, Colbert's successors issued new laws exempting these manufactures from certain aspects of the ordinances of the 1660s and specifying new standards for these particular fabrics. Thus the process was not so much one of increasing the heavy hand of government on the individual *fabricant* as of substituting regional statutes for national ones. Colbert himself had granted numerous exceptions to his general regulations,[15] and his successors should not be blamed for continuing to do so.

Both Colbert and his successors urged severe penalties for those guilty of abuses. The punishment for a first offense was the confiscation of the defective goods and the exposure of the goods on a pillory in front of the guild hall. Also the worker was fined anywhere from a few to several hundred livres, which were divided among the accuser, the guild, the king, and sometimes the local hospital. For a second offense, the guilty party suffered all the above and in addition was reprimanded in a public meeting of his guild. For a third offense, the malefactor paid a fine and was pilloried for several hours standing beside his confiscated goods.[16]

Most historians have decried this entire system as detrimental to the public good. Emile Levasseur has termed the above-mentioned punishments as a "sad example of the excesses of a despotic power,"[17] but the main charge against this regulatory program is simply that it hurt rather than helped textile production. Certainly there is evidence to support this claim. Manufactures in some regions of France did decline in the latter part of Louis XIV's reign, and there are many examples of French merchants or manufacturers either violating or protesting against what they believed to be unfair or overly harsh regulations. Historians such as Levasseur and Martin have made ample use of this evidence.[18]

There is also evidence to support an opposite conclusion. At least two historians have noted the utility of many of these rules. Charles Woolsey Cole, though critical of many of the controls, nevertheless admits that they were a first step in the way of much-needed consumer protection.[19] Tihomir J. Markovitch goes even further. Markovitch has extensively studied the French woolens industry of the seventeenth and eighteenth centuries,[20] and his conclusion has been that the system of controls generally had a beneficial impact on industrial growth.

To the twentieth-century reader, a lengthy manufacturing *règle-ment* might seem like bureaucratic nonsense intended for the sole purpose of vexing poor, illiterate peasants and artisans. The guilds, however, had actually had such regulations for centuries. Fur-thermore, the artisans following these rules were—in theory at any rate—experienced in their crafts and had been trained either at home or through apprenticeship in a guild. Thus the lengthy *rè-glements* to which seventeenth-century craftsmen had to conform were really no more complicated than the blueprints that many twentieth-century factory workers have to follow.

Our principal concern here is not whether French manufactures were or were not helped by royal intervention,[21] but rather how contemporaries viewed the situation. Although there was opposi-tion to various aspects of royal regulation, there is just as much, if not more, evidence of businessmen supporting the program of central control. As noted in Chapter One, the central government had a long tradition of consultations with the merchant community on business matters. One can affirm categorically that neither Colbert nor any of his successors ever issued an *arrêt* or ordinance concerning manufactures without first getting the advice of traders and manufacturers.[22] Colbert encouraged the calling of local *assemblées des manufactures*, in which *fabricants* and municipal of-ficials met with royal representatives to discuss ways to encourage manufactures.[23]

The papers of the controller general and the letter books of Daguesseau and Amelot reveal dozens of instances in which mer-chants or guilds complained about abuses and even requested tighter government controls. In August 1713, for example, mer-chants in Bayonne complained that the cloths they were receiving from other provinces were so defective that Bayonne's commerce was "almost entirely lost."[24]

The best evidence of popular support for the Colbertian regula-tions, however, lies in the Council of Commerce. Not once during the years under consideration here did the *commissaires* or the deputies urge a relaxation of the Colbertian regulatory system.[25] The deputies frequently deplored the many abuses that were perpetrated by artisans and merchants, and they urged the issu-ance of new regulations whenever they felt it to be necessary. The *procès-verbaux* mention thirty-eight specific cases involving manu-facturing abuses that were discussed in the council from 1700 to 1715, but it is clear that this is only a small fraction of the total number of cases with which the council as a whole or the deputies dealt. One could provide numerous examples of cases not reported in the *procès-verbaux*. In May 1714, for example, the deputies exhorted the intendant at Rouen to prevent workers there from excessively stretching their woolen cloths on tenter frames; the extra length that the cloths gained in this manner disappeared once they were washed by their purchasers. After condemning this abuse, the deputies bemoaned the fact that despite all the precautions that they and the government took to perfect and encourage manufactures, some workers would always be eager for "a sordid gain."[26]

In order to prevent such abuses, to clarify existing rules, and to make way for new fabrics, the Council of Commerce helped draft approximately two hundred new *règlements* of various types during this fifteen-year period.[27] To keep track of all such laws issued before and after 1700, the council maintained an up-to-date *Recueil des règlemens concernant les manufactures*.[28]

THE INSPECTORS OF MANUFACTURES

It is impossible, however, to speak of royal regulation of industry without speaking of the machinery by which these laws were enforced. Traditionally this job was performed by the local artisanal guilds. Every piece of cloth had to undergo from four to six inspections, at different stages of the manufacturing process, before it could be sold. The job of inspecting belonged primarily to the guild wardens (called *jurés, syndics,* or *gardes*), and they were responsible for punishing any infractors. All disputes were taken before the *juges des manufactures*, who were the city magistrates.[29] This system of regulation worked fine in theory, but in practice it was extremely faulty. In many areas of the country, there were no guilds, and thus no guild regulations; and even where there were guilds, the wardens were frequently negligent or corrupt, permitting defective goods to be put on the market. Colbert nevertheless retained this system of regulation. He fostered the growth of new guilds and buttressed the power of old ones. As a result these corporations grew in number and in power during the latter part of the seventeenth century; and despite harsh criticism of them by the *philosophes* and Turgot, they wielded a major force in the national economy up to the Revolution.[30]

In 1669 Colbert superimposed over this method of control a network of royal inspectors of manufactures.[31] Like the intendants, these inspectors held commissions rather than venal offices. At first there were fourteen of them; by 1683 their number had expanded to twenty-four. They worked under the authority of the provincial intendants, and they themselves supervised the work of the guild wardens. They were each assigned a department, and they were expected to visit every center of manufactures within it one or more times each year. Periodically they sent reports on the textiles in their departments to the controller general.

From 1683 to 1700 Colbert's successors strove to consolidate and improve the corps of inspectors, and they increased their number to more than thirty. An *arrêt* of 8 November 1687, for example, declared that in the future no foreign cloths could enter the country except through the customs offices at Calais and Saint-Valéry-sur-Somme.[32] To guarantee that such cloths were properly marked, a new inspector was appointed to work in each of these two cities. An *arrêt* of 1 September 1693 established an inspector at Marseilles to check all French cloths destined for the Levant.[33]

But despite the work of Colbert and his successors, it is clear that the inspectors failed miserably in living up to the expectations of the government. They were unable to compel reluctant guild officials to cooperate with them, and several of the inspectors themselves were guilty of negligence or incompetence. On numerous occasions during the 1690s, Controller General Louis de Pontchartrain bemoaned the fact that the inspectors were not properly fulfilling their duties.[34]

Therefore, when the Council of Commerce was established in 1700 much remained to be done in the way of putting teeth into the Colbertian system of regulation. That the council reacted with vigor to this situation cannot be doubted. The number of archival documents pertaining to the inspectors of manufactures balloons markedly for the years after 1700.

The same bureaucratic impulse that contributed to the formation of the Council of Commerce likewise led to the formation of a better system of control over the inspectors of manufactures. Prior to 1700 the inspectors had been little more than a neglected appendage of the central government. The royal ministers who had control of the inspectors (Colbert, Louvois, and Louis de Pontchartrain) each had charge of more than one governmental ministry. Weighed down as they were with the problems of finance, the army, and the navy, these ministers had little time to direct the day-to-day activities of the inspectors. In the 1690s Henri Daguesseau was charged with supervising them, but this improved the situation little, since Daguesseau was expected, single-handedly, to administer all internal commerce and industry. This came in addition to his work in numerous government councils and commissions.

As noted earlier, Daguesseau resigned the direction of commerce in 1699 in favor of his nephew Amelot. Amelot, as director of commerce, and Daguesseau, as president of the newly formed Council of Commerce, thereafter shared control over the inspectors of manufactures. Although Amelot and Daguesseau personally directed the appointment of, and correspondence with, the inspectors, they depended on the council for advice on general problems and particular disputes. They were assisted in particular by Amelot's personal secretary, de la Vigne,[35] and by the council's secretary, Valossière. De la Vigne was influential in the appointment and control of inspectors, and Valossière drew up commissions for new inspectors.[36] Each also helped in the drafting of letters and the preservation of records.

The letter books of Amelot and Daguesseau for the years after 1700 reveal that now, for the first time, the government could keep a close eye on the daily operation of the inspectors. The director of commerce continually urged individual inspectors to perform their duties with energy and thoroughness. Amelot and Daguesseau often shifted inspectors from one department to another in order to prevent them from establishing "strong connections" with local favorites.[37] They were quick to dismiss inspectors who were found to be wanting due to old age, negligence, or corruption. Thus in October 1714 Daguesseau decided that Inspector Duplessis, whose department included part of Auvergne, Limousin, and La Rochelle, had become "so fat and so slow" that he could no longer perform his duties; a replacement was therefore named to take his place.[38] Intendants were reminded of their duty to support inspectors against any possible opposition. When the inspector in Montauban was late in submitting his semiannual *état* to the government in March 1701, Amelot was quick to write to him and to the provincial intendant to see what was wrong.[39]

Lest one get the impression that the regime under which the inspectors worked was overly harsh, it should be noted that Amelot and Daguesseau also were swift to compliment inspectors for jobs well done;[40] and the director of commerce often reminded inspectors that, though they were to work steadfastly to wipe out abuses, they were, nevertheless, to use discretion and to avoid "fatiguing" manufacturers.[41]

In the opening years of the eighteenth century, the Council of Commerce strove to consolidate the work of the past and to get a better grip on the network of inspectors. Amazing as it may seem, it was not until sometime after 1700 that the crown, through the Council of Commerce, endeavored to establish a list of all the inspectors and their departments and to find out how, and if, they were paid. In this respect a document located in the controller general's papers in the Archives Nationales proves to be highly instructive. The document is entitled "Etat des appointements des inspecteurs des manufactures pour l'année 1701."[42] This *état* lists the names of fourteen inspectors who were to be paid various sums from the *trésor royal*, ranging from a few special grants of 300 to 500 livres to full salaries of 1,800 to 2,000 livres. This document is extremely valuable for two reasons. First, it contradicts what virtually every historian has heretofore written concerning the mode of payment of the inspectors. Colbert had determined that inspectors should be paid from the product of a one-sous duty collected on each piece of cloth examined. Bacquié—and those who have relied on his account—assumed that this had always remained the case.[43] The fact is, however, that only the inspectors of woolen cloths were to be remunerated in this fashion. After 1683 other types of inspectors were created, and these new inspectors were paid directly by the crown. The second reason for the importance of this document is that it tells us who these new inspectors were. Included among them were the two men posted at Calais and Saint-Valéry, who have already been mentioned. In addition, there were two inspectors posted in Brittany for the purpose of guaranteeing that no foreign (i.e., English and Dutch) textiles entered there in fraud. There were also two inspectors in Paris charged with examining all cloths entering the city. Finally, there were six inspectors appointed to examine all *toiles*[44] manufactured in France.[45] These six men were assigned to the three areas where *toiles* were chiefly produced: the Lyonnais, Brittany, and Normandy. The existence of these six inspectors at least as early as 1701 corrects the assertion of Hayem and Markovitch that there were no inspectors of *toiles* until 1727.[46]

In addition to the inspectors named in this list, there were twenty-three or twenty-four inspectors of woolens at the turn of the century. The earliest list of all the inspectors that I have uncovered dates from November 1704.[47]

The total number of inspectors increased slightly in the early years of the century. Up until 1701, for example, one man had been responsible for inspecting all the *toiles* produced in the *généralités* of Caen and Alençon. Amelot decided that this area was too large for one person; he therefore divided that department into two and appointed a second man.[48] In 1706 the deputies of trade concluded that two men were not sufficient to eradicate all the defects appearing in Languedoc and appointed a third man to cover it.[49]

Generally, however, the Council of Commerce was reluctant to create any new inspectors and preferred instead to increase the diligence and effectiveness of the inspectors already in existence. New inspectors might cause more delays in the production process, and, in addition, new inspectors would have to be paid—either by the crown or by the workers themselves. Thus the council turned down several proposals for new inspectorships—usually submitted by individuals hoping to profit from them.[50]

By far the greatest achievement of the council in its early years concerning French manufactures occurred in 1704. It came as a result of a decision made by the crown to transform the inspectors' posts into venal offices. One of the devices that the crown used to stave off bankruptcy during the last two wars of the reign was the creation and sale of dozens of types of such positions. It was therefore not extraordinary when, by the edict of October 1704, it decided to transform its inspectors of manufactures from holders of commissions into owners of hereditary offices.[51] This edict proclaimed the establishment of two inspectors general in each *généralité*; it also created special *commissaires-contrôleurs et visiteurs* and *concierges-gardes* in each place of manufacture. The latter two types of offices were to replace guild wardens in the task of inspecting. Since there were thirty-two *généralités* in all, this meant that sixty-four inspectors general would be created. The new offices of controllers and warehouse guards would have numbered in the hundreds. The crown hoped that the sale of these offices would bring in more than three million livres.[52]

Almost immediately merchants and manufacturers from throughout France raised an outcry against the new creations, and the deputies of trade spearheaded a drive to repeal the October edict.[53] The deputies had two main objections to the new creations. First, the army of new inspectors was to be paid from new duties collected on textiles, and this would drive prices so high that neither Frenchmen nor foreigners would be able to afford them. Second, the deputies feared that these new officials would cause "continual trouble and infinite damage, because if these persons become fixed in their places by the acquisition of venal offices they will become more concerned with their own particular interests than with the good of manufactures."[54] The deputies preferred to maintain the present system of inspectors and guild wardens. The inspectors held mere commissions, and they were frequently moved from place to place; they could be dismissed if they did not do a good job. Similarly, the guild wardens served for only limited periods and thus did not enjoy the security of hereditary offices.

The deputies were supported in all their claims by Amelot. He wrote several lengthy memoirs against the project, and in the hallways and antechambers of Versailles, he lobbied doggedly for its annulment.[55] Amelot's work in this regard led Thévenin, the man who had contracted to sell the new offices, to hold a special grudge against him[56]

The deputies and Amelot were soon victorious: a declaration of 30 December 1704 abolished the recently created offices and reinstituted the regular inspectors and guild wardens.[57] The declaration made special mention of the work of the Council of Commerce in influencing its decision.

In order that the king be indemnified for the loss of revenue from the sale of the offices, the government accepted a plan proposed by the Council of Commerce. The deputies had suggested that the merchant guilds in the major commercial and manufacturing cities of France join together to pay the king 1,200,000 livres for the repurchase and dissolution of the venal offices. In 1705 and 1706 a series of *arrêts* finalized this plan.[58] The total sum was divided among approximately twenty-five *généralités*,[59] the merchants of which had to pay anywhere from 4,000 to 150,000 livres. A glance at the distribution of the 1,200,000 livres reveals an industrial hierarchy among French *généralités*. Rouen and Lyons had to pay the most: 150,000 livres each. Next came Amiens (80,000 livres), Rheims, Caen, Toulouse, Montpellier, Montauban, and Bordeaux (50,000 livres each). The *généralité* of Paris (including Beauvais) was charged 37,000 livres, whereas the *généralité* of Soissons had to pay only 10,000 livres.[60]

The repeal of the October edict was a tremendous victory for the Council of Commerce and for Amelot personally.[61] It was Amelot, working with his secretary, de la Vigne, who drew up the declaration of 30 December 1704.[62] This episode proved to be a mild political setback for Nicolas Desmaretz. As a director of finances, Desmaretz had supported the sale of the new offices, and he had been skeptical of the plan to have merchants put up 1,200,000 livres to repurchase the new offices.[63] He noted dryly in a letter to Amelot: "I do not notice that merchants in the provinces are generally disposed to pay what is asked of them."[64]

As it turned out, Desmaretz was partially correct on this point. The 1,200,000-livre debt was scheduled to have been paid off by the end of 1706. But merchants continually bickered among themselves, complaining that one group or one city was being forced to pay more than its fair share, and evidence reveals that as late as 1710 the debt had not been liquidated.[65]

Under the controller generalship of Desmaretz, royal concern for the inspection of manufactures increased markedly. Soon after assuming that office, he commanded each of the inspectors to draw up a detailed description of his department, listing all the places of manufacture and giving figures concerning the amount of production.[66] The resulting survey was then compiled into a single volume, and it remains today a precious index of the French economy in the early eighteenth century.[67]

Also in 1708 Desmaretz created the six intendants of commerce, in an effort to facilitate the work of the Council of Commerce.[68] As noted earlier, each intendant was charged with a fixed department, consisting of several *généralités*. The intendants received and analyzed the semiannual reports submitted by each of the inspectors.[69] After 1708 these reports began to include not only data but also small samples of the cloths being inspected.[70] These samples, several of which were attached to a single piece of paper, enabled the members of the Council of Commerce to decide for themselves whether or not the fabrics were of the prescribed quality.

The actual number of inspectors likewise increased after 1708. A list drawn up in 1714 reveals that the total number of inspectors had risen to thirty-nine. There were twenty-seven inspectors for woolens, eight for *toiles*, four for incoming foreign manufactures, and two special inspectors charged with examining all cloths sold in Paris.[71]

Throughout the War of the Spanish Succession, the area of manufactures to which the Council of Commerce devoted the most attention was the high-quality woolens destined for the Levant. In the course of the seventeenth century, England and the United

Provinces had gradually won over a large share of this market, despite the fact that Languedoc's numerous producers and Marseilles's geographical proximity seemed to ensure that the Eastern Mediterranean trade belonged to France. Thus during this fifteen-year period, the Council of Commerce was repeatedly concerned with the Levant question, and it watched the inspectors of manufactures in Languedoc more closely than any of the others. At the first sign of defect in Languedoc woolens or of a complaint against one of the inspectors there, the council was quick to write to the intendant (Basville) for an accounting.

When news arrived in 1707 that many Levant customers were dissatisfied with the quality of some of the cloths being shipped from France, the council set about to rectify the situation. Throughout 1708 it worked—in consultation with Basville and local businessmen—on a new *règlement* for Languedoc's cloths. Many of the area's manufacturers themselves requested a new statute that would help protect the good name of their products.[72] The result was the *arrêt* of 20 November 1708, which laid out specifications for cloths destined for the Levant.[73] It contained thirty-four articles, and was as detailed as any regulation issued by Colbert and his immediate successors.

When even this new statute failed to eradicate all abuses committed by unscrupulous manufacturers, Intendant Basville suggested that another inspector be appointed in Languedoc to examine all woolens destined for the Levant.[74] The Council of Commerce agreed, and an *arrêt* issued on 7 May 1714 established a new inspector in Montpellier.[75] Thereafter every piece of cloth produced in Languedoc had to be transported to Montpellier to be scrutinized and to receive the seal of the inspector there. This new inspection came in addition to the other ones already in place for such woolens: those of the various guild wardens, the regular inspectors in Languedoc, and the inspector in Marseilles.

PROBLEMS OF ENFORCEMENT

The above-mentioned difficulties in preventing abuses in Languedoc's woolen manufactures points up a general question involving the crown's entire regulatory system: How well were the manufacturing statutes actually enforced? Although the controller general and the Council of Commerce worked steadfastly to improve the network of controls, the results were, at best, mixed.

Financial difficulties, problems of communication, and local opposition helped ensure that many things would fall through the net of regulation.

The question of how the inspectors of manufactures were to be paid is illustrative of this entire situation. From their creation in 1669 until the Revolution, the inspectors continually faced the problem of lack of payment, and the government seems not to have been able to rectify that situation.[76] The plight of the inspectors of woolens was particularly acute. It should be recalled that these inspectors were paid from the duty of one sou, collected by the guild wardens, on each piece of cloth inspected. The problem was that the wardens often pocketed the money themselves or neglected to collect it in the first place, and the inspectors were thus in the delicate situation of having their salaries depend on the very people whom they were charged with supervising and possibly even punishing. Several inspectors therefore found their positions compromised; in order for the guilds to pay them, they had to put their stamp of approval on defective goods. Even before 1700 provincial intendants had been charged with making sure that such difficulties did not arise for the inspectors, but most intendants were already overworked and could spare little time for the inspectors of manufactures.

The inspectors who were paid by the royal treasury[77] were no better off. They often found that the *états* for their payment had not been drawn up or that the special fund they were to be paid from had disappeared.

This general problem grew even worse in time of war. From 1700 to 1715 virtually all the inspectors encountered financial difficulties at one time or another. Their letters to the controller general or to the Council of Commerce were often desperate. In April 1711, for example, Boré, the inspector of *toiles* in Alençon, wrote to Desmaretz bemoaning the fact that he had not been paid his salary since 1708. He complained that his creditors were pressing him and that he would not be able to continue his work if his financial plight got any worse.[78]

This inspector, however, was not alone. By 1713 Desmaretz had received so many complaints that he charged one of his *premiers commis*, de la Garde, with finding out the names of all the inspectors and how they were paid.[79] Since the controller general did not even know the names of the inspectors, it is not surprising that he often neglected to have them paid.[80]

In carrying out his mission, de la Garde worked closely with the members of the Council of Commerce. Daguesseau had already complained of the penury of most of the inspectors, and he provided the information that was needed.[81] As a result of de la Garde's inquiry, *états* were drawn up in 1714 ordering that the *trésor royal* pay all special inspectors and inspectors of *toiles* for years 1709 through 1714.[82] Another result was that de la Garde drew up a large register of approximately three hundred pages in which he listed the names of all the inspectors and described in careful detail each of their departments.[83] This register remains our best source of information concerning the composition of the corps of inspectors and the makeup of their departments at that time.

The inference to be drawn from all of this is that the inspectors could not be fully effective if they were continually hampered by financial problems. Even when they were paid, their salaries (usually 1,500 to 2,000 livres per year) were far from munificent. Out of this they had to maintain a residence and cover the expenses they encountered in traveling from place to place throughout the year. Boré, in Alençon, lamented that even when his salary was paid he could not afford to visit all the places where he was expected to go.[84] It goes without saying, therefore, that when the inspectors were not paid they cut even more corners and neglected to make the required number of tours in their departments each year.

The inspectors faced many other problems as well. The very size of their departments made it physically impossible for some of them to execute their duties to the fullest extent. The inspectors of woolens in Amiens and Rouen had to visit only about twelve to fifteen different towns in their departments each year; but the inspectors in Orléans and Champagne each had more than thirty places to visit, and the unfortunate inspector in Montauban had more than seventy.[85] Since most of the inspectors were forbidden to have subinspectors, this meant that the burden of visiting each of these manufacturing centers several times a year fell on a single man.[86]

The network of inspection was further weakened by the fact that the entire structure was superimposed over the existing guild system. The inspector's job was to supervise the work of guild wardens and to scrutinize the *bureaux de visite* to which guild workers brought their goods for examination by the wardens. An inspector could not properly perform his functions in areas where there were no guilds, and Colbert therefore had intended for every city and every craft to have its own guild or guilds. Even though the number of such bodies did increase in the decades after Colbert, however, the process was never finally completed. A survey of guilds taken in 1708, for example, revealed that in Poitiers only thirty-five of sixty-five trades were organized in guilds. The provinces of Roussillon, Berry, and La Rochelle had few guilds, and Béarn had none at all.[87]

What was worse, many manufacturers were moving their trades, heavy looms and all, to the countryside, where they could escape the bothersome regulations of the urban guilds. This ruralization of manufactures, sometimes referred to as the *usine dispersée*, made the inspection of manufactures increasingly difficult. Noëtte, inspector in Beauvais, complained to the controller general in 1713 that weaving looms (*métiers*) were "scattered in diverse villages in secret places, sometimes in a barn and sometimes in a loft, and often they are moved from place to place in order to hide the fraud."[88] It is virtually impossible to estimate the percentage of total production that escaped inspection in this manner.[89]

Another problem faced by the inspectors of manufactures was the resistance or, at times, outright hostility with which local merchants and manufacturers greeted them. The inspectors constantly had to beware of attempted frauds by local businessmen, and there were also at least a half-dozen open revolts against inspectors in various towns or villages during the period under study here.[90] Whenever Amelot or Daguesseau received a report of such an incident, he ordered the local intendant to imprison the leaders of the revolt for several days.[91]

In addition, the inspectors' jobs were frequently made more difficult by the very people who were supposed to help them; that is, the guild wardens and local *juges de police*. The wardens and city magistrates often proved reluctant to enforce regulations that might offend or cause hardships for their relatives and neighbors. Wardens therefore were prone to marking defective cloths, and both the wardens and the *juges* frequently neglected to levy the fines that were called for by law as a punishment for various abuses. During the years 1700 to 1715, the government received scores of complaints from inspectors or intendants against guild wardens or city magistrates.[92] The Council of Commerce and the controller general invariably cautioned these recalcitrant officials that unless they performed their duties better they would face possible fines or dismissal from office.

On several occasions during this period, some of the inspectors of manufactures also ran into problems with the parlements. These sovereign courts, acting on appeals, occasionally revoked decisions made by the inspectors. The inspector in Toulouse complained, for example, in 1708 that many of his confiscations of defective goods were appealed to the Parlement of Toulouse, which more often than not voted for the release of the goods that had been seized.[93] Bertrand exclaimed that under such circumstances it was impossible for him to enforce the law.

Invariably, the controller general, with the firm backing of the Council of Commerce, acted to support the power of the central government against the local-minded parlements. Either the courts' decisions were annulled by royal *arrêts*, or the cases were evoked to the provincial intendants or to the king's council.[94]

Although it is true that the amount of local resistance to the inspectors of manufactures was far from negligible, there is reason nevertheless to believe that historians have tended to exaggerate its extent.[95] Like the proverbial squeaky hinge, conflicts and quarrels always seem to get the most attention. One can argue, however, that this open or clandestine resistance was the exception rather than the rule. The overwhelming majority of letters and reports submitted by the inspectors to the controller general mention no opposition or upheavals. This has led at least one historian to conclude that the system of inspection "functioned very well for over a century."[96]

There is also other evidence to indicate that the inspectors were well received in many quarters. First of all, the deputies in the Council of Commerce, who represented business interests and who themselves were businessmen, wholeheartedly supported the upholding of royal laws by the inspectors. Local merchants and manufacturers likewise made known their support for the inspectors. Although the papers of the controller general, of Amelot, and of Daguesseau present many examples of opposition to the inspectors, they present many more instances of local businessmen pleading for better enforcement of textile regulations. Businessmen realized how important it was to protect the good name of a city's or a province's products. The letter books of Amelot and Daguesseau contain dozens of references to *marchands* or *fabricants* complaining about inspectors of manufactures—complaining not that the inspectors were trying to enforce the laws but that they were not working hard enough to enforce them. The businessmen wanted more, not less, government intervention.[97]

Their dissatisfaction with inspectors covered a wide spectrum of offenses: laziness, negligence, incompetence, favoritism, dishonesty.[98] The intendant in Provence, Lebret, reported in May 1713, for example, that Cauvière, the inspector in Marseilles, was suspected by many honest merchants of receiving bribes from certain *négociants* and *fabricants* in return for permitting defective cloths to be shipped to the Levant.[99] The inspector in Carcassonne, de la Marque, was accused of being too severe on some manufacturers while being overly lenient to his friends and family.[100]

Amelot and Daguesseau generally responded to such allegations by having the intendant in the area study the matter. If an inspector was indeed remiss, he was either reprimanded or fired. More often than not, however, the inspectors were not personally at fault. Barolet, inspector in Champagne, responded to charges against him in April 1713 by arguing that his department was too big for one man; he also noted that he was not paid enough—when he was paid at all—to cover all his expenses.[101] But the inspectors who, for one reason or another, were felt to be doing an inferior job were in the minority. The government and the greater part of the business community seem to have been convinced that most of them were doing as well as could be expected.

Up to this point this chapter has dealt with the work of the Council of Commerce in issuing new manufacturing regulations and in helping to supervise the inspection of manufactures. Also, the discussion has been limited solely to the textile industry because textile output was far more important to both the internal and external markets than all other industries combined. It was therefore natural that the Council of Commerce should concentrate overwhelmingly on this sector of the economy. The inspectors of manufactures likewise were charged almost exclusively with the examination of finished cloths of various types.[102]

This is not to say that other industries were neglected. The Council of Commerce was also active in issuing new, or revising old, regulations concerning the manufacture of hosiery, blankets, soap, leather goods, paper, and glass, and concerning the mining and processing of coal, tin plate, iron ore, and other such products.[103] The inspectors of manufactures were expected to keep an eye on these industries in a general fashion. Occasionally their letters and reports to the controller general contain detailed information regarding them. The guild wardens, the *juges des manufactures*, and the provincial intendants were also charged with supervising the work and enforcing quality standards in the non-textile sectors. In some cases there were special officials appointed to do work similar to that of the inspectors of manufactures. For example, all mining in France was under the surveillance of the *grand-maître des mines, minières, et substances terrestres.*[104]

ENCOURAGEMENT OF MANUFACTURES

In addition to regulation by statute and by means of inspectors, the central government employed yet other means by which it administered and promoted French manufactures. These included the granting of privileges, the protection of established industries from newly introduced ones, and the protection of the supply of raw materials.[105] Every industry—not merely textiles—benefited from these kinds of encouragement.

The granting of privileges of one sort or another by the French crown to manufacturers went back to at least the fifteenth century, but the practice became regular only under Henry IV and reached its climax with Colbert. There were basically four types of manufacturing enterprises in France.[106] First, there were the *manufactures du roi*, which the government owned and administered and whose chief customers were the king and his court. These establishments thus included the renowned tapestry and carpet factories—Gobelins, Beauvais, Savonnerie—and the various artisans who had workshops at the Louvre or who followed the court. Second, there were the *manufactures royales*, which were privately owned but which the crown had recognized by means of *brevets* or *lettres patentes*. These manufactures had fairly extensive privileges, often including the exclusive right to produce a particular item. Next came the *manufactures privilégiées*, which were also privately owned and had royal charters. The privileges granted to these companies were usually less generous than those bestowed on the *manufactures royales*.[107] The fourth group comprised those enterprises which the crown never officially recognized. They were generally small shops with insignificant amounts of production, and royal officials, already overworked, tended to tolerate their existence. It was with the manufactures of the second and third types that the Council of Commerce principally dealt.[108]

Colbert often showed his favor to the inventor of a new manufacturing process or to a gifted entrepreneur by granting him the exclusive right to manufacture a particular item. Sometimes this monopoly extended to the whole country, but most often it extended only to a single province or area (usually a radius of three to ten leagues from a particular town). Financial subsidies or exemptions of various types generally accompanied such an exclusive privilege.

In their general memoirs of 1700–1701, most of the deputies of commerce denounced the notion of monopoly of any sort, and from this one would have expected them to oppose unalterably the granting of such exclusive privileges. Such was not the case in practice, however. From 1700 to 1715 the Council of Commerce supported the granting of thirteen exclusive privileges to various enterprises.[109] This number admittedly is relatively small when compared with the number of monopolistic privileges granted by Colbert. Charles Woolsey Cole, however, has asserted that as early as the 1680s the crown itself was already decreasing the number of exclusive privileges awarded to entrepreneurs.[110]

The point to be made here, however, is that the council did not in principle oppose giving an individual the exclusive right to produce an article in his town or province if the situation warranted it. Thus in 1701 the council agreed that the individuals who had devised a new way to make oil (used in preparing textiles and in paints) should be the only ones permitted to use the new method.[111] In 1709 Daguesseau recommended to Desmaretz that a man named Saint-Etienne be granted a nationwide exclusive privilege for the manufacture of porcelain by means of a new process he had invented; the monopoly would run fifteen years, however, and not twenty as Saint-Etienne had wished.[112]

In March 1715 two brothers, Jacques and Thomas Bourdon, requested authorization to establish at Andelys, in Normandy, a plant for the manufacture of fine English-style woolens. They asked for the exclusive right to make these goods in all the territory within three leagues of Andelys for the next twenty years. Not only did the Council of Commerce grant this local monopoly but it exempted the Bourdons and all their workers from quartering troops, from paying the *taille* and from numerous other charges, including the *milice, guet, tutelle,* and *curatelle.* In addition, the cloths sent from this factory to Italy or Spain were freed from several internal customs duties. Finally, the new business was designated the *manufacture royale des Andelys.*[113]

Although one might cite other examples of exclusive privileges accorded on the advice of the Council of Commerce, one must admit that the council turned down most of the requests it received for such national or local monopolies. It always did this in cases where an exclusive privilege granted to one manufacturer would have hurt other manufacturers already engaged in making the same product. If a man could not offer a new product or technique, or if he could not prove that his own enterprise would be the first of its kind in a particular area, then he was not likely to receive an exclusive privilege. Therefore, the council in 1703 rejected a request by some individuals that they be the only ones in France permitted to manufacture glue in the English fashion.[114] These persons had claimed that their new product would save Frenchmen from needing to purchase such glue from England. The council decided, however, that their new product was very similar to the ordinary glue already made in France and that an exclusive privilege might therefore drive many French workers out of business. For the same reason the council in 1705 turned down the request of a Marseilles businessman for the sole right to produce starch (*amidon*) in Provence; there were already many workers producing starch in the province, and such a monopoly would have thrown them out of work.[115]

If the council was rather hesitant about the granting of new exclusive privileges, it showed no reluctance when it came to reaffirming the exclusive privileges that had been originally granted by Colbert and others prior to 1700. Almost invariably the council voted to renew such monopolies whenever the terms of the original grants were about to expire. The council, for example, gave strong support to the *manufacture royale des glaces*, which continued to hold its virtual monopoly over all high-quality plate glass and mirrors throughout the eighteenth century.[116]

Another *manufacture royale* that had been founded by Colbert and that received the warm backing of the Council of Commerce was the van Robais firm in Abbeville. Colbert had lured the Protestant Josse van Robais from Holland in 1665 with promises of lavish royal patronage. In return for producing woolens of the highest quality, van Robais was granted an exclusive privilege in the Abbeville area. In addition, he received huge government loans and subsidies. By the early eighteenth century, the van Robais firm had more than 1,200 employees.[117]

The Council of Commerce had numerous opportunities to display its favor for this particular enterprise. In 1708 the van Robais family requested that all their workers be exempted from personal taxes and that throughout the remainder of the war their woolens be able to pass into Spain without any internal or export duties; both requests were granted.[118] In October 1710 van Robais's exclusive privilege for the production of high-quality woolen cloths within a ten-mile radius of Abbeville was renewed.

All was nearly lost in 1711, however, when the van Robais family was rocked by a scandal. The founder of the company, Josse van Robais, had left behind two sons, Josse and Isaac. Isaac, however, died in 1703 and thus the *lettres patentes* of October 1710 that renewed all the privileges of the company named as directors Josse and his sister-in-law Marie, the widow of Isaac. About this same time, however, Marie married the valet of her dead husband, a man named Vasseur. Josse van Robais and the children of Marie felt disgraced by "this shameful *mésalliance*" since Vasseur was "without education, without experience and without money."[119] The affair climaxed in 1711 when it was discovered that Vasseur, a former Huguenot, had relapsed to Protestantism.[120] He was compelled to flee to Holland, and Marie soon followed, taking many of her valuables with her. The van Robais family was shaken by this scandal, and their entire enterprise seemed about to founder. Josse van Robais asked that the recently issued *lettres patentes* be revised so as to exclude Marie van Robais from any ownership of the family business.

The whole affair was sent to the Council of Commerce. The council set to work at once to determine all the holdings of the van Robais factory and to draw up new plans for the administration of the company. *Arrêts* were issued on 12 May 1711 and 28 June 1712 naming Josse van Robais and two of his nephews (the two eldest sons of Marie) as directors and dividing up Marie's interest in the enterprise among her children.[121] Although this affair was somewhat unusual, it accurately reflects the care with which the council treated most of the established *manufactures royales*.

The bulk of French manufactures, of course, were on a scale much smaller than that of the van Robais family. Except for the very small enterprises, all of these manufactures were required, at least officially, to purchase royal charters. Hundreds of these establishments were in return granted nonexclusive privileges—hence the name *manufactures privilégiées*. These privileges often included exemption from billeting troops and from payment of the *taille*, or freedom from the *milice, guet, curatelle,* and *tutelle*. Frequently the government also presented new and promising entrepreneurs with gifts of money or loans at favorable rates of interest. Finally, the crown often favored manufacturers by allowing them to pay lower import duties on raw materials needed for their goods or lower export duties on the finished products being sold abroad.

Both Levasseur and Cole argue that government support for new manufacturers declined after Colbert's death. As proof they assert that the number of privileged manufactures created after 1683 dropped sharply. Levasseur says, in fact, that only twenty such enterprises were established between 1683 and 1715.[122] Neither Cole nor Levasseur cites any quantitative evidence, either from Colbert's period or later. To answer this question conclusively, one would have to uncover all the relevant *lettres patentes* issued from the 1660s to 1715—a task of formidable dimensions.

If one looks at the records of the Council of Commerce, however, one comes to a conclusion at odds with that of Cole and Levasseur. Certainly the government had less money to hand out to prospective entrepreneurs during the final two wars of the reign, but it continued eagerly to grant privileges of other sorts to newly created manufactures. From 1700 to 1715 the *procès-verbaux* mention specifically more than forty cases where the Council of Commerce discussed the formation of enterprises endowed with *privilèges ordinaires*.[123] It is certain that the number of such undertakings actually created during this period far exceeds this number. A typical example of these sorts of privileges occurred in May 1712 when the council approved the creation of two new bottle-making plants, one in Vivier (near Folembray) and the other in Ozouer-la-Ferrière (near Paris). The owner and employees at each establishment were to receive exemptions from the *taille, curatelle, tutelle*, and from quartering troops.[124]

Another type of favor granted to manufacturers was payment of a gratification to the entrepreneur for each piece of cloth produced. This acted as an incentive for production and generally applied to cloths destined for the foreign markets. Thus it happened that one of the encouragements given in 1714 to a merchant named Jacques Lefèvre to establish a woolens factory in Ariès was that the king would give him three livres for each piece of cloth he produced for the Levant.[125] In Languedoc it had been the practice—begun probably under the prodding of Colbert—for the provincial estates to give each *manufacture royale* in the province one *pistolle* (approximately ten livres) for each bolt of cloth dispatched to the Levant. At least three different times during the first fifteen years of the eighteenth century, the estates asked to be relieved of this obligation.[126] The deputies of commerce vigorously criticized this proposal, arguing that French manufacturers needed all the help they could get at a time when they had a chance to drive the English and Dutch out of the Levant market. The *commissaires* agreed with the deputies, and the estates were told to continue the gratification, which they did.[127]

In addition to bestowing such privileges as these on hundreds of businessmen, the crown sought to protect old, established industries from new products and techniques. It may be argued that in so doing the monarchy was impeding progress, but this policy had great popular support, including that given it by the Council of Commerce.

The policy of protecting older industries from new ones had originated early in the seventeenth century, but its practice grew apace under Colbert and his successors. The use of indigo in dyeing cloths, for example, had long been restricted so as not to compete with woad. In 1664 the making of half-beaver hats was prohibited in order to protect the sale of hats made entirely of beaver. This ban was lifted by an *arrêt* of 10 August 1700 when the government realized that the freedom to mix beaver hair with other types of hair or wool might actually increase the consumption of beaver. The government likewise sought to protect button-makers from new competition. Traditionally, buttons had been made of metal, silk, or the horns of animals, and each type was made by a particular guild. In the 1690s, however, a new kind of button began to be made by tailors and haberdashers. The new buttons were made of the same material as the garment to which they were attached (wool, linen, etc.). The makers of old-style buttons protested vociferously against this innovation, and the crown responded by issuing a declaration on 25 September 1694 outlawing the new buttons. The new law proved to be difficult to enforce, but the government did its best to see that it was observed. One could cite several other similar cases where the crown sought to protect workers from new industries.[128]

This general policy was firmly supported by the Council of Commerce, chiefly in three areas. The first of these, the manufacture of brandy, has already been mentioned.[129] The council sought to protect the traditional wine and brandy industries from newly introduced brandies made from grape skins, apple cider, or honey. The new brandies were permitted to be made and consumed in only a few cities and provinces.

A second area in which the Council of Commerce was deeply

involved was the manufacture of woolen stockings. Since early in the seventeenth century, silk stockings had been made on stocking looms or frames, but woolen stockings continued to be knitted by hand. Countless thousands of workers—usually peasant women or the sick and poor confined to hospitals—depended on their knitting for their livelihoods. Beginning in the 1660s, however, workers in Lyons devised a method that also made possible the manufacture of woolen stockings on frames. One worker using a stocking frame could produce stockings faster and more economically than several persons toiling by hand. This practice grew despite a crescendo of opposition from hand-knitters and the merchants who sold their goods. The traditionalists won a victory in 1684 when the government issued an *arrêt* ordering that one-half of all frames had to be used exclusively for silk hosiery,[130] but the battle of hand-knitters (making *bas au tricot*) against modern machinery (*bas au métier*) continued. Finally the government issued an *arrêt* on 30 March 1700 that severely restricted stocking production on frames: the new *arrêt* henceforth limited stocking frames to eighteen cities.[131] Owners of stocking frames in other areas would have to move them to these cities.

After the Council of Commerce was established, it gave its fervent support to this *arrêt*. The deputies of trade, who in 1700 called for *liberté* and who represented business interests, were the most vocal opponents of the free enterprise of the owners of stocking frames. During the years studied here, the council rejected numerous requests by workers to set up, or to continue to operate, stocking frames in cities other than those listed in the 1700 *arrêt*.[132] By about 1713, however, it had become clear that the policy of restriction was losing the battle: stocking frames were continuing to spread. Begrudgingly, therefore, the Council of Commerce had to make concessions. One by one, new cities were added to the original list of eighteen. In 1714 and 1715 the cities of Falaise, Bayeux, and Valence won the right to have stocking frames, and this trend increased its pace in the years after 1715.[133]

The third, and most famous, area in which the Council of Commerce participated in an attempt to prevent the growth of a new industry concerned the importation into France of cottons from the East, especially India. By the mid-seventeenth century, these cottons were becoming highly fashionable all over Europe. They were roughly of two types: white cottons and cottons of various colors and designs. There were many varieties of the latter type, though they were all generally referred to in France as *toiles peintes* or *indiennes* and in England as calicos. Beginning in the 1660s, French workers began to imitate the *toiles peintes*. But whereas the original, Indian-made cloths actually had designs painted onto them with feathers or brushes, the French models had designs printed (*imprimées*) on them by means of a crude system of wooden blocks. The French cloths were inferior in design and in color, and their colors tended to mix or to fade quickly. Nevertheless, the French imitations soon also came to be termed *toiles peintes* or *indiennes*, and by the 1670s their production was thriving in France.

These new fabrics posed a deadly threat to the more traditional French cloths: woolens, silks, and linens. Workers from all over France virtually flooded the government with protests against the new cottons. The chief culprit was the East India Company, whose ships brought back more and more of the goods each year. By an *arrêt* of 26 October 1686, the crown at last decided to prohibit the sale of *toiles peintes* from the East and to forbid their manufacture in France.[134]

From the very beginning, the new policy of prohibition faced rough going. The government was forced at several points to come to the rescue of the East India Company by allowing it to sell the Indies cottons in France. Marseilles, as a free port, also claimed the right to sell and use *toiles peintes* within its own borders. Worst of all, calicos were smuggled into the country in huge quantities, and they continued to be the rage among French nobles and bourgeois, especially the women.

The story of *toiles peintes* in France—and the role played in it by the Council of Commerce—has been told at length elsewhere[135] and need not be described in detail here. Far from championing freedom of trade, the council became, in the words of Edgard Depitre, a "fierce partisan of the prohibition."[136] During the period 1700–1715, the council drafted over a dozen *arrêts* aimed at driving the new cloths out of the country. It successfully ended the rights of the East India Company to sell *toiles peintes* in France, although it failed to get the cloths banned from Marseilles.[137] The council reinforced or stiffened the penalties for breaking the law. Any merchant found handling the prohibited fabrics was subject to a fine of 3,000 livres and banishment from the profession for life. Two-thirds of all fines were to go the *dénonciateurs* who made known the crime. Any royal officials or employees of the tax farms who were discovered permitting the commerce of *toiles peintes* were to be put in the galleys for nine years. All captured goods were to be confiscated; half were to be burned, and the other half were to be sold, on condition that they be exported from the country.

The almost rabid hatred of the deputies of trade for the *toiles peintes* is, at least on the face of it, somewhat surprising. Only a minority of them were from manufacturing areas that would have been seriously hurt by the new fabrics (Lyons, Languedoc, Rouen). Most of the other deputies were from major commercial cities that would have benefited from the trade in *toiles peintes*. The fact that virtually all of them supported the policy of prohibition is perhaps a sign that the crown had been at least partially successful in getting the deputies to consider "the general good" above purely local interests.

So it was that throughout this period the deputies repeatedly deplored "the prodigious consumption" of *toiles peintes* in France, which was estimated to value twelve million livres a year.[138] They condemned the East India Company because, instead of bringing drugs and spices to France, it desired to bring products that caused "a considerable prejudice to manufactures and to all the trade of the kingdom."[139] On several occasions the deputies bitterly criticized "this degrading taste"[140] of "the ladies of the court," who dared to wear Indian cottons in the palace of the king himself.[141]

The effort to prevent the entry and use of printed or painted cottons was doomed to failure. As Depitre has explained, "That which, in the beginning, was just an affair of taste became a fashion, and fashion made it a necessity."[142] The more legislation that the government issued against *toiles peintes*, the more that people wanted them. In the years after 1715, the Council (later Bureau) of Commerce continued to legislate against them, with little more success. By the 1750s French workers had pirated from England the secret for using dyes on cotton, and this led the crown, in 1759, finally to repeal all prohibitions against the import or manufacture of *toiles peintes* in France.[143]

An obvious lesson to be learned from all the above examples concerning *toiles peintes*, stocking frames, brandy, and other items is that one cannot prevent innovation or dictate taste by means of legislation. In every instance where this was attempted, it failed. It might, in fact, be argued that such restrictions actually damaged the economic development of the nation. There can be no doubt of the fact that the strictures against *toiles peintes* hindered the development of the French cotton industry.

But, more important to our purpose here, two other points should be made. First of all, in each of these cases the crown acted out of a humanitarian impulse. Royal ministers and intendants repeatedly expressed their concern lest *les pauvres* or *le menu peuple* lose their jobs as a result of changing styles or techniques. Second, in each instance, at least in the early stages, the crown had wide popular support for its policies. When businessmen finally were given a voice in the formulation of royal programs, through the Council of Commerce, their deputies supported the same basic policies already espoused by the crown.

One final method by which the government, aided by the Council of Commerce, sought to help manufactures was through the conservation of raw materials. In Chapter Five it has already been noted how the council encouraged neutral and enemy countries to bring such goods to France. Similarly, the council strove to ensure that France's own natural resources were at the full disposal of its workers. This was done by controlling their use within the country and, if necessary, by prohibiting their export.

Since woolens were the single most important type of cloth made in France, it was only natural that the Council of Commerce be concerned about the production of wool in France and about the well-being of France's sheep. The council supported the government's policy of prohibiting the export of raw wool to France's competitors;[144] and when, in 1714, some French merchants made known their intention to export sheep to Spain, the crown, at the behest of the deputies of trade, issued an *arrêt* prohibiting such export.[145] Moreover, the council was always solicitous of the health and reproductivity of the nation's sheep. There were three to four million more sheep than people in France,[146] and the council wished to ensure that this situation would not change. At the first sign of an epidemic among sheep or a decrease in their numbers due to some other cause, the council drafted *arrêts* prohibiting the killing of sheep in one province or in the nation as a whole. These prohibitions lasted from several months to a year. At least six such *arrêts* were issued from 1700 to 1715. Stiff fines were imposed on butchers, tavern owners, and other individuals who violated these laws. A more lasting solution to the problem was brought by an *arrêt* of 5 November 1710 and a declaration of 16 February

1712.[147] These statutes forbade the slaughter of any lambs or sheep between Easter and Pentecost of each year. Since meat consumption was already down during Lent, this meant that France's twenty-four million sheep were—at least in theory—protected from mutton-loving Frenchmen for about one-third of each year.

The council also took other steps to protect or build up France's supply of raw materials. On numerous occasions it drafted *arrêts* that temporarily prohibited the export of thistles, linseed, resin, and other articles used in the preparation of textiles.[148] The council likewise proposed measures to conserve and augment the nation's dwindling timber supply.[149] Similarly, the council urged the adoption of tax incentives and other inducements to get people to plant mulberry trees, in the hope that France could grow enough silkworms on its own so that it would not need to import raw silk from Italy and the Levant.[150]

THE STATE OF FRENCH MANUFACTURES

This chapter has concentrated on the government's program of regulation and encouragement of French manufactures. One matter that has generally been avoided is the question of whether, in actuality, this regulatory system helped or hurt French manufactures. This question has not been posed basically because the attempt here has been to study the administration of manufactures rather than the manufactures themselves. Nevertheless, the question of the relationship between governmental control and economic growth—during early modern times or any other period—is of vital importance.

As a general rule, historians have assumed that royal intervention must have had a deleterious effect on the economy. Biollay, for instance, has avowed that the only inspectors of manufactures who helped the economy were the ones who were too lazy to do their jobs and therefore let things run themselves.[151] The underlying assumption beneath this historiographical aversion to the mercantilist program of regulation has been that French manufactures declined in inverse proportion to the growth of state controls. The classic portrait that historians have drawn of French commerce and industry late in the reign of Louis XIV is therefore one of gloom: entire cities whose industries were destroyed, plummeting trade figures, and decline in virtually every area of manufactures.[152] Of course, many factors are believed to have been responsible for this: the revocation of the Edict of Nantes, wars, famines, royal monetary manipulations, epidemics, and tariff policies, among others. But historians have assumed uniformly that the "economic statism" or *mercantilisme à outrance* of Colbert's successors was a major element in this decline.

Three responses might be made to this interpretation. First of all, no one as of yet has systematically endeavored to test the hypothesis that government intervention must automatically hurt economic growth. John U. Nef, it is true, studied the relationship between industry and government in France for an earlier period[153] and concluded that royal regulation had a damaging impact on industrial development. His conclusions are severely weakened, however, by his violent *parti pris*. He was writing in 1940—at a time when democracy seemed to be endangered—and he tended to equate Louis XIV with Hitler. We therefore desperately need a new analysis of the effect that royal controls had on manufactures.[154]

Second, the mournful portrait of the French economy late in the reign of Louis XIV has been overdrawn. Several recent studies have shown that many areas of French commerce and industry did rather well late in the reign. Languedoc's production of woolens for the Levant increased gradually throughout the War of the Spanish Succession and then soared spectacularly in 1713, continuing to rise until the 1780s.[155] J. S. Bromley has likewise demonstrated that the trade of several Atlantic ports increased during the war years.[156] Pierre Deyon has argued that Amiens's manufactures experienced a growth cycle that began in 1680 and extended throughout the remainder of the reign.[157] Markovitch has shown that the woolens industry grew in many regions (Toulouse, Alençon, Sedan, Montpellier, Poitiers, and others) between 1692 and 1708.[158] This fact is confirmed by two circular letters written to the inspectors of manufactures by Daguesseau—on behalf of Desmaretz—in September 1708. Desmaretz declared that he was "happy to be informed of the present state of all the manufactures" and then went on to encourage the inspectors to do their jobs well. In addition, he requested them to take a general survey of all the manufactures in their departments and to submit the results to him.[159] Although some manufactures did decline late in Louis XIV's reign, others grew. Indeed, much recent research in French demographic, industrial, agricultural, and commercial history is posing a sharp challenge to the traditional image of the economy at that time.[160]

A third, and final, reply to the usual evaluation of royal regulation of industrial growth is the message that this chapter has striven to convey. Royal statutes were born not of an overwrought *esprit de réglementation* within the royal ministries but out of a cooperative effort between the government and the business community. There *was* opposition to many of the regulations by unscrupulous, and even by honest, merchants and manufacturers, but there were probably even more who upheld the crown's efforts to regulate and promote native industries. The Council of Commerce in particular believed in the salubrious effects of royal intervention. Whatever the long-range impact of the crown's policies on the economy might therefore have been, it is clear that during the years under study here they had much popular support.[161]

1. See Chapter 1, n. 63; Chapter 2, n. 54.

2. AN, F¹² 114–15 (years 1700–1), 121–25 ¹⁻² (years 1705–9). Although these letters were written by Amelot and Daguesseau—as is noted on the frontispieces of the registers—they were always signed by the controller general.

3. The only exception to this was the inspector of manufactures in Marseilles, who was under the secretary of state for the navy.

4. Clément, *Histoire du système protecteur*, pp. 25–26.

5. Cobban, *A History of Modern France*, vol. 1: *1715–1799*, p. 43. Also see J. S. Bromley, *The New Cambridge Modern History*, 6:28; Deyon, *Le Mercantilisme*, pp. 29–30; Pierre Gaxotte, "Colbert impose la dictature du travail."

6. Heckscher, *Mercantilism*, vol. 1, pt. 1, chaps. 5–6. Also see Kurt Samuelsson, "Religion and Economic Action," in Robert W. Green (ed.), *The Weber Thesis Controversy*, p. 119.

7. Clément, *Histoire du système protecteur*, p. 25; Depping, *Correspondance administrative*, 3:55; Tihomir J. Markovitch, "Le triple tricentennaire de Colbert: l'enquête, les règlements, les inspecteurs," pp. 312–13. Clément does not provide the source of his information. Certainly his numbers are much too low, both for Colbert's period and for the years following. Literally hundreds of industrial regulations for the entire period can be found in the Collection Rondonneau at the Archives Nationales and in the huge *Recueil des règlemens généraux et particuliers concernant les manufactures et fabriques du royaume*, hereafter *Recueil des règlemens*. Emile Levasseur has counted 150 industrial statutes for Colbert's period alone, and even this figure is probably low (see Levasseur, *Histoire des classes ouvrières et de l'industrie en France avant 1789*).

8. See above, Chapter 3, nn. 101–2. Also see Levasseur, *Histoire des classes ouvrières*, vol. 2, bk. 6, chap. 6; Marchand, *Un Intendant*, pp. 300, 324, 340; Paul-M. Bondois, "L'Organisation industrielle et commerciale sous l'ancien régime: le privilège exclusif au XVIIIᵉ siècle"; Goubert, *L'ancien régime*, 2:211; Goubert, *Louis XIV*

and Twenty Million Frenchmen, p. 266; Léon, in Braudel and Labrousse, *Histoire économique et sociale,* 2:224–25; Davis, *Rise of the Atlantic Economies,* p. 224; Pierre Deyon, "La Production manufacturière en France au XVIIe siècle et ses problèmes"; Marc Raeff, "The Well-Ordered Police State and the Development of Modernity in Seventeenth and Eighteenth–Century Europe: An Attempt at a Comparative Approach," p. 1226.

9. See Chapter 3, nn. 71–79. Also, Mar., B[7] 507, fol. 59v, Machault to Pontchartrain, 25 October 1709.

10. *Recueil des règlemens,* 1:283–98.

11. Cole, *French Mercantilism, 1683–1700,* p. 143. Also see Martin, *La grande industrie . . . Louis XIV,* pt. 2, chaps. 4 and 10; Auguste Dubois, *Précis,* p. 215; Emile Levasseur, *Histoire des classes ouvrières,* vol. 2, bk. 6, chap. 6.

12. Cole, *French Mercantilism, 1683–1700,* pp. 29, 145–46.

13. *Recueil des règlemens,* 1:421 ff.

14. See Pierre Deyon, *Amiens, capitale provinciale: étude sur la société urbaine au 17e siècle,* p. 172.

15. For example, see Markovitch, "Le triple tricentennaire," p. 317. In speaking of the longer, more complex textile regulations issued in 1779–80, Harold Parker says that such laws actually indicated flexibility on the part of the government (*The Bureau of Commerce in 1781 and Its Policies with Respect to French Industry,* pp. 38–39).

16. This final punishment seems to have been executed only rarely (see Levasseur, *Histoire des classes ouvrières,* 2:234).

17. Ibid.

18. Ibid., 2:213–14, 313–33; Martin, *La grande industrie . . . Louis XIV,* pt. 2, chaps. 4, 10. Also see Goubert, *L'ancien régime,* 2:211.

19. Cole, *French Mercantilism, 1683–1700,* pp. 143–44.

20. In addition to the works already cited, consult: "La première industrie lainière à Paris"; "L'Industrie lainière française au début du XVIIIe siècle"; "L'Industrie française au XVIIIe siècle: l'industrie lainière à la fin du règne de Louis XIV et sous la régence."

21. This will, however, be discussed briefly at the end of this chapter.

22. The ordinances that Colbert issued in 1669 provide a good illustration of this. These statutes were the product of seven years of study. Colbert had intendants and specially appointed officers (including two *drapiers* from Paris) confer with merchants and *maîtres-ouvriers* throughout France before issuing the new laws. (Levasseur, *Histoire des classes ouvrières,* 2:211–13.)

23. See Chapter 1, n. 19.

24. AN, G[7] 1701, piece 148, Louis Itier to Desmaretz, 24 August 1713. For other examples see AN, F[12] 123, fol. 15, Chamillart to Collet, 23 November 1706; G[7] 8, Pontchartrain to Foucault, 29 October 1697; F[12] 124, fol. 85, Chamillart to d'Harouis, 8 November 1707. Concerning the problems resulting from the production of defective goods, see Octave Teissier, *Inventaire des archives historiques de la chambre de commerce de Marseille,* p. 14; Fernand Braudel, *The Mediterranean World in the Age of Philip II,* 1:627; Pierre Léon, *La Naissance de la grande industrie en Dauphiné: fin du XVIIe siècle–1869,* 1:115; Andrew Trout, *Jean-Baptiste Colbert,* p. 127.

25. On a few occasions, extenuating circumstances did prompt the council to relax certain rules for particular individuals. In 1709 the council urged that, because of that year's economic disaster, fines levied for infractions be lowered (see AN, G[7] 1694, piece 60, Lescalopier to Desmaretz, 12 February 1709).

26. AN, F[12] 1349, "Mémoire sur l'usage des rames pour la perfection de la fabrique des draps," dated 11 May 1714.

27. This figure is tentative. It is based on the *Recueil des règlemens* and on the materials I have found thus far in other sources. Further work, particularly in the Collection Rondonneau at the Archives Nationales, should provide a more accurate figure. The number 200 does, however, correspond with the 219 *règlements* that Germain Martin has found for the period 1715–30. (see Martin, *La grande industrie . . . Louis XV*, p. 27).

28. See AN, G⁷ 1689, piece 129, untitled memoir, dated 18 June 1724. In addition to preserving individual copies of newly issued laws, the council had a copy of the *Recueil des règlemens des manufactures et teintures d'étoffes*, edited by Saugrain and published in 1701. The 1724 memoir states that a new *recueil* is needed. It is highly probable that the council (after 1722 the Bureau of Commerce) was involved in the preparation of the new *Recueil des règlemens*, the first volume of which was published in 1730.

29. An edict issued in October 1699 created lieutenants general of police in most of the larger cities in France. After that date these new officials performed the functions of *juges des manufactures* in these cities. This edict is partially reprinted in Isambert, *Recueil général*, 20:346. The editors of this collection mistakenly imply that lieutenants general were established only in the cities where parlements met; they were also formed in cities that had any of the following: a *cour des aides*, a *chambre des comptes*, a presidial court, or a court of the *bailliage* or *sénéchaussée*.

30. Good descriptions of guilds and their operations during the seventeenth and eighteenth centuries can be found in Levasseur, *Histoire des classes ouvrières*, vol. 2, bk. 6, chap. 9; François Olivier-Martin, *L'Organisation corporative de la France d'ancien régime*, chap. 2; E. Coornaert, *Les Corporations in France avant 1789*.

31. Inspectors had, however, been appointed at various times before 1669, largely on an *ad hoc* basis. The most detailed account of the inspectors of manufactures is Franc Bacquié, *Les Inspecteurs des manufactures sous l'ancien régime, 1669–1792*.

32. Cole, *French Mercantilism, 1683–1700*, p. 295.

33. A copy is in AN, F¹² 730.

34. Boislisle, *Correspondance des contrôleurs généraux*, 1:558–60; AN, F¹² 673, circular letter to inspectors of manufactures, 28 February 1694.

35. See above, Chapter 2, n. 70. De la Vigne also worked on tariff questions for the Council of Commerce as a whole (see below, Chapter 7).

36. Numerous references to the work of these two men can be found in AN, F¹² 730.

37. AN, F¹² 123, fol. 79–79v, Chamillart to Boislisle, 11 January 1707.

38. AN, G⁷ 1703, piece 42, Daguesseau to Desmaretz, 6 October 1714.

39. AN, F¹² 115, fol. 34. Chamillart to Le Gendre, 8 March 1701 and Chamillart to Leyrat, 8 March 1701.

40. For example, AN, F¹² 122, fol. 102v, Chamillart to Pichol, 20 July 1706.

41. AN, F¹² 115, fol. 12, Chamillart to Timouecourt (?), 23 January 1701.

42. AN, G⁷ 1689, piece 99.

43. Bacquié, *Les Inspecteurs des manufactures*, pp. 248 ff. Bacquié's description of this topic errs in many respects. He fails to note that some inspectors were paid by the *trésor royal*, and he mistakenly asserts that in *pays d'états* inspectors were paid by the provincial estates.

44. Fabrics made of linen or hemp.

45. This document also lists payments to men charged with special missions concerning manufactures, and it notes payments to Grandval (a farmer general) and de la Vigne, both of whom were working under Amelot toward the establishment of a balance of trade.

46. Julien Hayem, "Les Inspecteurs des manufactures," in Hayem (ed.), *Mémoires et documents pour servir à l'histoire du commerce et de l'industrie en France*, 2d ser., p. 229; Markovitch, "Le triple tricentennaire," p. 309.

47. AN, F¹² 730, "Etat général des inspecteurs des manufactures," November 1704. As with all subsequent lists, this one divides the inspectors into four categories: inspectors of woolens, inspectors of *toiles*, inspectors of foreign manufactures, and inspectors stationed in Paris.

48. AN, F¹² 115, fol. 35–35v, Chamillart to Pinon and Foucault, 14 March 1701; ibid., fol. 108v, same to same, 9 June 1701.

49. AN, F¹² 122, fols. 82–83, Chamillart to Basville, 22 June 1706. In 1697 Louis de Pontchartrain had decided to increase the number of inspectors in Languedoc from two to four, but apparently nothing was done about it. See AN, G⁷ 8, Pontchartrain to Bosson and de la Marque, 20 October 1697; ibid., Pontchartrain to Basville, 9 December 1697.

50. AN, F¹² 51, fols. 114, 283–86, 402v, 433v–35; F¹² 54, fols. 62–64, 87–88v.

51. A copy may be found in AN, AD XI, 42.

52. See Wallon, *La Chambre de commerce de la province de Normandie*, p. 35; AN, G⁷ 9, Chamillart to *juges* and *consuls* of the *juridiction consulaire* of Beauvais, 25 November 1704.

53. Wallon, ibid.; AN, G⁷ 359, piece 158, Trudaine to Chamillart, 28 November 1704; also piece 180, directors of the Chamber of Commerce of Lyons to Chamillart, 9 December 1704; and piece 183, Trudaine to Chamillart, 9 December 1704.

54. These sentiments of the deputies are noted in the declaration of 30 December 1704, a copy of which is in AN, AD XI, 42. Also see AN, F¹² 673, various untitled memoirs and notes concerning this affair.

55. See AN, G⁷ 1688, piece 80, "Observations sur l'Edit de création des Inspecteurs en titre d'office"; piece 134, Amelot to Desmaretz, 14 February 1704; piece 137, same to same, 6 November 1704; piece 138, Amelot to Chamillart, 11 November 1704.

56. Ibid., piece 17, *placet* by Thévenin and partners to Chamillart. They complain that "the affair would have succeeded as had been projected if it had not been for the extraordinary actions taken by Monsieur Amelot to make it fail.".

57. A copy is in AN, AD XI, 42.

58. There is some evidence that the new offices were not selling well and that the government would gain little by them. This could very well have helped persuade the government to settle for 1,200,000 livres. Of this amount, 1,000,000 livres were to go to the king and 200,000 to the men who had contracted to sell the offices. See various letters and untitled notes in AN, G⁷ 1688 and F¹² 673. Also consult AN, AD XI, 42, *arrêt* 10 February 1705. Numerous *arrêts* were issued concerning the amounts due by particular cities or *généralités*. For Bourges, *arrêts* were issued on 28 July 1705, 18 May 1706 and 28 December 1706. (See AN, G⁷ 1687, pieces 120, 129, 130.)

59. Areas with little or no manufactures were not asked to pay. French Flanders (with important textile centers such as Lille) was also not included. I have not, as yet, been able to determine the reasons for this exemption.

60. See AN, F¹² 750, dossier entitled "Etats de répartition des sommes auxquelles ont été taxées les généralités de Poitiers, Pau, Moulins, La Rochelle, Auvergne, Tours, Orléans, Paris, Rouen, Châlons, Toulouse, Montpellier, Alençon, Caen, et de la Bretagne"; and "Etat des villes dont les corps de marchans doivent estre taxés."

61. Unfortunately, some historians have seen the edict of October and have not realized that it was soon after revoked. Thus Charles Woolsey Cole (*French Mer-*

cantilism, 1683–1700, p. 155) and Eli Heckscher (*Mercantilism*, 1:154) conclude that the inspectors' positions were venal after 1704.

62. A draft of the declaration can be found in AN, G⁷ 1688, piece 103. Also see G⁷ 867–881, de la Vigne to de la Garde, 28 January and 30 January 1705.

63. Actually, merchants were not to pay directly toward this reimbursement. The money was to be raised indirectly, through small duties collected on all cloths produced in the various towns that were held accountable for the debt.

64. AN, G⁷ 9, register 2, Desmaretz to Amelot, 26 December 1704.

65. For example, AN, G⁷ 1689, piece 82, La Cour de Beauval to Le Gendre, 16 December 1710; piece 86, Fouillé de Martangis to Desmaretz, 3 March 1710.

66. Desmaretz's circular letter to the intendants, dated 11 September 1708, is reprinted in Boislisle, *Correspondance des contrôleurs généraux*, 3:11. Also see AN, G⁷ 1708, piece 242, "Expéditions concernant le commerce et les manufactures du 10 septembre 1708."

67. This survey is contained in BN, MSS. fr., 8037. This was the fourth such survey taken in France. Similar ones had been commissioned in 1664 (by Colbert), in 1692 (by Louis de Pontchartrain), and in 1703. The origins of the latter survey are not clear. Colbert's survey has not been preserved, but those of 1692 and 1703 have been (in AN, G⁷ 1685 and 1688 respectively). The surveys of 1692 and 1703 are analyzed in Fontvieille, "Les premières enquêtes industrielles de la France." Markovitch discusses all four of these surveys in the various works of his that have already been cited. The 1692 survey is also discussed in Cole, *Colbert and a Century of French Mercantilism*, 2:573–88.

68. See above, pp. 23, 45 n. 63.

69. Although these semiannual reports were submitted regularly by the inspectors of manufactures from 1700 on, very few of them have been preserved for the period to 1715. Markovitch errs, however, in concluding from this that the requirement of submitting a detailed report every six months was not enforced until after 1715 (Markovitch, *Histoire des industries françaises: les industries lainières de Colbert à la Révolution*, p. 475). The weekly lists of materials submitted by the controller general to the Council of Commerce (see above, Chapter 2, n. 64) and the letter books of Amelot and Daguesseau (F¹² 114–15, 122–25 A) make clear mention of these reports. Several inspectors, in fact, submitted *états* more often than twice a year.

70. In 1691 Controller General Pontchartrain had requested that inspectors include such *échantillons* with their reports, but this does not seem to have taken effect (see Boislisle, *Correspondance des contrôleurs-généraux*, 1:560). On the council studying these samples, see AN, G⁷ 1697, piece 23, Valossière to [de la Garde?] 12 February 1712. Many of these samples of cloth have been preserved in various cartons of series F¹² at the Archives Nationales. For example, F¹² 649 contains pieces of *serges, camelots, estamines, droguets*, and other fabrics.

71. Two of the inspectors of *toiles* doubled as inspectors of woolens, thus making the total 39, not 41. The departments of the inspectors did not necessarily correspond to *généralités*. The following departments each had one inspector of woolens: Beauvais, Aumale, Amiens, Rouen, Alençon, Caen, Nantes, Saint-Malo, Tours, Crévecoeur-Granvilliers, Berry, Orléans, Poitou, Bordeaux, Montauban, Brionde (parts of Auvergne, Montpellier, Quercy, and Rouergue), Auvergne-Limousin-Xaintonges, Toulouse, Montpellier, Carcassonne, Nîmes, Castres-Saint-Pons, Dauphiné, Dijon, Troyes-Châlons, Rheims, and Sedan. There were two inspectors in Paris, one at the *bureau de la douane* and one at the *halle aux draps*. The departments of the inspectors of *toiles* were Rouen, Caen, Alençon, Brittany, Laval, and Lyonnais-Beaujolais. Of the four inspectors of incoming foreign manufactures, two were in Calais and Saint-Valéry. The other two, who also served as inspectors of

woolens, were in Brittany. As noted earlier, their job was not so much to inspect as to prevent the entry of foreign textiles. In addition to these inspectors, special inspectors were appointed from time to time for particular missions or projects; there were never more than one or two of these at a time. See AN, G⁷ 1702, piece 187, "Etat général des inspecteurs des manufactures"; piece 188, "Mémoire"; piece 189, *Etat* for payment of inspectors from the *trésor royal*, 1711; G⁷ 1703, piece 253, untitled register.

72. That complaints from the Levant arose before 1707 can be seen in AN, F¹² 115, fols. 79v, 100; F¹² 122, fols. 177v–80; F¹² 123, fols. 21–22v, 113. On the preparation of the new regulation, see F¹² 123, fol. 113; F¹² 124, fols. 86–87, 153–54; F¹² 125, fol. 118–18v; AN, G⁷ 1692, piece 54; G⁷ 1704, piece 8; Boislisle, *Correspondance des contrôleurs généraux*, 3:17, Desmaretz to Le Bret and Caurière [Cauvière], 12 April 1708.

73. A copy can be found in AN, AD XI, 42.

74. AN, G⁷ 1702, fols. 128v–32v, "Mémoire sur le commerce des draps du Levant," by Basville, dated 22 January 1714. Also see AN, F¹² 58, fols. 270–71, 308v–9v, 313–13v, 320v–21v.

75. A copy is located in AN, AD XI, 42.

76. Cole, *French Mercantilism, 1683–1700*, p. 154; Bacquié, *Les Inspecteurs des manufactures*, pp. 256–65.

77. That is, the inspectors of *toiles*, the inspectors of foreign manufactures, the inspectors stationed in Paris, and the inspectors who were occasionally appointed for special purposes.

78. AN, G⁷ 1696, piece 95, Boré to Desmaretz, 18 April 1711.

79. AN, G⁷ 1701, piece 214, Desmaretz to de la Garde, 24 November 1713.

80. Bacquié (*Les Inspecteurs des manufactures*, pp. 100, 181) discusses this episode and concludes that Desmaretz must have been referring to the special inspectors appointed by some provincial estates. Bacquié's reasoning is that Desmaretz certainly must have known the names of the royal inspectors, since it was he who selected and supervised them. But it is clear from the letters written on this matter by Desmaretz, de la Garde, Daguesseau, and Valossière that Desmaretz was indeed referring to the royal inspectors (see Boislisle, *Correspondance des contrôleurs généraux*, 3:516, circular letter from Desmaretz to intendants, 3 December 1713). There are two possible explanations for Desmaretz's ignorance on this point. First of all, the supervision of the inspectors was something that the controller general usually delegated to the director of commerce and the Council of Commerce. Second, to expect that anyone in the finance ministry should automatically have a list of all its functionaries, with descriptions of their departments, is to place twentieth-century bureaucratic standards back into the early modern period.

81. De la Garde labored to clarify the administration of the inspectors throughout 1714 (see AN, G⁷ 1703, piece 6, Valossière to de la Garde, 10 July 1714; piece 28B, Daguesseau to Desmaretz, 14 September 1714; and various other letters and documents in this carton).

82. AN, G⁷ 1702, pieces 159, 186–99.

83. AN, G⁷ 1702, piece 200, Desmaretz to de la Garde, 19 June 1714. The register itself is also in the same carton.

84. AN, G⁷ 1694, piece 293, Boré to Desmaretz, 17 August 1709.

85. These figures are based on the reports of the inspectors in AN, G⁷ 1685, 1688. The *généralité* of Amiens actually produced many more woolens than did Montauban, but in the latter the production was dispersed over a wider area (see Markovitch, *Histoire des industries françaises: les industries lainières de Colbert à la Révolution*, chaps. 4, 12).

86. Throughout the greater part of the reign of Louis XIV, no inspector was allowed to have an assistant. Late in the reign, however, the government gave tacit permission for a few of them—in especially large or busy departments—to appoint subinspectors (see AN, F¹² 114, fol. 110v, Chamillart to David, 18 November 1700). Bacquié is correct in stating that subinspectors were not regularly created until about 1740 (*Les Inspecteurs des manufactures*, p. 108). Even then they remained few in number.

87. See Cole, *French Mercantilism, 1683–1700*, p. 187; Levasseur, *Histoire des classes ouvrières*, 2:224–25. The *subdélégué* of the intendant in Béarn reported: "In this little department we do not have any corporations of craftsmen or merchants, since each trader or artisan carries out his affairs freely and independently, as at Nay and Bruges, where *bavettes* and *cadis* are made without any regulations; at Oloron, stockings, *cordeillats, bures* and serges are made; . . . " (Boislisle, *Correspondance des contrôleurs généraux*, 3:6).

88. AN, F¹² 1362 ᴬ, Noette to Desmaretz, 19 April 1713.

89. Markovitch argues repeatedly that most rural manufactures were eventually inspected, either *sur place* or when they were brought to town to be sold. Although he admits the possibilities of fraud, he affirms that only about five percent of total production escaped inspection in this manner. Other historians, without attempting to give percentages, argue that a far greater amount escaped inspection. See Heckscher, *Mercantilism*, 1:203–12; Deyon, *Amiens*, pp. 199–200; Pierre Goubert, *Beauvais et le Beauvaisis de 1600 à 1730*, 1:127–32. Also consult E. Tarlé, *L'Industrie dans les campagnes en France au XVIIIᵉ siècle*; William M. Reddy, "The Textile Trade and the Language of the Crowd at Rouen 1752–1871," pp. 66–67; the January 1979 issue of the *Revue du Nord* deals extensively with this subject.

90. For example, AN, F¹² 122, fol. 161, Chamillart to intendant of Paris, 21 September 1706; AN, G⁷ 1689, piece 4, undated and unsigned letter to Desmaretz; AN, F¹² 1891, Vallery to Desmaretz, 1 June 1713. Also see Boislisle, *Correspondance des contrôleurs généraux*, 3:28; Heckscher, *Mercantilism*, 1:140; Goubert, *Beauvais et le Beauvaisis*, 1:128; Léon and Labrousse, in Braudel and Labrousse, *Histoire économique et sociale*, 2:225–26, 355; James N. Hood, "Patterns of Popular Protest in the French Revolution: The Conceptual Contribution of the Gard," pp. 265–66.

91. See AN, F¹² 121, fol. 152v, Chamillart to Bignon, 12 January 1706.

92. See Bacquié, *Les Inspecteurs des manufactures*, pp. 327–33; Levasseur, *Histoire des classes ouvrières*, 2:340–41; Deyon, *Amiens*, p. 188; Heckscher, *Mercantilism*, 1:168; AN, F¹² 115, fols. 63, 66, 77, 78, 83v; F¹² 123, fols. 175v–77, 180v; F¹² 55, fols. 257v–58; F¹² 58, fols. 86–86v, 88v; AN, G⁷ 1694, piece 95, de la Marque to Desmaretz, 3 December 1708.

93. AN, G⁷ 1692, piece 125, Bertrand to Desmaretz, 19 December 1708.

94. For example, AN, G⁷ 1694, pieces 349–50, concerning the annulment of an *arrêt* of the Parlement of Metz in 1709; AN, F¹² 115, fol. 185v; F¹² 123, fols. 13v–14.

95. Levasseur, *Histoire des classes ouvrières*, 2:213–214; Martin, *La grande industrie . . . Louis XV*, pp. 95–96; Goubert, *Beauvais et le Beauvaisis*, 1:127–32, 307; Deyon, *Amiens*, pp. 199–200.

96. Markovitch, "Le triple tricentennaire," p. 321. Bacquié's *Les Inspecteurs des manufactures* presents the strongest defense of the inspectors. Indeed, Bacquié himself was an inspector of manufactures early in the twentieth century, and his admiration for his predecessors at times leads him to be overly apologetic. Heckscher, though not liking what the inspectors were doing, admits that they were often very effective in performing their jobs (see *Mercantilism*, 1:154–55, 169).

97. Many examples are contained in AN, F¹² 730, as well as in other cartons in series F¹² and G⁷. See F¹² 121, fols. 155v, 157; F¹² 122, fol. 159v; G⁷ 1693, piece 60; Bonnassieux, *Les Assemblées*, pp. 14–15, 22.

98. Some historians have stressed the ignorance or incapacity of many of the inspectors (Martin, *La grande industrie . . . Louis XV*, pp. 97–99; Biollay, *Etudes économiques*, pp. 455–60). Bacquié and Markovitch, on the other hand, note that the government generally sought men experienced in manufactures. Oftentimes a man had to pass a test before being appointed (see Bacquié, *Les Inspecteurs des manufactures*, pp. 142–57, 282–97; Markovitch, "Le triple tricentennaire," p. 320). During the period under consideration here, Daguesseau and Amelot were extremely scrupulous in their search for competent administrators. I have discovered only one instance where an appointment went to a man primarily because of court patronage. In this case a relative of a *femme de chambre* of Mme de Maintenon was chosen as inspector of Orléans (see Boislisle, *Correspondance des contrôleurs généraux*, 3:57, Desmaretz to de Bouville, 30 September 1708).

99. AN, F¹² 730, Le Bret to Desmaretz, 3 May 1713.

100. AN, F¹² 123, fols. 64v–65, Chamillart to Basville, 28 December 1706.

101. AN, F¹² 730, Barolet to Desmaretz, 22 April 1713. Plessart, inspector in Amiens, defended himself in the same manner two years later (see ibid., Plessart to Desmaretz, 18 June 1715).

102. The cotton and silk industries largely escaped inspection. French cotton production was relatively unimportant in this period and did not grow significantly until the second half of the eighteenth century. Lyons, the chief center for silk production, had bargained with the government and successfully defended its right to inspect silk itself (chiefly through the guilds).

103. The statutes concerning these industries, as well as for textiles, can be found principally in the *Recueil des règlemens* and in the Collection Rondonneau (AN, series AD XI).

104. Bacquié, *Les Inspecteurs des manufactures*, p. 195.

105. As noted earlier, there were also two other means of helping manufactures. One, the exclusion of foreign manufactures, is described in Chapter 5. The other, tariff policies, is discussed in Chapter 7.

106. See Warren C. Scoville, *Capitalism and French Glassmaking, 1640–1789*, p. 125; and Parker, *The Bureau of Commerce*, p. 53.

107. Although *manufactures royales* tended to be larger than *manufactures privilégiées* and to have greater privileges, often there was no significant difference between individual enterprises in the two groups.

108. The council did, however, occasionally deal with the *manufactures du roi*—in particular with the tapestry factory at Beauvais. This establishment was experiencing severe financial problems during this period. See, for example, AN, G⁷ 1693, piece 13, letters and memoirs referred by Desmaretz to the Council of Commerce, 22 February 1709; G⁷ 1695, piece 113, d'Orsay to Desmaretz, 30 May 1710.

109. The number 13 is probably too low. Others may have been accorded on the advice of the council without being mentioned in the *procès-verbaux*.

110. Cole, *French Mercantilism, 1683–1700*, p. 116.

111. AN, F¹² 115, fols. 134–34v, "Mémoire sur la proposition concernant une huille nouvelle."

112. AN, F¹² 1694, piece 197, Daguesseau to Chamillart, undated.

113. AN, F¹² 58, fols. 336v–40, 22 March 1715. The *milice* was the city militia; the *guet* was the night watch. The *tutelle* obliged a man (chosen by a local judge) to take care of orphans and other minors who had no parental control. The *curatelle*, which was very similar to the *tutelle*, obliged a man to watch over the legal interests of such a minor. Whenever exemption from the *taille* was granted, it was on condition that the person had not previously paid it in the district where the manufacture was to be

established. Thus in practice this exemption generally worked only for foreign workers and skilled artisans brought in from other areas of France.

114. AN, F¹² 51, fols. 164, 180–80v, 9 February and 21 April 1703.

115. Ibid., fol. 335, 10 June 1705.

116. See Scoville, *Capitalism and French Glassmaking*, passim. AN, G⁷ 1690 contains much information on the *manufacture royale des glaces* for this period; on the role of the Council of Commerce, see especially pieces 148–51.

117. Levasseur, *Histoire des classes ouvrières*, 2:261–62. A survey of the van Robais business taken in 1711 described it as "a little world" and listed nearly 1,300 employees (see AN, G⁷ 1696, pieces 185–97).

118. AN, G⁷ 1692, piece 9, "Mémoire pour les Srs. van Robais entrepreneurs de la manufacture de draps fins establie à Abbeville," by Daguesseau, 3 May 1708.

119. AN, F¹² 55, fols. 262–65v, 8 May 1711.

120. The members of the van Robais family themselves had been permitted, by special grace, to remain Protestant. None of their French employees, however, could be Protestant.

121. AN, F¹² 58, fols. 107–8, 27 January 1713.

122. Cole, *French Mercantilism, 1683–1700*, p. 116; Levasseur, *Histoire des classes ouvrières*, 2:334. Cole himself admits that Levasseur's figure is too low. Boislisle has shown that in the period 1683–1700 in the *généralité* of Paris alone there were at least 25 privileged manufactures established. Furthermore, Boislisle admits that his research was far from exhaustive. (See *Mémoires des intendants*, pp. 605–6.)

123. See AN, F¹² 55, fol. 348v, 11 December 1711.

124. AN, F¹² 58, fols. 49, 50v–52v, 13 May and 27 May 1712.

125. Ibid., fols. 304v–6, 1 September 1714.

126. AN, F¹² 51, fols. 209–9v (3 August 1703), 211–11v (11 August 1703), 213–14 (17 August 1703); F¹² 121, fols. 102–3v, 134, 158–59v, 182v; F¹² 125ᴬ, fols. 98–98v; G⁷ 1692, piece 250, letters from the controller general concerning commerce, 12 November 1708; G⁷ 1693, piece 24, letters and memoirs sent from controller general to Council of Commerce, 17 May 1709, and piece 196, 5 January 1714.

127. This should not be taken to mean that the Estates in Languedoc did not wish to promote manufactures. The role of local authorities in encouraging the woolens industry is briefly described in Eugène Guitard, "L'Industrie des draps en Languedoc et ses protecteurs sous l'ancien régime," in Hayem, *Mémoires et documents*, 1:9–34.

128. The examples given here, as well as others, are discussed in Cole, *French Mercantilism, 1683–1700*, pp. 164–87.

129. See above, Chapter 4, n. 8–9.

130. Cole, *French Mercantilism, 1683–1700*, p. 179.

131. A copy may be found in AN, F¹² 1396. The eighteen cities were Paris, Dourdan, Rouen, Caen, Nantes, Oléron, Aix, Toulouse, Nîmes, Uzès, Romans, Lyons, Metz, Bourges, Poitiers, Orléans, Amiens, and Rheims.

132. For some illustrations see AN, F¹² 123, fol. 174; F¹² 124, fol. 2; G⁷ 1762, piece 101, Landivisiau to Desmaretz, 4 April 1714; G⁷ 1696, piece 218, Caumartin de Boissy to Desmaretz, 26 October 1711.

133. AN, F¹² 58, fols, 329v–31, 350–50v.

134. The entire question of *toiles peintes* in France is treated thoroughly in Edgard Depitre, *La Toile peinte en France au XVIIᵉ et XVIIIᵉ siècles*. On the 1686 *arrêt* see Chapter 1. The reason for excluding foreign *toiles peintes* is clear: the protection of native manufactures. The reason for prohibiting the manufacture of *toiles peintes*

within France is perhaps less clear, since it had the effect of wiping out a new industry. This action was taken because Frenchmen had not yet perfected the art of applying dyes to cotton. The crown therefore feared, with good reason, that most Frenchmen would prefer to purchase *toiles peintes* from the East or from England and Holland.

135. Depitre, *La Toile peinte*, especially pp. 47–48.

136. Ibid., p. 48.

137. This again points to the power of Marseilles's lobbying interests in Paris. The *arrêt* of 10 July 1703, which reconfirmed Marseilles's privileges as a free port, prohibited the entry and use there of *toiles peintes* from India but permitted them from the Levant. It was easy, however, for Marseilles's merchants to get around this distinction and to import printed cottons from the Far East. From Marseilles these cloths were smuggled into the rest of France.

138. AN, F¹² 1403, memoir by deputies, dated 25 May 1701. This carton contains dozens of memoirs and letters by members of the Council of Commerce on this subject.

139. AN, G⁷ 1686, piece 150, "Mémoire contre l'arrest des toilles peintes," 10 November 1702.

140. AN, F¹² 1403, "Mémoire contre la proposition d'un fort petit nombre de marchands de Paris qui distribuent des étoffes des Indes," by Anisson of Lyons (May 1705).

141. AN, G⁷ 1692, piece 240, "Les Députez au conseil de commerce informez de la nouvelle fureur avec laquelle des Dames de la cour et de la ville se servent de toiles peintes, pour leurs habits. . . ." Two copies of this memoir may also be found in F¹² 54, fols. 231–32; Depitre, *La Toile peinte*, pp. 69–70, 72–73. Also see Boislisle, *Correspondance des contrôleurs généraux*, 3:577, d'Argenson to Desmaretz, 14 June 1715.

142. Depitre, *La Toile peinte*, p. 66.

143. Ibid., pp. 228–39.

144. When reports showed in 1703 that the supply of French wool was more than sufficient for domestic needs, all the deputies (except Anisson, of Lyons) supported permitting a limited export of wool on a temporary basis. This did not come about, however, and by 1705 all the deputies were once again defending the traditional policy of prohibiting its export. This prohibition extended only to French wool; wool from Spain, Italy, and elsewhere could be reexported. In AN, F¹² 1903 see "Mémoire du député de Lyon concernant la défense de la sortie des laines originaires," 2 March 1703; "Mémoire pour répondre seulement à deux ou trois objections que M. le Député de Lyon fait par son mémoire," 2 March 1703; "Sentiment des députez au conseil de commerce sur le mémoire du commis de Chaparillan au sujet de la défense de sortir les laines du Royaume," 5 January 1705. Also, *arrêt* of 7 April 1714, in AN, AD XI, 42.

145. *Arrêt* of 7 April 1714; see AN, AD XI, 42.

146. Markovitch calculates the total number of sheep in France early in the eighteenth century to have been 24.5 million ("L'Industrie lainière française au début du XVIIIᵉ siècle," p. 562).

147. AN, F¹² 58, fols. 233v–34, 19 January 1714.

148. For example: *arrêt* of 23 October 1708, prohibiting export of linseed through 10 October 1709 (AN, F¹² 55, fol. 301–1v, 17 July 1711); *arrêt* of 20 May 1714, prohibiting export of thistles (*chardons*), a copy of which is in AN, AD XI, 42.

149. This whole question is discussed at length in Paul W. Bamford, *Forests and French Sea Power, 1660–1789*. Also see AN, F¹⁰ 256, "Mémoire de Mrs les deputez du commerce sur les bois et forests à restablir en France et sur les bois de construction,

les merreins, et les masts qu'on peut tirer de Canada," 20 July 1701; a copy may also be found in F¹² 647–48. Other related memoirs are in F¹² 647–48 and Boislisle, *Correspondance des contrôleurs généraux*, 2:80–81, 100–102.

150. AN, F¹² 51, fols. 209, 219, 272–72v; F¹² 55, fol. 50v. G⁷ 1692, piece 222, "Mémoire sur la proposition du Sr Silvestre de Ste Catherine;" F¹² 115, fol. 132.

151. Biollay, *Etudes économiques*, p. 460.

152. Among many examples, see Scoville, *The Persecution of Huguenots*, chap. 11; Levasseur, *Histoire des classes ouvrières*, vol. 2, bk. 6, chap. 6; Léon, "La Crise de l'économie"; Martin, *La grande industrie . . . Louis XIV*, pt. 2, chap. 2, and pt. 3, chap. 4; Henri Sée, *L'Evolution commerciale et industrielle de la France sous L'ancien régime* (Paris, 1925), pp. 152–53; Sagnac, "L'Industrie et le commerce de la draperie en France à la fin du XVIIe siècle," pp. 36–40; Bingham, "Louis XIV and the War for Peace," pp. 619–28; Cole, *French Mercantilism, 1683–1700*, pp. 112–15, and passim.

153. *Industry and Government in France and England, 1540–1640*.

154. A recent study of economic trends in Marseilles has concluded that there is very little correlation between royal regulatory policies and business cycles (see Charles Carrière, *Négociants marseillais au XVIIIe siècle: contribution à l'étude des économies maritimes*, vol. 2, pt. 2, chap. 4).

155. See Markovitch, *Histoire des industries françaises: les industries lainières de Colbert à la révolution*, pp. 271 ff. Precise figures for the entire eighteenth century are provided in Michel Morineau and Charles Carrière, "Draps du Languedoc et commerce du Levant au XVIIIe siècle."

156. Bromley, "Le Commerce de la France de l'ouest."

157. Deyon, "Variations de la production textile aux XVIe et XVIIe siècles: sources et premiers résultats," pp. 947–55; Deyon, *Amiens*, pp. 171–72.

158. Markovitch, *Histoire des industries françaises: les industries lainières de Colbert à la révolution*, passim.

159. AN, F¹² 125^A, fols. 55v–58v, Desmaretz to inspectors of woolens, and Desmaretz to inspectors of *toiles*, both 11 September 1708. The reports that the inspectors submitted are in BN, MSS. fr., 8037.

160. See Schaeper, *The Economy of France*.

161. Concerning popular support for government regulation in the period after 1715, consult the following works, among others: C. Schnakenbourg, *Communautés de métiers contre liberté économique à la fin de l'ancien régime*; Steven L. Kaplan, *Bread, Politics, and Political Economy in the Reign of Louis XV*; Parker, *The Bureau of Manufactures*; Serge Chassagne, *Oberkampf: un entrepreneur capitaliste au siècle des lumières*.

7

FISCAL PROBLEMS

Although its duties related primarily to trade and industry, the Council of Commerce often dealt with issues pertaining to the king's revenues. In particular it concerned itself with the questions of taxes and customs duties, for these directly influenced commerce and manufactures. As noted earlier, two farmers general were appointed in 1700 to sit on the council. These men, Charles de Poyrel de Grandval and Jean-Rémy Hénault, attended the council whenever matters directly pertained to the tax farms or to the king's revenues. It appears that this generally occurred in from fifteen to twenty meetings a year.[1]

Before going any further, a word should be said about the farmers general and the fiscal organization of France. Going back at least as far as the fourteenth century, the French crown had found itself incapable of directing and carrying out all the tasks incumbent on it. The practice therefore arose of leasing out to private businessmen various functions that we today normally consider to be tasks of the government. As the country grew in size and as the central authority expanded its power, so also the private contractors who performed public services increased in number. By the seventeenth century these individuals were known by several names: *gens d'affaires, partisans* (from the *partis*, or syndicates, into which they grouped themselves), and *traitants* (from the *traités* they signed with the government). These individuals or groups carried out a host of functions, such as supplying the army and navy, selling government offices, and managing the postal and transportation networks.

These enterprisers also frequently became involved in state finances; hence they were called *financiers*. By definition these were men who were charged, in one capacity or another, with either the collection or the expenditure of royal funds.[2] Broadly speaking, financiers can be divided into two groups. First, there were those who held a venal office of some sort and who were a part of the bureaucratic machinery at work under the controller general of finances. These men held the posts of *gardes du trésor royal, trésoriers généraux, payeurs des rentes,* and *receveurs généraux,* among others. In theory they were royal servants, but their ownership of the positions they held made them relatively independent of any strict control from above. Although these officeholders were compelled to lend large amounts of money to the crown (in the form of notes based on future revenues), many of them were able to amass huge fortunes by using royal funds in their personal business ventures. For the most part, these financiers regarded their royal offices as only one part of their larger schemes of private investment and speculation.

A second group of financiers were the tax farmers. The French crown had long before discovered that it could not manage the cumbersome job of collecting the myriad indirect taxes that were placed on the movement of goods involved in internal and foreign trade.[3] Therefore it had become accustomed to farming them out to individuals, who signed leases valid for a certain number of years and took it upon themselves to collect them. Whatever money these tax farmers collected above the lease price was their own personal profit. As a result of this arrangement, the crown guaranteed itself a definite income without having to worry about the uncertainties and headaches arising from the task of collection. By the seventeenth century, the number of different tax farms was in the hundreds.

Colbert sought to simplify this complex system by consolidating many of the local customs duties and by replacing the host of small tax farms with a few larger ones. His greatest step in this direction occurred in 1680, when he created the *fermes générales unies.* Into these general farms were placed most of the indirect taxes collected in the entire country. These impositions had dozens of names, but they can roughly be divided into the following categories: the *gabelles* (salt tax); the *aides* (excise duties, mostly on wine and other alcoholic beverages); the *domaines* (taxes from the king's lands or old prerogatives); the *traites* or *douanes* (customs duties); and the *octrois* (duties collected on goods passing into or out of certain towns).[4]

The collection of these taxes was leased to a group of men called the farmers general. These men (who at first numbered forty and later sixty) formed the most important group of tax farmers in France from 1680 until the Revolution.[5] Their headquarters was in Paris, but they had clerks (*commis*) and inspectors all over the country. Their employees numbered perhaps 35,000, of whom 15,000 served in armed brigades that constantly patrolled the countryside searching for smugglers. The 20,000 others manned bureaus and collection points in more than 1,000 places in France; more than half of these were located in the interior of the kingdom. At regular intervals (usually every six years), the Company of the General Farms renegotiated the terms of its contract and signed a new lease with the government. As was true with financiers in general, the crown relied heavily on the farmers general as a source of short-term credit; in this manner the government could spend money that would not be collected for one or more years in the future. In order to guarantee that they would make a good profit from the lease they held, the directors of the company made sure that their entire operation worked as efficiently as possible. The cool determination of their *commis* in the provinces to collect all that was due to them made the farmers general, and tax farmers as a whole, a favorite target for discontented subjects throughout the eighteenth century.

In their general memoirs of 1700–1701, several of the deputies of trade attacked various abuses being committed by the employees of the farmers general. They also criticized the existing system of French tariffs and internal tolls. Judging from this one would have expected the deputies to become ardent crusaders against the tax farmers and the tax system. Indeed, several historians have assumed that there must have been a basic antipathy between the two sides.[6]

Such was not the case. To be sure, the deputies often bitterly disagreed with the farmers general on major questions, but just as often they sided with them. The remainder of this chapter will explore the ways in which the deputies, and the council as a whole, cooperated with, or tried to reform, the French fiscal system.

BALANCE OF TRADE

One question on which all members of the Council of Commerce, including the farmers general, agreed was the need to establish a favorable balance of trade. Only by doing this could France guarantee healthy markets for its manufactures and agricultural goods and conserve its supplies of gold and silver. Several of the deputies mentioned this in their general memoirs of 1700–1701. The entire system of the "equivalent"[7] that the council enforced throughout most of the war was part of an effort to ensure that France sold more than it bought from other countries.

It is hardly surprising to learn that plans for a favorable balance of trade were not new in 1700. The bullionist element of mercantilism naturally required that a government seek to have one. Thus in 1664 Colbert ordered the tax farmers charged with customs duties to draw up and submit to him alphabetized tables of all exports and imports.[8] Armed with this information, he hoped to be better able to determine if France was buying more than it was selling abroad. Nothing much resulted from this project, however, and in 1692 Daguesseau, director of commerce, tried to resurrect it. Working with de Lagny, Daguesseau ordered the *commis* posted on all French borders and in all ports to submit periodic, detailed reports on all exports and imports. In 1693 Daguesseau wrote to Controller General Louis de Pontchartrain that

> there is nothing so necessary, Monsieur, for administering trade than having exact records of all the imports and exports of the kingdom and to compare these two sets of figures every year.[9]

The controller general approved this plan. Sometime late in the 1690s, he appointed one of the farmers general, Hénault, to compile records of imports and exports for the entire kingdom.[10] The *règlement* of September 1699 that distinguished the commercial responsibilities of the controller general from those of the secretary of state for the navy included among the former's duties the tabulation of France's foreign trade statistics.[11]

Despite all these initiatives, however, the program never really worked. The *commis* in the provinces were often either too overworked or too irresponsible to send in the reports and figures requested of them. The disruption produced by the final two wars of the reign also helped undermine the project.

Nevertheless, after the Council of Commerce was erected, a majority of its members adamantly insisted that France needed reliable trade statistics. Without such figures the government could not determine a proper tariff posture, they affirmed, since it would not know whether too many or too few foreign goods were entering the country. These considerations led the deputies to clamor repeatedly for better records on French foreign trade. They were seconded by Amelot and Daguesseau, who, as directors of commerce, had direct contacts with the farmers general and their *commis*. On several occasions these two men reminded the *commis* of their obligation to send in trimestral reports listing all goods passing through their bureaus.[12] Amelot's secretary, de la Vigne, recorded all the figures that were submitted.[13] Imperfect as these data were, they formed the basis for much of the commercial legislation of the period.

But despite these actions, few concrete results were achieved. In April 1710 Mesnager announced to Desmaretz that a new project for obtaining accurate trade statistics had been worked out with the farmers general.[14] Daguesseau was to present this plan to the controller general in person sometime soon thereafter, but once again the project languished. The Council of Commerce and the farmers general continued to work on the plan for a few months afterward, but then it was dropped.[15]

Not until 1713 was the government finally prompted to act decisively on the notion of firmly establishing a balance of trade. The reason for its sudden haste was the treaty of commerce signed with Great Britain at Utrecht in April of that year. This treaty made it seem probable that trade barriers between the two nations would be significantly lowered. During the negotiations at Utrecht, it had become clear that the English representatives were well informed on their country's trade and were thus in a position to know what demands they should make and what concessions they could afford to grant. The basis for their self-assurance was the commercial statistics that had been kept regularly since 1697 by the inspector general of imports and exports.[16]

The French delegates at Utrecht, however, had no such stock of commercial figures to guide them in their decisions. It became clear that the French envoys who were going to travel to England later that year to iron out the final details of a trade agreement would be at a tremendous disadvantage if they did not have accurate statistics on their nation's foreign commerce.[17] It was in order to provide them with this information that the crown created a *bureau de la balance du commerce* on 18 April 1713.[18] This bureau was headed by Grandval, one of the two farmers general in the Council of Commerce. He was assisted by a handful of specially appointed *commis* who were posted in several of the major cities of the country. These *commis* gathered data from the ordinary *commis* situated on the frontiers. All this information was then forwarded to Grandval, who constructed tables each year showing the general picture of French trade. In return for this work, Grandval and his *commis* were granted a small subsidy from the royal treasury.[19]

The *bureau de la balance du commerce* functioned from 1713 until 1791.[20] The figures that it furnished often were incomplete, but they nevertheless provided an approximate estimate of the state of French trade. They were the basis for much of France's economic planning in the eighteenth century.

TARIFFS

The standard view of the Council of Commerce leads one to expect it to have been a staunch proponent of lower tariffs[21] and an unremitting foe of tax farmers. These latter, according to the popular consensus, defended high customs duties at every available opportunity. The evidence afforded by the deputies' general memoirs of 1700–1701 is not conclusive on these points. To be sure, the deputies decried what they considered to be extravagant taxes imposed on trade, and they excoriated the abuses perpetrated by many *commis* of the various tax farmers. As noted earlier, however, they did not attack the system of tax-farming itself, and they did not oppose the idea of protective tariffs.[22]

The testimony of the next fifteen years is likewise mixed. On dozens of occasions, the Council of Commerce helped establish new, or revise old, tariff agreements and customs duties. In general the council did endeavor to moderate what it judged to be excessively high impositions; but in a significant number of cases, it either refused to lower, or it actually raised, tariffs. Furthermore, there was a much higher degree of cooperation and basic agreement between the deputies and the farmers general than might have been anticipated.

It is impossible here to mention every incident relating to this subject, so only a few of the more representative cases will be discussed. We have already seen, in Chapter 5, that the Council of Commerce helped formulate the *arrêt* of 6 September 1701. The *arrêt* drastically raised import duties on many articles coming from England, Scotland, and Ireland. In addition, the council agreed that during the war years the Franco-Dutch tariff of 1699 was void. Dutch mechandise entering the country therefore had to pay the same, higher duties imposed on goods from other nations.

After the accession of Philip V to the throne of Spain, everyone agreed that closer commercial ties were needed between that country and France. The first step in this direction was the negotiation of a new tariff agreement between Spanish and French Flanders. During the War of the League of Augsburg, trade between these two areas had been severely restricted; and because of high customs duties, the situation had improved little since the conclusion of the war in 1697.[23] In an effort to lower these tariff barriers, the two nations began commercial negotiations in Brussels sometime late in 1701. France was represented by the intendant of maritime Flanders, Dugué de Bagnols, and by the farmer general Grandval. The Spanish delegation was led by the treasurer general of Spanish Flanders, the comte de Bergeyck. Although both sides agreed in principle, they became bogged down over details. As a result, the discussions dragged on for nearly two years. The French attributed the delay to what they considered the traditional Spanish lethargy. In December 1701 Amelot wrote to Grandval, "It is true that one needs patience in any kind of neogotiation, and I see by that which you wrote to me that the Spanish phlegm has been transmitted to the ministers in Brussels.[24] Throughout the ensuing months of discussions, the Council of Commerce remained in close contact with the French delegation.[25] The opinions of the deputies were, as a rule, quickly forwarded to Brussels. Although the deputies agreed that some moderation of tariffs was necessary, they were unwilling to go as far as the Spanish desired.

The comte de Bergeyck favored an across-the-board lowering of duties by both sides. As the situation was at present, he declared, Spanish Flanders purchased 21 million livres worth of goods from France each year; but French tariffs prevented it from selling more than 6 million livres worth of goods in return.[26] What Bergeyck especially desired was that textiles from his territory have easy access to the entire French market.

The Council of Commerce, however, balked at the notion of reducing the tariff wall protecting French manufactures. The deputies further noted that the king's revenues would suffer if import duties were lowered too much.[27] But the chief concern the deputies had was that the government of Spanish Flanders was not doing enough to decrease its trade with the Dutch. They insisted that Bergeyck sever all trade with the enemy. They feared that unless this was done the Dutch would take advantage of any lowered tariffs and freely pass their goods into France via Spanish

Flanders. France, the deputies claimed, could supply the territory with all that it needed. Piécourt, of Dunkirk, went so far as to say that the question of whether the Flemish really needed goods from Holland was superfluous. He said that this was wartime and that the defeat of the Dutch—not the welfare of Spanish Flanders—was the only thing that mattered.[28]

The deputies were so stubborn on these points that French officials were forced to disagree with them. Intendant Bagnols admitted that Spanish Flanders was heavily dependent on supplies from Holland; to demand that the territory cut off all trade with the republic was totally unrealistic.[29] Even Farmer General Grandval voiced his support for lower French customs duties. He had fewer fears than did the deputies that France would be inundated with Dutch goods, and he argued that at times lower tariffs can increase trade and, in so doing, augment royal revenues. Thus, for example, Grandval argued that France should reduce the newly imposed taxes levied on coal entering France from Spanish Hainaut and on lime leaving French Flanders for the Spanish territory. He explained that new taxes such as these often have unforeseen, harmful consequences and cause more inconveniences than they are worth.[30] In several other instances, Grandval took a similarly flexible position. The highly ironical situation therefore arose in which a tax farmer favored a lower tariff in the interest of trade, but merchants (that is, the deputies) supported a higher tariff in the interests of royal revenues and protection of native manufactures.

An accord was finally reached on 15 March 1703 when Bagnols and Bergeyck signed a new tariff agreement.[31] The document provided a compromise solution to nearly every question. Duties were lowered on oils, hats, clothing, salt, glass, books, and a handful of other items entering Spanish Flanders from France. The latter reciprocated by lowering import duties on several types of articles coming from Spanish Flanders, including books, charcoal, coal, tapestries, and a few types of cloth. But whereas these goods could now enter French Flanders fairly easily, they were still subject to pay relatively high duties when passing into France's central provinces (the *cinq grosses fermes*). The Council of Commerce thus had succeeded in protecting the bulk of the country from foreign competition. The 1703 agreement did, however, grant free passage for the remainder of the war to manufactured goods passing through France from Spanish Flanders to either Italy or Spain.

The tariff of 15 March 1703 was satisfactory to neither side. The comte de Bergeyck and merchants in his territory complained that France got the best of the arrangement, and they persistently asked that France lower its import duties even further. The Council of Commerce, on the other hand, charged that the authorities in Brussels were not actively discouraging Flemish-Dutch trade. The deputies deplored the fact that *les républicains* were able to smuggle many of their goods into France through the "Flemish connection." After 1706 the tariff became basically a moot question. Most of the Spanish territory was captured by the allied armies in the summer of 1706, and the areas that remained under the control of the comte de Bergeyck had few goods to exchange with France. Following the conclusion of the war, a new tariff had to be negotiated with what had become the Austrian Netherlands.

Other examples might also be cited to show that the deputies or the other members of the council were not always enthusiastic about lowering customs duties. For example, in 1708 the council rejected a proposal to reduce import duties on foreign tin.[32] During and even after the war, the council also argued in favor of maintaining the high taxes imposed on English products by the *arrêt* of 6 September 1701.[33]

But on nearly two dozen occasions during this period, the council supported—and obtained—a reduction of various duties. In 1701, for instance, the council drafted an *arrêt* abolishing the *droit de marque* on all hats made in France.[34] Several times the council was instrumental in moderating import duties on butter and cheese coming from Holland, Ireland, and Scotland.[35] It likewise helped decrease tariff impositions on foreign merchandise brought to France in prize vessels.[36] In 1708 the deputies, working with the farmers general, thwarted a plan to raise export duties on French wines and brandies.[37] This added tax would have forced up the prices of these products and thereby damaged their sale abroad.

It should be mentioned that in a majority of cases where the council either lowered taxes or opposed their increase it had the complete support of the farmers general. The company's two representatives in the council, Grandval and Hénault, usually agreed with the deputies that the needs of commerce or the good of the state demanded the lower rates. They likewise agreed that lower taxes did not necessarily decrease the king's revenues, for if the level of trade rose, then too would the number of taxable transactions. But as will be demonstrated below, relations between the farmers general and the other members of the council were not always harmonious.

TARIFF REFORM

The previous section has shown that the Council of Commerce did occasionally act to change individual parts of the French tariff system. Of much greater importance during this period, however, was a movement within the council to reform the entire tariff structure. By the late seventeenth century, the French customs network had become so complicated that it virtually defies a clear explanation.[38] Export and import duties were collected not only on the borders of the country but also at hundreds of points within. These duties, which went by various names, were a medieval heritage, dating back to the time when France consisted of dozens of autonomous or semi-autonomous principalities and fiefs. The taxes that were levied at the borders of these territories remained in effect even after the lands themselves were incorporated into France proper. Numerous examples of these duties could be cited. Every article passing through the territory of Lyons had to pay the *douane de Lyon*. A *traite foraine* was collected on virtually all goods passing into or out of Provence, Languedoc, and Dauphiné. If a merchant wished to transport merchandise by land across France, he most likely had to pay several such export and import duties.[39]

The one exception to this rule was the area of France known as the *cinq grosses fermes*. This area received its name from the fact that most of the indirect taxes collected within it were at one time leased out to five large companies of tax farmers. The *cinq grosses fermes* were formed in the fourteenth century and included most of the provinces in the northern half of the country.[40] Together they constituted a large free trade area. Merchandise traveling from Rheims to Rouen, for instance, did not have to acquit any customs dues along the route.

The *cinq grosses fermes* constituted one of three basic customs regions within France. The other two were the *provinces réputées étrangères* and the *provinces de l'étranger effectif*. To pass from one of these three areas into another was very nearly like entering another country insofar as tariffs went. The subdivision of France into these three regions was largely due to the failure of one of Colbert's plans. Colbert had hoped to unite France into a single customs union. His vehicle for achieving this was the tariff of 1664. He had intended for the new import and export dues of this tariff—collected on the frontiers of the country—to replace all internal customs duties. Unfortunately for Colbert, however, the plan encountered fierce opposition among many French provinces, who feared royal encroachment and the loss of their various particular fiscal privileges. In the end Colbert managed to get his tariff accepted only by the provinces of the *cinq grosses fermes*. The new tariff wall that now surrounded this area set it even further apart from the rest of France. Items entering the *cinq grosses fermes* were subject to the same uniform duties, whether they came from another country or from another part of France.

In an effort to protect all French manufactures from foreign competition, Colbert established a second, higher tariff in 1667. This tariff was truly national, for it encompassed the *cinq grosses fermes* as well as most of the remainder of France (the *provinces réputées étrangères*).[41] A few scattered areas remained outside this tariff wall, and they were therefore truly foreign territories insofar as tariffs were concerned.[42]

At first the 1667 tariff had applied to only fifty-seven foreign products and to four French products; these were primarily manufactures that the crown did not want to enter France and raw materials that it did not want to leave. From 1667 to 1700 a large number of other items were added to this tariff. These additions came to be known as the *nouveaux droits*. Together with the 1667 tariff, they were referred to as the *droits uniformes*—from the fact that each type of article was subject to the same duty regardless of where it entered the country.

It was these *droits uniformes* that aroused the ire of most of the deputies of trade. In their general memoirs, they complained that many of these tariff duties were excessively high. As a result, they claimed, foreign merchants directed their business away from France, and other nations erected high tariff walls against French products. The new, higher duties also caused internal problems. They added to the perplexing array of customs duties that had to be paid on goods passing through the country. Many unscrupulous *commis* of the farmers general took advantage of the confusion to levy whatever taxes they wished, and unsuspecting merchants were therefore frequently overcharged.

The government was aware of all these problems before the Council of Commerce brought them to its attention. Late in the 1690s Controller General Pontchartrain established an informal commission to study ways of reforming the nation's tariff structure. The individuals involved in it included Daguesseau, Amelot, de Lagny, Grandval, Hénault, Anisson, and several Parisian merchants.[43] The group met regularly in the homes of Amelot and the farmers general. It accumulated a large inventory of recommendations, and it worked to reconcile differences between the needs of the tax farms and the needs of trade. Although nothing definite resulted from these meetings, at least a start had been made toward a genuine reevaluation of the customs system.

When the Council of Commerce was created in 1700, it continued where this commission had left off. The question of tariff reform remained of crucial importance during the first ten years of the council's existence. The *projet du nouveau tarif*, as it was called, was mentioned specifically in the *procès-verbaux* seventy-seven times from 1701 to 1710,[44] but this reflects only a small part of its general importance. It was also the subject of regular meetings held outside the council proper. These meetings were held in the homes of Amelot, Anisson, d'Ernothon (one of the *maîtres des requêtes* in the council), and Valossière. De la Vigne helped collect information needed for the study, and he preserved all the relevant data.[45]

The quest for a new customs system was much broader than the "single duty project" described by John Bosher. It also involved an attempt to lower, or at least to readjust, both export and import duties. The most salient episode in this regard took place from 1701 to 1703. In the meeting of 10 June 1701, the council appointed a three-man committee to study ways of altering the 1664 tariff so as to help French manufactures.[46] This committee consisted of Anisson, Mesnager, and Peletyer. They did not take long in reporting back to the council. They suggested first that higher duties plus some prohibitions be placed on English manufactures. This proposition aroused the opposition of a few of the other deputies, but the issue was quickly settled. The result was the *arrêt* of 6 September 1701. A second set of proposals recommended that export duties either be reduced or abolished on six basic kinds of French manufactures: cloths made of silk or of silver or gold thread; cloths made of wool or wool mixed with either silk or hair; hats (in particular those made of beaver from Canada); paper and playing cards; linens; and cotton cloths.[47] The council agreed to lower export duties on these commodities, and an *arrêt* to that effect was issued on 24 December 1701.[48]

The farmers general were quick to voice their displeasure with this *arrêt*,[49] claiming that the tax farms would lose more than 400,000 livres a year.[50] They further argued that the *arrêt* was a breach of the contract they had for the tax farms and that they would have to be idemnified by the crown for any losses they suffered.

Horrified by the prospect of being further indebted to the Company of General Farms, the crown capitulated and issued the *arrêts* of 2 April and 3 October 1702.[51] The first of these nullified or watered down the tariff reductions announced in the *arrêt* of 24 December 1701. The second declared that many internal customs duties still had to be paid, both on goods destined for abroad and on those traveling from one part of France to another.

Despite this setback the deputies continued in succeeding years to campaign for various reductions in the French tariffs. A memoir drawn up sometime after 1707 lists 116 types of goods for which they believed that export duties should be lowered.[52] For reasons that will be discussed below, few of these recommendations were ever enacted; but lest one assume that the farmers general were always the ones responsible for defeating proposals for lower tariffs, one should note that frequently the deputies themselves were divided on the question. A debate that took place in 1703 concerning a moderation of import duties on foreign manufactures illustrates this point. The deputies of Nantes, Saint-Malo, and Bordeaux attacked the 1667 tariff and the *nouveaux droits*. These high customs dues drove foreign merchants away from France and made it difficult for Brittany and Guienne to sell their wines and other products abroad. These deputies therefore desired that foreign manufactures be able to enter everywhere, not just through Calais and Saint-Valéry. They further demanded that import duties on foreign manufactures be reduced to ten percent of value, attacking those deputies who supported import duties as high as thirty or forty percent.[53]

Other deputies, chiefly those from the more industrialized provinces, fervently supported the high tariff wall that protected French manufactures. They explained that if this barrier was lowered, then English and Dutch textiles would sell more cheaply than those produced within the country and France would soon be deluged with foreign goods. These deputies finally exclaimed that their adversaries in the council, "the partisans of the vineyard," were filled with "a blind passion" to sell their wine, no matter the cost to the general good.[54]

Interspersed with these discussions about raising or lowering customs duties was the ongoing examination of what Bosher has aptly termed the "single duty project."[55] This plan aimed at creating a uniform tariff wall around all of France, thereby eliminating all internal customs dues. Its goal therefore was to erase the tariffs that separated one province from another and that set the *cinq grosses fermes* apart from the *provinces réputées étrangères* and the *provinces de l'étranger effectif*.

The primary crusader for the *droit unique* was Jean Anisson, deputy from Lyons. His chief allies were Mesnager (Rouen) and the various deputies from Paris and Languedoc. These men were generally supported by the two chief members of the council, Daguesseau and Amelot. Over a period of several years, Anisson wrote numerous memoirs in which he enumerated the benefits that his project would bring.[56] By reducing all customs levies to a single export or import duty paid on the frontiers of the country, French goods would be subject to fewer taxes; they could therefore be sold abroad at lower prices and be better able to compete on the international market. They could also be sold more cheaply on the domestic market, thereby eliminating much foreign competition. By making France into a single customs area, one could bolster the political and economic unity of the kingdom. Finally, Anisson countered possible objections by positing that the king's revenues would not be damaged by the proposal. Because trade would be increased, the tax farms would actually benefit from the change. He likewise noted that Colbert himself had had the original idea for abolishing all internal tariff barriers,[57] and thus the project could not, according to Anisson, be labeled a dangerous innovation.

The general reformation of French tariffs, of which the single duty project was but a part, failed for a number of reasons. The farmers general heatedly criticized it. They remonstrated that the decrease or abolition of various customs duties would do irreparable harm to the royal treasury—and thus to their own also. It would be unfair, however, to accuse the farmers general of being hidebound doctrinaires opposed to any changes in the tax farms. As noted above, they frequently supported the moderation of different taxes. The deputies had great respect for Grandval and Hénault and had a good working relationship with them.[58]

One must take into consideration the dire straits into which the general farms as a whole were thrown during the latter part of

Louis XIV's reign. The Wars of the League of Augsburg and the Spanish Succession were no less disastrous for the farmers general than they were for the king's revenues. The leases signed by the Company of General Farms in 1691, 1697, 1703, and 1706 steadily decreased in value.[59] This meant that the company had to pay the government less for the right to collect the taxes, but the receipts from these farms also plunged dramatically during these years. The farmers general therefore were losing money themselves, and the government found it to be increasingly more difficult to find groups of financiers willing to take over the enterprise. In 1709 the crown finally had to put the general farms in *régie*.[60] Not until 1714 could the government persuade the company to take over the farms again.

The farmers general, who were after all businessmen, should not be too severely blamed if they did not wish to jeopardize further their position by accepting a potentially costly reformation of the tariff system. Grandval and Hénault agreed that the reforms proposed by Anisson and others would in the long run be beneficial for trade and for the king's revenues, but they argued that such changes would be unprofitable in the short run.[61] The genuine sympathy that the farmers general had for the reform plan was demonstrated by later developments. In the 1720s, when the country's economic and financial situation was somewhat brighter, the farmers general were numbered among the most ardent backers of the single-duty project.[62]

The Company of the General Farms was far from being the only opponent of this project during the War of the Spanish Succession: the crown itself also was leery of it. Even if the government did believe that in the long run a reduction of customs duties would help the royal treasury, it could not afford to sacrifice part of its income for several years while waiting for this to occur. Both Chamillart and Desmaretz realized this fact, and they made clear to the Council of Commerce that no such plan was feasible at that moment.[63]

If the troubled state of royal finances during wartime helped prevent adoption of the single-duty project, there were yet more profound factors militating against it. These obstacles arose, ironically enough, within the Council of Commerce itself. The plain fact is that most of the deputies of trade, and the majority of French merchants as a whole, were not ready for such a change. The mutual jealousies and the sensitivity about regional privileges that made themselves known on other issues likewise thwarted the implementation of the *droit unique.*

Throughout the nine years when the subject was debated in the council, the deputies constantly bickered among themselves concerning just how much the customs duties should be reduced. As noted earlier, deputies from manufacturing regions wished to retain a high tariff wall around French textiles, whereas those from agricultural regions wanted to lower these impositions. Deputies from the Atlantic ports attempted to slip into the draft of a new tariff plan a clause abolishing the 20 percent duty collected on Levant goods that did not pass through Marseilles. That city's deputy noticed the article and fulminated against the treachery of those who wished to destroy his city.[64] Similarly, Anisson uncovered a plan by other deputies to insert a clause in the new tariff that would have removed Lyons's monopoly on the silk trade.[65] He listed numerous reasons as to why "the good of the general trade of the kingdom" required that his city's privilege be maintained.

The most vehement adversaries of the single-duty project were the deputies of Nantes, Saint-Malo, Bordeaux, and La Rochelle.[66] With the exception of the latter, all these cities were in the *provinces réputées étrangères.* Thus, it was much easier for them to trade with other countries than with the rest of France. The duties imposed on goods entering and leaving their ports were in many cases lower than the taxes that would have been chargd if the goods traveled inland to the *cinq grosses fermes.* If a new tariff wall were placed around the borders of the country, it would limit the foreign trade of these cities and compel them to seek markets within France. Such a move, according to these deputies, would severely disrupt the customary business patterns of their cities, thereby seriously damaging their economies. In some cases the possibilities for increased trade with the interior of the country were slim. Nantes's trade with the central provinces was sorely handicapped by a long line of privately and publicly owned tolls (*péages*) along the Loire River.[67] Saint-Malo lacked both a river and a rich hinterland with which to trade. Bordeaux's neighboring provinces had little need of that city's wines and brandies, since they were already well stocked with these goods. The deputies from these cities also claimed that if Brittany and Guienne lost their ancient fiscal privileges, the "natural constitution" of these provinces would be destroyed.[68]

One might also ask if the other deputies were truly prepared to make France into a huge free-trade area. The manner in which they treated France's northern provinces leads one to wonder. French Flanders, Hainaut, Cambrésis, and Artois were all *provinces réputées étrangères*. Goods passing between them and the *cinq grosses fermes* were subject to duties set down in a special tariff issued in 1671. Throughout the period under study here, merchants in these territories continually requested a moderation of the tariff barrier between their cities and the rest of France. After the tariff of 1703 was signed between France and Spanish Flanders, merchants in Lille and other northern French towns protested that it was now easier for foreigners to trade with France than it was for them.[69] Despite the justice of some of these claims, the Council of Commerce was very reluctant to reduce the tariff between these provinces and the rest of the nation. Merchants and manufacturers in other provinces feared competition from the well-developed textile industries in French Flanders and Artois. Therefore, most of the requests for low duties were rejected. The council also feared, during the war years, that the Dutch would fraudulently pass many of their own goods into France through French Flanders. When the city of Lille was captured by the allies in 1708, its merchants were literally shut off from the French market. At the same time the Council of Commerce abrogated the privilege of free passage across France for all Flemish textiles destined for Spain.[70]

Even after the conclusion of the war, the deputies retained their inflexible posture toward French Flanders. In 1716 they opposed a suggestion by the farmers general that the 1671 tariff be lowered in the interests of trade.[71] The deputy of Lille described the devastating impact of the war on his city's industries, and he beseeched the council to make it easier for Flemish textiles to reach markets in the interior of the country.[72] The other deputies, however, stridently defended the existing tariff barriers. If one were to lower the existing customs duties on Lille's manufactures, they argued, "one should be resolved to see collapse the greater part of the manufactures of the interior of the kingdom."[73]

The general reformation of tariffs therefore had little chance to succeed early in the eighteenth century. The subject was not formally debated in the Council of Commerce after 1710.[74] Some discussion concerning it did arise in 1714, when a new lease on the

General Farms was negotiated;[75] but for all practical purposes, the project had reached a standstill. It was revived at several points later in the century, but that is not part of our story here.

THE DEPUTIES AND THE FARMERS GENERAL

It should be clear by now that there was no unbridgeable wall of hostility between the deputies and the farmers general who sat on the Council of Commerce. Indeed, Grandval and Hénault proved at times to be more flexible than the deputies on questions of tax reform. Nonetheless, the deputies did speak harshly of the tax farms in their general memoirs of 1700–1701, and it would be wrong to mitigate the importance of the merchant–tax farmer conflicts during this period.

A memoir written sometime about 1708 describes as one of the most important functions of the Council of Commerce the settling of disputes between *marchands* and the *commis* of the farmers general and other tax farmers.[76] These disputes usually arose when *commis* seized goods that were thought to be entering or leaving the country illegally or when merchants thought that the *commis* were arbitrarily collecting more money than was stipulated by law. Perhaps as much as 25 percent of the entire agenda of the council resulted from such quarrels. The council, however, usually treated these incidents under the heading of larger questions, such as the regulation of neutral and enemy trade during the war or the reformation of tariffs. In the chart in the appendix, most of these cases have therefore been placed in categories other than that of "conflicts between merchants and tax farmers."

Out of the hundreds of disputes that were brought before the council during this period, the *commissaires* and deputies decided in favor of the farmers general and their *commis* well over 60 percent of the time. In other words, the council agreed that the tax officials had only been doing their jobs and that it was the merchants who were at fault. In May 1708, for example, a Rouen merchant named Gidéon Vincent demanded the release of forty-three bales of cow and goat hair that had been seized by a customs official in that city upon their arrival in a Dutch ship because these goods were not on the list of items permitted from the United Provinces. Furthermore, Vincent evidently knew this, since he had tried to hide them under a pile of other goods that were permitted to enter France. The deputies decided that the employee of the farmers general had been correct in seizing the merchandises. Since this was Vincent's first offense, he was treated leniently: he was granted the release of the goods in question, on the condition that they be returned to Holland.[77] Scores of other similar cases could be cited. In the great majority of instances, merchants had made honest mistakes, due to oversight or ignorance of the law, and had not intended to commit any frauds.

On many occasions, however, the *commissaires* and the deputies decided that it was the farmers general or their employees who were in the wrong. Several times the council discovered that the farmers had been collecting taxes at rates higher than those prescribed by law.[78] Most frequently the council uncovered incidents where the *commis*, not the farmers general themselves, were at fault. This usually involved cases in which the *commis* had unjustly confiscated goods that were legally entering or leaving the country. A substantial number of *commis* were found guilty of negligence or outright corruption for frequently demanding gifts or bribes from innocent merchants. Many were accused of treating businessmen with contempt and of needlessly interfering with the flow of trade. In these cases the *commissaires* and the deputies generally requested that the farmers general take the necessary steps to dismiss or reprove their employees.

Although it would be virtually impossible to prove, it seems that the Council of Commerce was instrumental in at least partially improving relations between the merchant community and the farmers general early in the eighteenth century. With only a few exceptions, the deputies of trade were on cordial terms with the two representatives of the general farms who sat on the council.[79] For their part the farmers general willingly participated in the attempts to eradicate all the sources of friction between their employees and the general public. Action was taken in this regard as early as February 1701. In that month Amelot met with Grandval and Hénault, and together they drew up a new code of behavior for the *commis* in the provinces.[80] In 1705 the deputies admitted that on every occasion when they had brought to the council complaints by merchants against the *commis* they had obtained from the farmers general "all the justice which they had requested of them."[81] Indeed, the farmers general had cooperated "with infinite courtesy and all the diligence that could be desired." This had led, according to the deputies, to a reduction in the number of legal suits brought by merchants against the *commis* before the *juges des traites.*

Of course, the farmers general and the other tax farmers were still disliked by the great majority of Frenchmen. Perhaps the most that one can say is that the spirit of conciliation engendered in the Council of Commerce during these years helped delay the more virulent popular outcries against the farmers general that began around the middle of the century.[82]

MONETARY PROBLEMS

The worrisome state of royal finances during the last twenty-five years of Louis XIV's reign has been too well documented to require description here.[83] The controllers general of the period all struggled valiantly to obtain money and credit for the state through a variety of fiscal expedients. Nonetheless, the crown became more and more indebted as each year passed. By the time that the king died, the government had already spent money that would not be collected for several years in the future.

Occasionally the Council of Commerce was asked to give its advice on financial matters. Needless to say, the question of tariff reform and other issues surrounding trade and industry had already involved the council in matters that pertained indirectly to the king's revenues. But at several points from 1700 to 1715 the council helped determine policies that immediately concerned royal finances.

One of the first subjects to which the council turned its attention after it was founded was royal monetary manipulations. In order to understand this, one must know the basic elements of the French monetary system. All goods and services in the country were evaluated in livres, which formed the money of account.[84] But livres did not circulate; instead, French currency consisted of a variety of coins (*espèces*) the most important of which were the *louis d'or* (as its name implies, made of gold) and the silver *écu*. The government assigned to these coins a value in livres. The problem was that, beginning in 1689, the controllers general of finances began increasingly to tinker with the value of these coins, raising or lowering their value with respect to the livre. The crown had various reasons for doing this. If it was expecting to receive a large payment, it was to its advantage to lower the value of the coinage (called *diminution des espèces*). In this way relatively more coins would have to be paid to the government in order to equal the amount of livres that was owed. On the other hand, when the government paid out money, it was to its advantage to raise the value of the currency, so that it would have to pay out fewer coins (an *augmentation des espèces*). From 1689 to 1715 the crown performed these two operations more than forty times. During this period the value of the *louis d'or* fluctuated between the low of 11 livres 10 sous and a high of 20 livres, and the *écu* between 3 livres and 5 livres.[85]

Both contemporaries and historians have agreed that this tinkering with the currency had a debilitating impact on the economy.[86] In their general memoirs of 1700–1701 and in subsequent writings, the deputies of trade were quick to catalog these evils. The basic result was that there was complete monetary instability. Not only was internal trade disrupted but many foreign merchants were reluctant to trade with France. What was worse, many Frenchmen deposited or invested their money abroad, where they could be sure of its value.

This general problem was submitted to the Council of Commerce for discussion in 1701, and for the next three years, the members discussed it on several occasions. All the deputies were united on two points: first, that the monetary fluctuations must be brought to an end; second, that Frenchmen should be discouraged from sending their money abroad. Unfortunately for the government, however, that was as far as any agreement went. From 1701 to 1704 the deputies, *commissaires*, and farmers general wrote numerous memoirs on this subject.[87] In these memoirs they dwelt on matters that seem arcane to the twentieth-century reader. They discussed, in minute detail, the metallic composition of French and foreign coins, and they pondered the exchange rates then in effect between the various European currencies. A debate that occurred in 1701 between several of the deputies reflects the general tone of all these memoirs and discussions. Descasaux du Hallay argued in favor of a *diminution* that would reduce the value of the *louis d'or* to 11 livres and the *écu* to 3 livres.[88] He noted that these were the values that had existed under Colbert and up to the late 1680s, and by returning to these old, traditional standards, he averred, faith would be restored in the currency. This would encourage foreigners to increase their trade with France. It would also raise the value of French *lettres de change* on the international money market in Amsterdam, which in turn would mean that less money would leave the country. Opposed to this position were Samuel Bernard, Joseph Fabre, and several other deputies. They favored maintaining the *louis d'or* and *écu* at a higher level—12 livres and 3 livres 5 sous respectively.[89] They argued that if French coinage were valued at a fairly high rate, then Frenchmen would prefer to keep it within the country. In addition, foreigners would also be more willing to send their own coins into France, where they would be able to purchase relatively more French goods. In between these two positions, the deputies of Bordeaux and Lyons favored placing the *louis d'or* at 11 livres 5 sous and the *écu* at 3 livres 2 sous.[90]

Although the deputies used numerous "obscure reasonings" in examining this "abstract matter," they were unable to arrive at a solution satisfactory to all of them.[91] Perhaps that is why the government no longer asked the council to discuss the subject after 1704.

In later years the council became involved in two other financial affairs that were of crucial importance to the crown. The first of these concerned the ill-fated *billets de monnaie* that the government began to issue in 1702.[92] At first these treasury notes were accepted well by the public, for the crown promised to redeem them for currency to anyone bringing them to a *hôtel des monnaies*. In 1703 there were only 6.7 million livres worth of them in existence. But as the crown's financial plight deteriorated, it issued more and more of them, until by 1706 there were over 180 million livres worth of them circulating. Their value declined correspondingly, and by the end of 1706 they were worth only fifty-six pecent of their face value.[93] Up until this time the *billets* circulated only in the area around Paris; and by an *arrêt* of 12 April 1707, Controller General Chamillart decreed that they should be accepted all over the kingdom. Henceforth one could use *billets de monnaie* to pay up to one-third of one's debts to the government or to other individuals. Merchants throughout the country immediately protested against this move. No one liked the idea of being paid in discredited paper notes, nor would foreign merchants willingly accept this paper in return for merchandise they sold in France. The deputies of trade made all these objections known to the controller general.[94] As a result of this popular outcry, the crown issued a second *arrêt* on 10 May 1707 that once again restricted the circulation of these notes to Paris and its environs.[95]

The second affair in which the council was involved concerned plans for the establishment of a state bank in France. Several projects for such an institution were brought before the government during these years.[96] Without a national bank, France lacked the credit facilities and the monetary stability that state banks had brought to Venice, England and the United Provinces. The most serious—and perhaps the only tenable—project for a royal bank during this period came from Samuel Bernard and his associates in 1709. Despite the promising aspects of this plan, it possessed a fatal defect: the chief assets of the bank would be in paper (mostly *billets de monnaie*), not in gold and silver. Controller General Desmaretz neverthelsss considered Bernard's plan carefully, and he had several of the deputies of trade study it.[97] In a memoir written late in 1709, the deputies mockingly compared the proposed French bank to the one in Holland:

> This image, true and sincere as it is, clearly shows that the Bank of Paris could resemble the Bank of Amsterdam in name only. The funds of the latter are composed entirely of gold and silver. One proposes to form the funds of the former with a material that is doubtful and discredited in the marketplace, that is to say paper bills which suffer a loss of 50 to 60 percent. One is therefore shocked to see that there are plans for erecting an edifice for credit and confidence on such a shaky foundation. Things being thus, what comparison can one make between the trade of France and Holland?[98]

Desmaretz already had his own misgivings about the plan, and many financiers (especially Bernard's enemies) opposed it. It seems safe to assume that the doubts expressed by the deputies also had some bearing on the government's decision to reject the proposal.

Another question relating to royal finances in which the Council of Commerce became involved was venality of office. The creation and sale of government offices was one of the expedients to which the hard-pressed crown increasingly turned during this period. Although historians have perhaps exaggerated the extent of this development, it is nevertheless true that during the last three decades of the reign dozens of new types of venal positions were established.[99] Many of these were directly related to trade and industry—for example, examiners or guild officials of various sorts. Although the Council of Commerce never attacked venality of office *per se*, it did seek to limit its impact on the business community. New venal officers usually meant more inspections, more delays in the transportation of goods, and more fees to be paid. Although it was not always successful, on more than a dozen occasions during this period the council did help defeat plans for the establishment of new venal positions. The most important such episode, involving the creation in 1704 of inspectors general of commerce, has already been described.[100] In other cases the council rebuffed a recommendation for sixty special cloth measurers in Paris and a proposal to set up saffron examiners throughout the country (saffron, or crocus, was used in dyeing textiles).[101] The council even had to reject a plan for making into a venal office the post of secretary in the Council of Commerce and in the chambers of commerce.[102]

It should be obvious from what has been said in this chapter—as well as in previous ones—that during this period the council clung to a staunchly bullionist position on most fiscal questions. The system of the "equivalent," the drive to establish a favorable balance of commerce, the attempt to discourage individuals and companies from exporting gold and silver, all exemplified the traditional view of precious metals. This is not to say that the council viewed gold and silver alone to be a proper gauge of a nation's wealth. In their general memoirs of 1700–1701, several of the deputies acknowledged that the country's prosperity was also based on its large and industrious population, its size, its natural resources, and its geographical location. Nevertheless, in these memoirs and in subsequent writings, the deputies repeatedly exhorted the government to do everything possible to build up its supplies of the precious metals.[103] They pointed to the pitiful fate of Spain, which had permitted its huge hordes of gold and silver to escape to other lands. The deputies said that this example should make France "tremble," lest the same thing happen to her.[104] The apparent shortage of metallic currency in France during the War of the Spanish Succession only reaffirmed the deputies' worst fears.[105] This fervent attachment to precious metals led the council to distrust all forms of paper money and contributed to the deputies' opposition to a royal bank.

In summary, one can see that during this period the Council of Commerce offered invaluable aid to the crown on a wide range of matters relating to tariffs and royal finances. The council did not always win acceptance for its views, most notably in the case of general tariff reform. But it did help establish a bureau for the collection of trade statistics, and it did achieve some moderation of customs duties. In addition, it acted as a conduit through which the interests of trade could be reconciled—at least partially—with the financial needs of the state. The policies that the council advocated were almost invariably of a traditional, mercantilist nature.

1. It is impossible to say precisely how often the farmers general attended the Council of Commerce. Sometimes the *procès-verbaux* state that they were present, but other evidence shows that they occasionally attended meetings and yet were not mentioned in the *procès-verbaux*. During the period 1701–8, the two directors of finances, who each sat on the council, often assumed the task of safeguarding the king's financial interests.

2. On French finances and financiers, see J. F. Bosher, *French Finances, 1770–1795: From Business to Bureaucracy*; Julien Dent, *Crisis in Finance: Crown, Financiers, and Society in Seventeenth-Century France*; Guy Chaussinand-Nogart, *Les Financiers de Languedoc au XVIII*e *siècle*.

3. The crown kept the collection of direct taxes under closer control. These taxes included the *taille, capitation, dixième*, and *vingtième*. The persons charged with collecting these taxes were the *receveurs généraux*, ordinary *receveurs*, and a number of other officials. For a general desription of the various taxes, direct or indirect, see François Hinckner, *Les Français devant l'impôt sous l'ancien régime*.

4. Any revenue farm that covered most of the country was called a *ferme générale*. The consolidated national company discussed here was the company of the *fermes générales unies*. But often it was simply called the *fermes générales*, and its directors were virtually always referred to as *fermiers généraux*. The taxes that the *fermes générales unies* included changed at different points from 1680 to 1789. From 1680 to 1697 and again after 1730, for example, the royal tobacco monopoly was a part of them. On this, consult Jacob Price, *France and the Chesapeake*, 1:37–38, 52, and passim. For a brief description of the *fermes générales unies*, see George T. Matthews, *The Royal General Farms in Eighteenth-Century France*. Yves Durand studies the social and economic backgrounds of the farmers general in *Les Fermiers généraux au XVIII siècle*. Unfortunately for the present work, this book concentrates on the period after 1715.

5. There remained numerous other tax farms, although none could compare in size and scope with the General Farms. Other tax farmers included those charged with the posts, the *domaine d'occident*, and the *domaines* of Flanders and Metz.

6. For example, Bosher, *The Single Duty Project*, p. 29.

7. See Chapter 5.

8. Biollay, *Etudes économiques*, p. 485.

9. AN, G⁷ 1685, Daguesseau to Pontchartrain, 24 August, 1693.

10. Mar., B⁷ 499, fols. 380–81, de Lagny to Jérôme de Pontchartrain, 12 December 1699.

11. Mar., A² XXXI, p. 162; reprinted in Neuville, *Etat sommaire*, p. 247.

12. AN, F¹² 115, fols. 213–18, letters from Chamillart to various farmers general, 30 December 1701; F¹² 124, fols. 138v–39, Desmaretz to farmers general, 27 March 1708; F¹² 125ᴬ, fol. 64–64v, Desmaretz to various intendants, 18 September 1708.

13. At times he was referred to as the "secrétaire du commerce et des manufactures de France" (see Pierre Goubert, *Familles marchandes sous l'ancien régime: les Danse et les Motte de Beauvais*, pp. 111–12, 120).

14. AN, G⁷ 1695, piece 70, Mesnager to Desmaretz, 7 April 1710.

15. Ibid., pieces 104 and 107, Mesnager to Desmaretz, 20 and 28 May 1710.

16. See Chapter 5, n. 13. Also see G. N. Clark, *Guide to English Commercial Statistics, 1696–1782*; Ian Kenneth Steele, *Politics of Colonial Policy: The Board of Trade in Colonial Administration, 1696–1720*. On the French deputies' high opinion of the English statistics, see AN, G⁷ 1704, "Mémoire sur la négociation . . . " by Anisson.

17. On these commercial negotiations with England, see Chapter 8.

18. The order of the king's council that created the bureau on 18 April 1713 was confirmed by an *arrêt* of 16 June 1716. Many of the records from the bureau are preserved in series F¹² in the Archives Nationales. The fundamental work on the bureau is Ambroise Arnould, *De la balance du commerce et des relations extérieures de la France*. Also see Biollay, *Etudes économiques*, pp. 485 ff.

19. In 1713 they received a total of 4,900 livres. In 1716 this was raised to an annual sum of 6,000 livres. Later in the century the bureau received as much as 15,000 livres per year. See AN, F¹² 1834^A, "Mémoire sur la balance du commerce."

20. In 1781 the bureau was transferred from the farmers general to the controller general's office. See Michel Beaud, "Le Bureau de la balance du commerce (1781–1791)." On the bureau's performance throughout the century, see Léon, in Braudel and Labrousse, *Histoire économique et sociale*, 2:407 ff.; Pierre H. Boulle, "The French Colonies and the Reform of Their Administration during and following the Seven Years' War," 1:234–35; 2:569.

21. The word "tariff" (*tarif*) was used in a variety of ways in the Old Regime (see Marcel Marion, *Dictionnaire des institutions de la France aux XVIIe et XVIIIe siècles*, p. 532). Here it is used in its most common sense, to denote a schedule of customs duties. The most famous examples were Colbert's tariffs of 1664 and 1667. As will be noted below, the Council of Commerce referred to its proposed revision of customs duties as the *projet du nouveau tarif*. The various taxes that were collected as part of a tariff were referred to in general as customs duties (*traites, douanes*). In practice, however the individual customs duties collected all over France went by a host of different names (*liard du baron, douane de Lyon, table de mer, traite foraine*, etc.). Customs duties were collected not only on the frontiers of the kingdom, but also at many regional borders located in the interior. Thus it is very easy to confuse the customs duties with the *péages* (internal tolls), and the *octrois* (taxes collected on merchandise entering or leaving certain towns), and the *aides* (excise taxes). Bosher explains that in general these latter types of impositions were mere taxes, whereas customs duties sometimes served to favor certain kinds of trade, or the trade of certain merchants, or certain areas, at the expense of others (see Bosher, *The Single Duty Project*, pp. 3–5).

22. See Chapter 2.

23. On commercial relations between France and Spanish Flanders prior to 1700, see AN, F¹² 662–70, "Traité des marchandises de la flandre espagnolle par terre," no date.

24. AN, F¹² 115, fol. 200v, Chamillart (i.e., Amelot) to Grandval, 9 December 1701.

25. Grandval did not remain continuously in Brussels. As a farmer general and as a member of the Council of Commerce, he had many affairs that called him back to Paris. Bagnols therefore became the chief French spokesman at the discussions. The bulk of the correspondence and memoirs concerning these negotiations is in AN, F¹² 646. Also see F¹² 51, fols. 78, 80v, 83v, 84, 128, 129v–30, 131–31v.

26. AN, F¹² 646, piece 178, Bergeyck to Chamillart, May 1704.

27. Ibid., piece 19, "M. le député de Lion sur la prétention des marchands de la flandre espagnolle," 7 July 1702.

28. Ibid., piece 210, memoir dated 14 November 1702.

29. Ibid., piece 200, memoir dated 22 September 1702.

30. Ibid., piece 13, "Mémoire du Sieur de Grandval touchant le droit de cinq sols ordonné estre levé sur le charbon venant du Hainaut espagnol . . . ," 21 July 1702; ibid., piece 22, "Mémoire du Sieur de Grandval sur l'introduction dans le Royaume des ouvrages de soye . . . "

31. A copy can be found in ibid., piece 88.

32. AN, F^{12} 54, fols. 172, 173v.

33. AN, F^{12} 58, fol. 206–6v.

34. AN, F^{12} 51, fol. 69v.

35. Ibid., fols. 365–65v; F^{12} 54, fols. 216v–17; F^{12} 55, fol. 116; F^{12} 58, fols. 303–3v, 383.

36. See above, pp. 138–39.

37. AN, G^7 1692, piece 259, fols. 338v–40, "Mémoire des députez au conseil de commerce sur la proposition d'augmenter de 10 livres des droits de sortie sur chaque tonneau de vin et sur chaque pipe d'eaux de vie"; ibid., piece 30, "Mémoire des fermiers généraux."

38. A concise description of it can be found in Bosher, *The Single Duty Project,* chap. 1.

39. In addition to customs duties the merchant also would have paid *péages, octrois,* and *aides,* among other taxes.

40. See Cole, *Colbert and a Century of French Mercantilism,* 1:416–23. The provinces of the *cinq grosses fermes* included the Ile de France, Normandy, Picardy, Champagne, Bourgogne, Bresse, Poitou, Aunis, Berry, Bourbonnais, Anjou, Maine, Orléannais, Perche, Nivernais, Touraine, Thouars, Beaujolais, Bugey, Châtellenie, Chantoceaux, Dombes.

41. On the tariffs of 1664 and 1667, see Elzinga, "Le Tarif de Colbert." The *provinces réputées étrangères* included Angoumois, Artois, Auvergne, Béarn, Brittany, Cambrésis, Dauphiné, Flanders, Foix, Forez, Franche Comté, Gascony, Guienne, Hainaut, Ile-de-Rhé, Ile d'Oléron, Languedoc, Limousin, Lyonnais, Marche, lower Navarre, Provence, Roussillon, Rouergue, Saintonge, and Vivarais. The duties specified in the 1667 tariff and in later *arrêts* were not collected in Brittany and Guienne until 1692. See AN, F^{12} 1910, memoirs by the deputies of Nantes, La Rochelle, and Bordeaux, all dated 25 March 1703.

42. The *provinces de l'étranger effectif* were Alsace, Trois Evêchés (Metz, Toul, Verdun), Lorraine (after it became French), the county of Venaissin, and the free ports of Marseilles and Dunkirk. These areas remained outside the royal customs system either because of their late annexation to France or because they wished to retain their relatively open trade with other nations.

43. Many provincial intendants also participated in the commission's work by sending in reports on the customs duties collected in their provinces. On the commission's work, see AN, F^{12} 114, fol. 58, Chamillart to Grandval and Hénault, 4 July 1700; ibid., fols. 84v–85, circular letter to Chamillart to intendants, 4 September 1700; AN, KK 1340, p. 509; AN G^7 532, Anisson to Chamillart, 20 November 1699; AN, F^{12} 51, fols. 312–13v; Bosher, *The Single Duty Project,* pp. 26–27.

44. Bosher (*The Single Duty Project,* p. 29 n. 1) counts only 62 references to the project during this period. In addition to those instances where the *prochain bail des fermes* or *le projet du nouveau tarif* is directly referred to, I have included those cases where discussions immediately pertained to the reformation of the tariff system. This has produced a figure slightly higher than Bosher's.

45. De la Vigne received 3,000 livres a year for the work he performed in this regard. This sum was usually included in the same *états* as the salaries of those inspectors of manufactures who were paid by the royal treasury. (See AN, G^7 1702, pieces 193–97.)

46. AN, F^{12} 51, fol. 42v.

47. Most of the documents relating to this entire episode are in AN, F^{12} 1903, 1910. See especially F^{12} 1910, "Estat des marchandises sur lesquelles Mrs. les

députés du commerce suplient d'accorder une diminution de droits d'entrée et de sortie," 12 July 1701. A copy may also be found in Mar., B⁷ 500, fols. 201–3v.

48. A copy is in AN, F¹² 1910.

49. Ibid., "Réponse des fermiers généraux," 19 August 1701 (also in Mar., B⁷ 500, fols. 204–8); AN, F¹² 1903, farmers general to Chamillart, 3 January 1702.

50. AN, F¹² 1903, "Etat de ce à quoi monte la totalité des droits des marchandises énoncées dans l'arrest du conseil du 24 décembre 1701"; ibid., "Estat pour justifier la perte que sufrira la ferme"; ibid., "Mémoire sur l'arrest des six espèces"; ibid., "Mémoire du M. Chartier." The farmers general declared that in an average year the *droits de sortie* on these six types of goods amounted to 713,000 livres, but would plummet to about 300,000 livres if the *arrêt* of 24 December 1701 took effect.

51. Copies are in AN, F¹² 1910. On these *arrêts* see Bosher, *The Single Duty Project*, pp. 29–31.

52. AN, F¹² 1910, "Marchandises sur lesquelles Mrs les députés estiment qu'il y a lieu de faire quelques changemens pour les droits de sortie." On the frontispiece the year 1702 is written, but a later page contains a reference to an *arrêt* issued in 1707.

53. AN, F¹² 1910, "Mr. le député de Bordeaux sur le projet du nouveau tarif," 25 March 1703; ibid., "Mrs. les députez de Nantes et de Saint-Malo sur le projet du nouveau tarif," 25 March 1703; ibid., "Sentimens d'une partie des députés . . . ," 11 July 1703. The deputies from La Rochelle and Lille were also sympathetic to the arguments of the deputies from Brittany and Guienne (see ibid., "Mr. le député de la Rochelle sur la projet du nouveau tariff," 25 March 1703 and "Réflexions de Mr. Taviel sur le projet cy-joint," undated).

54. Ibid., "Réponse au mémoire par lequel on demande l'entrée des manufactures étrangères a 10 pour cent de droit," undated.

55. Bosher, *The Single Duty Project*, especially pp. 25–36. Most of the documents relating to this project during the early part of the eighteenth century are in AN, F¹² 641, 646, 693, 1903, 1910.

56. Bosher, *The Single Duty Project*, pp. 31–33.

57. It is therefore impossible to argue that the single-duty project was in any way antimercantilist or opposed to traditional royal policies. Another mercantilist spokesman who supported it was Pottier de la Hestroye (see Bib. de l'Arsenal, MS. 4069, p. 262). On other officials and private citizens who favored the measure, see Bosher, *The Single Duty Project*, p. 34.

58. See the final passages of the "Mémoire sur la réformation du tarif des cinq grosses fermes," written by several of the deputies in May 1705. It can be found in AN, G⁷ 1687, piece 138, and F¹² 1910.

59. Matthews, *The Royal General Farms*, pp. 54–58.

60. Taxes were either farmed out or they were in *régie*. Taxes in *régie* were administered by officials within the controller general's office.

61. AN, F¹² 1910, "Réponse des fermiers généraux au mémoire par lequel on propose la décharge des droits de sortie sur six espèces de marchandises," 19 August 1701.

62. Bosher, *The Single Duty Project*, pp. 44–52.

63. AN, G⁷ 1687, piece 138, "Mémoire sur la réformation du tarif des cinq grosses fermes," 20 May 1705 (also in AN, F¹² 1910). The Council of Commerce realized that "la conjoncture présente" (i.e., war) was a major obstacle to the project (see F¹² 51, fol. 237v).

64. AN, F¹² 1910, "Mr. le député de Marseille sur le projet du nouveau tarif," 25 March 1703.

65. Ibid., "Mr. le député de Lyon sur le projet du nouveau tarif," 25 March 1703.

66. See above, note 53. Although Fénellon, of Bordeaux, originally was one of the most vocal detractors of the single duty project, by 1707 he had changed his views and began to support it. This could be cited as one example of a deputy sacrificing the particularist desires of his constituents in order to work for the common good. La Rochelle's major objections to the plan were that it would continue the high import duties on foreign manufactures and that it would raise the duties paid on fish brought to the city both by Frenchmen and by foreigners.

67. The question of the *péages* on the Loire River was discussed in the Council of Commerce several times in 1701 and 1702 (see AN, F¹² 51, fols. 58v, 62, 66, 68v, 85, 85v, 89, 93, 97, 120v, 124v, 125v, 129, 337). On the benefits that Nantes continued to receive throughout the eighteenth century as a result of its being excluded from the *cinq grosses fermes*, see Pierre H. Boulle, "Slave Trade, Commercial Organization, and Industrial Growth in Eighteenth-Century Nantes."

68. AN, F¹² 1910, "Mrs. les députez de Nantes et de Saint-Malo sur le projet du nouveau tarif," 25 March 1703.

69. These claims were partially correct. From 1703 to 1708, for example, *camelots* (cloths of goat or camel hair mixed with silk or wool) from Spanish Flanders paid fewer import duties when entering the *cinq grosses fermes* than did similar cloths made in French Flanders. This situation was corrected by an *arrêt* of 17 January 1708. A copy can be found in AN, F¹² 827.

70. Since 1669 manufactured goods from French Flanders had enjoyed the right of free passage across France when destined for Spain, Italy, and other nations. This *transit* was repealed by an *arrêt* of 30 July 1709. The Council of Commerce refused to approve its reestablishment until after the war had ended. See AN, F¹² 1908, "Mémoire sur le transit de Lille" undated; ibid., *avis* of the deputies of trade, undated.

71. AN, F¹² 827, "Avis des fermiers généraux," 12 March 1716.

72. Ibid., "Réponse du député de Lille à l'avis des députés."

73. Ibid., "Avis des députés," 1 April 1716; F¹² 1910, "Sur la demande des états et chambre de commerce de Lille d'une réduction de droits pour les manufactures de laine."

74. AN, F¹² 55, fol. 194v, 2 August 1710.

75. AN, F¹² 1911, Grandval to [?], 17 December 1714; ibid., "Extrait du projet de tarif pour les droits d'entrée;" ibid., "Article surcis du projet de tarif pour les droits d'entrée de l'acier étranger;" ibid., "Estat de tous les droits que payent les harengs tant de la pesche estrangère que de la pesche françoise."

76. AN, F¹² 725, "Mémoire pour les départemens des six intendants du commerce."

77. AN, F¹² 54, fols. 188v, 196–96v.

78. AN, F¹² 1910, *arrêt* of 2 April 1702; ibid., "Mémoire des députés du commerce sur les cires blanches," 18 August 1702.

79. Descasaux du Hallay (Nantes) and Joseph and Mathieu Fabre (Marseilles) were generally always hostile toward the farmers general. See, for example, AN, G⁷ 1686, piece 86, "Griefs du commerce de la Bretagne . . . ," 1 June 1701; Mar., B⁷ 502, fols. 321–22, Joseph Fabre to Pontchartrain, 20 January 1703.

80. AN, F¹² 1924, note added to the reverse side of letter from de Vaubourg to Chamillart, 6 February 1701; F¹² 51, fol. 21.

81. AN, G⁷ 1687, piece 138, and F¹² 1910, "Mémoire sur la réformation du tarif des cinq grosses fermes," 20 May 1705.

82. Many Frenchmen, including Saint-Simon and La Bruyère, had already attacked the farmers general in a very bitter fashion. Hinckner and Durand argue, however, that these criticisms became more serious and wider in scope after the 1760s (Hinckner, *Les Français devant l'impôt*, pp. 84–85; Durand, *Les Fermiers généraux*, bk. 3, pt. 1, "Le Fermier devant l'opinion").

83. Among other things, see François Véron Duverger de Forbonnais, *Recherches et considérations sur les finances de France depuis l'année 1595 jusqu'à l'année 1721*; Philippe Sagnac, "Le Crédit de l'Etat et les banquiers à la fin du XVIIe et au commencement du XVIIIe siècle"; A. Vuitry, "Un Chapitre de l'histoire financière de la France: les abus du crédit et le désordre financier à la fin du règne de Louis XIV"; Lüthy, *La Banque protestante*, 1:123–274; Boislisle, *Correspondance des contrôleurs généraux*, 3:672–87; René Dumas, "La Politique financière de Nicolas Desmaretz, contrôleur général des finances (1708–1715)."

84. Each livre contained 20 sous, and each sous was divided into 12 *deniers*. A livre was equivalent to approximately three dollars in today's American currency.

85. Such monetary manipulations had occurred prior to 1689, but they had been relatively infrequent. On this subject see Natalis de Wailly, "Mémoire sur les variations de la livre tournois"; Pierre Gaxotte, *The Age of Louis XIV*, pp. 266–68; Germain Martin and Marcel Bezançon, *L'Histoire du crédit en France sous le règne de Louis XIV, Vol. 1: Le Crédit public*, pp. iv–ix; Lüthy, *La Banque protestante*, 1:98–104. Paul Masson says that from 1701 to 1713 there were no fewer than 90 edicts or *arrêts* concerning French currency (Masson, *Histoire du commerce . . . XVIIe siècle*, p. 335 n. 4). Also see Scoville, *Persecution*, pp. 385 ff.; Lévy, *Capitalistes et pouvoir*, pp. 17–24, 42 ff., 358 ff.; Frank Spooner, *The International Economy and Monetary Movements in France, 1493–1725* pp. 60, 92, and passim; BN, MSS. fr., 21770, various *arrêts* and other pieces on this subject.

86. In 1726 monetary manipulations ended and the values of the *louis d'or* and the *écu* remained stable until the end of the Old Regime. On the return of *paix monétaire*, see Carrière, *Négociants marseillais*, pp. 811 ff.

87. BN, MSS. fr., 21769, passim; ibid., nouv. acq., 6828, fols. 560 ff.; *Memorials Presented by the Deputies*, pp. 93 ff.; AN, F^12 51, fols. 44v–45, 46–48v, 51v, 55v, 56v, 57v, 63, 66v, 77, 216–16v, 219, 266–67, 270–71v; AN, G^7 497, Mesnager to Chamillart, 30 October 1703, with accompanying memoir; G^7 1687, piece 80, "Réflexions des députez du commerce sur l'édit du mois de mai 1704 qui augmente le prix des espèces." The deputies returned to this subject in later years, but the major discussions on it occurred from 1701 to 1704 (see Mar., B^7 509, fols. 374–86; AN, F^12 58, fols. 216, 217). As noted earlier, Chamillart and Jérôme de Pontchartrain attended the Council of Commerce only two times after its establishment. On one of these two occasions, the currency question was one of the major issues being discussed (AN, F^12 51, fol. 44v, 23 June 1701).

88. AN, G^7 1686, piece 87, "Mémoire de Sieur Descazaux député de Nantes . . . .," 20 July 1701; copies of this memoir can be found in BN, MSS. fr., nouv. acq., 6828, fols. 570–78; *Memorials Presented by the Deputies*, pp. 110–20; Martin, *La grande industrie . . . Louis XIV*, pp. 392–400.

89. AN, G^7 1686, piece 89, "Mémoire de Mr. Bernard et des députez qui sont de son sentiment . . . ," 20 July 1701; Mar., B^7 500, fols. 249–52v, "Pour tenir les espèces au prix qu'elles sont plutôt que de les diminuer," by Joseph Fabre; Carrière, *Négociants marseillais*, p. 817.

90. AN, G^7 1686, piece 88, "Réflexions du député de Bordeaux sur la prix des espèces d'or et d'argent," 20 July 1701; ibid., piece 90, "Addition au mémoire de Mr. Fénelon," 20 July 1701.

91. These phrases were used by Descasaux du Hallay. See note 88 above.

92. On this subject see Boislisle (ed.), *Mémoires* of Saint-Simon, 14:603–16. It is treated extensively in a French law thesis that I have not yet been able to consult: A. Seligmann, "La première tentative d'inflation fiduciaire en France. Etude sur les billets de monnaie du trésor royal à la fin du régne de Louis XIV (1701–1718)."

93. Memoir of Chamillart, 16 October 1706, in Boislisle, *Correspondance des contrôleurs généraux,* 2:473–75.

94. AN, G⁷ 1618, Anisson to Chamillart, 15 May 1707; Fournier, *La Chambre de commerce de Marseille,* pp. 66–68; Boislisle, *Correspondance des contrôleurs généraux,* 2: 402–4, 518; ACCM, B 161, letters of Mathieu Fabre to chamber of commerce, 9 May, 11 May, 16 May, 18 May 1707.

95. A third *arrêt,* issued on 18 October 1707, partially reinstated that of 12 April 1707. The new *arrêt* stipulated that *billets de monnaie* could be used for up to one-fourth of any particular debt in most French provinces. These *billets* were never printed in denominations under 500 livres, so they were used mostly by the more prominent bankers, financiers, and businessmen. In 1708 and 1709 Desmaretz worked hard to eradicate the entire supply of them. Thanks to the arrival in 1709 of large amounts of gold and silver from the *mer du Sud,* he was able that year to repurchase 43 million livres worth of the notes. During 1709 and 1710 he converted most of those that remained in circulation into *billets des fermiers généraux, rentes,* and other more esteemed forms of credit.

96. Colonel Herlaut, "Projets de création d'une banque royale en France à la fin du règne de Louis XIV (1702–1712)"; Boislisle, *Correspondance des contrôleurs généraux,* 3:636–51; Paul Harsin, *Crédit public et banque d'état en France du XVIe au XVIIIe siècle,* pp. 15–53; McCollim, "The Formation of Fiscal Policy," pp. 248–61; Bib. Mazarine, MS. 2342.

97. Boislisle, *Correspondance des contrôleurs généraux,* 3:639, Bernard to Desmaretz, 9 November 1709.

98. Ibid., p. 642, "Mémoire des députés . . . "; also see AN, G⁷ 1696, piece 329, "Sur le mémoire concernant une société générale de commerce"; AAE, Mém. et doc., France, 137, fols. 130–32 and 1182, fols. 290–93.

99. The classic work on venality of office for an earlier period is Roland Mousnier, *La Vénalité des offices sous Henri IV et Louis XIII.* We are in need of a thorough examination of this topic during the reign of Louis XIV. In the 1690s Louis de Pontchartrain is supposed to have said to the king, "Every time that Your Majesty creates a new office God creates a fool to buy it." Historians often quote this sentence (apocryphal though it may be) and assume that throughout the second half of the reign the government recklessly created hundreds of new and useless offices. For example, see Levasseur, *Histoire des classes ouvrières,* vol. 2, bk. 6, chap. 7. From the archival evidence that I have seen for this period, it seems to me that the crown used as much restraint as possible in establishing new offices. Each year it received hundreds of proposals for new venal posts from individuals all over France, but it gave serious consideration to very few of them. Many of these proposals are contained or described in AN, G⁷ 694–727, 761–786. Also see Boislisle, *Correspondance des contrôleurs généraux,* 3: 44, Desmaretz to Daguesseau, 22 August 1708; McCollim, "The Formation of Fiscal Policy," pp. 210–48.

100. See above, pp. 159–61.

101. AN, F¹² 51, fols. 241v–43, 433v–35.

102. Ibid., fols. 305v–6v.

103. See ibid., fols. 85, 87v, 91, 100; F¹² 55, fols. 10v, 11, 15v; BN, MSS. fr., nouv. acq., 6828, pp. 557–60; *Memorials Presented by the Deputies,* pp. 93–95.

104. AN, F¹² 1910, "Mrs. les députés sur le projet du nouveau tarif," 15 March 1703.

105 On the *disette d'argent,* as it was called, see AN, G⁷ 1694, piece 158, Mesnager to [Clautrier?], 25 May 1709; ibid., piece 167, Hosdier to [?], undated; G⁷ 1704, piece 10, Mathieu Fabre to Desmaretz, January 1715; ibid., piece 96, Garnison to Desmaretz, 13 May 1715; ibid., piece 136, *juges consuls* of Orléans to Desmaretz, 29 July 1715; Boislisle, *Correspondance des contrôleurs généraux,* 2: 268, 3:142; Rambert, *Histoire du commerce de Marseille,* 6:271; Georges Livet, *L'Intendance d'Alsace sous Louis XIV, 1648–1715,* pp. 873–81; Carrière, *Négociants marseillais,* p. 794; Heutz de Lemps, *Géographie du commerce,* pp. 38–40; Webster, "The Merchants of Bordeaux," pp. 355 ff. Spooner, on the other hand, argues that an influx of gold from Brazil and silver from the *mer du Sud* made the shortage of precious metals less serious than it had been earlier in the reign (*The International Economy,* pp. 40, 52, 196 ff.).

8

FOREIGN RELATIONS AND OTHER EXTERNAL PROBLEMS

The Council of Commerce helped shape French policies on matters that extended beyond the country's borders, and I shall demonstrate in this chapter the important ways in which it did so. These matters included Franco-Spanish relations, privileged trading companies, colonies, commercial negotiations, the French fishing industry, and the spread of plagues. Because most of these subjects have received extensive treatment from other historians, there is no need to dwell on them at length here. I hope merely to call attention to an aspect of these topics that has been overlooked by most authorities: namely, the role of the Council of Commerce.

FRANCO-SPANISH RELATIONS

During the War of the Spanish Succession, French influence in the Iberian peninsula reached a height that it had never seen before or would ever see again—except perhaps under Napoleon. Acting as a loving grandfather and as a concerned ally, Louis XIV sent to Madrid a large number of officials and advisers to counsel the youthful and inexperienced Philip V. These individuals helped direct the Spanish war effort and sought to bind France and Spain together economically.[1]

The highpoint of French involvement in peninsular affairs came in the period 1705–9. This was so mainly because of the work of two members of the French Council of Commerce: Michel Amelot and Nicolas Mesnager. From May 1705 to September 1709, Amelot served as French ambassador to the Spanish court.[2] Thanks to his ingratiating personality, undisputed abilities, and unquestioned integrity, he was able to work with Spanish nobles and officials as none of his predecessors had been able to do. His power was so great that he functioned virtually as a royal minister. He sat on the

Council of State (the *despacho*). From there he advised the king, appointed Spanish officials, and began to reform the government along French lines. His achievements were so remarkable that one historian has hailed him as "the Colbert of Spain."[3]

Amelot's activities in Spain have been amply documented by various scholars,[4] but Mesnager's work in Madrid has received much less attention.[5] The Rouen deputy made two separate journeys to Spain, remaining there from December 1704 to April 1706 and from May to July 1708. Although Amelot, as ambassador, dealt with all manner of affairs, Mesnager's expeditions were purely commercial in aim. He was sent to Madrid by Controller General Chamillart to work with Spanish officials toward establishing closer commercial ties between the two countries. Along with Ambroise Daubenton, an agent of Jérôme de Pontchartrain,[6] Mesnager for a time sat on the Spanish junta of commerce. His chief goal was the formation of a "union" of Franco-Spanish commerce that would have given Frenchmen greater privileges in the profitable Spanish colonial trade. Although he won many Spanish officials over to his project, little ever came of it.

In addition to the work of two of its members in Spain, the Council of Commerce itself participated actively in advising the French government concerning trade relations with its ally. Only a small fraction of this activity is reported in the *procès-verbaux* of its meetings,[7] but other evidence demonstrates clearly the important role that the council played. Jérôme de Pontchartrain in particular seems to have relied heavily on it. I have discovered in the naval archives more than 250 letters relating to Spanish affairs from Pontchartrain to various members of the council for the period 1700–1715.[8] Evidence in the financial archives likewise testifies to the constant contact that Chamillart and Desmaretz had with the council on Spanish matters. Because Franco-Spanish relations were considered to be matters of state, and therefore secret, the ministers preferred to consult with the individual *commissaires* and deputies rather than have an open debate in a council. This fact is often mentioned in ministerial correspondence. Pontchartrain frequently asked Daguesseau to discuss delicate matters with those "deputies who are the most knowledgeable and capable," in whom one could "have confidence."[9] On a question involving French and Spanish privateering, Desmaretz wrote to Pontchartrain in March 1711 that he had obtained the views of Daguesseau and Amelot; the controller general added that in such matters he never hesitated in following their advice.[10]

Undoubtedly the most important question involving Franco-Spanish relations during this period concerned the latter country's colonies in the New World. Indeed, both Louis XIV and Queen Anne of England avowed that the fate of Spanish America was the most important issue at stake in the entire war.[11] Officially, the Spanish government had always prohibited its colonies from trading with anyone but the mother country. Foreigners wishing to participate in this trade had to take their goods to Cadiz and work through Spanish commissioners. Twice each year a fleet left Cadiz. Upon reaching the Caribbean, some of the ships went to Mexico and others to Central and South America. Although Spain jealously guarded her colonies, the increasingly weaker government of the late seventeenth century was unable to prevent ships of foreign nations from trading illegally with her empire. By the year 1700, the richest part of this empire was Peru, whose vast silver mines provided the money to keep the Spanish monarchy afloat. The Pacific waters off Peru and Chile were called the *mer du Sud* (South Sea).

Throughout the seventeenth century, Frenchmen had often traded illegally with Mexico and the Spanish West Indies. Late in the 1690s, French ships began to traverse the Magellan straits and penetrate to the *mer du Sud*. The Spanish monarchy protested bitterly against these intrusions, but it was unable to make even its own colonial officials uphold the ban on commerce with other nations. French encroachments in the *mer du Sud* remained a constant source of friction between the two states during the succession war. On the one hand, France did not want to irritate its ally, nor did it wish for England and the United Provinces to fear that it was working to capture the entire Spanish Empire for itself. On the other hand, the Spanish colonists were in dire need of European food supplies and manufactured goods, and they could afford to pay for them with silver coins and plate. Perhaps as many as 175 French ships ventured to the *mer du Sud* from 1700 to 1715, bringing back as much as 400 million livres worth of silver.[12]

Officially the French government always prohibited trade with the Spanish colonies in the *mer du Sud*, but unofficially it oscillated between at least a dozen different positions throughout the war. At times it earnestly endeavored to prevent Frenchmen from partaking in this illicit trade, but at other times it allowed French vessels to go there, under the pretext that they were on "voyages of discovery." At still other times the government merely closed its eyes to this traffic and made little effort to prevent it.

Jérôme de Pontchartrain reversed his position on this whole problem so often that historians have called him weak and vacillating.[13] The truth is, however, that Pontchartrain's personal position remained fairly constant throughout this period. He opposed the illicit trade with Spanish colonies for three reasons: first, it created much ill feeling between France and Spain; second, it deprived the French navy of many able-bodied seamen;[14] third, it diverted the attention of French merchants and led them to neglect France's own colonies, especially the fledgling settlement in Louisiana.[15]

But Pontchartrain had to contend with other forces. Controllers General Chamillart and Desmaretz steadfastly supported French trade in the *mer du Sud* because of the huge supplies of silver that it brought to France. They frequently worked behind Pontchartrain's back by ordering local officials to tolerate illegal trade and by persuading the king to adopt a more lenient attitude toward it.[16] The Council of Commerce also generally supported French merchants and worked to win approval for their "voyages of discovery." Several of the deputies themselves were actively involved in this trade.[17] In 1705 the council drew up plans that greatly increased the amount of tacit permissions that merchants were granted for their expeditions.[18]

The council was also busy in other ways concerning the *mer du Sud*. It frequently acted as an arbitrator of disputes that arose between investors in the various expeditions destined for Peru.[19] It served as final judge in all legal suits in which the government prosecuted merchants who had sent vessels there illegally.[20] The council also helped regulate the number of ships departing on "voyages of discovery" in the Pacific; it did not want the South American market to be glutted with an oversupply of European goods.[21] In January 1712, when the government finally decided in earnest to stop this trade, it fell to the Council of Commerce to draft the ordinance that embodied the new policy.[22]

In addition to the *mer du Sud* question, the wartime alliance between France and Spain brought other opportunities and problems relating to trade.[23] The Council of Commerce fully supported the French effort to have Spain cut off all trade with the enemy.[24] France claimed that she herself would be able to supply her ally with everything that she needed. Although this effort to make Spain totally dependent on France failed, the Spanish market for French goods did increase noticeably during the war.[25] The Council of Commerce encouraged French artisans to imitate the

Dutch and English textiles that were so well liked in Spain, and it worked diligently to guarantee the high quality of every article exported across the Pyrenees.[26] The council also helped develop the entrepôt trade of Bayonne: the city was granted numerous tax exemptions for goods that it received from other parts of France and from Holland for transshipment to Spain.[27] The council had less success in its efforts to win for France a monopoly of the highly prized Spanish wools. Although Spain did reduce export duties on a limited amount of wool going to France, she refused to prohibit its export to England and Holland.[28]

PRIVILEGED TRADING COMPANIES

The Council of Commerce played no role in administering the chartered trading companies. That job belonged primarily to the secretary of state for the navy, although the controller general had to give his consent to the various privileges that each company was granted. But because the Council of Commerce played a major role in determining French trade policies in general, it was inevitable that many of its decisions should have a direct bearing on these companies.

When the council was established in 1700, there existed seven great trading companies. These were the East India Company, the Senegal Company, the Guinea Company,[29] the China Company, the North Africa Company, the Company of Saint-Domingue, and the Company of the *mer du Sud*.[30] To these might also be added the royal tobacco monopoly, which at that time belonged to a group of financiers headed by Samuel Bernard.[31] Each of these companies possessed exclusive trading rights with the area of the world or in the commodity listed in its charter. Each one also enjoyed a variety of privileges and tax exemptions.

Despite these advantages, however, every one of these companies—with the possible exception of the tobacco monopoly—was in dire straits throughout the period under consideration here. They were all in debt and being hounded by their creditors and stockholders. A number of factors contributed to their problems. These included the hazards of wartime, stiff competition from English and Dutch traders, and general mismanagement. The Company of the *mer du Sud*, which was founded only in 1698, was formally prohibited from trading with the area of its concession for most of the period after 1700. Several of the companies quarreled among themselves, charging one another with violating their respective trading monopolies, and these quarrels led to long and costly legal suits. By 1715 all these companies had either ceased to function actively or had leased their privileges to private individuals.

As was noted in an earlier chapter, most of the deputies of trade criticized these companies in their general memoirs of 1700–1701; but at the same time, the deputies recognized the potential value of such chartered enterprises.[32] They chiefly objected to the real or supposed abuses of which some of the companies were guilty. Several of the deputies in fact were members of one or more of the companies—either at the time when they served on the Council of Commerce or later.[33] Although on more than one occasion from 1700 to 1715 the deputies deplored the existence of trading monopolies, in actuality they were anything but hardened foes of the companies.

The rather evenhanded approach that the Council of Commerce adopted toward the companies is demonstrated by the fact that the government generally relied on its members to judge the legal suits in which the trading enterprises often became embroiled. The naval and financial archives reveal scores of instances in which either *commissaires* or deputies were charged with investigating the affairs of the privileged companies. It is not surprising that the government should rely on the *commissaires*. As *conseillers d'état* and *maîtres des requêtes*, they were already involved in many of these cases in various ministerial bureaus and in the *conseil d'état privé*. But it is rather remarkable that the crown also frequently called on the deputies to perform this service. In order for legal squabbles to be taken out of the ordinary law courts and brought before the Council of Commerce or some of its members, both parties in the confrontation had to consent to it. The trading companies would never have done this if the council's members were known to be indomitable critics of such bodies. As it was, however, virtually all the members of the council participated in examining and judging disputes in which the companies were involved. For example, in 1707 Fénelon, Anisson, and Mesnager were charged by Pontchartrain with examining the financial problems of the Senegal Company in an effort to see what could be done to protect it from its creditors.[34] These same deputies as well as Laurencin, Piou, Moreau, Vilain, and others worked at different times on the affairs of the China, Guinea, and East India companies.[35] More often the *commissaires* alone met and sat as judges in cases involving the companies.[36] Occasionally the council as a whole assembled to arbitrate disputes. In September 1706, for instance, it decided that the Company of the *mer du Sud* should be paid 220,000 livres by Noël Danycan (a wealthy Saint-Malo merchant) and the China Company. The latter two parties had amassed huge profits as a result of their trade with Peru.[37]

The undogmatic, flexible approach that the council took with regard to the companies is perhaps best illustrated in the case of the East India Company. Throughout this period the council and the deputies frequently attacked the company for its practice of exporting precious metals and importing Indian *toiles peintes*. By 1715 the council succeeded in totally prohibiting the company from transporting to France any sort of printed cottons and muslins.[38] In thus limiting the rights of the company, the council acted more out of a program to protect French bullion supplies and French manufactures than out of a desire to cripple the company. In fact, the council acknowledged that the company deserved most of its exclusive privileges, in order that it be recompensed for the heavy expenses incurred in establishing trade with the Orient. The council wanted the company to work harder at exporting French manufactures and at importing things that France really did need—especially drugs and spices.[39] On several occasions the council decided issues in favor of the company. In 1713 it defended the company's right to import coffee from Moka;[40] and in 1714 it agreed that the company should be able to import raw silk from the Far East, but, as noted earlier, Controller General Desmaretz chose instead to protect the traditional silk-importing privileges of the city of Lyons.[41]

The Guinea Company was the only one whose actual charter was directly influenced by the Council of Commerce. Traditionally that company had an exclusive privilege over the African slave trade from the Sierra Leone River south to the Cape of Good Hope. In the fall of 1701, the company was reorganized and its privileges were renegotiated. The deputies of trade insistently demanded that the new company not retain that exclusive privilege. The old company had never been able to supply the French West Indies with enough slaves, and the colonies were suffering as a result of this lack of workers. The deputies therefore clamored for a complete opening of the slave trade to all individuals. The new Guinea Company did maintain its monopoly, but, as a result of the deputies' remonstrances, the government ordered it to grant permissions free of charge to any merchant who wished to enter that trade.[42] During the next twelve years, the Council of Commerce made sure that the company obeyed this rule. The council was quick to complain to the government whenever it heard that the company was refusing to issue permits or was trying to make merchants pay for them.[43] In November 1713 the company was reorganized once again, and this time the council succeeded in completely abolishing its monopoly. Henceforth the Guinea slave trade was open to anyone wishing to engage in it.[44]

The trading company for which the council had the least sympathy was the royal tobacco monopoly. The deputies[45] charged that Saint-Domingue and other French colonies were languishing because the monopolists refused to pay them a fair price for their product. What was worse, the company often sent money from France in order to purchase tobacco in Holland.[46] But one should not make too much of this opposition to the tobacco monopoly. In the fifteen-year period under study here, this company was discussed by the council on fewer than ten occasions. During the war years the major complaint against it was not that it was a monopoly but that it traded too freely with the Dutch and that it occasionally used Dutch ships in preference to French ones.[47]

COMMERCIAL NEGOTIATIONS

Although diplomatic relations with other countries were chiefly in the department of the secretary of state for foreign affairs, the controller general and the secretary of state for the navy retained extensive rights in this area in matters relating to trade. It is therefore not surprising to learn that the Council of Commerce or its individual members also were quite influential in determining French trade agreements. Despite the fact that the *commissaires* and deputies clung to a basically protectionist position, they did nevertheless help promote friendlier commercial contacts with virtually all of Europe. The pages that follow will first briefly discuss trade with Muscovy and Persia and then will treat the series of negotiations that were connected with the peace treaties signed at Utrecht in 1713.

Throughout the period under review, the Council of Commerce worked earnestly to establish better trade relations with Muscovy. In April 1701 the great Rouen banker Thomas Le Gendre proposed to Controller General Chamillart that France sign a trade agreement with the tsar,[48] and the Council of Commerce, to which this matter was referred, heartily concurred.[49] Muscovy could supply France with a host of raw materials, including hemp, furs, hides, and tallow; and it could provide a great market for French wines, brandies, sugar, woolens, and other items. As the situation then stood, however, there was virtually no direct trade between the two nations. Instead, the Dutch middlemen had become the "sole masters" of this commerce; they sent two fleets each year to Archangel. The deputies of trade urged that an agreement be signed in which the tsar would grant Frenchmen the same privileges enjoyed by English and Dutch shippers.

Nothing came of this proposal. The succession war and the war between Sweden and Muscovy were largely to blame. In the succession war Dunkirk privateers captured several Russian vessels, and, to the consternation of the tsar, French admiralty courts judged them to be valid prizes.[50] What was worse, France refused to give up its traditional alliance with Muscovy's enemy, Sweden. Although Louis XIV and Peter the Great exchanged diplomatic envoys during the war, no commercial accord was reached,[51] and Franco-Russian trade therefore continued for the most part to be channeled through the Dutch.[52]

After the war the prospects for a commercial treaty improved. In the summer of 1713, the tsar sent an envoy to Paris to negotiate the terms of such an agreement.[53] Various members of the Council of Commerce set to work, in secret, to help bring this matter to a successful conclusion. Once again the project became snagged on several items, and the discussions dragged on into 1715. The tsar refused to lower import duties on French wines and brandies; he was at that moment trying to promote Russian viniculture, and he did not want it to be crushed in its infancy by foreign competition. Also at that particular juncture the French government was irritated that the tsar had endeavored, unsuccessfully, to lure some French artisans to leave their country and come to Moscow.[54] But the major obstacle to a settlement lay elsewhere. France secretly agreed that Peter the Great should be permitted to retain Saint Petersburg, his cherished port on the Baltic. The trouble was that this port recently had been won at the expense of Sweden. France could not sign any official treaty with Muscovy without alienating its old Scandinavian ally. For the time being no formal convention was signed between the two states,[55] but the Council of Commerce did encourage Frenchmen to go directly to Russia, even though they would not enjoy the special privileges that a treaty would have brought. In 1714 a company in Saint-Malo began to send ships to Archangel and Saint Petersburg, and by 1715 there were hopes of even greater direct links between the two nations.[56]

French contacts with Persia were even more modest during this period. In 1708 a treaty of commerce was signed by the king of Persia and a French envoy to that country (one Sieur Michel).[57] This treaty established direct tariff regulations, and it catalogued the rights and obligations of all Frenchmen trading in Persia. Despite this encouraging opening of commercial relations, however, virtually no direct contacts were made between the two countries in ensuing years. There were two reasons for this. First, the English and the Dutch dominated the Arabian Sea during the war years, and their ships would have prevented any French vessels from trading with Persia. Second, French merchants complained that several articles in the treaty were either unfavorable to France or ambiguous. They claimed that England and Holland had received much better terms from the Persian government. Under such conditions as these, no Frenchmen were willing to risk huge sums of money to open trade with that distant country.

In February 1715 a Persian ambassador arrived at Versailles, and he opened negotiations for a revision of the 1708 treaty.[58] One member of the Council of Commerce (Landivisiau) met with the ambassador in person on several occasions to discuss this issue. Several of the deputies also were asked by Pontchartrain and Desmaretz to give their advice. Landivisiau worked out a series of compromises with the ambassador, and he hoped that a new treaty would be signed.[59] But the members of the Council of Commerce were sharply split into three mutually contradictory positions. First, the deputy of Marseilles objected to any treaty with Persia, on the grounds that it would ruin the trade of his city.[60] Traditionally France obtained Persian goods indirectly, purchasing them from merchants in the Levant. As we have seen, Marseilles held a virtual monopoly over this trade. It did not want to lose it by seeing Frenchmen from other cities trade directly with Persia (which Marseilles considered to be a part of the Levant). The deputies of Lyons and Languedoc (Anisson and Gilly) championed a second position. They argued in favor of caravans across Turkey and Armenia that would establish direct links with Persia. They further believed that Persian merchants should be allowed personally to bring their merchandise to Marseilles and other ports and receive all the privileges usually accorded to foreign businessmen residing in France.[61] A third position was supported by Moreau (deputy of Saint-Malo) and Antoine Crozat (the financier and merchant who in 1712 had acquired a lease on all the privileges of the East India Company). They argued that all the trade with Persia rightly belonged to that trading company.[62] Therefore this commerce should not go through the Mediterranean, but rather it should travel by means of the ocean. This would have the effect of giving the Persian trade to the Atlantic ports. The deputies of Lyons, Marseilles, and Languedoc joined together to refute this position. They pointed out that a Mediterranean route would save both money and time. They also noted that the privilege would be of no use to the company. The chief article imported from Persia was silk, and the *arrêt* of 13 March 1714 had already reaffirmed the exclusive right that Lyons, Marseilles, and Pont-de-Beauvoisin had over the entry of that merchandise into France. Eventually the government decided in favor of the Mediterranean deputies. More Frenchmen did begin to venture to Persia, but the privileges of Marseilles in the Eastern Mediterranean trade were preserved. This story really extends beyond 1715. What is important here is that the Council of Commerce was instrumental in negotiating a treaty with a foreign prince.

The council—and especially its individual members—played an even greater role in the commercial and diplomatic negotiations that preceded and accompanied the conclusion of the War of the Spanish Succession.[63] The search for peace began long before the Congress of Utrecht actually assembled in 1712. As early as 1706, Louis XIV sent out peace feelers to various member of the enemy coalition. Foreign Minister Colbert de Torcy employed a variety of individuals in these diplomatic forays, but none was more important than Nicolas Mesnager, deputy of trade from Rouen. In his *Mémoires* Torcy himself explains how he first came to use Mesnager.[64] Throughout the latter part of 1706 and in 1707, Mesnager wrote a series of memoirs for Chamillart and Pontchartrain concerning trade with Spain and the Spanish colonies. Mesnager's intelligence and his firsthand experience in Madrid made him the acknowledged expert on Spanish affairs. At the same moment, the Dutch Republic was intensely suspicious of French aims in the Spanish empire. The Dutch feared that France was endeavoring to win a trading monopoly with this empire for itself. Torcy therefore tells us that Mesnager was the natural choice to be envoy to the United Provinces. Mesnager was already planning a trip to Holland on private business, and this would serve as an ideal ruse to camouflage his mission so that Holland's allies would not learn of it. In December 1707 Torcy therefore dispatched Mesnager to meet with representatives of the Dutch Republic in Rotterdam. He was instructed to discuss commercial affairs only. His chief goal was to work out a plan by which France, the United Provinces, and Spain would share the latter's colonial trade—to the exclusion of England and other countries. During the months of January and February 1708, Mesnager conferred with a series of Dutch representatives, including Grand Pensionary Antonie Heinsius. Mesnager was able to win approval of most of his commercial propositions, but the Dutch insisted on discussing political topics. In particular they demanded the cession of territories in Flanders (for the "barrier" that they so much desired). They also repeated their demands that Philip V abandon the Spanish throne. Louis XIV was not yet prepared to discuss these issues, and so Torcy recalled Mesnager to France early in March.[65]

Although this expedition to Holland had largely failed, Mesnager himself had displayed a keen grasp of the issues and a shrewd bargaining style. On two other occasions, therefore, Torcy used him on similar missions. The first of these occurred early in 1709. Mesnager set out in January of that year for Holland, but he never got beyond Ypres. The States-General in Amsterdam was feeling especially truculent and suspicious of France at that moment, and it refused to grant Mesnager a passport to enter its territory. The Dutch claimed, somewhat petulantly, that if France was really negotiating "in good faith," then it would send "persons of character" to treat with them.[66] Consequently Mesnager was forced to return to Paris, and, in order to placate the Dutch, Foreign Minister Torcy himself journeyed to Holland late in the spring of 1709. He worked out a set of peace proposals known as the Preliminaries of the Hague, but because the Dutch demanded that Louis XIV send French troops to Madrid to remove Philip V from the Spanish throne, France was forced to reject this agreement.

By 1711 a series of domestic and international events led England to make known its desire for peace. That country's new Tory ministry tired of the uncompromisingly belligerent attitude of its Dutch ally. In the spring and summer of 1711, the English government initiated a series of secret discussions at London and Paris concerning a possible Anglo-French *rapprochement*. In August, Torcy decided that the negotiations required the presence in London of an official French envoy. The man chosen for this mission was Nicolas Mesnager. From August to October 1711, Mesnager negotiated a general peace settlement with Bolingbroke and other Tory ministers. The Preliminaries of London, signed by Mesnager on 8 October, laid the basis for the political and commercial agreements worked out at Utrecht in 1712 and 1713. When Mesnager returned to France late in October, the king received him personally at Versailles and lauded him for his achievements. In December 1711 Mesnager was further rewarded when Louis XIV appointed him to serve as one of the three French plenipotentiaries at the upcoming peace conference at Utrecht.[67]

Mesnager served in Holland and England as the personal agent of Torcy, and the Council of Commerce was not directly involved in any of these negotiations. The situation at Utrecht, however, was vastly different. The three French plenipotentiaries there (Mesnager, the marshal d'Huxelles, and the abbé de Polignac) were officially under Torcy, but they also received advice and instructions from Desmaretz and Jérôme de Pontchartrain.[68] Through these latter two ministers, the Council of Commerce likewise came to play a significant role in the peace talks.

The Congress of Utrecht opened in January 1712 and did not complete its work until 1715. On 11 April 1713, however, the French delegates signed seven treaties with representatives of foreign nations. These included treaties of peace with Portugal, Savoy, Prussia, the United Provinces, and Great Britain. In addition treaties of commerce were signed with the last two nations.[69]

Throughout the months of consultations and bargaining at Utrecht, the Council of Commerce was always kept informed of the progress that was being made. Because tariffs and commercial agreements lay chiefly in his department, Desmaretz was constantly in contact with the French plenipotentiaries, especially Mesnager; and the evidence clearly reveals that Desmaretz relied heavily on the Council of Commerce for the instructions that he sent to Utrecht.[70] Because the negotiations were confidential and extremely delicate, the council did not usually discuss them in its regular meetings.[71] Instead, a special bureau was set up to deal with matters on which Desmaretz needed assistance. This bureau met at the home of Daguesseau, and in addition to him it consisted of Amelot, de Nointel (one of the *commissaires*), and several of the deputies. Of the latter, Anisson and Fénellon attended most often. Desmaretz also requested memoirs from individual members of the council. Anisson in fact drew up the initial set of instructions that Desmaretz presented to the plenipotentiaries before they left Paris.[72] One would probably not be too far from the truth in saying that the commercial clauses of the treaties signed at Utrecht were largely the work of the French Council of Commerce.

The articles concerning trade in the peace treaties can be quickly summarized. Although Savoy had joined the coalition against France in 1703, economic relations between the two nations had remained fairly unchanged throughout the war. Article 10 of the Franco-Savoyard treaty therefore merely affirmed that trade between the two states would continue to be based on the various tariffs and conventions that had been agreed to in the 1680s and 1690s.[73]

Commerce with Portugal, however, had been severely restricted ever since that country had signed the Methuen Treaty in 1703 and thereby joined the allied cause.[74] Articles 5 through 13 of the treaty signed at Utrecht related to trade.[75] By the terms of these articles, trade between the two countries basically returned to its *status quo ante bellum*. A few problems remained (such as a Portuguese prohibition on the import of French brandies), but these were to be worked out in later negotiations. The treaty also settled questions concerning the border between French Guiana and Portuguese Brazil. In addition, France promised not to permit its merchants or missionaries to enter the Portuguese colony.

Throughout the early months of 1713, the French and Prussian plenipotentiaries worked feverishly to conclude a treaty of commerce. Its details could not be completed by the time when the general peace treaty was signed on 11 April, so the diplomats reassembled in May to continue work on it. Each side was eager to achieve a formal accord, but the discussions were immediately hung up over a series of technicalities. The Prussians objected to what they considered to be overly burdensome sanitary regulations that had recently been established in French ports as a safeguard against the plague, which was then spreading through parts of Germany. In addition, Frederick William I demanded that his newly acquired territory of Neuchâtel receive the same privileges in its trade with France that were granted to most of the Swiss cantons. These and other problems doomed the negotiations to failure, and in July the assembly broke up.[76]

Prussian-French trade throughout the remainder of the eighteenth century was based on a rather ambiguous clause in Article 1 of the peace treaty signed on 11 April. This clause was interpreted by both sides to mean "reciprocal freedom of trade, both on sea and on land,"[77] which meant that there would be no restrictions on what each country could export to the other. Although the French government would have preferred a formal commercial agreement, it was not unhappy with the situation that resulted from the lack of one. Trade with Prussia began to grow in 1713 and continued to increase modestly throughout most of the century.[78] France did not have any fears about being inundated with Prussian manufactured goods: Daguesseau, Mesnager, and Desmaretz all agreed in February 1713 that Prussia had virtually no industries.[79]

The treaty of commerce signed by French and Dutch diplomats on 11 April 1713 was almost literally a carbon copy of the Treaty of Ryswick.[80] Furthermore, an *arrêt* issued on 30 May 1713 reinstated the 1699 Franco-Dutch tariff.[81] Thus *les hollandois* succeeded in reacquiring all the trading privileges that they had held in France prior to the war.

Throughout 1712 and early 1713, the question of a treaty of commerce with Great Britain was perhaps the single most important topic in the minds of Desmaretz and the members of the Council of Commerce. Ever since 1700 the *commissaires* and deputies had espoused the hope that a trade agreement of some sort might be signed with France's cross-channel neighbor. Only with such a convention could one begin to dismantle the extravagant customs barriers that had been erected between the two nations.

Yet, despite the sincere efforts of Louis XIV and the Tory ministers in England, no such treaty every emerged. The treaty of commerce that was signed at Utrecht on 11 April 1713[82] needed to be ratified by the English Parliament, but the Parliament refused to do this. The chief stumbling blocks were Articles 8 and 9 of the treaty. Article 8 declared that each country would accord most-favored-nation status to the other. Article 9 proclaimed that each nation would reduce its import duties on goods from the other to the rates that had existed in 1664, but it specified that woolen cloths, sugar, salted fish, and whale products were to be exempted from this stipulation. France feared (probably correctly) that if it lowered its import duties on these four articles, they would then pour into the country from England, ruining French industries and fishing.

This is not the place to describe in detail the lengthy negotiations that took place toward working out a trade agreement. The main point to be stressed here is the role of the Council of Commerce. Late in 1712 Desmaretz decided to send two deputies of trade to London to negotiate secretly with Bolingbroke and the other Tory ministers. He chose for this task Anisson, of Lyons, and Fénellon, of Bordeaux. In January 1713 they left for England with the new French ambassador to that country, the duc d'Aumont. From January to July of that year, they worked alongside English representatives to hammer out an acceptable treaty. Their mission proved fruitless, however, and they returned to France empty-handed. Desmaretz sent them to London a second time in 1714, and they continued their work from February to September of that year. Once again, however, they failed to achieve any results.[83]

Throughout both of these missions, they remained in close contact with Desmaretz. The controller general, in turn, relied almost exclusively on the members of the Council of Commerce for advice. The bureau that had assembled at Daguesseau's home throughout the Utrecht conference continued to meet during the negotiations with England. Desmaretz also sought help from individual members—Daguesseau and Mesnager in particular.[84]

The negotiations with England failed for several reasons. The French were divided among themselves concerning what concessions could be made. Anisson and Desmaretz wished to protect French manufactures and fishing; therefore they refused to grant the relatively low 1664 tariff to England for the four articles mentioned above. Fénellon, however, was less interested in protecting French manufactures. His main goal was the lowering of English duties on French wines—especially those of his native Bordeaux—and, consequently, he was more willing to make compromises with the English.[85] In this he seems to have had the support of foreign minister Torcy.[86]

The domestic political situation in England was perhaps even more to blame for the failure of the negotiations. The Whig party lambasted the Tories, then in power, for not having won enough concessions from the French and Spanish at Utrecht. They charged that the same mistake would be repeated if the proposed treaty of commerce was signed. The Whigs contended, perhaps falsely, that France possessed a favorable balance of commerce with England, and that the French advantage would increase even more if England lowered most of its customs duties on French goods.[87] The Tories were unable to win a majority vote on the issue in

Parliament, and when the Whigs returned to power under the new king, George I, Anisson and Fénellon were recalled to France for the final time. Legal trade between the two nations therefore remained at a fairly low level until a treaty of commerce was finally signed in 1786. Both French and British merchants continued, of course, to smuggle goods back and forth throughout the century.

No peace treaty was signed at Utrecht between Louis XIV and the emperor,[88] but in 1713 a trade agreement was worked out in that city between France and the Austrian (formerly Spanish) Netherlands. To negotiate this treaty, Desmaretz sent to Utrecht a merchant named Vaultier and a deputy of trade (Piécourt, of Dunkirk). These two men worked with Austrian representatives from July through December 1713. The bureau that met at the home of Daguesseau once again was the source of most of the instructions sent to the French delegates.[89] The major topics of the discussions were the tariffs of 1670 and 1680, which had regulated trade between the Spanish Netherlands and France. The Austrians demanded that the parts of those tariffs favorable to Flemish exports into France be reinstated and that the relatively high import duties on French goods remain intact. The resulting tariff of 27 January 1714[90] was largely a compromise, although the French made more concessions than they would have liked. French duties on woolens, silk fabrics, and other goods coming from the Austrian Netherlands were lowered. On the other hand, duties on French wines, vinegars, and other products entering the Austrian dependency remained rather steep. But Desmaretz and the Council of Commerce decided that these irritations were small compared with the potential benefits to be gained from amicable trade relations with Brussels and its surrounding territory.

Another series of commercial negotiations in which the Council of Commerce became involved concerned the Hanseatic cities of Hamburg, Bremen, and Lübeck. In the summer of 1713, these cities each sent deptuies to Paris to request a treaty of commerce with France.[91] These negotiations continued, off and on, through the next two years. Jérôme de Pontchartrain seems to have taken control of these discussions, even though commercial treaties and tariffs were more properly in the department of the controller general.[92] Under Pontchartrain's aegis the Council of Commerce held a series of "extraordinary assemblies" to examine the matter in June and July of 1715.[93] In these meetings the Hanseatic representatives and the French deputies of trade drafted a mutually acceptable treaty of commerce. This convention granted to Hanseatic ships and merchants the same privileges and tariff rates that the Dutch enjoyed in France. Furthermore, it guaranteed Hanseatic vessels the status of neutrality in the event of future wars. In return Frenchmen were to receive all the same advantages enjoyed by English and Dutch traders in Hanseatic ports. Although the final details of this treaty were worked out in the fall of 1715, it was not formally signed until 28 September 1716.[94]

One final area should be mentioned with regard to the role of the Council of Commerce in foreign diplomacy. In 1712 a long-simmering feud between the county of Venaissin and the city of Lyons erupted into acrimonious debate.[95] The papal enclave of Venaissin, whose capital was Avignon, had always enjoyed preferential treatment in the French customs system, even though it was, technically, a foreign territory. Through a series of understandings dating back to the sixteenth century, silks produced in Avignon had been exempted from having to pass through Lyons before entering other parts of France. In addition, Avignon's textiles were subject to relatively low tariff duties upon entering French territory. The provinces of Languedoc, Lyons, and Dauphiné complained that Avignonese products were underselling their own textiles. The deputies of trade, led by Anisson, therefore demanded that Avignon's special privileges be revoked.[96] Controller General Desmaretz and the farmers general, on the other hand, generally sided with Avignon. They thought that its textiles were subject to enough duties and that forcing its silks to pass through Lyons would be an unnecessary disruption of the normal flow of trade.[97]

The debate continued, however, and since Avignon belonged to the papacy, it was inevitable that this question should become enmeshed in the Franco-Roman controversy concerning the papal bull *Unigenitus*. Issued late in 1713, this bull condemned many of the theological tenets of French Jansenism. Originally Louis XIV had requested that the Pope officially censure this religious movement, but when the bull was finally issued, most Frenchmen decried it as a violation of the liberties of the Gallican church. In December 1714 Louis XIV appointed Michel Amelot to serve as special minister in Rome.[98] Amelot's major task was to win acceptance for a French episcopal council that would be free to regulate the practices and dogmas of the French church. He was also charged with finding a solution to the Avignon question, and on at least one occasion, he spoke personally with Clement XI concerning the matter.[99] But Amelot's mission was probably doomed from the start. The Pope refused to tolerate anything resembling conciliarism. It seems also that he refused to countenance any modification of Avignon's trading privileges in France.

ADDITIONAL PROBLEMS

At first glance it appears that the Council of Commerce played a minor role in administering the trade and industry of the French colonies. The council's *procès-verbaux* mention the colonies only rarely.[100] It is clear that Jérôme de Pontchartrain wished for Canada, Louisiana, the French West Indies, and other such dependencies to be run by himself and a few specially chosen *premiers commis*.[101]

Nevertheless, the Council of Commerce constantly made decisions that either indirectly or directly affected French overseas territories. Several examples of this have already been cited. For instance, the council protected the monopoly that La Rochelle, Nantes, Bordeaux, Dieppe, and Marseilles had on trade with the West Indies, thereby excluding other cities from that commerce.[102] The *commissaires* and the deputies also decided many questions concerning the privileges of the trading companies, and several of these organizations had the responsibility of supplying the colonies with slaves, food, and other commodities. Also, as noted above, the council helped end the exclusive monopoly of the Guinea Company, enabling private individuals to start supplying the Caribbean islands with the slaves they needed. The council's actions with regard to tariffs and general trading policies likewise had an inevitable impact on the French colonies. For example, many of the permissions that it granted for trade with Holland concerned Dutch merchandise that was needed in the African slave trade. Finally, the French islanders would have starved if the council during the war had not permitted Irish salted meat to enter France, thence to be reshipped to the Caribbean.

In general the *commissaires* and deputies supported the standard mercantilist tenet which held that colonies existed only to serve the mother country. Thus the deputies wanted to restrict severely the growth of sugar refineries in the West Indies, lest they compete with refineries at home.[103] Throughout this period the council also steadfastly refused to allow colonists to trade freely with foreigners.

Only ships possessing valid passports issued in cities permitted to trade with the colonies were supposed to be received by colonial port officials. Although on a few occasions during the war Jérôme de Pontchartrain allowed foreign (mostly Dutch) vessels to transport food supplies to the Caribbean islands, he was on all other occasions in complete agreement with the council's views on this matter.[104]

During these years Pontchartrain frequently consulted individual members of the council on a wide variety of problems relating to the colonies. In the spring of 1709, for instance, Nicolas Mesnager cautioned the secretary of state not to accept a proposal offered by some individuals for establishing an exclusive company to trade with Louisiana. He thought that the plan lacked sufficient financial backing. Also he feared that the company might bring attention to the fledgling colony and lead England to demand its cession at a future peace conference.[105] On another occasion Pontchartrain requested that the council as a whole examine the problems caused by French sailors who were deserting merchant ships that stopped in Martinique.[106]

Most often the Council of Commerce became involved in colonial matters as an examiner and arbitrator of disputes. This was particularly true in the case of Canada. Throughout the period under review here, the Canadian beaver trade was in the hands of a private company (the *Compagnie de castor*). Colonists had to sell all their beaver pelts to this company, and only the company's beaver could be sold in France. Despite these and other advantages, however, the company failed to prosper. It was obligated to purchase (at fixed prices) all the pelts that French Canadians brought to it, but the market for its product was declining in France. Many French artisans smuggled cheaper pelts into France from England and Holland. They also substituted other furs for beaver, creating half-beaver hats. Compounding these problems was the fact that the company had expended huge sums in establishing its trade. It also was embroiled in difficulties with the administrators of the *domaine d'occident* (the tax farm whose principal responsibility was the collection of import duties on goods coming from the West Indies). These officials had operated the beaver trade from 1675 until they sold it to the company in 1700. The company was unable to pay off its debts to the tax farmers, and by 1705 it owed over 1,600,000 livres to them and other creditors.[107]

These and other problems led Jérôme de Pontchartrain to rely on various members of the Council of Commerce for help in solving the company's problems. He often asked Daguesseau or Amelot to examine the company's records in order to ascertain the extent of its liabilities, and on several occasions these two men helped work out compromises between the company and its creditors. They also obtained additional tax exemptions for the company.[108]

On a few occasions, the council as a group considered the problems of the Beaver Company. In November 1707 the directors of the enterprise asked for permission to import a shipment of whale oil from Holland,[109] claiming that they needed this oil for the finishing process used on their pelts. The deputies of trade, however, rejected this request, declaring that it would only serve to help the Dutch fishing industry. Cod fish oil was generally used on beavers, they said, and there was much of that in France.[110] In 1709 and 1710, however, the council did help the company, even when this meant going against its own principles. Early in 1709 the company's directors beseeched the government to allow a few Dutch ships to go to Canada in order to purchase beavers, which would then be sold in Holland. They claimed that this would help decrease the glut of unsold pelts accumulating in its warehouse in Québec and in France, and the profit from the sale would help them honor bills of exchange whose terms were about to expire. Despite misgivings about permitting foreign vessels to trade openly with French colonies, Pontchartrain and the Council of Commerce approved a few such passports during the next two years. These were granted on the condition that the ships leave Holland empty and that they purchase no Canadian goods other than beaver.[111]

Another external problem to which the Council of Commerce devoted its attention during this period was the French fishing industry. The deputies and *commissaires* moved in a number of ways to upgrade and protect this vital sector of the economy. Perhaps the most significant action taken was the prohibition on the import of fish caught by the enemy during the war. Even before hostilities began, the council virtually prohibited the entry of English fish and whale products into the country. The *arrêt* of 6 September 1701 placed unprecedentedly high customs duties on these and other English exports, and the *arrêt* of 28 August 1703 forbade the import of fish and all other merchandise from enemy powers. Although France did begin as early as 1704 to lift some interdictions on trade with its adversaries, the deputies continually rejected all requests for the importation of enemy-caught fish. The only exception to this was salted salmon, which was permitted to enter from Scotland. Even though the depredations inflicted by enemy privateers prevented French fleets from supplying the country with all the fish that it needed, the *commissaires* and deputies did not want Frenchmen to adopt the habit of purchasing supplies from other countries. The deputies further pointed out that fishing was an essential industry in England and the United Provinces and that by forbidding the import of their catches into France irreparable harm would be done to their economies. Time and again from 1702 to 1713, the council therefore refused to permit enemy fish or fish oil to enter France, and it counseled vigilance lest these enemy goods be smuggled in via Spain, Venice, or other channels.[112]

At the behest of Secretary of State Pontchartrain, the council in 1708 helped formulate a fishing treaty that was signed with England.[113] This accord applied strictly to the home fisheries—that is, the fishing that was done off of the coasts of each nation. Hundreds of small boats participated in this trade, and during the war enemy privateers repeatedly confiscated them or forced their owners to pay ransom. Both countries agreed that most of the small boats that plied coastal waters belonged to "the unfortunate poor" and that their business was of no consequence to the outcome of the war.[114] The two governments therefore pledged that henceforth their privateers would no longer harass these small fishing vessels. The larger ships that participated in cod fishing off the Newfoundland coast and whaling near Greenland, however, were still fair game for the corsairs of both sides. In ensuing years each nation occasionally complained of infractions committed by ships of the other,[115] but by and large the treaty was a success.

From 1708 to the end of the war, the council also contributed to negotiations concerning a similar fishing convention with the United Provinces. Late in 1707 a verbal agreement had been made between the intendant of Dunkirk and a Dutch representative from Zeeland.[116] By the terms of this accord, the coastal fishing of these two provinces was to be respected by privateers of both nations. After the Dutch heard of the Anglo-French treaty, they demanded a similar one—one that would protect the coastal shipping of all the Dutch provinces. In return they promised not to interfere with French fishing boats, and they even offered to guarantee the security of French vessels sailing to Newfoundland.

The Council of Commerce had two objections to such a treaty with the Dutch. First, the promise of security for French cod fishing in the Atlantic was useless, since French ships still could have been captured by English privateers. Second, the deputies argued that France must do nothing to help Dutch fishing. The industry was a "gold mine" for the republic, employing twelve to thirteen thousand sailors. The deputies also rejected Dutch requests that the Frisian island of Texel be included in the 1707 agreement, and they heatedly rebutted all proposals for extending Dutch privileges to the rich herring fisheries of the Dogger Bank in the North Sea. No broadening of the 1707 agreement therefore came about.[117]

In other ways as well, the council aided and regulated the French fishing industry. In 1702 it drafted an *arrêt* that outlawed many fishing preserves along the coasts of Normandy and Brittany.[118] On another occasion it deliberated the legality of using certain types of dredges in coastal fishing.[119] Throughout these years the council firmly upheld the *arrêt* of 24 March 1687, which forbade any fishing for herring after 31 December each year. From January through the spring, herring spawned in the channel and North Sea waters, and they were judged to be of poor quality during this period. In order to protect the good reputation of French-caught fish, the deputies therefore rejected all requests for a permit to fish for herring during this part of the year.[120]

Throughout the peace negotiations at Utrecht, various members of the council worked, along with Jérôme de Pontchartrain, to protect French fishing interests in the New World. Thanks to their efforts, France managed to hold on to a good amount of its North American empire. It ceded Newfoundland, Nova Scotia, and the Hudson Bay territory to England; but it retained New France (Québec), Cape Breton Island, a shore on Newfoundland, and the fisheries off the Newfoundland coast.

One final extraterritorial problem in which the Council of Commerce played an important part was the series of plagues (affecting both humans and animals) that ravaged many areas of Europe—especially Eastern Europe, Germany, and Scandinavia—from 1712 through 1715. Ever since the Black Death of the fourteenth century, Europe had from time to time been subjected to epidemics of varying intensity. Whenever news of a plague reached a country or a territory, elaborate safety precautions were erected at all border crossings and ports in order to prevent the *peste* from entering. With the creation of the Council of Commerce, France now had a central agency to organize its sanitary regulations. That the task should fall upon this council was understandable: the most common transmitters of plague were merchants, sailors, and the goods that they transported.

In 1712, therefore, Desmaretz and Pontchartrain began to forward to the council all information that they received concerning the extent of the various epidemics. During the next three years, the *commissaires* and deputies drafted a series of ordinances that restricted trade with countries and cities suspected of being infected. These measures included a total severance of trade with some cities for certain periods of time, along with regulations for quarantine procedures. Ships arriving from areas suspected of having the plague were usually forced to stay anchored out in French harbors for a forty-day waiting period. Even after trade was reopened with formerly infected cities, the council forbade the importation of certain goods for long periods of time. Wools, furs, and several other materials were known to be good carriers of the *maladie contagieuse*, and therefore they could not enter France until all danger of infection had passed. Desmaretz and Pontchartrain did not always agree with the council's decisions. At times they thought that it was being too rigorous and at other times too lax. Nevertheless, they generally followed the guidelines it laid down.[121]

This chapter has endeavored to point up the crucial role that the Council of Commerce exercised in affairs stretching beyond the country's borders. Its members served the government in a variety of ways: as advisers, as arbitrators, and as diplomats. Just as this body helped give central direction to internal economic programs, so also it helped coordinate French foreign policy. Because the *commissaires* and deputies were involved in virtually every area of trade and industry, they were able to approach problems from a wide perspective. Even though they clung to a bullionist, protectionist view of foreign commerce, they also realized that trade must be reciprocal and of benefit to all parties concerned. If France's economic ties with other nations were friendlier in 1715 than they had been in 1700, one can attribute much of this development to the work of this body.

The council's involvement in external issues also posed difficulties. Even before 1700 the royal ministers had occasionally quarreled among themselves concerning jurisdiction over certain matters involving relations with other countries. Nominally this was the province of the secretary of state for foreign affairs, but as we have seen in this chapter, the secretary of state for the navy and the controller general of finances also possessed extensive rights in this field. Foreign Minister Colbert de Torcy frequently relied on various members of the Council of Commerce for advice or personal service, but the council was used even more by Jérôme de Pontchartrain, Michel Chamillart, and Nicolas Desmaretz when they intervened in foreign affairs. Torcy was bitterly irritated by what he considered to be undue interference in matters belonging to his department, but the other ministers could point to royal sanction of their activities in that realm.[122] Thus although the Council of Commerce marked a great step forward in the administration of trade and industry, it also helped aggravate a nagging defect in another area of the Old Regime's bureaucracy.

1. Franco-Spanish relations during this period have received exhaustive study in Alfred Baudrillart, *Philippe V et la cour de France*, vol. 1; C. Hippeau, *L'Avènement des Bourbons au trône d'Espagne*; and Henry Kamen, *The War of Succession in Spain, 1700–1715*.

2. Amelot had had prior experience as an ambassador, serving in Venice (1682–85), Portugal (1685–88), and Switzerland (1688–97).

3. Baudrillart, *Philippe V et la cour de France*, 1:229. Although attention here is given to the work done by Amelot and Mesnager, one should not neglect the important contributions to Spanish governmental affairs that were made by other Frenchmen during this period. In particular one should mention Jean Orry, sieur of Vignory. Orry did much to reorganize Spanish finance. He worked at the Spanish court from June 1702 to August 1704; from May 1705 to July 1706; and from April 1713 to February 1715. On Orry see Kamen, *The War of Succession*, pp. 11–12, 111–17, and passim.

4. Baudrillart, *Philippe V et la cour de France*, 1:220–30, 272–82, and passim; Kamen, *The War of Succession*, pp. 45–46, 86–90, and passim; E. W. Dahlgren, *Les Relations commerciales et maritimes entre la France et les côtes de l'océan pacifique (commencement du XVIIIᵉ siècle)* vol. 1: *Le Commerce de la mer du Sud jusqu'à la paix d'Utrecht*, pp. 329–42, and passim. Also see Baron de Girardot (ed.), *Correspondance de Louis XIV avec M. Amelot son ambassadeur en Espagne, 1705–1709*; Saint-Simon, *Mémoires*, 16:652–58, 18:449–51.

5. Baudrillart does not even mention him. Kamen, who devotes nearly two chapters to commercial affairs (*The War of Succession*, pp. 126–66) mentions him in passing on only three occasions. Mesnager receives more attention in Dahlgren, *Les Relations commerciales*, especially pp. 321–24, 498–515.

6. Daubenton served in Spain from 1702 to 1709. On him see Dahlgren, *Les Relations commerciales*, pp. 243 ff.; Neuville, *Etat sommaire*, pp. 268–69.

7. See the chart in the Appendix.

8. Most of these are in series B² of the Archives de la Marine.

9. Mar., B² 189, pp. 279–86, Pontchartrain to Daguesseau, 12 May 1706; B² 196, pp. 671–78, same to same, 2 February 1707; ibid., pp. 783–85, Pontchartrain to Amelot, 9 February 1707.

10. Mar., B³ 202, fol. 172, Desmaretz to Pontchartrain, 19 March 1711.

11. On 18 February 1709 Louis XIV wrote to Amelot: "Le principal objet de la guerre présente est celui du commerce des Indes et des richesses qu'elles produisent" (Girardot [ed.], *La Correspondance de Louis XIV avec M. Amelot*, 2:121). In an address to the Parliament in 1712, Queen Anne said, "The apprehension that Spain and the West Indies might be united to France was the chief inducement to begin this war" (cited in R. Marx, *Histoire du Royaume-Uni*, p. 245).

12. E. W. Dahlgren lists the details of many of these expeditions in his *Voyages français à destination de la mer du Sud avant Bougainville (1695–1749)*. He found records of 130 ships departing for the *mer du Sud* from 1700 through 1715. Dahlgren admits that his figures are incomplete, and from the correspondence I have read, it seems that at least 175 vessels went to Peru during this period. Only about half of the silver brought back from the *mer du Sud* was officially reported to the government. Dahlgren estimates that from 250 to 400 million livres worth of precious metals were brought to France in this manner during these years. Since Dahlgren's figures for the total number of ships is low, it appears safe to assume that the higher sum is closer to the truth. In the mid-eighteenth century, the marquis d'Argenson (son of Louis XIV's lieutenant general of police in Paris) noted in his *Journal* that earlier in the century the *mer du Sud* trade brought 100 million livres per year to France (cited in Frostin, "Les Pontchartrain," pp. 310–11). This estimate is far too high. For the Spanish point of view on this subject, see Geoffrey J. Walker, *Spanish Politics and Imperial Trade, 1700–1789*, pp. 19–63.

13. Dahlgren, *Les Relations commerciales*, pp. 195, 280, 338, 355, 493; Dahlgren, "Le Comte Jérôme de Pontchartrain et les armateurs de Saint-Malo (1712–1715)," pp. 247–49; Giraud, "Crise de conscience," pp. 181–86.

14. See Mar., B² 170, fols. 336–38, Pontchartrain to Amelot, 4 November 1703; B² 181, fols. 311v–12, Pontchartrain to Daguesseau, 22 April 1706; AN, Col., B 28, pp. 323–24, Pontchartrain to Daguesseau, 8 December 1706.

15. See Frostin, "Les Pontchartrain," pp. 323–24.

16. Dahlgren, *Les Relations commerciales*, pp. 185, 278, 337, 437, 458, 585–86, 663–66, 698–99; Mar., B³ 189, fol. 158, Desmaretz to Pontchartrain, 9 July 1710. Occasionally the government was able to collect fines from merchants who had sent ships to the *mer du Sud* without permission. In 1714 a bitter quarrel erupted between Pontchartrain and Desmaretz over whether this money should go the *trésorier général de la marine* or to one of the *gardes du trésor royal*. On this see various letters and memoirs in Mar., B² 237.

17. Descasaux du Hallay (Nantes) and Piécourt (Dunkirk) were among the leaders in sending ships to the *mer du Sud*. They each sent perhaps as many as ten vessels there during this period. Piou (Nantes), and La Motte-Gaillard, Grandville-Locquet, and Moreau (all of Saint-Malo) also participated in this trade. Letters concerning their affairs are scattered throughout the financial and naval archives. Also see Dahlgren, *Voyages français* and *Les Relations commerciales*, passim.

18. Mar., B² 175, fols. 169–70, memoir by merchants of Saint-Malo; AN, F¹² 121, fol. 47, Chamillart de Pontchartrain, 25 August 1705; Dahlgren, *Les Relations commerciales*, pp. 336–38.

19. For example, see Mar., B² 222, p. 918, Pontchartrain to Amelot, 17 September 1710; B² 226, pp. 164–65, Pontchartrain to Daguesseau, 14 January 1711; Mar., B² 231, pp. 183–84, Pontchartrain to Landivisiau, 27 July 1712; B² 238, pp. 141–42, same to same, 24 January 1714; B² 238, pp. 165–66, Pontchartrain to Amelot, 23 May 1714.

20. Dahlgren, "Le Comte Jérôme de Pontchartrain et les armateurs," pp. 245–46.

21. AN, F¹² 55, fols. 80v–81v, 19 July 1709.

22. Ordinance of 18 January 1712. A copy is in Mar., A² 23, pp. 22–23. As so often happened in the Old Regime, this ordinance was not actually drafted and published until more than two weeks after its official date. See Mar., B² 230, pp. 183–84, Pontchartrain to Daguesseau, 27 January 1712; AN, F¹² 58, fols. 9v–10, 5 February 1712. By 1712 it was too late for the government to try to prevent Frenchmen from entering into the profitable *mer du Sud* trade. Merchants and even some naval officials opposed and disobeyed the prohibition. This failure of royal authority is well documented in Giraud, "Crise de conscience"; Dahlgren, "Le Comte Jérôme de Pontchartrain et les armateurs"; and Lévy, *Capitalistes et pouvoir*, pp. 444 ff.

23. Many of these are discussed in Kamen, *The War of Succession in Spain*, pp. 126 ff.

24. Mar., B² 181, fols. 764v–65, Pontchartrain to Amelot, 20 June 1705; B² 189, pp. 165–66, Pontchartrain to Daguesseau, 8 May 1706; B² 199, pp. 127–28, Pontchartrain to Mesnager, 8 October 1707; F¹² 1923, de Machault to Pontchartrain, 15 March 1710; Mar., B⁷ 508, fols, 142–44, de Machault to Pontchartrain, 13 February 1712.

25. See Kamen, *The War of Succession in Spain*, p. 135.

26. AN, F¹² 51, fols. 101v. 103–4, 162, 169, 196, 220, 280v, 319–19v, 324, 335–35v; F¹² 55, fols. 73, 207–8; F¹² 58, fol. 149.

27. AN, F¹² 54, fols. 124–25, 145v–46, 172v, 174v–75, 177, 219, 233v–34, 269; F¹² 55, fols. 114v–15; F¹² 58, fols. 28–28v.

28. AN, F¹² 51, fols. 134, 135, 245; F¹² 58, fol. 392; Mar., B² 182, fols. 252–53, Pontchartrain to Daguesseau, 5 August 1705; Mar., B⁷ 503, fols. 280–94, memoirs by Amelot, Daubenton, and Daguesseau, 1705; Mar., B² 183, fols. 441–43v, Pontchartrain to Amelot, 4 November 1705; Kamen, *The War of Succession in Spain*, pp. 132–34.

29. In October 1701 France purchased the Spanish Asiento contract from a Portuguese company and gave it its own Guinea Company. Until 1713 the latter company was known as the Asiento Company. By means of this contract, the company could transport slaves from Africa to Spain's American colonies. At Utrecht, Great Britain acquired the Asiento.

30. The number of books written on these companies is quite large. For a rapid summary of all of them, see Pierre Bonnassieux, *Les grandes compagnies de commerce*. More detailed accounts of particular companies can be found in Paul Kaeppelin, *Les Origines de L'Inde française: la Compagnie des Indes et François Martin;* Claudius Madrolle, *Les premiers voyages français à la Chine, 1698–1719;* Georges Scelle, *Histoire politique de la traite négrière aux Indes de Castile,* and Dahlgren, *Les Relations commerciales.* Also see Cole, *French Mercantilism, 1683–1700* pp. 3–105. Parts of this chapter are taken from Schaeper, "Colonial Trade Policies Late in the Reign of Louis XIV."

31. See Price, *France and the Chesapeake,* 1:52 ff.

32. See above, p. 64.

33. See above, p. 51.

34. Mar., B² 197, pp. 153–54, Pontchartrain to Mesnager and Anisson, 6 April 1707; B² 198, pp. 1360–61, Pontchartrain to Fénellon, 7 September 1707; B⁷ 504, Fénellon to Pontchartrain, 21 September 1707; AN, G⁷ 1704, piece 293, extract of an assembly held concerning the company's affairs.

35. For some illustrations of this work, see Mar., B² 176, fols. 197–98, Pontchartrain to Anisson, Laurencin, and Fénellon, 18 July 1704; ibid., fol. 293, same to same, 3 August 1704; B² 182, Pontchartrain to Anisson and Fénellon, 2 September

1705; B² 190, p. 724, Pontchartrain to Anisson, 4 August 1706; B² 199, pp. 907–8, Pontchartrain to Héron and Fénellon, 30 November 1707; B² 207, fol. 276v, Pontchartrain to Fénellon, 18 April 1708; B² 227, pp. 187–88, Pontchartrain to Anisson, 8 April 1711; B² 230, p. 344, Pontchartrain to Anisson and Fénellon, 18 May 1712. *Arrêt* of 7 April 1705 appointing Villian (of Paris) to judge a dispute between Sieur Danycan (Saint-Malo) and the China Company; cited in Bonnassieux, *Les grandes compagnies*, p. 342.

36. For example, see Mar., B² 190, pp. 924–25, Pontchartrain to d'Armenonville, 18 August 1706; B² 228, pp. 280–81, Pontchartrain to Amelot, 19 August 1711; B² 234, p. 79, Pontchartrain to de Machault, 11 January 1713.

37. AN, F¹² 51, fols. 449v–60, 15 September 1706. Also see Dahlgren, *Les Relations commerciales*, pp. 189–93.

38. See above, p. 175, and Depitre, *La Toile peinte*, pp. 47–80.

39. See AN, F¹² 1403, "Mémoire de Mrs. les Députés du Commerce sur la commerce de la Compagnie des Indes orientales," 25 May 1701; ibid., "Marchandises d'Orient qu'il peut estre permis à la Compagnie des Indes d'aporter du dit pays," 21 June 1706.

40. See Chapter 4, n. 94.

41. Ibid., n. 98–9.

42. AN, G⁷ 1686, piece 96, Amelot to Chamillart, 15 September 1701; AN, Col., B 24, fol. 368, Pontchartrain to Massiot, 1 March 1702; ibid, fol. 376, Pontchartrain to Daguesseau, 15 March 1702; AN, F¹² 51, fol. 101, 3 March 1702.

43. AN, F¹² 54, fols. 281v–82, 289; AN, G⁷ 1692, piece 259, fols. 328–29, memoir by deputies, October 1708; AN, Col. B 31, pp. 88–89, Pontchartrain to Daguesseau, 18 July 1708.

44. Although anyone could thereafter enter the Guinea slave trade, ships participating in it had to leave and reenter France at the ports of Nantes, La Rochelle, Bordeaux, and Rouen (see Mar., B³ 216, fol. 76, Desmaretz to Pontchartrain, 4 September 1713; AN, Col., B 35, fols. 195–95v, Pontchartrain to the marquise de la Vieuville, 24 November 1713; AN, Col., B 36, fols. 229–30, Pontchartrain to Desmaretz, 5 August 1714; AN, G⁷ 1701, piece 151, Pontchartrain to Desmaretz, 30 August 1713). The Senegal Company retained its monopoly of the slave trade in that section of the African coast extending from Cape Blanc to the Sierra Leone River. All historians agree that the French slave trade grew rapidly after 1713, but most of them say that the Guinea Company lost its monopoly only in January 1716, when *lettres patentes* to that effect were issued. According to the evidence that I have uncovered, the 1716 measure merely reaffirmed the above-mentioned actions of 1713. On the 1716 decision, see Robert Louis Stein, *The French Slave Trade in the Eighteenth Century: An Old Regime Business*, pp. 13–14; Huetz de Lemps, *Géographie du commerce*, p. 570.

45. With the exception of Samual Bernard, who headed the monopoly.

46. See BN, MSS. fr., nouv. acq., 6828, pp. 501–12; *Memorials Presented by the Deputies*, pp. 20–21; Price, *France and the Chesapeake*, 1:63–66; AN, F¹² 51, fols 88–88v, 13 January 1702.

47. AN, F¹² 123, fol. 190v, Chamillart to Pontchartrain, 7 June 1707; Mar., B² 226, pp. 681–83, Pontchartrain to Desmaretz, 25 February 1711; AN, G⁷ 1696, piece 99, Anisson to Desmaretz, 21 April 1711; ibid., piece 116, same to same, 7 May 1711.

48. Mar., B⁷ 500, fol. 256, "Commerce de Moscovie," by Le Gendre, April 1701; fols. 257–58, "Mémoire sur le commerce de Moscovie," by Le Gendre, May 1701.

49. AN, G⁷ 1688, piece 82, "Sentiment du député de Languedoc au conseil de commerce sur le commerce de Moscovie et de la mer Baltique"; AN, F¹² 51, fols.

37v, 38v, 69–69v; Mar., B⁷ 500, fol. 259, "Sentiment de Mrs. les Députez du commerce sur la proposition faite par M. le Gendre . . . ," 20 May 1701; ibid., fol. 261, "Mémoire pour un projet de commerce en Moscovie," attached to a letter from Torcy to Chamillart dated 12 December 1701.

50. Mar., B³ 132, fol. 69, Torcy to Pontchartrain, 1 December 1705; Alfred Rambaud, ed., *Recueil des instructions données aux ambassadeurs et ministres de France* vol. 8, *Russie, des origines jusqu'à 1748*, pp. 109–10.

51. On Franco-Russian relations during this period see ibid., pp. 91–135. Philippe Sagnac errs in saying that a treaty of commerce was signed between the two countries in 1708 ("La Politique commerciale," pp. 273–74).

52. AN, F¹² 54, fols. 264–65; F¹² 58, fols. 133v–34; Huetz de Lemps, *Géographie du commerce*, pp. 167, 180, 551.

53. AN, G⁷ 1701, piece 184, Anisson to Desmaretz, 20 October 1713.

54. On these negotiations see AN, G⁷ 1704, piece 341, "Objets principaux des convenances de la France sur le commerce de Moscovie et des obstacles qui empêchent le progrez," undated; Mar., B³ 226, fol. 6, Pontchartrain to comte de Toulouse, 4 February 1714; Mar., B² 237, p. 534, Pontchartrain to Landivisiau, 4 April 1714; B² 239, p. 151, Pontchartrain to Amelot, 20 October 1714; ibid., p. 416, Pontchartrain to Landivisiau, 21 November 1714; Mar., B² 241, p. 811, Pontchartrain to Daguesseau, 26 June 1715.

55. See Mar., B³ 233, fols. 211–13, Landivisiau to Pontchartrain, 24 February 1714, ibid., fols. 215–216, extract of letter from M. de Campredon to Pontchartrain, 12 January 1715; ibid., fols, 217–25, Landivisiau to Pontchartrain, 12 April 1715; ibid., fols. 230–33, same to same, 21 May 1715; ibid., fols. 243–45, "Mémoire touchant le commerce de la Grande Russie," by Landivisiau, 7 July 1715.

56. AN, G⁷ 1704, piece 190, "Mémoire sur le commerce exclusif que les Malouins demandent à faire dans les Etats du Czar par le port de Petersbourg en Livonie," undated; AN, G⁷ 1704, piece 341, "Objets principaux"; Mar., B² 235, pp. 77–78, Pontchartrain to Amelot, 16 October 1713; ibid., pp. 216–17, same to same, 1 November 1713; ibid., pp. 368–69, same to same, 22 November 1713; ibid., p. 467, same to same, 6 December 1713; Mar., B⁷ 509, fols. 265–66v, seven *négociants* of Saint-Malo to Pontchartrain, 18 April 1714; B² 241, p. 28, Pontchartrain to Daguesseau, 2 January 1715. A strictly political treaty of friendship between Russia, Prussia, and France was signed in August 1717 (see J. H. Shennan, *Philippe, Duke of Orleans: Regent of France*, p. 62).

57. AN, G⁷ 1702, fols. 21–31, "Capitulations entre la France et la Perse du Septembre 1708 faites et aportées par le Sr Michel."

58. Many of the documents relating to negotiations with Persia during this period were recopied by Desmaretz's *premier commis*, de la Garde, in "Commerce de Perse," AN, G⁷ 1704, piece 339.

59. AN, G⁷ 1704, piece 339, Landivisiau to Desmaretz, 19 July 1715; ibid., same to same, 3 August 1715; ibid., "La manière dont le commerce de Perse peut estre fait avec avantage," by Landivisiau.

60. Ibid., *maire, échevins*, and deputies of commerce of Marseilles to Desmaretz, 2 August 1715, with accompanying "Mémoire de la chambre de commerce de Marseille.".

61. AN, G⁷ 1702, piece 14, Anisson to Desmaretz, 4 February 1714; ibid., piece 40, "Mémoire sur le commerce de Perse," by Anisson; G⁷ 1704, piece 16, Anisson to Desmaretz, 10 February 1715, with accompanying memoir entitled "Observations sur la lettre icy à costé"; ibid., "Observations sur ce commerce" and "Sur le commerce de Perse," both by Anisson and Gilly.

62. Their position is described in the pieces listed in notes 58 and 61.

63. On these peace negotiations, consult the following works: Arsène Legrelle, *La Diplomatie française et la succession d'Espagne*, vol. 4; J. G. Stork-Penning, *Het Grote Werk; vredesonderhandelingen gedurende de Spaanse successieroorlog, 1705–10*; Mark Thomson, "Louis XIV and the Grand Alliance 1705–1710"; Ottokar Weber, *Der Friede von Utrecht*.

64. Torcy, *Mémoires de M. de Torcy pour servir à l'histoire des négociations depuis le traité de Riswick jusqu'à la paix d'Utrecht*, 1:181.

65. On this mission to the United Provinces, see *Recueil des instructions données aux ambassadeurs et ministres de France*, vol. 22: *Hollande*, ed. Louis André and Emile Bourgeois, pp. 159–77; Dahlgren, *Les Relations commerciales*, pp. 566–572; Lévy, *Captitalistes et pouvoir*, pp. 267 ff., 322 ff.

66. AN, G⁷ 1694, piece 56, Mesnager to Le Blanc, 8 February 1709 (copy). Mesnager detailed his attempts to get into Holland in a series of letters to Desmaretz. These letters are dated from 6 January 1709 to 10 April 1709 and are all in this same carton. Dahlgren errs when he says that Mesnager actually reached Holland and pursued further talks with Dutch officials early in 1709 (*Les Relations commerciales*, p. 575).

67. On Mesnager's work in England, see *Recueil des instructions données aux ambassadeurs et ministres de France*, vol. 25, pt. 3, *Angleterre (1698–1791)*, ed, Paul Vaucher, pp. 75–105; G. M. Trevelyan, "The 'Jersey' Period of the Negotiations Leading to the Peace of Utrecht"; Dahlgren, *Les Relations commerciales*, pp. 629 ff.; Lévy, *Capitalistes et pouvoir*, p. 438.

68. Letters and memoirs by Desmaretz and Pontchartrain relating to the discussions at Utrecht can be found in AAE, Mém. et Doc., France, 1426; and in AN, G⁷ 1700, register B. On Pontchartrain's involvement in foreign affairs, also see John C. Rule, "Jérôme Phelypeaux, Comte de Pontchartrain, and the Establishment of Louisiana, 1696–1715," p. 197.

69. All are reprinted in Henri Vast (ed.), *Les grands traités du règne de Louis XIV*, vol. 3. From April 1713 to 1715 the Congress worked on the questions of a treaty between France and the empire, treaties between Spain and its enemies, and the Dutch Barrier Treaty.

70. Register B in AN, G⁷ 1704 contains most of the Mesnager-Desmaretz correspondence. It also has letters from Desmaretz to all three plenipotentiaries, and letters from Daguesseau to Desmaretz. Also see G⁷ 1697, piece 172, "Second mémoire des Députez au conseil de commerce sur le tarif des hollandois;" and G⁷ 1700, register B.

71. The *procès-verbaux* of the council mention the Utrecht negotiations, in passing, on only three occasions. See chart in Appendix.

72. See AN, G⁷ 1696, piece 258, Anisson to Desmaretz, 26 October 1711; ibid., piece 270, same to same, 9 November 1711; ibid., piece 280, same to same, 21 November 1711; ibid., piece 314, same to same, 31 December 1714.

73. Vast, *Les grands traités*, 3:138.

74. See above, p. 126.

75. Vast, *Les grands traités*, 3:114–18.

76. See Prosper Boissonnade, "Histoire des premiers essais de relations économiques directes entre la France et l'état prussien pendant le règne de Louis XIV (1643–1715)," pp. 376–416.

77. Ibid., pp. 409–10; Vast, *Les grands traités*, 3:121.

78. Boissonnade, "Histoire des premiers essais," pp. 414–16.

79. AN, G⁷ 1700, register B, Desmaretz to Mesnager, 12 February 1713.

80. Vast, *Les grands traités*, 3:161.

81. A copy is in Mar., A² 23.

82. Vast, *Les grands traités*, 3:87–111.

83. On these two missions, see AN, G⁷ 1699, which contains letters and memoirs by Anisson, Fénellon, Desmaretz, Daguesseau, and others: also see G⁷ 1704, piece 338, "Mémoire sur la négociation faite à Londres pour le traité de commerce des années 1713 et 1714," by Anisson.

84. See ibid.; also G⁷ 1697, Anisson to Clautrier, 29 December 1712; ibid., piece 194, "Mémoire des députés au conseil de commerce sur la navigation et le commerce entre les deux nations françoise et angloise;" G⁷ 1702, piece 4, Mesnager to Desmaretz, 15 January 1714; AAE, Corr. pol., Angleterre, 249, fols. 141–49, Mesnager to Torcy, 4 July 1713, with accompanying memoir. Also see the letters of Mathieu Fabre and François Philip in ACCM, B 161–66.

85. AN, G⁷ 1704, piece 338, "Mémoire sur la négociation.".

86. AN, G⁷ 1701, piece 221, Anisson to Desmaretz, 2 December 1713. The negotiations in London provide a good example of the manner in which French ministers competed among themselves in the conducting of foreign affairs. During this period Torcy was represented in England by the French ambassador or envoy (the duc d'Aumont in 1713, Charles François d'Iberville in 1714). Desmaretz, on the other hand, supervised the work of Anisson and Fénellon. Jérôme de Pontchartrain likewise had a commercial agent in London (a man named Vergier), who was charged with pursuing discussions related to the navy; on him see G⁷ 1699, Anisson to Desmaretz, 24 February 1713.

87. In 1712 Charles Davenant, the English inspector general of imports and exports, published a book showing that England by far had the advantage in its trade with France, but Whig-inspired public pressure led Davenant to disavow having written the book. On this episode see AN, G⁷ 1704, piece 338, "Mémoire sur la négociation." Concerning English opposition to the treaty of commerce, see also D. A. E. Harkness, "The Opposition to the 8th and 9th Articles of the Commercial Treaty of Utrecht"; Emory Crokett Bogle, "A Stand for Tradition;" D. C. Coleman, "Politics and Economics in the Age of Anne: The Case of the Anglo-French Trade Treaty of 1713."

88. Treaties were signed with the emperor at Rastadt (6 March 1714) and Baden (7 September 1714) (Vast, *Les grands traités*, 3:162–92).

89. The bulk of the correspondence and memoirs concerning this affair are recorded in AN, G⁷ 1700, register A.

90. Most of it is reprinted in ibid., pt. 2, fols. 51–84.

91. See Mar., B⁷ 509, fols. 5–14, de Boissy to Pontchartrain, 10 July 1713.

92. I have no evidence of any animosity between Desmaretz and Pontchartrain concerning this particular affair, although Desmaretz was aware that these negotiations belonged in his own jurisdiction (see AN, G⁷ 1702, piece 123, Vaultier to Desmaretz, 12 May 1712).

93. Mar., B³ 233, fols. 176–77, Rouillé de Fontaine to Pontchartrain, 11 June 1715; ibid., fols. 178–79, same to same, 22 June 1715; ibid., fol. 189, same to same, 29 July 1715; ibid., fols. 193–97, same to same, 10 August 1715; ibid., fols. 199–208, "Demandes des Messieurs les députés de Hambourg, Lubeck et Bremen"; also see various letters from Pontchartrain to Daguesseau and Rouillé de Fontaine in Mar., B² 242.

94. Pierre Dardel, *Navires et marchands dans les ports de Rouen et du Havre au XVIIIᵉ siècle*, p. 83.

95. See AN, G⁷ 1703, especially pieces 209–47.

96. Ibid., piece 211, "Mémoire sur l'affaire qui est entre les habitans de la ville et Comtat d'Avignon et la ville de Lyon.".

97. Ibid., piece 211 and piece 213, "Instance entre les marchands et habitans de la ville et Comtat d'Avignon et les prevost des marchands et échevins de la ville de Lyon"; piece 234, untitled memoir by farmers general.

98. See A. Le Roy, *La France et Rome de 1700 à 1715: histoire diplomatique de la Bulle Unigenitus jusqu'à la mort de Louis XIV*, pp. 612–14, 681, and passim. The cardinal de la Trémoille was the regular French ambassador in Rome at the time. He remained there during Amelot's stay in the city, and his personal jealousy of the special minister may have contributed to Amelot's failure.

99. AN, G⁷ 1703, piece 247, Amelot to Desmaretz (the date has been eaten away).

100. See chart in Appendix. On this general topic, see Schaeper, "Colonial Trade Policies."

101. These were de Lagny, Des Haguais, Sallaberry, and Fontanieu. The first two have been mentioned several times already. Charles de Sallaberry served as head of the *bureau du Levant* from 1688 to July 1709. Colonial affairs were taken care of in this bureau until January 1710 when a *bureau des colonies* was created. Pontchartrain chose Moyse Augustin de Fontanieu, a *trésorier général de la marine*, to direct this new bureau. (See Mar., B⁸ 18, "Bureaux de la marine," June 1749.)

102. See above, pp. 61–62.

103. On the restriction of refineries in the colonies and their growth in France in the eighteenth century, see Cole, *French Mercantilism, 1683–1700*, pp. 87–90; Bondois, "L'Industrie sucrière en France au XVIIIe siècle," p. 342; Bondois, "Les Centres sucriers.".

104. See above, p. 125.

105. Marcel Giraud, *Histoire de la Louisiane française*, 1:123–24.

106. AN, Col., B 28, Pontchartrain to Daguesseau, 10 March 1706.

107. Cole gives the figure 1,607,249 livres (*French Mercantilism, 1683–1700*, p. 77). An anonymous memoir written at about that time set the company's debts at 1,700,000 livres and its assets at 700,000 livres (AN, F¹² 799 A, "Mémoire sur l'état de Canada"). A memoir from a year later put the company's total liabilities at 1,397,936 livres (AN, Col., B 27, fol. 262v, "Mémoire sur la nécessité de la vente génćralle des castors," 9 June 1706).

108. On the beaver trade in general and other problems of the *Compagnie de castor*, see Cole, *French Mercantilism, 1683–1700*, pp. 66–77, and the other works cited therein. Sources of letters by Pontchartrain, Daguesseau, and Amelot on this question can be found throughout AN, Col., B 21–37 and in series B² and B³ of the Archives de la Marine. Among other things, see Mar., B² 154, fol. 683, Pontchartrain to Amelot, 22 June 1701; B² 160, fol. 282, same to same, 8 February 1702; B² 157, fols. 157–65, Pontchartrain to Daguesseau, 6 March 1706; AN, Col., B 29, fol. 135, Pontchartrain to Daguesseau, 30 November 1707; AN, F¹² 799 A, Pontchartrain to Daguesseau, 9 March 1706.

109. AN, Col. B 29, fol. 134, Pontchartrain to Daguesseau, 16 November 1707; AN, F¹² 54, fol. 104v, 18 November 1707.

110. AN, F¹² 1903, *avis* of deputies, 23 November 1707.

111. See above, p. 125.

112. AN, F¹² 51, fols. 150v–51v, 201v, 333, 336, 374v, 375; F¹² 54, fols. 149–49v; F¹² 55, fols. 141–41v, 255v, 267; F¹² 58, fol. 233v. Among other things also see AN, G⁷ 1694, piece 34, de Machault to Desmaretz, 27 January 1709; G⁷ 1695, piece 120, Daguesseau to Desmaretz, 4 July 1710.

113. It was first signed in May 1708 and then renewed in September 1710 (see Bromley, "The French Privateering War," p. 214).

114. AN, F^{12} 54, fols. 208v, 212v.

115. For example, see AN, G^7 1692, piece 94, memoir by deputies of trade, August 1708; Mar., B^7 507, Sunderland to Pontchartrain, 7 June 1710, fols. 409–10; Mar., B^3 189, fol. 14, Pontchartrain to admiralty officers in Cherbourg, 30 July 1710.

116. Mar., B^7 508, fols. 375–79, "Mémoire de ce qui s'est passé entre la France et la Hollande à l'égard de la pesche du poisson frais," March 1712, by a M. Raudot.

117. On these negotiations see AN, F^{12} 54, fols. 163v, 170, 179v, 180v, 189–89v, 240v, 287–87v, 295–96; F^{12} 55, fols. 12v–13, 75–77v, 241–42; F^{12} 58, fols. 69v–70; AN, G^7 1691, piece 190, *avis* of deputies, 4 May 1708; ibid., piece 194, *avis* of deputies, 11 May 1708; ibid., piece 200, *avis* of deputies, 18 May 1708; Mar., B^7 507, fols. 117–19, "Réflexions des députez au conseil de commerce sur la proposition faitte par les hollandois"; ibid., fols. 370–407, various memoirs. Working under instructions from Torcy, Desmaretz, and Pontchartrain, Nicolas Mesnager left Paris for Holland in January 1709. One of his many objectives was the negotiation of a Franco-Dutch fishing treaty. On this see AN, G^7 534, Pontchartrain to Desmaretz, 4 January 1709. As noted above, however, Mesnager was not granted a passport to enter Dutch territory.

118. AN, F^{12} 51, fols. 40, 79, 130v–31, 133v. Fishing preserves (*parcs*) consisted of long series of nets by which individuals enclosed large areas of the sea, thereby reserving the sea life of those areas for themselves.

119. AN, F^{12} 54, fols. 146v, 158v–60v; AN, G^7 1692, piece 259, fols. 77–79, memoir by deputies, March 1708.

120. AN, F^{12} 54, fols. 146v, 158v–60v; F^{12} 55, fols. 45, 81v–82, 140v, 227–28, 255. Also see Mar., B^2 220, p. 77, Pontchartrain to de Boissy, 1 January 1710; B^2 223, p. 152, Pontchartrain to Daguesseau, 15 October 1710; B^2 226, pp. 524–25, Pontchartrain to de Boissy, 11 February 1711; B^2 227, pp. 80–81, 672–73, Pontchartrain to de Boissy, 1 April and 13 May 1711; B^2 230, p. 585, Pontchartrain to Daguesseau, 23 March 1712; B^2 231, p. 417, Pontchartrain to de Boissy, 31 August 1712; B^2 234, pp. 324–25, same to same, 15 February 1713; B^2 237, p. 423, same to same, 14 March 1714; B^2 239, p. 451, Pontchartrain to Desmaretz, 28 November 1714.

121. AN, F^{12} 58, fols. 13–13v, 16v–17, 25–27, 34–35v, 95–97v, 142–45, 156–59, 172–72v, 192–94, 202v–5v, 213–15v, 225–25v, 226–26v, 234, 255, 271v, 283v–84v, 306v–7v, 329. Correspondence concerning this subject is in Mar., B^2 230–42, and in Mar., B^7 507–8. Also see Boislisle, *Correspondance des contrôleurs généraux*, 3:531 ff; McCloy, *Government Assistance*, pp. 106–8; Ragnhild Hatton, *Europe in the Age of Louis XIV*, pp. 10–12.

122. The *règlement* 13 September 1699 detailed the rights of the controller general and the secretary of state for the navy in all matters relating to commerce; on this *règlement* see Chapter 1, n. 66. In 1698 the new foreign minister Colbert de Torcy endeavored to curb naval secretary Louis de Pontchartrain's powers in external affairs. The latter defended his prerogatives in this regard. A *règlement* issued in October 1698 reaffirmed the naval secretary's traditional rights in corresponding with the French ambassadors and envoys on matters relating to commerce and the navy. See Mar., G 222, piece 20, "Mémoire de M. de Pontchartrain au Roy concernant les fonctions de la charge de secrétaire d'état de la marine, et de celle de M. de Torcy ayant le département des affaires étrangères" (1698); Mar., A^2 21, pp. 130–33, "Règlement fait par la Roy entre M. de Pontchartrain ministre et secrétaire d'état de la marine et M. de Torcy ministre des affaires étrangères sur les fonctions de leurs charges," October 1698. On interministerial conflicts or confusion sur-

rounding the conduct of foreign affairs, see Rule, "Jérôme Phélypeaux, Comte de Pontchartrain," p. 197; Rule, "King and Minister," pp. 223–24; William J. Roosen, "The Functioning of Ambassadors under Louis XIV," p. 323; Camille Georges Picavet, *La Diplomatie française au temps de Louis XIV (1661–1715): institutions, moeurs, et coutumes*, pp. 42–47; Lévy, *Capitalistes et pouvoir*, pp. 304 ff; Frostin, "Les Pontchartrain," pp. 330–31; Frostin, "L'Organisation ministérielle sous Louis XIV: cumul d'attributions et situations conflictuelles, 1690–1715."

9

CONCLUSIONS

The study of the Council of Commerce demonstrates clearly that this body rendered an invaluable service to the royal government early in the eighteenth century. Far from being the product of opposition to the monarchy, the council actively and eagerly participated in the government's administration of trade and industry. The monarchy had consulted with the business community on a regular basis throughout the seventeenth century, and this council merely marked the culmination and consolidation of this practice.

An examination of the personnel and the functioning of the council reveals plainly that it was much more than a mere decorative advisory panel. The *commissaires* who sat on it included several of the most powerful and most respected officers in the upper echelons of the bureaucracy. Through their personal and official contacts with royal ministers, they ensured that the council's opinions were not only listened to but also generally followed. The council—or its individual members—became involved in virtually every important issue surrounding trade or manufactures during this period.

The factor that gave the council its uniqueness was the presence on it of merchant representatives from several of the leading commercial cities in the kingdom. These deputies were nearly always chosen from among the most knowledgeable and competent members of their communities and were thus well equipped to transmit to the government the needs and aspirations of their regions. In their general memoirs written in 1700 and 1701, the deputies were given a rare opportunity to express themselves on a wide range of topics relating to commerce and industry. Although most historians have seen in these memoirs much evidence of a general attack on traditional mercantilist policies, a close analysis of them reveals that the deputies actually had few real disagreements with the

Colbertian legacy. They repeatedly called for "liberty of trade," but this "liberty" was far from our contemporary conception of the word. Often the deputies employed this phrase in a distinctly medieval fashion, wherein "liberty" signified a vested privilege or a right. Furthermore, the idea of freedom—meaning a lessening of restrictions—was by no means alien to Colbert and other practitioners or theorists of mecantilism.

Just as the royal government established the Council of Commerce, so also it endeavored to create chambers of commerce in those cities represented in the Parisian body. Despite constant royal prodding, however, most cities dragged their feet in setting up such bodies. There were several reasons for the delays encountered: lack of money; disputes concerning the composition of the chambers; satisfaction with traditional modes of discussing local economic problems and presenting grievances to the central government; fear of royal encroachments on local privileges; and the distraction of war. Nevertheless, by the year 1715 there were a total of eight chambers of commerce in the country. Contrary to the designs of the monarchy, these chambers tended to become staunch defenders of regional interests, unmindful of the general good. At the behest of their constituents, the deputies in Paris therefore were compelled to devote a large part of their time to the defense of local privileges, which frequently resulted in bitter feuds between deputies upholding the conflicting claims of two or more competing cities or provinces. Notwithstanding these shortcomings, however, the chambers of commerce did provide valuable service by supplying the government with expert advice and information concerning local trade and manufactures. In addition, the deputies of trade often were able to subsume their regional loyalties when these loyalties markedly contradicted the general good.

The question of wartime trade with enemy and neutral powers was the subject that recurred most frequently in the Council of Commerce during this period. Although in their general memoirs the deputies had propounded the benefits of "liberty of trade" and of reduced barriers and restrictions on international commerce, they performed an abrupt *volte-face* after the outbreak of war. From 1702 through 1713 the Council of Commerce relentlessly taxed, restricted, proscribed, or otherwise intervened in all areas of foreign trade in an effort to protect and encourage French trade and shipping. Its trade policies fell generally into two parts. The first was directed against enemy nations. Early in the war, the council prohibited all trade with France's adversaries. The chief targets of this measure were England and the United Provinces. The council especially wished to wreck the carrying trade of the Dutch; again and again the deputies fulminated against "ces républicains," who had managed to become the masters of many areas of Europe's commerce. The impracticality of this trade ban soon became apparent, and little by little the council had to expand the limits on trade with hostile powers. Thousands of passports were reluctantly granted to Dutch vessels bringing Dutch, German, and Scandinavian goods to France. The second aspect of the council's policies involved neutral trade. The council was responsible for defining and determining the legitimate rights of neutral shipping. In addition, it granted a host of privileges to neutral vessels in order to induce them to trade directly with France. As a means of enforcing all these trade policies, the council helped broaden—within limits—the rights of French privateers.

The regulation and encouragement of manufactures was second in importance—in terms of frequency of discussion—among matters dealt with by the council during these years. Far from rejecting the multifarious *règlements, ordonnances,* and *arrêts* that controlled all aspects of textile production, the council reaffirmed them and increased their number. In an effort to ensure that these laws were enforced, the council expanded the number of inspectors of manufactures and encouraged their work. Although this policing of manufactures brought only a very qualified success, one must point out that the regulations and the inspectors had far more popular support than many historians would have us believe. The council strove to encourage manufactures in other ways as well. It granted subsidies and monopolies to individual entrepreneurs, and it afforded French products some measure of protection from foreign competition by means of outright prohibitions or elevated tariffs.

The members of the council also became involved in a wide variety of matters related to royal finances. The council was in large part responsible for establishing the *bureau de la balance du commerce* in 1713. By means of this agency, the *commissaires* and deputies hoped to guarantee that France would always have a favorable balance of trade, thereby conserving the nation's stocks of gold and silver. The council's work concerning tariffs was rather mixed. Although virtually all of its members supported the principle of lower tariff walls and of amicable trading relations with other nations, the council followed no set pattern in its proposals in this area. Although it helped lower several import and export duties, it raised, or refused to lower, perhaps just as many other ones. In general, the council worked to facilitate the import of raw materials and the export of manufactures, wine, and other goods. On the other hand, it supported rather high duties imposed on foreign manufactures. Despite the fact that the council was the center of discussion for the "single duty project," several *commissaires* and deputies opposed this measure. Thus the possibility of tariff reform was never very great. With regard to the farmers general, one must conclude that on the whole the council had a good—though not warm—working relationship with them. In a number of ways, the farmers general were more flexible and open to change than were several of the deputies and *commissaires*. Almost without exception the monetary policies advocated by the council were conservative and bullionist. Thus the council clamored for a stable currency and deplored the frequent currency manipulations to which the crown resorted. The council likewise helped defeat the rather risky plans for establishing a state bank and for extending the use of *billets de monnaie* to the entire kingdom.

Finally, the council (or its individual members) played a significant role in foreign relations and other areas relating to external trade. The council helped formulate virtually all policies pertaining to trade with Spain and with the *mer du Sud*. Although the council itself did not administer the chartered trading companies, its members were continually involved in judging disputes concerning the debts or the privileges of these bodies. Far from being hardened foes of the trading companies, the *commissaires* and deputies adopted a rather undogmatic approach toward them. In many instances they defended the rights of the companies, provided that the latter carried out their obligations. The council as a whole (or its individual members) also participated in virtually all the diplomatic negotiations that accompanied the close of the War of the Spanish Succession. In large measure, France's new trading postures toward other European nations were the work of the members of the Council of Commerce. The council was active in other areas as well, including the French colonies and the fishing industry. With regard to the colonies, the council pursued a policy of regulating the trade and industry of French dependencies in a way that would be advantageous for the mother country; and the council considered the native fishing industry to be so important that it expended much time in regulating it and protecting it from foreign competition.

The fact that the Council of Commerce was thoroughly mercantilist—in the sense of favoring strong regulation of all aspects of the economy—did not go unnoticed by contemporaries. For an illustration of this, one could cite an anonymous memoir preserved in the foreign affairs archives. [1] Written in 1730, the memoir gives a brief description of the administration of trade and industry from 1660 to 1730. It praises Colbert and his immediate successors, asserting that they realized the necessity of some individual freedom in such matters. The author declares, however, that the creation of the Council of Commerce undid much of the good work accomplished prior to 1700. The deputies, he claims, spent all their time defending the privileges of the particular regions. In addition, the council strove to perfect French manufactures, but in so doing it issued many "nouveaux règlemens" that destroyed an infinity of private enterprises. Although this memoir is overly biased against the council, it does demonstrate that contemporaries judged the council to be thoroughly traditional—possibly even too traditional.

Perhaps one would be most accurate in viewing the council as part of the ongoing process of bureaucratization that was at work in most of the European countries throughout the early modern era. During the last third of the seventeenth century and the first third of the eighteenth, special bodies dealing with commercial matters were created or revived in England, Sweden, Denmark, Muscovy, Prussia, Spain, Austria, Portugal, the Dutch Republic, and perhaps other states. These institutions were remarkably similar to one another, although they went by different names (council, college, board, junta). Like the French Council of Commerce, they were all mostly consultative rather than administrative in function. Louis XIV therefore was not alone in seeking the advice of economic experts and in creating a special body to deal with the problems of commerce and manufactures, but he was noticeably progressive and in advance of other rulers in two respects. The French council seems to have had a wider scope of interests and to have been more active than any of the other bodies; and, with the possible exception of the trade commission in Muscovy, [2] the French council was alone in giving such a prominent role to private businessmen. Indeed, the study of the Council of Commerce reveals that there was a much higher degree of cooperation between the

crown and the merchant community in the Old Regime than heretofore has been recognized.

1. AAE, Mem. et Doc., France, 1990, fols. 163–68, "Comparison de ce qui s est passé pour l'administration du commerce de France depuis 1660."

2. See AN, G⁷ 1704, piece 341, "Objets principaux des convenances de la France sur le commerce de Moscovie."

APPENDIX A
THE "COMMISSAIRES" IN THE COUNCIL OF COMMERCE

Controller general of finances
Michel Chamillart, 1700–1708
Nicolas Desmaretz, 1708–15
Secretary of state for the navy
Jérôme Phélypeaux, comte de Pontchartrain, 1700–1715
Ordinary *commissaires*
Henri Daguesseau, 1700–1716
Michel Jean Amelot de Gournay, 1700–1724
François-Joseph d'Ernothon, 1700–1708 (His position was abolished when the intendants of commerce were created in 1708.)
Nicolas-Prosper Bauyn d'Angervilliers, 1700–1702 (He was replaced by Etienne-Hyacinthe-Antoine Foullé de Martangis, 1702–8; this position was also abolished in 1708.)
Marc-René de Voyer de Palmy, marquis d'Argenson, 1705–20
Louis Béchameil de Nointel, 1708–18
Jean-Baptiste Desmaretz de Vaubourg, 1715
Director of finances
Hilaire Rouillé du Coudray, 1701–3, 1716–18 (During the regency he attended as a representative from the Council of Finances; in 1703 he was replaced by Nicolas Desmaretz, 1703–8.)
Joseph-Jean-Baptiste Fleuriau d'Armenonville, 1701–8
(These offices were suppressed in 1708.)
Intendants of commerce
Denis-Jean Amelot de Chaillou, 1708–15
Louis-François Lefèvre de Caumartin de Boissy, 1708–15
Louis-Charles de Machault, 1708–50 (After 1715 he was an ordinary *commissaire*.)
Jean Rouillé de Fontaine, 1708–15

Charles Boucher d'Orsay, 1708–11 (replaced by Noël Danycan de Landivisiau, 1711–15)

César-Charles Lescalopier, 1707–11, 1713–14 (For part of 1711–12 he was replaced by Samuel Bernard; in 1714 his department was given to another intendant of commerce, Caumartin de Boissy.)

Bayonne
   Léon de Rol, 1700–1702
   Vacancy, 1703–11
   Gérard Heusch de Janvry, 1711–18
Bordeaux
   Jean-Baptiste Fénellon, 1700–1718
Dunkirk
   Noël Piécourt, 1700–1715
Languedoc
   (?) Mourgues, 1700–1701
   Vacancy, 1701–3
   Syndics généraux
      Pierre Roux de Montbel, 1703–4
      André de Joubert, 1704–5
      (?) de Boyer d'Odars, 1705–6
      Jean-Antoine du Vidal de Montferrier, 1706–7
      André de Joubert, 1707–8
      Jean-Jacques de Boyer, fils, 1708–9
   Vacancy, 1709–13
   Simon Gilly, 1713–32
Lille
   François-Eustache Taviel, 1700–1702
   Vacancy, 1709–13
   Michel Vandercruysen, 1715–17
Lyons
   Jean Anisson, 1700–1722
Marseilles
   Joseph Fabre, 1700–1704
   Mathieu Fabre, 1704–14
   François Philip, 1714–17
Nantes
   Joachim Descasaux du Hallay, 1700–1702
   Germain Laurencin, fils, 1702–5
   Jean Piou, 1705–19

Paris
  Samuel Bernard, 1700–1720
  Antoine Peletyer, 1700–1702
  Denis Rousseau, 1702–3
  Claude Vilain, 1703–8
  Léonard Chauvin, 1708–19
La Rochelle
  Antoine Héron, 1700–1712
  Vacancy, 1712–15
  François Mouchard, 1715–19
Rouen
  Nicolas Mesnager, 1700–1712
  David Le Baillif, 1712–15
  Georges Godeheu, 1715–20
Saint-Malo
  Alain de La Motte-Gaillard, 1700–1702
  Charles de Grandville-Locquet, 1702–6
  René Moreau de Maupertuis, 1706–46

APPENDIX C
THE AGENDA OF THE COUNCIL

The table that follows is based on the *procès-verbaux* of the council. It lists the general categories of topics studied in the council and the frequency with which they were discussed. A glance at it reveals, for example, that the question that recurred most often was that of France's trade with enemy and neutral powers during the War of the Spanish Succession. Other topics that lead the list include the regulation of manufactures, tariff policies, and relations with Spain.

The difficulties encountered in coding each item into a single category make it impossible to give the chart total precision. In many instances an individual item overlapped several categories. In creating the chart, I therefore sometimes counted one particular case under two or, in a few occasions, three categories. Even those questions that were assigned to only one category were usually intimately related to others. For example, the council judged every request by a French merchant to import merchandise from another country by several criteria: Was this article needed by French manufactures? Was it needed for French trade with the Levant? With Spain? With French colonies? Would this trade in some way help Dutch commerce, thereby hurting French traders? Was this merchandise to be paid for by gold and silver (which was undesirable) or by the export of French manufactures and other products (which was encouraged)?

Although the chart does indicate the variety of things reported in the *procès-verbaux*, these minutes themselves fail to present a complete account of the council's work. The secretary did not record the reports and debates *in toto*, but rather gave brief summaries. What is even less satisfactory about the *procès-verbaux* is that they do not mention all the affairs that external evidence reveals were discussed in the council. Frequently, at the end of the record of a meeting the secretary wrote that "diverses autres choses" also had been examined. Fortunately, one can discover what most of these "other things" were by consulting the financial and naval archives. Many of the issues that the council discussed were of a trivial and a repetitive nature, and explicit mention of them was unnecessary; but in a handful of instances, extremely important matters discussed in the council were not reported in the *procès-verbaux*. One example is the affair of 1704 concerning the creation and sale of offices of inspectors general and collectors-visitors of woolens and linens. The Council of Commerce, responding to protests by merchant-manufacturers from all over France, was instrumental in getting these offices abolished (see Chapter 6). Yet, inexplicably, the *procès-verbaux* do not mention this episode.

Despite its shortcomings, however, the chart does represent in a general way the concerns of the council and (by implication) the concerns of the government and the business community.

Table 2

Subjects Reported in the *Procès-Verbaux* by Year

	1700–1701	1702	1703	1704	1705	1706	1707	1708	1709	1710	1711	1712	1713	1714	1715
The deputies' general memoirs of 1700–1701	14	0	0	0	0	0	0	0	0	0	0	0	0	0	0
Regulation and encouragement of manufactures	27	39	37	14	14	16	28	15	35	18	20	22	30	33	35
General problems concerning commerce with enemy and neutral nations	16	2	6	1	4	5	12	51	17	42	5	4	2	1	1
Trade with the Dutch	10	13	14	9	34	20	34	121	62	42	9	11	26	16	6
Trade with England, Scotland and Ireland	5	19	5	3	15	31	17	33	28	10	20	23	22	12	4
Trade with Denmark and Sweden	5	13	12	6	20	25	13	26	16	9	20	14	4	0	0
Trade with Muscovy	3	0	0	0	4	4	1	1	0	0	0	0	2	0	0
Trade with Germany (including Hanseatic cities)	1	2	0	4	7	9	0	10	11	12	60	51	29	8	2

Table 2 (*continued*)

	1700–1701	1702	1703	1704	1705	1706	1707	1708	1709	1710	1711	1712	1713	1714	1715
Trade with other enemy and neutral nations	1	6	5	3	7	5	6	6	12	8	20	11	9	2	2
Tariffs and internal customs duties	46	51	46	14	32	21	15	19	20	21	11	6	7	7	6
Relations with Spain (including French commerce in Spanish America)	10	13	9	2	6	10	6	18	6	9	15	6	2	5	4
French privateering	0	3	4	4	6	26	10	9	12	9	13	7	2	1	0
French and Spanish Flanders	4	3	12	3	7	11	6	7	10	12	14	5	14	1	0
French fishing industry	9	6	3	5	1	2	1	19	4	5	3	4	3	1	0
Conflicts between merchants and tax farmers	16	6	6	3	3	7	6	6	4	1	4	1	2	2	0
Disputes over Marseilles's privileges	10	7	11	9	3	2	7	2	2	2	1	2	2	4	7
Establishment and organization of chambers of commerce	22	9	7	7	3	3	7	0	0	1	3	0	3	1	1

Table 2 (continued)

	1700–1701	1702	1703	1704	1705	1706	1707	1708	1709	1710	1711	1712	1713	1714	1715
The French West Indies and Louisiana	8	8	1	3	1	1	0	6	6	3	1	2	0	3	4
Privileged trading companies	21	10	4	5	0	3	1	5	5	3	2	2	5	3	3
French currency, financial problems	12	11	9	3	0	0	0	7	1	1	0	0	2	1	0
Threats of plagues entering France	0	0	0	0	0	0	0	0	0	0	0	7	10	6	1
Powers of *juridictions consulaires*	4	3	6	9	1	2	0	0	0	2	1	0	0	0	6
Relations between businessmen (legal suits, *lettres de change,* marine insurance, etc.)	3	13	13	13	3	0	1	2	1	3	0	0	8	5	9
Shortages of wood in France	5	2	0	1	0	0	0	0	0	0	0	0	0	0	0
Diplomatic negotiations concerning trade	0	0	0	0	0	0	0	0	0	0	0	1	2	0	1
Creation of venal offices affecting trade or manufactures	2	0	4	8	3	1	1	1	1	0	0	0	0	0	0

Table 2 (*continued*)

	1700–1701	1702	1703	1704	1705	1706	1707	1708	1709	1710	1711	1712	1713	1714	1715
The grain trade, grain shortages	0	3	0	1	0	2	1	15	15	2	2	2	1	0	0
Importation of foreign silks	3	0	4	2	0	3	1	0	1	0	0	0	0	1	0
Importation of Indian cottons	5	5	0	0	4	2	1	4	5	5	0	0	1	3	3
Honoring trade and industry	8	1	0	0	0	0	0	0	0	0	0	0	0	0	0
Protection of French trade from enemy privateers	0	2	0	0	0	2	5	15	3	2	0	1	0	0	0
French livestock (especially sheep)	2	1	0	0	0	0	0	0	1	0	0	0	0	3	0
Canada	0	2	0	0	0	0	1	1	0	3	0	0	0	0	0
Quality of French brandies	1	0	5	2	0	0	0	0	0	2	2	0	2	1	1

APPENDIX D
THE COUNCIL OF COMMERCE AFTER 1715

A study of the Council of Commerce for the period from 1715 to its abolition in 1791 would be different in several ways from this one. As the problems facing French trade and industry changed through the century, so also did the major concerns of this council. An even greater difference would arise from the fact that the council itself was transformed after the death of Louis XIV. From 1715 until its dissolution during the Revolution, the council underwent numerous alterations, and never again does it seem to have wielded quite as much authority as it did under Louis XIV.[1] On the death of the king, the council and the intendants of commerce were abolished; this was part of the bureaucratic reshuffling that accompanied the beginning of the regency. In November 1715 a reorganized Council of Commerce began to meet. It became one of the seven councils that replaced the secretaries of state at that time. Although most of the ordinary *commissaires* remained on it (including Daguesseau and Amelot), the titular heads of the new council were Marshal Villeroy and the duc de Noailles. The merchant deputies attended meetings, but the intendants of commerce continued to be suppressed. Their departments were divided among the other *commissaires*. After the death of Daguesseau in 1716, Amelot became the de facto leader of the group; he reported its affairs to the Council of the Regency.

Early in 1722 the Council of Commerce was disbanded, as were all the others. Later in the same year, however, it was reestablished, but its name was changed to Bureau of Commerce. Its new title was more in keeping with its functions, but the titular demotion also probably signified a real loss of influence. One historian has suggested that the new controller general, Le Pelletier de la Houssaye, gave it the name *bureau* to signify that henceforth he would keep more control over economic planning within his own ministry.[2] The bureau had basically the same organization as the council created in 1700. In 1724 four newly reinstituted intendants of commerce were added to it. From 1724 to the 1780s, the bureau witnessed only minor changes.

In 1730, however, a new Council of Commerce was formed. This council bore absolutely no relation to the council that has been the focus of the present work. It consisted solely of royal ministers and councillors and was intended to issue laws and to administer trade and industry in much the same way that the Council of Finances acted on financial matters. The new council met rarely, however; and although the *Almanach royal* always listed it alongside the other royal councils, it was never more than a decoration. The examination and administration of economic matters continued to be performed in the Bureau of Commerce and in the finance and naval ministries.[3] Many historians who have written about mid- or late eighteenth-century French history have confused the new, relatively unimportant Council of Commerce with the still active Bureau of Commerce. Although it continued to be influential, the bureau seems to have suffered a severe curtailment of its power in 1744. Up to that date the president of the council (or bureau) had always held simultaneously the post of director of commerce in the finance ministry. On the death of the bureau's president in 1744 the two positions were separated.[4] Thereafter the man appointed president of the bureau was always a *conseiller d'état*, but he did not have the administrative control over intendants, inspectors of manufactures, and the farmers general that his predecessors had enjoyed. After 1744 the direction of commerce was assigned to an intendant of finances—Daniel-Charles Trudaine (1744–69) and then his son Jean-Charles-Philibert Trudaine de Montigny (1769–77). The bureau remained active under the supervision of the director of commerce, although it appears to have been used less than heretofore had been true. Under Louis XIV the council had assembled, on the average, more than forty times each year; beginning in the 1740s the number for the bureau fell to about thirty.[5]

One reason for this decline in authority may have been the strong mercantilist bias of the bureau. Throughout the eighteenth century, it continued to advocate protectionist, heavily regulatory policies. At the same time, however, several royal ministers and other officials began to adopt more flexible, "liberal" views. This led them to rely less on the bureau and even, on occasion, to avoid consulting it. This development became more noticeable in the 1750s, when Jacques-Claude-Marie Vincent de Gournay became an intendant of commerce and a close collaborator of the Trudaines. Gournay was a proponent of *laissez-faire, laissez-passer*, and he was put off by the heavy-handed regulatory system defended by the Bureau of Commerce. He therefore tended to disregard that body's advice whenever it did not suit him.[6]

The bureau's influence deteriorated even more in the 1770s, when Gournay's friend Turgot assumed the controller generalship. This tendency climaxed in the 1780s, when the intendants of commerce began to meet in a *comité* apart from the bureau. They often bypassed the bureau completely when studying important issues.

These remarks concerning the council (or bureau) for the years after 1715 are not based on exhaustive research. Thus they must be considered tentative until further research is made into the later history of this institution.

1. This statement is in direct contrast to the thesis of Jacqueline-Lucienne Lafon, who contends that only after 1715 did the council (or bureau) become important (*Les Députés du commerce*, passim).

2. Bosher, *The Single Duty Project*. pp. 43–44.

3. Bonnassieux and Lelong, pp. xiii–xiv; Antoine, *Le Conseil du roi*, pp. 138–39.

4. Louis Fagon became president in 1724 after the death of Amelot and served until his own death in 1744.

5. On the period after 1715, see Bonnassieux and Lelong, *Conseil de commerce*, pp. xi–xviii.

6. Ibid., pp. xvii–xviii, 1; G. Scelle, *Vincent de Gournay* (Paris, 1897), passim. In his private papers, Pierre Bonnassieux refers to a work published in 1761, in which the marquis de Mirabeau bitterly criticizes the regulatory excesses of the Bureau of Commerce (AN, AB XIX, 368). Throughout the eighteenth century, many businessmen continued to oppose free trade and to support the government's regulatory policies. For some illustrations see the works cited in Chapter 6, n. 161 above.

BIBLIOGRAPHY

MANUSCRIPTS

Archives Nationales
    Series AB XIX, numbers 368–77.
    Series AD XI, numbers 9, 29, 42, 53.
    Series E, numbers 707 C, 806 C–7 A, 824 A, 1916, 1932, 1940.
    Series F^4, number 2341.
    Series F^{10}, number 256.
    Series F^{12}, numbers 14, 51–59, 114–25 B, 551–52, 641–50, 662–70, 671 A–73, 692–94, 725–30, 750, 792–95, 799 A, 827, 855, 861 B, 847–54 A, 863, 875, 880–910, 1329, 1349, 1362 A, 1396, 1403, 1438, 1456 A, 1499, 1503 B, 1646–50, 1834 A–B, 1891, 1903, 1904, 1908, 1910, 1911, 1920, 1922, 1923–25, 1933 A, 2427, 2637 A.
    Series F^{13}, number 887.
    Series F^{14}, number 1870.
    Series G^7, numbers 8–9, 115, 181–83, 260, 265, 270–71, 304–6, 339, 341, 359, 431, 464–65, 496–97, 532–37, 540–41, 543 C, 544–50, 552–59, 598, 637–38, 694–700, 716, 736, 761, 815–27, 832–33, 839, 867–81, 906, 1618, 1685–1717, 1826–30, 1903–6.
    Series K, numbers 907, 1351.
    Series KK, numbers 1340–41.
    Series M, numbers 757, 760.
    Series MM, number 825.
    Colonies
        Series B, numbers 21–37.
        Series F^2 A, number 2.

Series F² B, numbers 1, 8, 10.

Series F² C, numbers 4, 9.

Series F³, number 8.

Archives de la Marine

Series A², numbers 20–23.

Series B², numbers 150–244.

Series B³, numbers 111, 115, 119, 122, 126, 132, 140, 152, 163, 175, 189, 202, 209, 216, 217, 226, 233.

Series B⁷, numbers 67, 495–517.

Series B⁸, number 18.

Series C², number 55.

Series C⁷, numbers 2, 4, 79, 108, 169, 177.

Series G, numbers 67, 72, 121, 127, 221–22.

Bibliothèque Nationale

Manuscrits français, numbers 1735, 6198, 7939, 8037–38, 9166–67, 9360, 11103, 14294, 16736, 16909, 18592, 18597, 18979, 21547, 21769–78, 21785, 22806.

Manuscrits français, nouvelles acquisitions, numbers 885, 6828.

Dossiers bleus, numbers 5, 16.

Nouveau d'Hozier, numbers 4, 264.

Pièces originales, numbers 14, 52, 2257.

Cabinet d'Hozier, number 3.

Collection Joly de Fleury, numbers 1720–21.

Collection Clairambault, numbers 297, 1174.

Cabinet d'estampes, Collection Hennin, numbers 6430, 6492.

Archives du Ministère des Affaires étrangères

Mémoires et Documents, France, numbers 137, 991, 1182, 1980.

Correspondance politique, Angleterre, numbers 233, 249.

Correspondance politique, Venice, number 160.

Bibliothèque Mazarine

Manuscrits, numbers 2342, 2626, 2762, 2882.

Bibliothèque de l'Arsenal

Manuscrits, numbers 3186, 4069, 4496, 4561.

Bibliothèque Sainte-Geneviève

Manuscrits, numbers 2012, 2015, 2077, 3509.

Bibliothèque Municipale de Poitiers

Manuscrits, number 548.

Archives Départementales
  Loire-Atlantique
    Series C, numbers 611, 694–95, 700, 754.
    Series E, Supplément, Dossier "Descazeaux."
  Charente-Maritime
    Series C, number 92.
  Gironde
    Series C, numbers 4300–4301.
  Ile-et-Vilaine
    Series C, numbers 1582–83.
  Hérault
    Series C, number 2757.
  Haute-Garonne
    Series C, number 2346.
Archives de la Chambre du commerce de Marseille
  Series A, numbers 15–19.
  Series B, numbers 152–66.
Newberry Library
  Manuscript Collection, Case, MS, F, 3925.56
                  Case, MS, H, 7045.372.

PRINTED SOURCES

Almanach royal, 1699–1715.

André, Louis, and Emile Bourgeois (eds.). *Recueil des instructions données aux ambassadeurs et ministres de France.* Vol. 22, *Hollande, 1698–1730.* Paris: E. de Boccard, 1923.

Beaurepaire, Charles, "Election d'un député au conseil de commerce," *Bulletin de la Société de l'Histoire de Normandie* 7(1893–95):305–7.

Boislisle, Arthur André Gabriel Michel de (ed.). *Correspondance des contrôleurs généraux des finances avec les intendants des provinces.* 3 vols. Paris: Imprimerie nationale, 1874–97.

————. *Mémoires des intendants sur l'état des généralités dressés pour l'instruction du duc de Bourgogne.* Vol. 1, *Mémoire de la généralité de Pairs.* Paris: Imprimerie nationale, 1881.

Champollion-Figeac, (?) (ed.). *Mélanges historiques.* Paris: Firmin Didot, 1848.

Clément, Pierre (ed.). *Lettres, instructions, et mémoires de Colbert.* 7 vols. Paris: Imprimerie impériale, 1861–82.

Colbert, Jean-Baptiste, marquis de Torcy. *Journal inédit de Jean-Baptiste Colbert, marquis de Torcy, ministre et secrétaire d'état des affaires étrangères, pendant les années 1709, 1710 et 1711.* Ed. F. Masson. Paris: Plon, 1884.

————. *Mémoires de Monsieur de Torcy pour servir à l'histoire des négociations depuis le traité de Ryswyck jusqu'à la paix d'Utrecht.* 3 vols. London: Nourse and Vaillant, 1757.

[Courtilz de Sandras, Gatien de.] *Testament politique de Messire Jean Baptiste Colbert.* The Hague: Henri van Bilderen, 1693.

[————.] *Testament politique du marquis de Louvois.* Cologne: Chez le Politique, 1695.

Daguesseau, Henri-François. *Oeuvres complètes.* 16 vols. Paris: Pardessus, 1819.

Dangeau, Philippe de Courcillon, marquis de. *Journal.* Ed. E. Soulié and L. Dussieux. 19 vols. Paris: Firmin Didot, 1854–60.

Depping, Georg (ed.). *Correspondance administrative sous le règne de Louis XIV.* 4 vols. Paris: Imprimerie nationale, 1850–55.

Fargès, Louis (ed.). *Recueil des instructions données aux ambassadeurs et ministres de France.* Vols. 4–5, *Pologne.* Paris: Félix Alcan, 1888.

Girardot, Auguste Théodore, baron de (ed.). *Correspondance de Louis XIV avec le marquis Amelot, son ambassadeur en Portugal, 1685–1688.* Nantes: V. Mellinet, 1863.

————. *Correspondance de Louis XIV avec M. Amelot, son ambassadeur en Espagne, 1705–1709.* Paris: Aubry, 1864.

Isambert, F. A., et al. (eds.). *Recueil général des anciennes lois françaises depuis l'an 420 jusqu'à la révolution de 1789.* 29 vols. Paris: Le Prieur, 1821–33.

Lebeau, Sylvain (ed.). *Nouveau code des prises, ou recueil des édits, déclarations, lettres patentes sur la course et l'administration des prises, depuis 1400 jusqu'à présent.* 3 vols. Paris: Imprimerie de la République, An VII–IX.

Memorials Presented by the Deputies of the Council of Trade in France, to the Royal Council in 1701. London: J. J. and P. Knapton, 1736.

Rambaud, Alfred (ed.). *Recueil des instructions données aux ambassadeurs et ministres de France.* Vol. 8, *Russie, des origines jusqu'à 1748.* Paris: Félix Alcan, 1890.

Recueil des règlemens généraux et particuliers concernant les manufactures et fabriques du royaume. 4 vols. and 3 supplementary vols. Paris: Imprimerie royale, 1730–50.

Saint-Simon, Louis de Rouvroy, duc de. *Mémoires.* Ed. A. de Boislisle. 41 vols. Paris: Hachette, 1879–1928.

Sée, Henri, and Léon Vignols. "Quelques documents sur les relations commerciales entre la France et la Hollande au début du 18e siècle," *Economisch-Historische Jaarboek* 15 (1929):287–306.

Sourches, Louis François de Bouchet, marquis de. *Mémoires.* 13 vols. Ed. Gabriel-Jules de Cosnac and Arthur Bertrand. Paris: Hachette, 1892–93.

Vast, Henri (ed.). *Les grands traités du règne de Louis XIV.* 3 vols. Paris: Picard, 1893–99.

Vauban, Sebastien Le Prestre de. *Projet d'une dixme royale.* Ed. E. Coornaert. Paris: Alcan, 1933.

Vaucher, Paul (ed.). *Recueil des instructions données aux ambassadeurs et ministres de France.* Vol. 25-2, *Angleterre, 1698–1791.* Paris: Centre national de la recherche scientifique, 1965.

Waddington, Albert (ed.). *Recueil des instructions données aux ambassadeurs et ministres de France.* Vol. 16, *Prusse.* Paris: Félix Alcan, 1901.

SECONDARY WORKS

Aalbers, J. "Holland's Financial Problems (1713–1733) and the Wars against Louis XIV." In A. C. Duke and C. A. Tamse (eds.), *Britain and the Netherlands. Vol. VI. War and Society. Papers Delivered to the Sixth Anglo-Dutch Historical Conference*, pp. 79–93. The Hague: Martinus Nijhoff, 1977.

Antoine, Michel. *Le Conseil royal des finances au XVIIIe siècle et le registre E 3659 des Archives nationales.* Geneva: Droz, 1973.

―――――. *Le Conseil du roi sous le règne de Louis XV.* Geneva: Droz, 1970.

Appleby, Joyce. *Economic Thought and Ideology in Seventeenth Century England.* Princeton, N.J.: Princeton University Press, 1978.

―――――. "Ideology and Theory: The Tension between Political and Economic Liberalism in Seventeenth-Century England." *American Historical Review* 81 (1976): 499–515.

Arnould, Ambroise. *De la balance du commerce et des relations extérieures de la France, dans toutes les parties du globe, particulièrement à la fin du règne de Louis XIV et au moment de la révolution.* 2 vols. and 1 supplementary vol. Paris: Buisson, 1791.

Ashley, W. J. "The Tory Origin of Free Trade Policy." In W. J. Ashley, *Surveys Historic and Economic.* London: Longmans, Green, 1900.

Bacquié, Franc. *Les Inspecteurs des manufactures sous l'ancien régime, 1669–1792.* Mémoires et documents pour servir à l'histoire du commerce et de l'industrie en France. Edited by Julien Hayem. 11th series. Paris: Hachette, 1927.

Bamford, Paul W. *Forests and French Sea Power, 1660–1789.* Toronto: University of Toronto Press, 1956.

————. "French Shipping in Northern European Trade, 1660–1789." *Journal of Modern History* 26 (1954): 207–19.

Barrie, Viviane. "La Prohibition du commerce avec la France dans la politique anglaise à la fin du XVIIᵉ siècle." *Revue du Nord* 59 (1977): 343–64.

Baudrillart, Alfred. *Philippe V et la cour de France.* 5 vols. Paris: Firmin Didot, 1890–1901.

Beaud, Michel. "Le Bureau de la balance du commerce (1781–1791)." *Revue d'histoire économique et sociale* 42 (1964): 357–77.

Bercé, Yves-Marie. *Croquants et nu-pieds: les soulèvements paysans en France du XVIᵉ au XIXᵉ siècle.* Paris: Gallimard/Julliard, 1974.

Berger, Patrice. "Pontchartrain and the Grain Trade during the Famine of 1693." *Journal of Modern History.* Supplement, 48 (1976): 37–86.

————. "Rural Charity in Late Seventeenth Century France: The Pontchartrain Case." *French Historical Studies* 10 (1978): 393–415.

Bernardini, Laura. "Le Conseil du commerce." *Mémoire* in fulfillment of Diplôme d'Etudes Supérieures, Faculté de Droit, Paris, 1961.

Bezard, Yvonne. *Fonctionnaires maritimes et coloniaux sous Louis XIV: Les Bégon.* Paris: A. Michel, 1932.

Bingham, Richard. "Louis XIV and the War for Peace: The Genesis of a Peace Offensive, 1686–1690." Ph.D dissertation, University of Illinois at Chicago Circle, 1972.

Biollay, Léon. *Etudes économiques sur le XVIIIᵉ siècle: le pacte de famine; l'administration du commerce.* Paris: Guillaumin, 1885.

Blaich, Fritz. *Die Epoche des Mercantilismus.* Wiesbaden: Steiner, 1973.

Bogle, Emory Crockett. "A Stand for Tradition: The Rejection of the Anglo-French Commercial Treaty of Utrecht." Ph.D. dissertation, University of Maryland, 1972.

Boissonnade, Prosper. "Histoire des premiers essais de relations économiques directes entre la France et l'état prussien pendant le règne de Louis XIV (1643–1715)." *Mémoires de la société des antiquaires de l'ouest* 6 (1912): 1–484.

Bondois, Paul-M. "Les Centres sucriers français au XVIIIᵉ siècle." *Revue d'histoire économique et sociale* 19 (1931): 27–76.

————. "L'Industrie sucrière en France au XVIIIᵉ siècle." *Revue d'histoire économique et sociale* 19 (1931): 316–46.

————. L'Organisation industrielle et commerciale sous l'ancien régime: le privilège exclusif au XVIIIᵉ siècle." *Revue d'histoire économique et sociale* 21 (1933): 140–89.

Bonnassieux, Pierre. *Les Assemblées représentatives du commerce sous l'ancien régime*. Paris: Berger-Levrault, 1883.

————. *Les grandes compagnies de commerce*. Paris: Plon, 1892.

————, and Eugène Lelong. *Conseil de commerce et Bureau du commerce, 1700–1791: inventaire analytique des procès-verbaux*. Paris: Imprimerie nationale, 1900.

Bosher, John F. *French Finances, 1770–1795: From Business to Bureaucracy*. Cambridge: Cambridge University Press, 1970.

————. *The Single Duty Project: A Study of the Movement for a French Customs Union in the Eighteenth Century*. London: Athlone, 1964.

Boulle, Pierre H. "The French Colonies and the Reform of Their Administration during and following the Seven Years' War." Ph.D. dissertation, University of California, Berkeley, 1968.

————. "French Mercantilism, Commercial Companies, and Colonial Profitability. In Leonard Blussé and Femme Gaastra (eds.), *Companies and Trade: Essays on Overseas Trading Companies during the Ancien Régime*, pp. 97–117. The Hague: Martinus Nijhoff, 1981.

————. "Slave Trade, Commercial Organization, and Industrial Growth in Eighteenth-Century Nantes." *Revue française d'histoire d'outre-mer* 59 (1972): 70–112.

Braudel, Fernand. *The Mediterranean and the Mediterranean World in the Age of Philip II*. 2 vols. New York: Harper and Row, 1972.

————, and Ernest Labrousse (eds.). *Histoire économique et sociale de la France*. Vol. 2. *1660–1789*. Paris: Presses universitaires de France, 1970.

Briggs, Robin. *Early Modern France, 1560–1715*. New York: Oxford University Press, 1977.

Bromley, J. S. "The Channel Island Privateers in the War of the Spanish Succession." *Transactions de la Société guernesiaise* 14 (1949): 444–78.

————. "Le Commerce de la France de l'ouest et la guerre maritime (1702–1712). *Annales du Midi* 65 (1953): 49–66.

————. "Les Corsaires zélandois et la navigation scandinave pendant la guerre de succession d'Espagne." In Michel Mollat (ed.), *Le Navire et l'économie du nord de l'Europe*, pp. 93–109. Paris: S.E.V.P.E.N., 1960.

———. "The French Privateering War, 1702–1711." In Henry Esmond Bell (ed.), *Historical Essays 1600–1750 Presented to David Ogg,* pp. 203–31. London: Adam and Charles Black, 1963.

———. "The Importance of Dunkirk (1688–1713) Reconsidered." In Commission internationale d'histoire maritime, *Course et piraterie: Etudes présentées à la commission internationale d'histoire maritime à l'occasion de son XVᵉ colloque international pendant le XIVᵉ congrès international des sciences historiques,* pp. 231–70. Paris: CNRS, 1975.

———. "The Jacobite Privateers in the Nine Years War." In Anne Whiteman et al. (eds.), *Statesmen, Scholars, and Merchants: Essays in Eighteenth Century History Presented to Dame Lucy Sutherland,* pp. 17–43. Oxford: Clarendon Press, 1973.

———. (ed.). *New Cambridge Modern History.* Vol. 6. *The Rise of Great Britain and Russia, 1688–1715/25.* Cambridge: Cambridge University Press, 1970.

———. "The North Sea in Wartime (1688–1713)." *Bijdragen en Mededelingen Betreffende de Geschiedenis der Nederlanden* 92 (1977): 270–99.

———. "Projets et contrats d'armement en course marseillais." *Revue d'histoire économique et sociale* 50 (1972): 74–108.

———. "Some Zeeland Privateering Instructions: Jacob Sautign to Captain Salomon Reynders, 1707." In Ragnhild Hatton and J. S. Bromley (eds.). *William III and Louis XIV.*

———. "The Trade and Privateering of Saint-Malo during the War of the Spanish Succession." *Transactions de la société guernesiaise* 17 (1964): 631–47.

Brutails, Jean-Auguste. "Etudes sur la chambre du commerce de Guienne." *Actes de l'Académie nationale des sciences, belles-lettres et arts de Bordeaux* 55 (1893): 255–350.

———. (ed.). *Inventaire du fonds de la chambre du commerce de Guienne.* Bordeaux: G. Gounouilhou, 1893.

Cain, Julien. "Les Mémoires des députés au Conseil de commerce de 1700." *Revue d'histoire moderne et contemporaine* 18 (1913): 5–20.

Carrière, Charles. *Négociants marseillais au XVIIIᵉ siécle: contribution à l'étude des économies maritimes.* 2 vols. Marseilles: Institut historique de Provence, 1974.

Chassagne, Serge. *Oberkampf: un entrepreneur capitaliste au siècle des lumières.* Paris: Aubier Montaigne, 1980.

Chaussinand-Nogaret, Guy. *Les Financiers de Languedoc au XVIIIᵉ siècle* Paris: S.E.V.P.E.N., 1970.

Chinault, Jules. *La Chambre de commerce de Toulouse du XVIIIe siècle: esquisse historique.* Toulouse: Mémoires de l'Académie de Législation, 1956.

Clark, Sir George N. *The Dutch Alliance and the War against French Trade, 1688–1697.* London: Longmans, Green, 1923.

————. *Guide to English Commercial Statistics, 1696–1782.* London: Royal Historical Society, 1938.

————. "Neutral Commerce in the War of the Spanish Succession," *British Year Book of International Law* (1928), pp. 69–83.

————. "War Trade and Trade War, 1701–1713." *Economic History Review* 1 (1927): 262–80.

Clément, Pierre. *Le Gouvernement de Louis XIV, ou la cour, l'administration, les finances, et le commerce de 1683 à 1689.* Paris: Guillaumin, 1848.

————. *Histoire de Colbert et de son administration.* Preface by A. Geffroy. 2 vols. 3d ed. Paris: Perrin, 1892.

————. *Histoire du système protecteur en France depuis le ministère de Colbert jusqu'à la révolution de 1848.* Paris: Guillaumin, 1854.

Cobban, Alfred. *A History of Modern France.* Vol. 1: *1715–1799.* 3d ed. Baltimore: Penguin Books. 1963.

Cole, Charles Woolsey. *Colbert and a Century of French Mercantilism.* 2 vols. New York: Columbia University Press, 1939.

————. *French Mercantilism, 1683–1700.* New York: Columbia University Press, 1943.

Coleman, D. C. "Mercantilism Revisited." *Historical Journal* 23 (1980): 773–91.

————. "Politics and Economics in the Age of Queen Anne: The Case of the Anglo-French Trade Treaty of 1713." In D. C. Coleman and A. H. John (eds.), *Trade, Government. and Economy in Pre-Industrial England: Essays Presented to F. J. Fisher,* pp. 187–211. London: Weidenfeld and Nicolson, 1976.

————. (ed.). *Revisions in Mercantilism.* London: Methuen, 1969.

Coombs, Douglas. *The Conduct of the Dutch: British Opinion and the Dutch Alliance during the War of the Spanish Succession.* The Hague: Martinus Nijhoff, 1958.

Coornaert, E. *Les Corporations en France avant 1780.* Paris: Gallimard, 1941.

Corvisier, André. *La France de Louis XIV, 1643–1715: ordre intérieur et place en Europe.* Paris: S.E.D.E.S., 1979.

Dahlgren, E. W. "Le Comte Jérôme de Pontchartrain et les armateurs de Saint-Malo (1712–1715)." *Revue historique* 88 (1905): 225–63.

————. *Les Relations commerciales et maritimes entre la France et les côtes de l'océan pacifique (commencement du XVIIIe siècle).* Vol. 1. *Le Commerce de la mer du Sud jusqu'à la paix d'Utrecht.* Paris: Honoré Champion, 1909.

————. *Voyages français à destination de la mer du Sud avant Bougainville (1695–1749).* Paris: Imprimerie nationale, 1907.

Dardel, Pierre. *Navires et marchands dans les ports de Rouen et du Havre au XVIIIe siècle.* Paris: S.E.V.P.E.N., 1963.

Dareste de la Chavanne, Antoine Elisabeth Cléophas. *Histoire de l'administration en France et des progrès du pouvoir royal, depuis le règne de Phlippe-Auguste jusqu'à la mort de Louis XIV.* 2 vols. Paris: Guillaumin, 1848.

Davis, Ralph. *The Rise of the Atlantic Economies.* Ithaca, N.Y.: Cornell University Press, 1973.

Delumeau, Jean. "La Guerre de course française sous l'ancien régime." In Commission internationale d'histoire maritime, *Course et piraterie: Etudes présentées à la commission internationale d'histoire maritime à l'occasion de son XVe colloque international pendant le XIVe congres international des sciences historiques,* pp. 271–98. Paris: CNRS, 1975.

Dent, Julien. *Crisis in Finance: Crown, Financiers, and Society in Seventeenth-Century France.* Newton Abbot, England: David and Charles, 1973.

Depitre, Edgard. *La Toile peinte en France aux XVIIe et XVIIIe siècles.* Paris: Marcel Rivière, 1912.

Deyon, Pierre. *Amiens, capitale provinciale: étude sur la société urbaine au 17e siècle.* The Hague: Mouton, 1967.

————. *Le Mercantilisme.* Paris: Flammarion, 1969.

————. "La Production manufacturière en France au XVIIe siècle et ses problèmes." *XVIIe siècle* Nos. 70–71 (1966) pp. 47–63.

————. "Variations de la production textile aux XVIe et XVIIe siècles: sources et premiers résultats," *Annales, E.S.C.* 18 (1963): 939–55.

Dubois, Auguste. *Précis de l'histoire des doctrines économiques dans leurs rapports avec les faits et avec les institutions.* Vol. I: *L'Epoque antérieure aux Physiocrates.* Paris: Arthur Rousseau, 1903.

Duchêne, Albert. *La Politique coloniale de la France: le ministère des colonies depuis Richelieu.* Paris: Payot, 1928.

Dumas, François. *La réglementation industrielle après Colbert.* Toulouse: Douladoure-Privat, 1908.

Dumas, René. "La Politique financière de Nicolas Desmaretz, contrôleur général des finances (1708–1715)." Thèse pour le Doctorat, Faculté de Droit, Paris, 1927.

Dupâquier, Jacques. *La Population rurale du bassin parisien à l'époque de Louis XIV*. Paris: Edition de l'Ecole des hautes études en sciences sociales, 1979.

Durand, Yves. *Les Fermiers généraux au XVIIIᵉ siècle*. Paris: Presses universitaires de France, 1971.

Elzinga, S. "Le Tarif de Colbert de 1664 et celui de 1667 et leur signification." *Economisch-Historische Jaarboek* 15 (1929): 221–73.

Fontvieille, Louis. "Les premières enquêtes industrielles de la France, 1692–1703." *Economies et Sociétés. Cahiers de l'Institut de science économique appliquée* 2 (1968): 1089–1290.

Forbonnais, François Véron Duverger de. *Recherches et considérations sur les finances de France depuis l'année 1595 jusqu'à l'année 1721*. 6 vols. Liège, 1758.

Fournier, Joseph. *La Chambre de commerce de Marseille et ses représentants à Paris, 1599–1875*. Marseilles: Barlatier, 1920.

———. (ed.). *Inventaire des archives de la chambre de commerce de Marseille*. Marseilles. Chambre de commerce, 1940.

Francis, A. D. *The Wine Trade*. London: Adam and Charles Black, 1972.

Frostin, Charles. "La Famille ministérielle Phélypeaux: esquisse d'un profil Pontchartrain (XVIᵉ–XVIIIᵉ siècles)." *Annales de Bretagne* 86 (1979): 117–40.

———. "L'Organisation ministérielle sous Louis XIV: cumul d'attributions et situations conflictuelles, 1690–1715." *Revue historique de droit français et étranger* 58 (1980): 201–26.

———. "Les Pontchartrain et la pénétration commerciale française en Amérique espagnole (1690–1715)." *Revue historique* 246 (1971): 307–36.

Garnault, Emile. *Le Commerce rochelais au XVIIIᵉ siècle*. 2 vols. La Rochelle: Mareshal & Martin, 1887–88.

Gaucheron, Roger. "Etude sur Michel Amelot et l'administration du commerce (1699–1724)." Thesis, Ecole des Chartes. Not locatable; summarized in *Ecole des Chartes: Positions des Thèses*. Paris: Picard, 1913. Pp. 41–49.

Gaxotte, Pierre. *The Age of Louis XIV*. Translated by Michael Shaw. New York: Macmillan, 1970.

———. "Colbert impose la dictature de travail." *Historia* 368 (1979): 62–72.

Gembruch, Werner. "Reformforderungen in Frankreich um die Wende von 17. zum 18. Jahrhundert: ein Beitrag zur Geschichte der Opposition gegen System und Politik Ludwigs XIV." *Historische Zeitschrift* 209 (1969): 265–317.

Gignoux, Claude-Joseph. *Le Commerce, du XVᵉ siècle au milieu du XIXᵉ. Histoire du commerce,* Vol. 6. Edited by Jacques Lacour-Gayet. Paris: SPID, 1951.

Giraud, Marcel. "Crise de conscience et d'autorité à la fin du règne de Louis XIV," *Annales, E.S.C.* 7 (1952): 172–90, 293–302.

————. "La France et la Louisiane au début du XVIIIᵉ siècle." *Revue historique* 204 (1950): 185–208.

————. *Histoire de la Louisiane française.* 3 vols. Paris: Presses universitaires de France, 1953–66.

————. "Tendances humanitaires à la fin du règne de Louis XIV." *Revue historique* 209 (1953): 217–37.

Goubert, Pierre. *L'ancien régime.* 2 vols. Paris: Armand Colin, 1969–73.

————. *Beauvais et le Beauvaisis de 1600 à 1730: contribution à l'histoire sociale de la France du XVIIᵉ siècle.* 2 vols. Paris: S.E.V.P.E.N., 1960.

————. *Familles marchandes sous l'ancien régime: les Danse et les Motte de Beauvais.* Paris: S.E.V.P.E.N., 1959.

————. *Louis XIV and Twenty Million Frenchmen.* Translated by Anne Carter. New York: Vintage Books. 1970.

Gras, L.-J. "Les Chambres de commerce." *Annales de l'école libre des sciences politiques* 10 (1895): 550–89, 680–740.

Grassby, R. B. "Social Status and Commercial Enterprise under Louis XIV." *Economic History Review,* 2d series, 13 (1960): 19–38.

Green, Robert W. (ed.). *The Weber Thesis Controversy.* Lexington, Mass.: D.C. Heath, 1973.

Guitard, E. "L'Industrie des draps en Languedoc et ses protecteurs sous l'ancien régime." In Julien Haymen (ed.), *Mémoires et documents pour servir à l'histoire du commerce et de l'industrie en France.* 1st series. Paris: Hachette, 1911.

Hajek, Jan. *Comparative Research into Mercantilistic Theories in Europe of the 16th and 17th Centuries.* Prague: Institute of Czechoslovak and World History of the Czechoslovak Academy of Sciences, 1980.

Harkness, D. A. E. "The Opposition to the 8th and 9th Articles of the Commercial Treaty of Utrecht." *Scottish Historical Review* 21 (1923–24): 219–26.

Harsin, Paul. *Crédit public et banque d'état en France du XVIᵉ au XVIIᵉ siècle.* Paris: Droz, 1933.

Hasquin, Hervé. "Sur les préoccupations statistiques en France au XVIIᵉ siècle." *Revue belge de philologie et d'histoire* 49 (1971): 1095–1118.

Hatton, Ragnhild. "Louis XIV: Recent Gains in Historical Knowledge." *Journal of Modern History* 45 (1973): 277–91.

————. "Louis XIV et l'Europe: éléments d'une révision historiographique." *XVIIᵉ siècle*, No. 123 (1979), pp. 109–35.

————. (ed.). *Louis XIV and Absolutism*. Columbus: Ohio State University Press, 1976.

————. (ed.) *Louis XIV and Europe*. Columbus: Ohio State University Press, 1976.

————. *Louis XIV and His World*. London: Thames and Hudson, 1972.

————. *Europe in the Age of Louis XIV*. London: Harcourt, Brace, and World, 1969.

————, and M. S. Anderson (eds.). *Studies in Diplomatic History: Essays in Memory of David Bayne Horn*. London: Longman Group, 1970.

————, and J. S. Bromley (eds.). *William III and Louis XIV: Essays 1680–1720 by and for Mark A. Thomson*. Liverpool: Liverpool University Press, 1968.

Hayem, Julien (ed.). *Mémoires et documents pour servir à l'histoire du commerce et de l'industrie en France*. 12 vols. Paris: Hachette, 1911–29.

Heckscher, Eli F. *Mercantilism*. Translated by Mendel Shapiro. Revised edition edited by E. F. Soderlund. 2 vols. London: Allen and Unwin; New York: Macmillan, 1955.

Herlaut, Colonel. "Projets de création d'une banque royale en France à la fin du règne de Louis XIV (1702–1712)." *Revue d'histoire moderne* 8 (1933): 143–60.

Hinckner, François. *Les Français devant l'impôt sous l'ancien régime*. Paris: Flammarion, 1971.

Hippeau, C. *L'Avènement des Bourbons au trône d'Espagne*. 2 vols. Paris: Didier, 1875.

Hood, James N. "Patterns of Popular Protest in the French Revolution: The Conceptual Contribution of the Gard." *Journal of Modern History* 48 (1976): 259–93.

Huetz de Lemps, Christien. "Le Commerce maritime des vins d'Aquitaine de 1698 à 1716." *Revue historique de Bordeaux* (1965), pp. 25–43.

————. *Géographie du commerce de Bordeaux à la fin du règne de Louis XIV*. Paris: Mouton, 1974.

Jacoby, Henry. *The Bureaucratization of the World*. Translated by Eveline Kanes. Berkeley: University of California Press, 1973.

Kaeppelin, Paul. *Les Origines de l'Inde française: la Compagnie des Indes orientales et François Martin. Etude sur l'histoire du commerce et des établissements français dans l'Inde sous Louis XIV (1664–1719).* Paris: Challamel, 1908.

Kamen, Henry. *The War of Succession in Spain, 1700–1715.* Bloomington: Indiana University Press, 1969.

Kaplan, Steven L. *Bread, Politics, and Political Economy in the Reign of Louis XV.* 2 vols. The Hague: Martinus Nijhoff, 1976.

Keohane, Nannerl O. *Philosophy and the State in France: The Renaissance to the Enlightenment.* Princeton, N.J.: Princeton University Press, 1980.

Klaits, Joseph. *Printed Propaganda under Louis XIV: Absolute Monarchy and Public Opinion.* Princeton, N.J.: Princeton University Press, 1976.

Labraque-Bordenave, V. "Histoire des députés de Bordeaux au conseil de commerce, au comité national, et à l'agence commerciale à Paris, 1700–1793." *Actes de l'Académie nationale des sciences, arts et belles-lettres de Bordeaux* 51 (1889): 277–466.

Lafon, Jacqueline-Lucienne. *Les Députés du commerce et l'ordonnance de mars 1673: les juridictions consulaires, principe et compétence.* Preface by Jean Imbert. Paris: Cujas, 1979.

La Morandière, Charles de. *Histoire de la pêche française de la morue dans l'Amérique septentrionale (des origines à 1789).* Paris: G.-P. Maisonneuve and Larose, 1962.

Landes, David S. "Statistics as a Source for the History of Economic Development in Western Europe: The Protostatistical Era." In Val R. Lorwin and Jacob M. Price (eds.), *Dimensions of the Past.* New Haven, Conn.: Yale University Press, 1972.

Lavisse, Ernest (ed.). *Histoire de France depuis des origines jusqu'à la révolution.* Vol. 8, Pt. 1. Paris: Hachette, 1908.

Legrelle, Arsène. *La Diplomatie française et la succession d'Espagne.* 4 vols. Ghent: Dullé-Plus, 1888–92.

Léon, Pierre. "La Crise de l'économie française à la fin du règne de Louis XIV, 1685–1715," *L'Information historique* 18 (1956): 125–37.

————. *La Naissance de la grande industrie en Dauphiné: fin du XVIIᵉ siècle-1869.* 2 vols. Paris: Presses universitaires de France, 1956.

Le Roy, Alfred. *La France et Rome de 1700 à 1715: histoire diplomatique de la Bulle Unigenitus jusqu'à la mort de Louis XIV.* Geneva: Slatkine, 1976 (Paris, 1892).

Levasseur, Emile. *Histoire des classes ouvrières en France avant 1789.* 2 vols. 2d ed. Paris: Arthur Rousseau, 1900–1901.

————. *Histoire du commerce de la France.* 2 vols. Paris: Arthur Rousseau, 1911–12.

Lévy, Claude-Frédéric. *Capitalistes et pouvoir au siècle des lumières: les fondateurs des origines à 1715.* Paris: Mouton, 1969.

Lheritier, Michel. "Histoire des rapports de la chambre de commerce de Bordeaux avec les intendants, le parlement, et les jurats, de 1705 à 1791," *Revue historique de Bordeaux et du département de la Gironde* 5 (1912): 73–104, 192–205, 256–68, 328–45, 400–418.

Livet, Georges. *L'Intendance d'Alsace sous Louis XIV, 1648–1715.* Paris: Les Belles Lettres, 1956.

Lonn, Ella. "The French Council of Commerce in Relation to American Trade." *Mississippi Valley Historical Review* 6 (1919–20): 192–219.

Lüthy, Herbert. *La Banque protestante en France de la révocation de l'Edit de Nantes à la Revolution.* 2 vols. Paris: S.E.V.P.E.N., 1959–61.

McCollim, Gary. "The Formation of Fiscal Policy in the Reign of Louis XIV: The Example of Nicolas Desmaretz, Controller General of Finances (1708–1715)." Ph.D dissertation, Ohio State University, 1979.

McCloy, Shelby T. *Government Assistance in Eighteenth-Century France.* Durham, N.C.: Duke University Press, 1946.

Madrolle, Claudius. *Les premiers voyages français à la Chine. La Compagnie de la Chine, 1698–1719.* Paris: A. Challamel, 1901.

Malettke, Klaus. *Opposition und Konspiration unter Ludwig XIV: Studien zu Kritik und Widerstand gegen System und Politik des französischen Konigs während der ersten Hälfte seiner persönlichen Regierung.* Göttingen: Vandenhoeck and Ruprecht, 1976.

Marchand, Joseph. *Un Intendant sous Louis XIV: étude sur l'administration de Lebret en Provence (1687–1704).* Paris: Hachette, 1889.

Marion, Marcel. *Dictionnaire des institutions de la France aux XVIIᵉ et XVIIIᵉ siècles.* Paris: Picard, 1923.

Markovitch, Tihomir J. *Histoire des industries françaises: les industries lainières de Colbert à la révolution.* Geneva: Droz, 1976.

————. "L'Industrie française au XVIIIᵉ siècle: l'industrie lainière à la fin du règne de Louis XIV et sous la régence." *Economies et Sociétés. Cahiers de l'Institut de science économique appliquée* 2 (1968): 1517–1697.

————. "L'Industrie lainière française au début du XVIIIᵉ siècle." *Revue d'histoire économique et sociale* 46 (1968): 550–79.

————. "La première industrie lainière à Paris." *Revue d'histoire économique et sociale* 45 (1967): 402–5.

————. "Le triple tricentennaire de Colbert: l'enquête, les règlements, les inspecteurs." *Revue d'histoire économique et sociale* 49 (1971): 305–24.

Martin, Germain. *La grande industrie en France sous le règne de Louis XV.* Paris: A. Fontemoing, 1900.

————. *La grande industrie sous le règne de Louis XIV.* New York: Burt Franklin, 1971 (1899).

————, and Marcel Bezançon. *L'Histoire du crédit en France sous le règne de Louis XIV.* Vol. I: *Le Crédit public.* Paris: Sirey, 1913.

Marx, R. *Histoire du Royaume-Uni.* Paris: A. Colin, 1967.

Masson, Paul. *Histoire du commerce français dans le Levant au XVIIᵉ siècle.* Paris: Hachette, 1896.

————. *Histoire du commerce français dans le Levant au XVIIIᵉ siècle.* Paris: Hachette, 1911.

Matthews, George T. *The Royal General Farms in Eighteenth-Century France.* New York: Columbia University Press, 1958.

Méthivier, Hubert. *Le Siècle de Louis XIV.* 6th ed. Paris: Presses universitaires de France, 1971.

Meuvret, Jean. "Les Temps difficiles." In *La France au temps de Louis XIV.* Collection Ages d'Or et Réalités. Paris: Hachette, 1965.

Minchinton, Walter E. (ed.). *Mercantilism: System or Expediency?* Lexington, Mass.: D. C. Heath, 1969.

Morineau, Michel. "La Balance du commerce franco-néerlandais et le resserrement économique des Provinces-Unies au XVIIIᵉ siècle." *Economisch-Historische Jaarboek* 30 (1965): 170–233.

————, and Charles Carrière. "Draps de Languedoc et commerce du Levant au XVIIIᵉ siècle." *Revue d'histoire économique et sociale* 46 (1968): 108–21.

Mousnier, Roland. *La Venalité des offices sous Henri IV et Louis XIII.* Rouen: Maugard, 1945.

Nef, John U. *Industry and Government in France and England 1540–1640.* Ithaca, N.Y.: Cornell University Press, 1957 (1940).

Neuville, Didier. *Etat sommaire des Archives de la marine antérieures à la révolution.* Paris: Baudoin, 1898.

Ogg, David. *England in the Reigns of James II and William III.* Oxford: Clarendon Press, 1955.

Olivier-Martin, François. *L'Organisation corporative de l'ancien régime.* Paris: Sirey, 1938.

Owen, J. H. *War at Sea under Queen Anne, 1702–1708.* Cambridge: Cambridge University Press, 1938.

Packard, Laurence B. "Some Antecedents of the Conseil du Commerce of 1700." Ph.D. dissertation, Harvard University, 1921.

Pariset, Ernest. "La Chambre de commerce de Lyon au dix-huitième siècle: étude faite sur les registres de ses délibérations." *Mémoires de l'Académie des sciences, belles-lettres, et arts de Lyon*, n.s., 24 (1887): 1–177.

Parker, Harold T. *The Bureau of Manufactures during the French Revolution and under Napoleon: The Bureau of Commerce in 1781 and Its Policies with Respect to French Industry*. Durham, N.C.: Carolina Academic Press, 1979.

Paul, Pierre. *Le Cardinal Melchior de Polignac (1661–1741)*. Paris: Plon Nourrit, 1922.

Perkins, Merle L. *The Moral and Political Philosophy of the Abbé de Saint-Pierre*. Geneva: Droz, 1959.

Picavet, Camile Georges. *La Diplomatie française au temps de Louis XIV (1661–1715): institutions, moeurs, et coutumes*. Paris: Félix Alcan, 1930.

Poinsard, Léon. "Les Chambres de commerce: étude sur leur rôle financier et sur les récents projets de réforme soumis au parlement français." *Annales de l'école libre des sciences politiques* 2 (1887): 165–89.

Price, Jacob M. *France and the Chesapeake: A History of the French Tobacco Monopoly, 1674–1791, and of Its Relationship to the British and American Tobacco Trades*. 2 vols. Ann Arbor: University of Michigan Press, 1973.

Quénet, Maurice. "Un Exemple de consultation dans l'administration monarchique au XVIIIᵉ siècle: les nantais et leurs députés au conseil de commerce." *Annales de Bretagne* 85 (1978): 449–86.

————. "Le Général du commerce de Nantes: essai sur les institutions corporatives coutumières des négociants au XVIIIᵉ siècle." Thèse de doctorat en droit, Nantes, 1973.

Raeff, Marc. "The Well-Ordered Police State and the Development of Modernity in Seventeenth- and Eighteenth-Century Europe: An Attempt at a Comparative Approach." *American Historical Review* 80 (1975): 1221–43.

Rambert, Gaston (ed.). *Histoire du commerce de Marseille*. Vol. 4. Paris: Plon, 1954.

Reddy, William M. "The Textile Trade and the Language of the Crowd at Rouen, 1752–1871." *Past and Present*, No. 74 (1977), pp. 62–89.

Reid, Allana G. "Representative Assemblies in New France." *Canadian Historical Review* 27 (1946): 19–26.

Reynaud, Félix, and G. Vinay. "Les Archives des chambres de commerce de France." *Gazette des archives*, No. 56 (1967), pp. 27–42.

Roosen, William James. *The Age of Louis XIV: The Rise of Modern Diplomacy.* Cambridge, Mass.: Schenkmann, 1976.

————. "The Functioning of Ambassadors under Louis XIV." *French Historical Studies* 6 (1970): 311–32.

Rothkrug, Lionel. *Opposition to Louis XIV: The Political and Social Origins of the French Enlightenment.* Princeton, N.J.: Princeton University Press, 1965.

Rozy, Henri. *La Chambre de commerce de Toulouse au XVIIIe siècle: esquisse historique.* Toulouse: Armaing, 1879.

Rule, John C. "Colbert de Torcy, an Emergent Bureaucracy, and the Formulation of French Foreign Policy, 1698 to 1715." In Ragnhild Hatton (ed.), *Louis XIV and Europe*, pp. 261–88.

————. "France and the Preliminaries to the Gertruydenberg Conference, September 1709 to March 1710." In Ragnhild Hatton and M. S. Anderson (eds.), *Studies in Diplomatic History*. pp. 97–115.

————. "Jérôme Phélypeaux, Comte de Pontchartrain, and the Establishment of Louisiana, 1696–1715." In John Francis McDermott (ed.), *Frenchmen and French Ways in the Mississippi Valley*, pp. 179–97. Urbana, Ill.: University of Illinois Press, 1969.

————. "King and Minister: Louis XIV and Colbert de Torcy." In Ragnhild Hatton and J. S. Bromley (eds.). *William III and Louis XIV*, pp. 213–36.

————. (ed.). *Louis XIV and the Craft of Kingship.* Columbus: Ohio State University Press, 1969.

————. "Royal Ministers and Government Reform during the Last Decades of Louis XIV's Reign." In Claude C. Sturgill (ed.), *The Consortium on Revolutionary Europe 1750–1850*, pp. 1–35. Gainesville: University Presses of Florida, 1973.

Sagnac, Philippe. "Le Crédit de l'état et les banquiers à la fin du XVIIe et au commencement du XVIIIe siècle." *Revue d'histoire moderne et contemporaine* 10 (1908): 257–72.

————. "L'Industrie et le commerce de la draperie en France à la fin du XVIIe et au commencement du XVIIIe siècle." *Revue d'histoire moderne et contemporaine* 9 (1907–8): 24–40.

————. "La Politique commerciale de la France avec l'étranger de la paix de Ryswyk à la paix d'Utrecht," *Revue historique* 104 (1910): 265–86.

————, and A. de Saint-Léger, *Louis XIV (1661–1715)*. 3d. ed. Paris: Presses universitaires de France, 1949.

Saint-Germain, Jacques. *Samuel Bernard, le banquier des rois*. Paris: Hachette, 1960.

Scelle, Georges. *Histsoire politique de la traite négrière aux Indes de Castille*. 2 vols. Paris: L. Larose and L. Tenin, 1906.

————. *Vincent de Gournay*. Paris: L. Larose and L. Tenin, 1897.

Schaeper, Thomas J. "Colonial Trade Policies Late in the Reign of Louis XIV." *Revue française d'histoire d'outre-mer* 67 (1980): 203–15.

————. "The Creation of the French Council of Commerce in 1700." *European Studies Review* 9 (1979): 313–29.

————. *The Economy of France in the Second Half of the Reign of Louis XIV*. Montreal: Interuniversity Centre for European Studies, 1980.

————. "The French Council of Commerce, 1700–1715: An Administrative Study of Mercantilism after Colbert." Ph.D. dissertation, Ohio State University, 1977.

————. "Government Regulation of Business: The Example of Early Eighteenth-Century France." *Delta Epsilon Sigma Bulletin* 26 (1981): 116–19.

————. "Government and Business in Early Eighteenth-Century France: The Case of Marseilles," *Journal of European Economic History* (forthcoming).

————. "The Interuniversity Centre for European Studies/Le Centre interuniversitaire d'études européennes." *French Historical Studies* 12 (1981): 139–43.

Schatz, Albert, and Robert Caillemer. "Le Mercantilisme libéral à la fin du XVIIe siècle: les idées économiques et politiques de M. de Belesbat." *Revue d'économie politique* 20 (1906): 29–70, 387–96, 559–74, 630–42, 791–816.

Schnakenbourg, C. *Communautés de métiers contre liberté économique à la fin de l'ancien régime*. Paris: Presses universitaires de France, 1976.

Scoville, Warren C. *Capitalism and French Glassmaking, 1640–1789*. University of California Publications in Economics, No. 15. Berkeley: University of California Press, 1950.

————. "The French Economy in 1700–1701: An Appraisal by the Deputies of Trade." *Journal of Economic History* 22 (1962): 231–52.

————. *The Persecution of Huguenots and French Economic Development, 1680–1720*. Berkeley: University of California Press, 1960.

Sée, Henri. "Aperçu sur la contrebande en Bretagne au XVIIIe siècle." Mémoires et documents pour servir à l'histoire du commerce et de l'industrie en France. Edited by Julien Hayem. Series 9.

―――. *Histoire économique de la France*. Preface by Armand Rébillon. Edited by Robert Schnerb. 2 vols. Paris: Armand Colin, 1939–42.

―――. "Notes sur le commerce des ennemis en France pendant la guerre de la succession d'Espagne." *Revue historique de droit français et étranger*. Ser. 4, 5 (1926): 106–15.

Shennan, J. H. *Philippe, Duke of Orleans: Regent of France, 1715–1723*. London: Thames and Hudson, 1979.

Solomon, Howard M. *Public Welfare, Science, and Propaganda in Seventeenth Century France: The Innovations of Théophraste Renaudot*. Princeton, N.J.: Princeton University Press, 1972.

Spooner, Frank C. *The International Economy and Monetary Movements in France, 1493–1725*. Cambridge, Mass.: Harvard University Press, 1972.

Steele, Ian Kenneth. *Politics of Colonial Policy: The Board of Trade in Colonial Administration, 1696–1720*. Oxford: Clarendon Press, 1968.

Stein, Robert Louis. *The French Slave Trade in the Eighteenth Century: An Old Regime Business*. Madison: University of Wisconsin Press, 1979.

Stork-Penning, J. G. *Het Grote Werk; vredesonderhandelingen gedurende de Spaanse successieoorlog, 1705–1710*. Groningen: J. B. Wolters, 1958.

Symcox, Geoffrey. *The Crisis of French Sea Power, 1688–1697: From the Guerre d'Escadre to the Guerre de Course*. International Archives of the History of Ideas, No. 73. The Hague: Martinus Nijhoff, 1974.

Tarlé, E. *L'Industrie dans les campagnes en France à la fin de l'ancien régime*. Paris: E. Cornély, 1910.

Teissier, Octave. *Inventaire des archives historiques de la chambre de commerce de Marseille*. Marseilles: Barlatier-Feissat, 1878.

Thomson, Mark. "Louis XIV and the Grand Alliance, 1705–1710." *Bulletin of the Institute of Historical Research* 34 (1961): 16–35.

―――. "Louis XIV and the Origins of the War of the Spanish Succession." *Transactions of the Royal Historical Society*, Ser. 5, 4(1954), pp. 111–34.

―――. "Louis XIV and William III, 1689–1697." *English Historical Review* 76 (1961): 37–58.

Trenard, Louis. *Les Mémoires des intendants pour l'instruction du duc de Bourgogne (1698): introduction générale.* Paris: Bibliothèque Nationale, 1975.

Trevelyan, George M. "The 'Jersey' Period of the Negotiations Leading to the Peace of Utrecht." *English Historical Review* 49 (1934): 100–105.

Trout, Andrew. *Jean-Baptiste Colbert.* Boston: Twayne, 1978.

Vignols, Léon. "Jean-Paul Vigneau, secrétaire de la représentation commerciale de Nantes (1730–1746)." *Annales de Bretagne* 6 (1890): 44–78.

Viner, Jacob. "Power versus Plenty as Objectives of Foreign Policy in the Seventeenth and Eighteenth Centuries." In D. C. Coleman (ed.). *Revisions in Mercantilism,* pp. 61–91.

Vuitry, A. "Un Chapitre de l'histoire financière de la France: les abus du crédit et le désordre financier à la fin du règne de Louis XIV." *Revue des deux mondes* 60 (1883): 748–83.

Wade, Ira O. *The Intellectual Origins of the French Enlightenment.* Princeton, N.J.: Princeton University Press, 1971.

Wailly, Natalis de. "Mémoire sur les variations de la livre tournois." *Mémoires de l'Académie des inscriptions et belles-lettres* 21 (1857): pt. 2.

Walker, Geoffrey J. *Spanish Politics and Imperial Trade, 1700–1789.* Bloomington: Indiana University Press, 1979.

Wallerstein, Immanual. *The Modern World System II: Mercantilism and the Consolidation of the European World-Economy, 1600–1750.* New York: Academic Press, 1980.

Wallon, Henri. *La Chambre de commerce de la province de Normandie, 1703–1791.* Rouen: Cagniard, 1903.

Weber, Max. *The Theory of Social and Economic Organization.* Translated by A. M. Henderson and Talcott Parsons. Edited by Talcott Parsons. New York: Free Press, 1968 (1947).

Weber, Ottokar. *Der Friede von Utrecht.* Gotha: Parthes, 1891.

Webster, Jonathan Howes. "The Merchants of Bordeaux in Trade to the French West Indies, 1664–1717." Ph.D. dissertation, University of Minnesota, 1972.

Wolf, John B. *Louis XIV.* New York: W. W. Norton, 1968.

Wolfe, Martin. "French Views on Wealth and Taxes from the Middle Ages to the Old Regime." *Journal of Economic History* 26 (1966): 466–83.

Woodbridge, Benjamin Mather. *Gatien de Courtilz, sieur du Verger: étude sur un précurseur du roman réaliste en France.* Johns Hopkins Studies in Romance Literatures and Languages, Vol. 6. Baltimore: Johns Hopkins Press, 1925.

Wybo, Bernard. *Le Conseil de commerce et le commerce intérieur de la France au XVIIIe siècle.* Paris: Domat-Montchrétien, 1936.

Zeller, Gaston. *Aspects de la politique française sous l'ancien régime.* Preface by Victor-L. Tapié. Paris: Presses universitaires de France, 1964.

INDEX

Abbeville, 170–71
Alençon, 159, 163, 164, 179
Almanach royal, 21, 23
Amelot de Chaillou, Denis-Jean (intendant of commerce), 136
Amelot de Gournay, Michel Jean, 87, 204; as diplomat, 26, 45 n. 63, 223–24, 236, 240–41; as director of commerce, 32–33, 150, 154, 157, 159, 166, 167, 195; role of, in Council of Commerce, 21, 26, 90, 160–61, 197, 209, 273; and royal ministers, 31, 33, 202, 243
Amiens, 153, 160, 164, 179
Amsterdam, 128, 234; and banking, 129, 211, 213; trade of, 116, 118
Anisson, Jean (deputy of Lyons), 22, 49, 50, 212, 228; as diplomatic agent and adviser, 81, 236, 238–39; general ideas of, on trade and industry, 57, 60, 61; and privileges of Lyons, 91–92, 93, 232, 240; and royal ministers, 40–41, 53; and tariff reform, 40, 96, 202, 204, 205, 206
Antilles. *See* West Indies, French
Argenson, Marc René de Voyer, marquis d' (lieutenant of Paris police), 23, 24
Asiento Company, 51, 125, 249 n. 29. *See also* Guinea Company
Assemblies des manufactures, 154
Assemblées représentatives du commerce, 5
Augsburg, War of the League of: French trade during, 4, 7, 8, 107, 108, 136, 197
Austria, 261. *See also* Holy Roman Empire; Netherlands, Austrian
Avignon, 240–41

Balance of trade, 61, 193–96, 259–60; and the equivalent system, 114, 119, 122, 124, 130, 132, 136–38. *See also* Money: bullionism
Baltic Sea: trade with cities on, 29, 64, 118. *See also* individual countries and cities
Bank, royal, 212–13
Basville, Nicolas de Lamoignon de (intendant of Languedoc), 82, 162
Bauyn d'Angervilliers, Nicolas-Prosper (*commissaire* in Council of Commerce), 21, 34
Bayonne: chamber of commerce in, 73, 75; trade of, 75, 93, 94, 125, 154, 227
Beauvais, 160, 165, 168
Béchameil de Nointel, Louis (*commissaire* in Council of Commerce), 24, 33, 236
Bergeyck, comte de (treasurer general of Spanish Flanders), 197–99
Bernard, Samuel (financier and deputy of Paris), 52, 211; as deputy of trade, 22, 49, 51, 54, 74, 77, 97–98; and East India Company, 51, 69 n. 41; plans of, for bank, 213; and royal tobacco monopoly, 51, 227
Billets de monnaie, 212, 213
Bordeaux: and brandy, 96–97; chamber of commerce in, 37, 73, 74, 79–80, 81, 85; foreign trade of, 125, 133, 137; and manufacturers, 160; and sugar refining and trade, 95–96; and tariffs, 203, 206; and West Indies, 58, 62, 94, 241. *See also* Fénellon, Jean-Baptiste; Wine trade
Bosher, John F. (historian), 202, 204
Boucher d'Orsay, Charles (intendant of commerce), 264
Brandy, 96–97, 173, 199, 206, 231, 236
Bremen. *See* Hanseatic cities
Bribery of goverment officials, 8, 85–87
Brittany, 158, 203, 206, 245. *See also* Nantes, Saint-Malo